The Longest Debate

The
Longest Debate

A legislative history
of the 1964 Civil Rights Act

Charles and Barbara Whalen

Seven Locks Press
Publishers
Cabin John, Md./Washington, D.C.

Library of Congress Cataloging in Publication Data

Whalen, Charles W.
    The longest debate.

    Bibliography: p.
    Includes index.
    1. United States. Civil Rights Act of 1964.
2. Afro-Americans—Legal status, laws, etc. 3. Discrimination—United
States. I. Whalen, Barbara, 1928–
II. Title.
KF4756.A315A168   1985   342.73'8073   84-20218
ISBN 0-932020-34-8   347.302873

Typography by Options Type Group, Takoma Park, Maryland
Printed by Thomson-Shore, Inc., Dexter, Michigan

Seven Locks Press
Publishers
7425 MacArthur Boulevard
P.O. Box 72
Cabin John, Maryland 20818

Seven Locks Press is an affiliate of Calvin Kytle Associates

To
Chip and Dan and Ted and
Joe and Anne and Mary
and
all those who read this story
so that we may not forget

Preface

J USTICE, observed Alexander Hamilton in the *Federalist Papers*, is the goal of government. All too frequently, however, Congress, constitutionally responsible for defining justice, has been blind to it. Simply stated, this is because Congress is organized in a way that makes it much easier to prevent legislation than to pass it. Fragmented by the disparate views of its 535 members, each with one vote, Congress is incapable of developing comprehensive, long-term programs. Instead, it usually relies on the executive branch for policy proposals and limits its own role to rejection or revision of these initiatives.

Too, consideration of legislative proposals often can be blocked by a relatively few representatives or senators. Prior to the parliamentary reforms of the 1970s, committees of the House of Representatives functioned as independent fiefdoms, dominated by elderly chairmen protected by the seniority system. Committee heads could pigeonhole bills with little fear of being forced to relinquish them for further consideration. Even bills approved by standing committees could be sidetracked if 8 members of the Rules Committee, whose principal duty is to prescribe procedures under which legislation is debated on the House floor, voted to withhold a rule. In the Senate 34 of its 100 members could allow a pending bill to be talked to death by refusing to permit a vote on final passage.

Finally, when citizen demands generate opposing pressures, paralysis inevitably results: the prospect of controversy is a sure prescription for congressional inertia. Throughout its history, therefore, Congress has played a reactive role, responding mainly when outcries from concerned groups were not seriously challenged by other groups with opposing views.

Although dependent on the executive branch for legislative leadership, Congress, because of its inability or unwillingness to confront controversial issues, often inhibits presidential initiatives. If a president is convinced that his plan to correct a social evil will be ignored or defeated by a hostile or apathetic Congress, he is likely to yield to the dominant mood on the Hill and may end up doing nothing. Thus, the presence of injustice frequently goes unacknowledged and unresolved by a federal government charged by the Constitution with its eradication.

Black Americans are a case in point. The United States was one of the last nations on earth to give freedom to its slaves. Then, having made them citizens, it ignored their rights as citizens. For another hundred years they were denied equal justice by the very government sworn to guarantee it.

But, periodically, presidential timidity and congressional indifference have been shaken by dramatic events. In the spring of 1963, events unleashed such a public clamor, such a torrent of indignation that, at last, the president and Congress were forced to confront the national disgrace of racial discrimination. The result was passage of the Civil Rights Act of 1964, which the *Washington Star* praised as "a historic achievement for American society." What follows is the story of this landmark legislation which, during its consideration, produced many heroes and revealed Congress in its finest hour.

Contents

Introduction

A DUTCH SHIP, sailing into the Chesapeake Bay in 1619, dropped anchor at Jamestown, Virginia, and, according to the journal of tobacco farmer John Rolfe, husband of Pocahontas,

> sold us twenty negars.

Thus came the black people, bound in chains, to the American colonies. Their new owners found them so profitable, especially in working the southern tobacco and cotton plantations, that soon the slave trade was a thriving industry. By 1776 there were nearly 500,000 slaves out of a total population of almost 2,500,000. Ironically, that year the Declaration of Independence proclaimed proudly to the world,

> We hold these truths to be self-evident, that all men are created equal....

Except some. For the second Continental Congress had removed Thomas Jefferson's impassioned attack on slavery.

> He [King George III] has waged cruel war against human nature itself, violating its most sacred rights of life and liberty in the persons of a distant people who never offended him, captivating and carrying them into slavery in another hemisphere, or to incure miserable death in their transportation thither. This piratical warfare, the opprobrium of infidel powers, is the warfare of the Christian King of Great Britain. Determined to keep open a market where Men should be bought and sold, he has prostituted his negative for suppressing every legislative attempt to prohibit or to restrain this execrable commerce.

Only a handful of delegates, from both North and South, had argued against this censure of the slave trade, but it was enough. Unity among the 13 colonies was of prime importance for a successful rebellion. So Congress agreed to wait until after the Revolutionary War. If they were not all caught and hanged as traitors, if they won their freedom and a new nation was formed, then they could do something about slavery. But after the war, when the

United States Constitution was being written, not one word mentioned the immorality of people owning people. Instead, the document merely stated how slaves should be counted in determining the number of congressmen a state should have. The southern states wanted to count them all, even though they would not be allowed to vote. The northern states objected. Finally they compromised:

a slave would be considered "three-fifths" of a person.

And so began 74 years of congressional compromise over the painful question of the black people in America and what to do about them, despite the growing clamor of abolitionists. It took the Civil War, in which more than 600,000 lives were lost, to resolve the problem. Amid the fighting, on January 1, 1863, President Abraham Lincoln issued the Emancipation Proclamation, which stated simply:

All persons held as slaves...shall be...forever free.

Their full rights as citizens were guaranteed when the postwar Congress passed, and the states ratified, the 14th Amendment to the Constitution:

All persons born or naturalized in the United States, and subject to the jurisdiction thereof, are citizens of the United States and of the State wherein they reside.

No State shall make or enforce any law which shall abridge the privileges or immunities of citizens of the United States; nor shall any State deprive any person of life, liberty or property, without due process of law; nor deny to any person within its jurisdiction the equal protection of the law.

Noble words. But after the assassination of President Lincoln, the country was without a strong, compassionate leader, one who might have found a way to ease the approximately 4,000,000 former slaves into the mainstream of American life. Instead, a vindictive Congress set up a Reconstruction program designed to humiliate the white people of the South. Their fear of black domination hardened into a bitter obsession, and when they regained their political and economic strength, they retaliated. New chains were clamped on the former slaves, chains of discrimination, padlocked into place by the United States Supreme Court with its 1896 decision (*Plessy v. Ferguson*) that there should be

...separate but equal facilities for white and Negro....

This decision pertained only to transportation within a state but was widely interpreted as applying to schools, trains, barbershops, theaters, restaurants, hotels, and churches throughout the South. And segregation, in fact, meant separate and unequal, designed to keep blacks ignorant and poor by denying them the legal and economic rights guaranteed other citizens. The hopelessness of their lives was told by black poet Paul Laurence Dunbar.

> A crust of bread and a corner to sleep in,
> A minute to smile and an hour to weep in,
> A pint of joy to a peck of trouble,
> And never a laugh but the moans come double.

The arrival of the twentieth century brought an explosion of inventions and an accompanying migration of blacks northward to find work in the factories. But they soon discovered that the North, which had sacrificed so many lives to free them, was not a place where they could work side by side or live next door to whites. Only menial jobs and the ghetto were open to them. And in desperation, W. E. B. DuBois, the first black to earn his Ph.D. at Harvard, shouted in print,

> We will not be satisfied to take one jot or tittle less than our full manhood rights. We claim for ourselves every single right that belongs to a free born American, political, civil and social; and until we get these rights we will never cease to protest and assail the ears of America.

But those ears were deaf to their cries. Most people were concerned about their own problems, not those of others. Most whites were not touched by discrimination, nor had they witnessed the more bestial forms of racism—the brutal beatings by law enforcement officers and the mob lynchings. Most whites, born into an environment that tolerated the segregation of blacks in both North and South, accepted the status quo as neither illegal nor immoral. And, too, most whites feared the complexities of a black and white society. So most turned the other way. And as America grew and prospered, America's ignored problem grew and festered. Until, finally, the bleak years of the Great Depression produced one voice of hope:

> The only thing we have to fear is fear itself.

Franklin Delano Roosevelt, persistently prodded by his humanitarian wife, Eleanor, was the first president since Lincoln to stretch out his hand to help the black people rise. Blacks benefited economically from the New Deal programs, and they benefited socially too. The Roosevelts had blacks as guests in the White House, which jolted a nation inured to the notion that they should be there only if they were carrying silver trays. But good intentions were no match for the realities of politics. In 1934, FDR explained why he could not push an antilynching bill then languishing in Congress:

> Southerners, by reason of seniority rule in Congress, are chairmen or occupy strategic places on most of the Senate and House Committees. If I come out for the antilynching bill now, they will block every bill I ask Congress to pass to keep America from collapsing. I just can't take the risk.

In 1941, threatened with a march by blacks on Washington, Roosevelt was forced to create the Fair Employment Practice Committee (FEPC) to prevent job discrimination in war industries. But never once during his 12 years in office did he dare confront the Congress with civil rights legislation. Finally, World War II exposed the hypocrisy of expecting blacks to accept oppression at home when they were fighting against oppression in Hitler's Germany. Race riots erupted in Detroit and Chicago. And in 1944 Gunnar Myrdal, the Swedish sociologist who wrote the massive study *An American Dilemma, The Negro Problem and Modern Democracy*, foretold the turmoil of the coming decades when he said:

> To get publicity is of the highest strategic importance to the Negro people.

After World War II, President Harry S Truman desegregated the armed forces by executive action and, in 1948, tried to get civil rights legislation through Congress, declaring:

> If we wish to inspire the peoples of the world whose freedom is in jeopardy, if we wish to restore hope to those who have already lost their civil liberties, if we wish to fulfill the promise that is ours, we must correct the remaining imperfections in our practice of democracy.

A number of civil rights bills, embodying the proposals contained in his speech, were introduced into Congress, but only one, pertaining to the rights of Americans of Japanese origins, passed. And in the meantime, the voices from the ghetto got louder. Writer Ralph Ellison cried out in *Invisible Man*:

> I can hear you say, "What a horrible, irresponsible bastard!" And you're right. I leap to agree with you. I am one of the most irresponsible beings that ever lived. Irresponsibility is part of my invisibility; any way you face it, it is a denial. But to whom can I be responsible, and why should I be, when you refuse to see me?

Dwight D. Eisenhower, the former supreme commander of the

Allied Expeditionary Force, was added to the list of presidents who faced the problem of getting civil rights legislation through a Congress dominated by southern committee chairmen. Fumed Eisenhower,

> I can't understand how eighteen southern Senators can bamboozle the entire Senate!

It was as if fear had frozen two-thirds of the United States government. Presidents feared the Congress, Congress feared its constituents, and the government itself was an iceberg of inaction. Then into the cold stepped the Judiciary. Free from fear of voter retribution and wielding the Constitution like an icepick, the United States Supreme Court chipped away at discrimination. In 1954, led by Chief Justice Earl Warren, the Court unanimously (including three southern justices) outlawed segregation in public schools in the case of *Brown v. the Board of Education of Topeka.* In overruling the earlier "separate but equal" decision, the Supreme Court split open the frozen wall of segregation and made sure it stayed open with its decision the next year that schools desegregate

> ...with all deliberate speed.

And so, as revolutions spring from hope rather than despair, six months later a single word was the opening cry of the long delayed rebellion of black America. It was a calm, undramatic, almost whispered word:

> No.

That word was uttered late one day in December 1955 by a black woman. On an overcrowded bus in Montgomery, Alabama, Rosa Parks refused to get up and give her seat to a white man. The reason was simple. She had been working all day. Her feet were tired and so was she. Tired as all her people were. Tired of standing while white folks sat, of working for a pittance of white folks' pay, of being called "coon" and "nigger." Tired of waiting and hoping and praying for a first-class world that would never come. Tired.

And so Mrs. Parks was jailed. It was lucky she was a woman. It would have been much worse for a man. That was how things were handled in the South when Negroes got uppity. But this time things were different. This time the Negroes decided to fight back. Rebellion was not new to the black people. Generations ago they had rebelled in the African forts, aboard the slave ships, and on the great plantations. But those rebellions had failed because they used the tool of their masters—violence. And their masters knew this tool better than they ever could.

This time a new style of leader stepped forward, a young minister named Martin Luther King, Jr., who offered them a new tool—nonviolence. From the pulpit he cried,

> Love must be our regulating ideal. If you will protest courageously and yet with dignity and Christian love, when the history books are written in future generations, the historians will have to pause and say, "There lived a great people—a black people—who injected new meaning and dignity into the veins of civilization."

Then, like India's Mahatma Gandhi, Dr. King led his people on a peaceful march. For 382 days almost 50,000 Montgomery blacks walked quietly to work, refusing to ride the segregated buses. And they discovered they could move mountains. The Supreme Court ruled that Alabama's "separate but equal" transportation policy was unconstitutional. Eight months later, reacting to public indignation throughout the country, Congress passed the first civil rights bill in 82 years, the Civil Rights Act of 1957. Three years later, reacting to publicity over lunch counter sit-ins by black students throughout the South, Congress again responded, this time by passing the Civil Rights Act of 1960. And while both were relatively innocuous laws, they raised hopes that a new day was dawning. Nineteen sixty was a presidential election year, and a dynamic young senator from Massachusetts, John F. Kennedy, was campaigning vigorously. Kennedy criticized Eisenhower's civil rights stance as largely passive and spoke eloquently of what blacks should expect of their next president.

> He must exert the great moral and educational force of his office to help bring about equal access to public facilities— from churches to lunch counters—and to support the right of every American to stand up for his rights—even if that means sitting down for them. If the President does not himself wage the struggle for equal rights—if he stands above the battle— then the battle will inevitably be lost.

John Kennedy won the presidency, but by a mere 118,500 votes, the closest presidential race of the century. His opponent, Richard Nixon, actually got 51 percent of the white vote, but Kennedy offset this by taking 68 percent of the black vote. Black leaders were elated. Their people had provided the margin of victory for a man committed to their cause. Now they expected a strong civil rights bill to eliminate discrimination in schools, jobs, housing, and public places. But even before he took office, it was evident this was not to be. John Kennedy, after savoring the joy of his victory, faced some disagreeable facts.

The new Congress was now more conservative than before; his Democratic party had lost 2 seats in the Senate and 21 seats in the House. Congress would continue to be controlled by a coalition of southern Democrats and conservative Republicans who not only would reject any civil rights proposals but might, in retaliation, torpedo his other New Frontier programs. In addition, the once solid Democratic South was no longer solid. Kennedy carried only 6 of the 11 southern states and might lose them all in 1964 if he proposed civil rights legislation. So now he had a choice. If he fulfilled the campaign promises he made to the black people, he would surely lose both the battle with Congress and any bid for reelection. It was morality against math. It was yearning to lead against yearning to win. Winning won. Nevertheless, his inauguration speech rang with eloquent optimism.

> Let the word go forth from this time and place, to friend and foe alike, that the torch has passed to a new generation of Americans, tempered by war, disciplined by a hard and bitter peace, proud of our ancient heritage, and unwilling to witness or permit the slow undoing of those human rights to which this nation has always been committed.

Blacks could not be blamed for wondering bitterly how Kennedy could talk about human rights for everyone else in the world but not for them. The new president tried to appease them by appointing blacks to high government posts, hoping that by his second term he would have the freedom to act. But token appointments would no longer satisfy the hopes that Kennedy himself had helped to raise. Other voices, too, were critical of his caution. The Reverend Theodore Hesburgh, president of Notre Dame University and a member of the Civil Rights Commission, said in the commission's 1961 annual report:

> Americans might well wonder how we can legitimately combat communism when we practice so widely its central folly: utter disregard for the God-given spiritual rights, freedom and dignity of every human person.

Finally, in the spring of 1963, Martin Luther King, as

knowledgeable as John Kennedy about the power of the press, decided to force the issue dramatically. He chose the tough steel town of Birmingham, Alabama, the most segregated city in the South, for his stage. Its Negro-baiting police chief, Bull Connor, was the perfect villain. In mid-April Dr. King started marching to protest segregated lunch counters and, predictably, Connor threw him in jail. While there, he was publicly denounced by a group of clergymen for disturbing the southern status quo, and from his cot he penned his now-famous reply,

> For years now I have heard the word "wait." It rings in the ear of every Negro with piercing familiarity. This "wait" has almost always meant "Never." We have waited for more than 340 years for our constitutional and God-given rights. The nations of Asia and Africa are moving with jet-like speed toward gaining political independence, but we still creep at a horse-and-buggy pace toward gaining a cup of coffee at a lunch counter; when you take a cross-country drive and find it necessary to sleep night after night in the uncomfortable corners of your automobile because no motel will accept you; when you are humiliated day in and day out by nagging signs reading "white" and "colored"; when your first name becomes "nigger," your middle name becomes "boy" (however old you are) and your last name becomes "John," and your wife and mother are never given the respected title "Mrs."; when you are harried by day and haunted by night by the fact that you are a Negro, living constantly at tiptoe stance, never quite knowing what to expect next, and are plagued with inner fears and outer resentments; when you are forever fighting a degenerating sense of "nobodiness"—then you will understand why we find it difficult to wait.

After he was released from jail, Martin Luther King decided that the moment had come to use his ultimate nonviolent weapon. He knew it would be widely criticized. But he also knew it would be widely publicized. So on May 2 more than one thousand black school children poured through the police-lined streets of Birmingham, some as young as 6, others as old as 16, some holding hands, others holding homemade signs, all singing in high clear voices:

> Deep in my heart I do believe
> We shall overcome some day.

As television cameras rolled, Bull Connor and his men descended on the culprits with billy clubs, police dogs, and fire hoses. One hundred pounds of water pressure knocked youngsters to the ground, swept them down streets, and threw them against buildings where they were handcuffed and hauled off to jail, still singing. That night Dr. King reassured their parents:

> Don't worry about your children who are in jail. The eyes of the world are on Birmingham. We're going on in spite of dogs and fire hoses. We've gone too far to turn back.

The eyes of the world were indeed on Birmingham. And what they saw was horrifying. But it had been happening for a long, long time, at night or in back alleys or in county jails. Martin Luther King gambled on his ability to goad Bull Connor into playing the villain in broad daylight on a national stage, and Connor's response was too good to be true. From tight-lipped Washington, D.C., came the question of how long children would be used. From Birmingham came the terse reply,

> Until we run out of children.

The country exploded. Whites were appalled and blacks were furious. Birmingham lit a fuse, and fires ignited in dozens of cities, both North and South: Raleigh, Knoxville, New Orleans, Chicago, Detroit, New York, Sacramento, and Philadelphia. As the pent up anger of three and a half centuries erupted, Dr. King cried,

> We're through with tokenism and gradualism and see-how-far-you've-comism. We're through with we've-done-more-for-your-people-than-anyone-elseism. We can't wait any longer. Now is the time.

For President Kennedy, it was also the time. There was no longer any choice. His brother Robert, the attorney general, was urging him to do something before the country split in open warfare. John Kennedy himself had described such a crisis in his book *Profiles in Courage.* He wrote that some men in political life acted with bold courage while

> ...others sailed with the wind until the decisive moment when their conscience, and events, propelled them into the center of the storm.

Birmingham had swept John Kennedy into the maelstrom. He was fully aware of the consequences of a strong civil rights bill. His political instincts told him not to present such a bill. Not only would it fail in Congress, but it would ruin his chance for a second term. Nevertheless, he had sworn to defend the Constitution. On June 11 Kennedy went on television to give what many considered his greatest speech in the two and a half years he had been in office.

> We are confronted primarily with a moral issue. It is as old as the Scriptures and it is as clear as the American Constitution. The heart of the question is whether all Americans are to be afforded equal rights and equal opportunities, whether we are going to treat our fellow Americans as we want to be treated....
>
> One hundred years of delay have passed since President Lincoln freed the slaves, yet their heirs, their grandsons, are not fully free. They are not yet freed from the bonds of injustice. They are not yet freed from social and economic oppression. And this Nation, for all its hopes and all its boasts, will not be fully free until all its citizens are free.
>
> Now the time has come for this Nation to fulfill its promise. The events in Birmingham and elsewhere have so increased the cries for equality that no city or state or legislative body can prudently choose to ignore them.
>
> We face, therefore, a moral crisis as a country and as a people. It cannot be met by repressive police action. It cannot be left to increased demonstrations in the streets. It cannot be quieted by token moves or talk. It is a time to act in Congress, in your state and local legislative body and, above all, in all of our daily lives.
>
> Next week I shall ask the Congress of the United States to act, to make a commitment it has not fully made in this century to the proposition that race has no place in American life or law.

Eight days later John F. Kennedy sent up to the Capitol a long overdue bill that would try to correct the wrongs of almost 350 years.

The Longest Debate

One

The Congressional Journey Begins

C ONGRESS, the 535-headed creature, whose strongest instinct was self-preservation, sprawled lazily on Capitol Hill, blinking in the morning sun and nervously eying the package that had been sent up from the White House—John F. Kennedy's civil rights bill.

In his accompanying message to Congress, the president said,

> The legal remedies I have proposed are the embodiment of this nation's basic posture of common sense and common justice. They involve every American's right to vote, to go to school, to get a job and to be served in a public place without arbitrary discrimination—rights which most Americans take for granted. In short, enactment of "The Civil Rights Act of 1963" at this session of Congress is imperative.

The Kennedy bill had eight provisions:

Title I enforced the constitutional right to vote in federal elections.

Title II prohibited discrimination in public accommodations, including all places of lodging, eating, and amusement and other retail or service establishments.

Title III desegregated public education and authorized assistance for solving problems of school segregation and racial imbalance.

Title IV established a Community Relations Service to assist individuals and communities involved in racial disputes.

Title V extended the Civil Rights Commission for four years.

1

Title VI prevented discrimination in federally assisted programs.

Title VII permitted the president to establish a Commission on Equal Employment Opportunity to deal with those firms having government contracts.

It was, for some, a most reasonable bill. A bill that promised to fulfill the promise. And yet, for most, a feared and hated bill. A ticking time bomb of a bill with a fuse long enough to stretch to the next election day and obliterate anyone unlucky enough to have touched it. A bill to be avoided at all costs. A most unreasonable bill.

But, of course, it was likely that most members of Congress would never have to summon the courage to vote on it, because in 1963 the long trip to the floor of either the House or Senate was routed through meddlesome, and often lethal, committees. After a bill was introduced, it was given a working number and referred to an appropriate committee. The committee chairman, acting with absolute power, decided whether to give it a hearing in the full committee, refer it to a subcommittee, or quietly put it in his desk drawer and suffocate it to death. If he sent it to a subcommittee, it was scrutinized in open hearings where witnesses testified for or against it. Then the subcommittee went into closed sessions to "mark up" the bill, after which it voted either to send it to the full committee or kill it. If it was sent to the full committee, the members might accept it in its entirety, completely reject it, or amend it. Or they might not act on it at all. If a bill was approved by a Senate committee, it was placed on the calendar and ultimately brought to the floor. In the House, however, before coming to the floor it first had to clear the Rules Committee.

Then as now, for a bill to become law, it must be passed by both House and Senate. And there are plenty of chances to cripple it along the way. Less than 10 percent of the legislation introduced into Congress ever sees the light of day; it is easier to kill a bill than to make it into a law.

Nevertheless, on the morning of June 26, Kennedy's bold civil rights bill began its journey through the labyrinthian corridors of the Hill. In the high-ceilinged hearing room of the Judiciary Committee of the House of Representatives, 19th-century Edwardian chandeliers burned brightly above the congressional aides who were filling pitchers with water. The first hearing of the bill was scheduled for 10:00 A.M., with the leadoff witness to be the president's brother Robert, the attorney general.

Shortly before the hour, Kennedy's Justice Department limousine rolled to a stop in front of the Cannon Building. As the attorney general pushed his way through the revolving door and strode to the elevator, people in the small rotunda stole sidelong glances at him. Robert Kennedy had a reputation for ruthlessness, earned during his seven years as legal counsel for the Senate Permanent Subcommittee on Investigations (chaired by the late Senator Joseph McCarthy of Wisconsin) and the Senate Select Committee on Improper Activities in the Labor and Management Field (better known as the McClellan committee). To this was added a renown for rudeness; according to his victims, the attorney general had the disconcerting habit of looking straight through anyone he deemed unimportant, without even giving one the dubious honor of being ignored.

This morning the redoubtable Robert Kennedy was accompanied by his aide, Burke Marshall, assistant attorney general for civil rights, who, like Kennedy, made little use of small talk. Both men rode the elevator to the third floor of the cavernous building, marched down the marble hallway thronged with people, and shouldered their way through the mahogany double doors into room 346.

The Judiciary Committee room was a handsome chamber that reeked of elite masculinity and expensive after-shave. Gold velvet drapes framed french doors and a view of the Capitol; thick carpeting muffled voices as well as footsteps. Men spoke in low, measured tones and had only to raise their eyebrows to bring aides hurrying to their sides. Here the problems of the pushing and prodding people of America came to be solved in slow and solemn style. Here the passing of laws began.

Today the place was packed. Newsmen, photographers, and assorted onlookers filled the 70 or so chairs behind the witness table, while dozens of additional spectators stood along the walls. Pages, aides, and legal counsels wove in and out, conferring with each other in whispered tones. Around the horseshoe-shaped mahogany hearing table on its raised marble dais were the 11 congressmen who sat on Subcommittee No. 5.

Reigning at the head of the table, his quick eyes scanning the room, was the tough and crusty chairman of both the full Judiciary Committee and this important subcommittee, Congressman Em-

3

anuel Celler, a Democrat from Brooklyn, New York. At his right sat William McCulloch, the gentle small-town lawyer from Piqua, Ohio, who was the senior Republican on the committee. Both men hid their considerable power behind facades of old-world courtesy.

"Good morning, Mr. Attorney General."

"Good morning, Mr. Chairman."

There were smiles all around. Emanuel Celler gaveled the hearing to order and glanced at his subcommittee. The six Democrats, handpicked by Celler, were all liberals: Peter Rodino (N.J.), Byron Rogers (Colo.), Harold Donahue (Mass.), Jack Brooks (Tex.), Herman Toll (Pa.), and Robert Kastenmeier (Wis.). The Republicans, chosen by William McCulloch, were a mixture: McCulloch was a fiscal conservative who was moderate on civil rights; William Miller (N.Y.) was a conservative who would seldom be present because of his time-consuming position as chairman of the Republican National Committee; George Meader (Mich.) was a conservative; and William Cramer (Fla.) was a conservative Southerner.

Newsmen noted that the subcommittee was dominated by liberal Democrats. Kennedy's bill would have gentler treatment here than anywhere else on the Hill. That was one reason why the president had started the bill in the House of Representatives rather than in the Senate. The Senate Judiciary Committee was chaired by James Eastland (D-Miss.), whose committee was infamously known as the graveyard of civil rights legislation. The House Judiciary Committee, on the other hand, had as its chairman a bona fide liberal and a longtime champion of civil rights. Emanuel Celler wanted a strong bill. In fact, he had introduced such a bill, based on the civil rights plank of the 1960 Democratic platform, shortly after Kennedy was inaugurated. But Kennedy, in the aftermath of his close election, had disavowed Celler's bill, and without the president's help, such a controversial measure did not have a chance. Clearly, Emanuel Celler was the logical sponsor for this fledgling bill.

Celler introduced it into the House on June 20, where it was given the working name H.R. (House of Representatives) 7152 and referred by Speaker John McCormack (D-Mass.) to the Judiciary Committee. Celler assigned it to Subcommittee No. 5 of which he was chairman, and scheduled immediate hearings. And now, in having Robert Kennedy this morning, the subcommittee was following the protocol of hearing first from the cabinet member whose department would be responsible for carrying out a bill's provisions, were it to become law.

At 37, Kennedy retained his boyish looks and seemed far too young to be attorney general of the United States. This had been the reaction of most people when the president-elect announced that he was appointing his younger brother to the important post. But John Kennedy had been firm. He wanted someone at the head of the Justice Department who would tell him the unvarnished truth. He got it. And Robert Kennedy drove himself relentlessly, working all night if necessary and expecting others to do the same.

While the president busied himself with international matters, it was the attorney general who had to deal with racial unrest. Almost immediately, Bobby Kennedy saw for himself the awful truth of what was happening in the South: the pathological hatred, the brutal beatings, the murders. In 1961, Kennedy's administrative assistant had been knocked unconscious by a club-wielding mob of whites and then left unattended on an Alabama sidewalk for half an hour. From then on the attorney general became immersed in the problem. During the Birmingham crisis, as he studied the map of the United States where pins showed trouble spots multiplying daily, he knew that the federal government could no longer run around the country like firemen putting out brushfires. They had to correct basic injustices. While the president continued to hesitate, the attorney general acted. On May 17, while on a flight to Asheville, North Carolina, he and Burke Marshall discussed the problem and began to shape a bill. Justice Department lawyer Harold Greene was given the outline to write into legislation, and Kennedy urged his brother to assume leadership, telling him civil rights was an issue that must be faced. When the president finally decided to act, the attorney general reassured him that the decision was the right one. Bobby Kennedy was no stranger to this bill.

Now, putting on his glasses, Robert Kennedy read his prepared statement in a high-pitched, Boston-accented voice.

> With respect to the bill [H.R. 7152] in its entirety, it must be emphasized that racial discrimination has been with us since long before the United States became a nation, and we cannot expect it to vanish through the enactment of laws alone. But we must launch as broad an attack as possible. If we fail to act promptly and wisely at this crucial point in our history, grave doubts will be thrown on the very premise of American democracy. The call to Congress is not merely for a law, nor does it come only from the president. This bill springs from the people's desire to correct a wrong that has been allowed

to exist too long in our society. It comes from the basic sense of justice in the hearts of all Americans.

As the attorney general answered questions, from the 11 subcommittee members and the 14 other members of the full committee who sat in as observers, it was plain that he wanted to return to his office without wasting time. After all, he almost singlehandedly brought the bill to life. Now let the Democrats on the Hill nurse it along. But the hours stretched on, broken only for lunch, and by midafternoon the discussion centered on the most controversial section, Title II, which guaranteed equal access to public places such as hotels and restaurants. Impatient with the tedious and often repetitive questions, Kennedy grew churlish and combative, often answering questions with counterquestions. When George Meader asked if he was familiar with a Republican public accommodations bill that had been introduced on June 3 by John Lindsay (R-N.Y.) and 23 other Republicans, Kennedy did not even attempt politeness.

"I am not," he retorted, implying that his time was too valuable to be spent reading Republican bills. "As the chairman said, there are 165 bills or 365. I have not read them all."

Liberal Republican John Lindsay, a member of the full committee who had been listening quietly, shot an astonished look at the attorney general. Lindsay was an outstanding champion of civil rights who had introduced a strong public accommodations bill weeks before the president's bill. And now, the president's brother was treating it like garbage. Lindsay's voice broke in sharply. "I am quite deeply disturbed, Mr. Attorney General, that you have never bothered to read this very important legislation...."

"Congressman," interrupted Kennedy, "I am sorry that I have not read all of the bills, and I am sorry that I have not read your bill."

When angered, the thin-skinned, patrician New Yorker had a habit of taking a pencil and knocking it on a table. Now the pencil started to tap. "In view of the fact," snapped Lindsay, "that you apparently did not consider these bills at all, I can't help but ask the question as to whether or not you really want public accommodations legislation or not. This is a question I would like to have the answer to. I should like to add this one comment to this question. Let us be frank about it. The rumor is all over the cloakrooms and corridors of Capitol Hill that the administration has made a deal with the leadership to scuttle the accommodations."

"I am surprised by this," Kennedy shot back, "but maybe I shouldn't be, that you would come out here in this open hearing and say that you heard these rumors in the cloakroom. I think it has been made clear...and I don't think the president nor I have to defend our good faith in our efforts, here to you or to really anyone else....I want this legislation to pass. I don't think, Congressman, that I have to defend myself to you about the matter."

Like two thoroughbreds they eyed each other across the several yards of gold carpeting that separated them, both prickly about their own prerogatives and wounded pride. But Lindsay had indeed touched a sore spot. Washington was abuzz with rumors that the administration had made a deal with the southern Democrats: after pretending to do battle, the Kennedy forces would abandon Title II, and the Southerners would let the president have the rest of his package. The administration could then claim credit for having tried to get a public accommodations section and blame the failure on the Republicans.

Swiftly, to prevent any further political bloodshed, Emanuel Celler intervened. He was a master at mediating quarrels between the temperamental prima donnas of the Hill.

After a minute or so, John Lindsay turned around and whispered to one of his legislative aides, "Do you think I was too hard on him?"

"Well, maybe a little," admitted the aide, "but I can understand why you were."

Lindsay muttered, still piqued, "I thought somebody should say something."

Both John Lindsay and Bobby Kennedy were young, bright, and extremely loyal to their respective parties. In this instance, however, Kennedy's political instincts failed him. His thoughtless remarks damaged his brother's bill, which would need 50 or 60 Republican votes to get through the House. *Wall Street Journal* reporter Joseph W. Sullivan noted that "since most Republicans take pride in their party's past attention to the cause of Negro betterment, the pain was deep and needless."

Actually, Bobby Kennedy made three mistakes that day on the Hill. First, he had not done his homework on the members of the Judiciary Committee, in whose hands H.R. 7152 would either live or die. If he had, he would have discovered that on January 31, four months before the president acted, ranking minority member William McCulloch had seized the initiative and introduced his own civil rights bill, cosponsored by 23 other Republicans, including 8 members of the Judiciary Committee. But while it was a good bill, it lacked a public accommodations section; and so, in the aftermath of Birmingham, John Lindsay had introduced the public accommodations bill that Kennedy so cavalierly dismissed.

Second, he should have remembered that the Hill is like the Tower of Babel. Members of Congress—all with different personal, regional, philosophical, and partisan interests—strive to be heard. Such a cacaphony makes it difficult, if not impossible, for Congress to construct a legislative agenda, much less act on one. The only clear note that can be heard above the din is the voice of the president. His proposals, of course, are not always granted (only 45 percent of John Kennedy's 1962 legislative requests cleared Congress), but without presidential push, a bill has little chance of becoming law. Consequently, Congress spends most of its time considering the president's proposals, rather than its own. When they start examining his bills, however, individual members often can gain acceptance for their own proposals by offering them as amendments. That was exactly what the Republicans planned to do with their versions of civil rights legislation; that was why they were so touchy about the attorney general's disdain.

Third, Kennedy neglected the unwritten rules of courtesy. When debating on the floor of the House or Senate, members invariably refer to each other in such grandiose terms as "the distinguished gentleman from New Hampshire" or "my learned colleague from Colorado." During committee hearings, congressmen are traditionally given the respected title, "Mr. Congressman," never a blunt "congressman," which is how Kennedy addressed Lindsay. And always, even though there might be fierce disagreement over issues, the code on the Hill is to disagree without being disagreeable. A member who might be against a colleague on one bill today could very well be his ally on another tomorrow. Thoughtlessness is unacceptable and rudeness a crime. Those who fail to observe these folkways do so at their peril.

This the attorney general was to discover. When his limousine pulled away from the Cannon Building late that afternoon, he left behind a lot of anger among GOP members. It was not a bright beginning for a bill that needed bipartisan support. However, a few key telephone calls were placed that night, and the next morning the administration tried to make amends when Secretary of Labor W. Willard Wirtz testified before the subcommittee.

"Yesterday," Wirtz said, "there was some unhappiness that prior witnesses had failed to mention or even read that [Republican] legislation. I hope that this testimony will be identified with a thorough reading of that legislation and that the approach to this matter will continue as it was throughout the past decade to be absolutely nonpartisan."

"I think the statement is well taken," Celler added. "I have come to rely greatly upon the support I have received on civil rights legislation from not only the Democrats but from the Republicans. Frankly, it would be extremely difficult to get a civil rights bill without the support of those on the other side of the aisle."

And there the matter rested while Congress went home for its 10-day Fourth of July recess. For the congressional staffs, it was a chance to relax, catch up on the filing, go to D.C. Stadium to see the hapless Senators play ball, or sneak a couple of days at the Delaware shore. Congressional families often went home, which was likely to be cooler and less humid than Washington. For the congressmen and senators themselves, the recess was a chance to get away from an often unreal world where people held doors open and told them how great they were and where there were endless rounds of cocktail parties, embassy dinners, and coveted invitations to the White House; a chance to return to a more down-to-earth life where people told them honestly what they thought of them and the way they were representing the district or state; a chance to find out whether at the end of their terms they would be returning to their jobs on the Hill with its door openers and flatterers and endless rounds of cocktail parties, embassy dinners, and coveted invitations to the White House.

Congressman William McCulloch, senior Republican on the House Judiciary Committee, went home to Piqua, in west central Ohio. His Fourth Congressional District was primarily a farming area, with seven counties, eight towns, 65 villages, and 356,994 people; largely middle-class, conservative, and white, much like its congressman. William Moore McCulloch was born on a farm and learned his ABCs in a one-room schoolhouse before going on to higher education, finally earning his law degree at Ohio State University. He was proud of his humble beginnings. While he could hold his own in any intellectual Washington conversation, McCulloch liked to shed his coat at county fairs (revealing his red suspenders) and carry on a good barnyard talk as well. By background and temperament, then, he should have been a conventional midwestern

Republican—cautious and tightfisted. On some issues he was; a strong proponent of limited government and fiscal integrity, he routinely opposed most big spending programs. In addition, the 62-year-old attorney was one of the few members of Congress who never used all his office allowance and who, year after year, returned the unspent money to the U.S. Treasury.

And yet, Bill McCulloch was more than he seemed. As a young man, he had practiced law for a time in Jacksonville, Florida, where he saw for himself that segregation was not only cruel but unconstitutional. That memory stayed with him when he returned north to establish a law practice in Piqua and serve in the Ohio legislature. When World War II came along, McCulloch was 40 years old, well past the age for going into battle; nevertheless, he resigned as Speaker of the Ohio House of Representatives and enlisted in the U.S. Army, serving almost 2 years in Europe. Elected to Congress after the war, he was appointed to the prestigious Judiciary Committee and, because of the seniority system, moved up gradually until he became its ranking member (most senior in the party out of power).

Bill McCulloch enjoyed wide popularity and respect at home, regularly winning reelection by a comfortable margin of 65 to 70 percent. And when the civil rights issues of the fifties arose, there was no reason for him to get involved. The black population in his district was an almost unseen 2.7 percent; there were no votes to be won in championing their cause. However, McCulloch considered himself a constitutional lawyer and felt that the Bill of Rights was meant for all the people, not just the white and the rich. So without fanfare, indeed so quietly that most of his constituents were only dimly aware of it, he played an important role in the passage of President Eisenhower's 1957 and 1960 civil rights bills.

To the citizens of Ohio's Fourth District, the civil rights dilemma was of little concern. Like most Americans, they would probably say, if they thought long and hard, that they wanted to live in a racially fair society. But it was not something they thought about, not long, hard, or at all. Other things were more important, like getting the crops harvested or making their businesses successful or finding the money to send their children to college. Quite frankly, they were glad to leave the difficult and unfamiliar problems of the country to Bill McCulloch. So when trouble came that spring to Birmingham, Alabama, they saw it on their television screens, but it was far away and did not touch their lives. Or so they thought.

On July 2, while the good people of Piqua were hanging the bunting on Main Street for their annual Fourth of July parade, Assistant Attorney General Burke Marshall slipped into town. In his briefcase was President Kennedy's civil rights bill.

The president's men had discovered, the day after Congress went home, serious trouble with H.R. 7152. In the Senate a secret poll taken by Robert (Bobby) Baker, secretary of the Senate majority, showed it would be impossible to get the necessary 51 votes to pass the bill; only 47 senators expressed support. And in the House the Republican votes that they had counted on were suddenly disappearing. The GOP liberals were furious with Robert Kennedy. The GOP conservatives, on the other hand, were delighted that the Democrats were in hot water and saw no reason why they should come to the rescue. The administration needed an influential moderate Republican to throw his support behind H.R. 7152 and to bring the two factions of his party along behind him. The logical person was Bill McCulloch; he commanded respect in both camps.

Deputy Attorney General Nicholas de B. Katzenbach had sent a memo to Robert Kennedy on June 28 in which he suggested that McCulloch "be sounded out before he is committed to a position publicly, and we should get to work on him immediately." Katzenbach wrote that Burke Marshall was the ideal man to contact him because Marshall's "familiarity with the bill should make him useful in discussions with McCulloch." The assistant attorney general, a brilliant negotiator, had been sent to Birmingham in May to work out a truce between Martin Luther King and the retail merchants. He successfully reached an agreement by meeting daily, first with white merchants, then with black leaders, and finally in the middle of the night with Dr. King, repeating this sequence each day until consensus was reached. He was just the man to persuade McCulloch.

Burke Marshall took a morning plane to Dayton and was met at the airport by the congressman's son-in-law, David Carver, a University of Michigan graduate student. The young man explained that McCulloch was busy speaking to the Piqua Rotarians; Carver would take Marshall to the country club for lunch and then to his father-in-law's office. The student did not tell Marshall that earlier in the day the congressman had observed with a little sly smile, "It won't hurt Marshall to cool his heels for awhile."

Bill McCulloch was not vindictive but he was proud. Balancing President Kennedy's need for Republican support against Bobby Kennedy's thoughtlessness, the congressman could not resist collecting a little satisfaction. If a Washington bigwig was kept waiting while a small-town lawyer tended to his constituents, well, that might be all right, too.

So Burke Marshall took a gratuitous tour of the prosperous Miami Valley while the earnest young man tried to engage the solemn lawyer from Justice in meaningful conversation. It was not easy. After a leisurely lunch they drove into Piqua (the name came from religious words of ancient Mound Builders and meant "he is risen from the ashes"), a quiet town of fine turn-of-the-century homes on a bend in the Miami River. Unfortunately, they were still too early for the meeting, so they killed time in a hardware store, where the man from Washington bought some nails for repairs around his house. Finally, stuffing the nails into his briefcase, Marshall shook hands with Carver, entered the lobby of the Piqua National Bank Building, and climbed the stairs to the second floor.

The congressman's office was a pleasant place overlooking the town square. The room belonged to a man of refined but spartan tastes; wood paneling, well-worn law books, comfortable leather chairs, and wall plaques that honored him for one reason or another. But it was also the room of a man practical enough to have painted on his window pane, in large letters, the name of his law firm—McCulloch, Felger, Fite, and Gutmann. Outside, they were seen easily from a distance. Inside, read backwards, they not only dominated the room but managed to make a visitor feel slightly dizzy.

McCulloch seemed as disarmingly provincial as his office. A courtly man of average height whose thinning red hair was now mostly gray, he welcomed his important guest to Piqua with a firm handshake and a few well-chosen words in a voice midwestern flat and nasal. As he seated himself behind his desk, one could glimpse the workaday red suspenders and the plain yellow pencils that he always carried in his shirt pocket.

But the hazel eyes behind the horn-rimmed glasses were canny; the nose and chin were Celtic sharp as befitted a man of Scottish ancestry; the mouth under the trim mustache always seemed on the verge of a smile. His was a face that, even in repose, looked secretly amused. It would have been a mistake for Burke Marshall to underestimate either the man or his surroundings.

Marshall, however, was inclined to do neither. Bill McCulloch's reputation for integrity, as well as his thoughtful philosophy on civil rights, was well known to the Justice Department. In introducing his bill on January 31, McCulloch had declared on the floor of the House that it was:

> A comprehensive bill which seeks to advance the cause of civil rights in the United States. At the same time, however, it is a bill keyed to moderation. And the reason for moderation is obvious. We members of the Republican Party are honestly desirous of proposing legislation which stands a chance of enactment. Anyone, of course, can introduce grandiose legislative schemes. But reaching for the sky, rather than aiming for the possible, is a form of showmanship we don't wish to engage in. Reality is what we live by and accomplishment is what we seek. For only in compromise, moderation, and understanding are we able to fashion our society into a cohesive and durable structure.

"The possible" was exactly what Burke Marshall aimed to find in Ohio. Actually, McCulloch's and the president's bills were not that different. But Marshall had to persuade the congressman to support H.R. 7152 and to meet privately with Justice officials to work out a compromise that everybody could accept. McCulloch was not hard to convince. And so, in the privacy that the small town of Piqua offered, the two men fashioned the strategy whereby McCulloch could put his own stamp on the president's measure and try to get the GOP liberals and conservatives to go along.

But McCulloch had his price. If he managed to shepherd a strong bill out of the House of Representatives, he wanted two ironclad agreements: (1) The administration would not allow the Senate to gut the measure, as it did in 1957 when Lyndon B. Johnson was the Senate majority leader. McCulloch insisted on having sole power to approve any change that the administration might accept in the Senate. (2) President Kennedy would publicly give the Republicans equal credit for passing the bill. These were tough terms. The plowboy could play hardball as well as any city slicker. Later in the day, when he bid goodbye to the assistant attorney general, there was more than a hint of a smile hovering around McCulloch's mouth. It had been a good day for the small-town lawyer.

It had also been a good day for H.R. 7152 in Washington and New York. On Capitol Hill a chastened Robert Kennedy appeared before the Senate Commerce Committee. With an ingratiating smile, Kennedy assured Republican senators that the Justice Department had examined all pending civil rights proposals and that he, per-

13

sonally, had studied the Voting Rights bill that Senator John Sherman Cooper (R-Ky.), who was sitting in front of him, had introduced on February 4. The administration was determined to make no more mistakes.

In New York City the National Association for the Advancement of Colored People (NAACP) rented the Terrace Suite of the Roosevelt Hotel to bring together several hundred members of the civil rights groups that would be lobbying Congress to pass H. R. 7152. The air was charged. This was the measure for which they had been working for most of their lives. There were representatives from the NAACP, the National Urban League, the Congress of Racial Equality (CORE), the Southern Christian Leadership Conference (SCLC), and the Student Nonviolent Coordinating Committee (SNCC), as well as some of the 74 organizations—such as labor unions and church groups—that made up the giant body known as the Leadership Conference on Civil Rights.

While these leaders were delighted that a strong bill had finally been submitted to Congress, like true zealots they were still not 100 percent satisfied. They wanted the bill to include (1) a so-called Fair Employment Practices Commission (FEPC) with the right to hear discrimination charges against any employer and the authority to order legally enforceable remedies; (2) strengthened authority for the attorney general to intervene in cases of alleged discrimination; and (3) the coverage of *all* public accommodations, including small retail stores. Most of them, however, were realists; they knew it would be tough, perhaps impossible, to get such a strong bill through Congress. However, they were determined to try, agreeing to set up a Washington Leadership Conference office in space offered by Walter P. Reuther, head of the United Auto Workers (UAW).

Plans were laid that afternoon for the massive job ahead. Arnold Aronson, whose work in the civil rights movement went back more than two decades, was named manager of the office. Journalist Marvin Caplan and Violet Gunther, former executive director of Americans for Democratic Action (ADA), would coordinate efforts behind the scenes. The lobbying would be done by veteran Washington civil rights spokesmen—Joseph Rauh, vice-chairman of ADA; former Wisconsin congressman Andrew Biemiller, who was now an AFL-CIO (American Federation of Labor and Congress of Industrial Organizations) lobbyist; Jack Conway of the AFL-CIO's Industrial Union Department; Rev. Walter

Fauntroy, head of the SCLC Washington office; and Clarence Mitchell, the NAACP's Washington representative.

The next weekend members of Congress trickled back into town from the Fourth of July recess. As they gathered for lunch in the House and Senate dining rooms, they shared the news from their home districts. The general consensus on the president's televised civil rights speech was that the people back home understood and accepted it. Larry O'Brien, special assistant to the president for legislative affairs, sent these welcome words in a memo to his boss.

The man in the Oval Office was pleased; he needed some good news. John Fitzgerald Kennedy, after two and a half years in the presidency, had changed in subtle ways. He still paced his office restlessly and still demanded excellence of himself and everyone else. But now the eyes were darker and graver, the face was fuller and more lined, the hair was starting to turn gray, and the six-foot frame was losing its slender boyishness. It had not been an easy first term. A president who believed that the right answers to all questions were within grasp if he and his band of brilliant men just worked hard enough had found success eluding his fingertips. And although Kennedy had campaigned for the presidency by promising to get the country "moving again," he all too frequently appeared to be only the stylish captain of a sluggish ship of state. Critics noted his failures:

Congress. During 1961, his first year in office, Congress had been reasonably cooperative, passing 48 percent of his programs. But in 1962, the balky lawmakers gave him only one major bill, the Trade Expansion Act. And this year relations between the White House and the Hill had so deteriorated that the slowest-moving Congress within memory had voted out only five minor administration bills. Kennedy could not get Congress to act.

International Relations. This had been John Kennedy's major interest when he was in Congress, and he expected that his greatest achievements as president would be in this field. But his stewardship was plagued with mishaps: the Bay of Pigs, the Berlin Wall, the Cuban missile crisis, and the chaos in Vietnam, where Buddhist monks were setting themselves afire in protest against the United States-backed Diem government.

Civil Rights. The one thing Kennedy did not want was civil rights legislation. And his persistent refusal was based in part on his own political philosophy. Although perceived in the presidential campaign as more liberal than Richard Nixon, John Kennedy

15

was not a liberal at all. As a congressman he had privately spurned the "real liberals,"as he called them, and the conservatives as well. He was embarrassed by the fervor of the one and bored by the up-tight stuffiness of the other. His philosophy was simple practicality: Will it help? Will it work? Will it pass?

Regardless of his campaign promises, civil rights was not a burning issue with Kennedy. As a three-term congressman, he had been relatively uninterested in the problems of the blacks. And as a U.S. senator in 1954, he took little notice of the Supreme Court desegregation decision. Nothing in his background prepared him for a civil rights battle. However, by mid-May of 1963, he could no longer avoid it. Increasingly, the nation's editors and columnists, to whose words he was very sensitive, called for leadership. And increasingly, his alter ego and brother, the attorney general, spoke of civil rights as a moral issue. Finally, on May 31, after debating with himself and his aides for two weeks, John Kennedy decided to go ahead with a strong bill. It was the toughest political decision of his presidency. He knew it could also be a self-destructive one.

Washington had been very quiet that Memorial Day weekend. Congress had gone home for a three-day recess, and the rest of the government was operating at half speed. In dozens of other cities throughout the country, however, black people were marching and shouting and protesting against their status as second-class citizens. Even as the president and his brother walked through the Rose Garden, 531 blacks were jailed in Jackson, Mississippi, for walking down the street. John Kennedy knew that when summer hit, tens of thousands of students would be eager to march. Open warfare between the races was more than likely, and it was the job of the president to prevent bloodshed. Ever the hard-headed realist, Kennedy acted that day with the full knowledge that he was morally right but politically wrong and that it might be, as he told his brother, his "political swan song."

"If we're going to go down," he said, "let's go down on a matter of principle."

At noon the next day, Saturday, June 1, the president met with 12 of his closest advisers in the Cabinet Room to discuss the legislation he had decided to send up to Congress. Regardless of his new resolve, he was more nervous and irritable than some had ever seen him. Many of his aides were against the idea, knowing that it was political dynamite. Larry O'Brien, his chief strategist, had warned him a week and a half earlier that it would cause "a straightout brawl that will position the extremes on both sides." But John Kennedy, with the firm backing of the attorney general, was going ahead. He told them he would wait, however, until after June 11 when two black students, Vivian Malone and James Hood, would try to enroll at the University of Alabama.

Alabama's governor, George Wallace, had campaigned in 1962 by promising "to stand in the schoolhouse door"and bar any black students from entering. The Kennedys wanted to avoid the kind of tragedy that had occurred the previous fall at the University of Mississippi when James Meredith had applied for entry. Violence had broken out on the Oxford campus between an armed mob of 2,500 and 400 U.S. deputy marshals. One hundred and sixty marshals were injured, and two civilians—a French journalist and a bystander—were killed.

This time the president and his brother were prepared. They sent Deputy Attorney General Nicholas Katzenbach to the University of Alabama to supervise the enrollment of the two students. With television cameras carrying the confrontation into millions of homes, Wallace stood defiantly in the doorway. Katzenbach gave him a presidential proclamation ordering him to "stand aside." Wallace refused; Katzenbach called Washington. The president immediately federalized the Alabama National Guard and ordered that the governor be removed. When confronted by his own people, Wallace backed off, and in a short time the two students were admitted peacefully.

Buoyed by this success and encouraged by his brother, John Kennedy decided to act quickly. Television time had been reserved for 7:00 p.m. that evening in case of violence, and the president decided to use the time, while attention was focused on the problem, to appeal to the nation for racial justice. With only a few hours' notice, speech writer Theodore Sorensen pounded out the address. Two minutes before air time, he stepped over television cables and handed the speech to Kennedy, who sat waiting at his desk.

Barely three hours after Kennedy's address, Medgar Evers, the NAACP director for Mississippi, pulled into his driveway and was shot by someone waiting in the dark. He died several hours later. The hate mongers were reacting in their own way to the new Kennedy leadership. The shocked president received Evers's widow and young children at the White House to offer his personal condolences. If before he had only wanted the votes of blacks, now John Kennedy became more committed to their cause than to anything else in his presidency.

"Sometimes you look at what you've done and the only thing you ask yourself is—what took you so long to do it?" he confided to a friend. The president immediately took over a project that the attorney general had begun some weeks before, meeting with large groups of influential citizens—state governors, hotel and restaurant owners, theater operators, labor officials, educators, lawyers, and religious leaders—asking them to show leadership by voluntarily desegregating their communities. When speaking to the clergymen, he said he knew that they, of all people, would "recognize the conflict between racial bigotry and the Holy Word."

"What about racial intermarriage?" asked one minister.

"I am not talking about private lives," replied the president with some vexation, "but public accommodations, public education, and public elections."

Polls showed a majority of white Americans favored the Kennedy bill but felt he was pushing too fast. The South was probably going to be lost. Right-wing Republicanism under Senator Barry Goldwater (R-Ariz.) began to rise. Hate mail poured into the White House. But now John Kennedy was determined to pass the best bill possible, at whatever cost to him politically.

"The issue could cost me the election," he confided privately to a black leader, "but we're not turning back."

Toughest to pass, of course, would be Title II (Public Accommodations). Senate majority leader Michael Mansfield (D-Mont.) discussed with the president the difficulty he would have getting it through the Senate. "You've got to get it done," insisted Kennedy. "It's the heart of the matter. These people are entitled to this consideration, and I'm depending upon you to see that what I recommended is passed."

And yet, for the president it remained a terrible challenge, and he found himself leaning more and more on his brother. People watching them were struck by their dissimilarities; the two figures were as different as an Irish setter is from an Irish terrier. Jack was cool; Bobby was feisty. Jack was well groomed; Bobby was disheveled. Jack moved with an elegant grace; Bobby dashed about impatiently. But both were fighters. Winning had been bred into them by their extremely competitive family. And so, referring to a secret poll taken in June that showed his popularity had dropped from

66 percent to below 50 percent, the president turned to his younger brother for reassurance.

"Do you think we did the right thing by sending the legislation up?" he asked. "Look at the trouble it's got us in."

Bobby reminded him that the issue "really had to be faced up to," that the tension in the country "was going to get worse during the summer."

The attorney general was right. Day by day the country, fueled by the murder of Evers, was heating up. In the 10 weeks following the childrens' march in Birmingham, there were 758 demonstrations, with 13,786 people arrested in 75 cities in the South alone. A July *Newsweek* poll revealed that 40 percent of black people had taken part in a sit-in, marched in a mass protest, or picketed a store. Birmingham had given them the impetus; they were aware that the risks included death, but they were determined to win. According to the poll, they believed strongly in John Kennedy and the Supreme Court, but only 1 in 10 expected Congress to pass legislation with a public accommodations section.

"You can't count on a Congress dominated by Southerners," said a black Dallas man. And indeed that was true. On Capitol Hill the Southerners were digging in. "Our backs are to the wall," admitted Senator Strom Thurmond (D-S.C.), "but we are not without weapons with which we can fight back."

Southerners chaired 12 of 18 committees in the Senate and 12 of 21 committees in the House. They implied that they would deliberately slow down their committees' work. They would force the president to shelve H.R. 7152 in order to get his money bills (to keep the government running) out of committee and onto the floor of the House and Senate. But slowing down Congress was hardly news.

"We are assigning ourselves a unique niche in history," complained Senator Jacob Javits (R-N.Y.), "as the biggest and longest running slow-motion show to hit Washington."

Ambitious plans, however, abounded to move Congress out of its lethargy. "This summer," Martin Luther King warned, "we will have a great deal of activity." It was rumored that blacks would throw themselves in front of buses, trains, and airplanes if their demands were not met. Blueprints were drawn for giant sit-downs in the halls of Congress. But even long-time civil rights advocate Emanuel Celler cautioned against overdoing it. In an open subcommittee hearing he warned Democratic congressman Charles Diggs, a Detroit black, that too many demonstrations might have an adverse effect on the public, which was at this point in sympathy with the black struggle. Celler told Diggs that black leaders must call off the planned sit-down at the Capitol. "This," admonished Celler, "would prejudice the cause of the Negro."

Congress, which could be extraordinarily tough when writing legislation, could be extraordinarily touchy about its own integrity. While lawmakers responded quickly to grass-roots movements of their constituents at home, most of them resisted being blatantly pressured by lobbyists in Washington. The trick was to know when to come on strong and when to hold back, when to talk to the congressmen and senators and when to see their staffs; but one always had to remember that subtlety was better than strong-arm tactics.

There was one lobbying plan, however, that could not be squelched. Black leaders were enthusiastically plotting a mammoth march on Washington similar to the one planned in 1941 that forced President Franklin D. Roosevelt to create the Fair Employment Practice Committee. President Kennedy first learned about the march during a June 22 meeting with civil rights leaders at the White House. He was not happy about the idea, questioning both the concept and the timing.

"We want success in Congress," Kennedy had stated, "not just a big show at the Capitol. Some of these people are looking for an excuse to be against us. I don't want to give any of them a chance to say, 'Yes, I'm for the bill, but I'm damned if I will vote for it at the point of a gun.' It seemed to me a great mistake to announce a march on Washington before the bill was even in committee. The only effect is to create an atmosphere of intimidation—and this may give some members of Congress an out."

"The Negroes are already in the streets," retorted A. Philip Randolph, president of the Brotherhood of Sleeping Car Porters. "Is it not better that they be led by organizations dedicated to civil rights and disciplined by struggle rather than to leave them to other leaders who care neither about civil rights nor about nonviolence?"

Martin Luther King added, "It could also serve as a means of dramatizing the issue and mobilizing support in parts of the country which don't know the problems at first hand. I think it will serve a purpose. It may seem ill-timed. Frankly, I have never engaged in any direct action movement which did not seem ill-timed. Some people thought Birmingham ill-timed."

"Including the attorney general," the president added. John Kennedy's wry humor surfaced a few minutes later during a discussion of Birmingham police chief Bull Connor and his brutality: "I don't think you should all be totally harsh on Bull Connor. After all, Bull Connor has done more for civil rights than anyone in this room."

Kennedy finally endorsed the march despite great concern by some members of the White House staff and against their advice. He did so because it was evident that, whatever his views, the civil rights organizations were going ahead with the plans. He felt that without his support, the march would appear to be against his administration. His support, he believed, would reduce the likelihood of disorder.

Plans went forward for the biggest lobbying event Washington had ever seen while the Kennedy administration hunkered down to survive both it and the coming sweltering season. Actually, there was no good reason for a city to be situated on what had been a swamp scattered with a few villages of Powhatan Indians. But in an uncannily prophetic move that foreshadowed much about the future doings of the place, the site of Washington was the result of a compromise. In 1790 the slavery issue made it difficult to choose a permanent location for the capital. Slave-owning Southerners opposed Philadelphia because the Quakers in that city favored abolition. Northerners did not want it in a southern area because they felt it would mean the new United States approved of slavery. So Secretary of the Treasury Alexander Hamilton worked out a compromise between the North and the South to locate the federal city on the Potomac River, and President George Washington picked a place convenient to his Virginia estate, Mount Vernon. That was why the nation's capital sat where the last hills of the Piedmont Plateau dropped down to meet the tidewater lowlands, a natural basin. Each summer hot, moist air from the Gulf Coast flowed in, was trapped, and grew stale without strong winds to blow it out. Rain made it worse, creating a steambath. On the worst July and August days, when the temperature hovered at 90 degrees and the humidity at 60 percent, Washington wallowed in a dense, fog-like thickness that was blue-gray in the morning and orange-white at noon and purplish-red in the evening. The sun hung over the city like a sullen, fiery ball, and people grew irritable from the tasks of breathing spongy air and fighting off gnats attracted by the sweat that made their clothes clammy by the time they arrived at work.

Before World War II, Congress traditionally quitted the city by the Fourth of July, declaring that no one could possibly concentrate in such weather. But with refrigerated rooms came summer-long sessions. And some questioned whether air conditioning was a blessing or a curse; most newsmen voted for the latter as they trudged from building to building to get their stories.

One of the major stories running throughout the long, hot summer was in the Cannon Building, where House Judiciary Subcommittee No. 5 continued its public hearings on H.R. 7152. There is a traditional pattern by which bills are heard in committee. Members of the president's cabinet are invited to testify first, followed by members of the House and Senate who have introduced similar measures. Finally, a limited number of private citizens are asked to voice their opinions, either for or against the bill.

Emanuel Celler announced on July 10 that he hoped to wind up all testimony by the end of the month. During the next several weeks, therefore, the subcommittee heard from 100 witnesses, including labor leaders—George Meany, president of the AFL-CIO; Walter P. Reuther, president of the UAW; and Gus Tyler, assistant president of the International Ladies Garment Workers—who all supported H.R. 7152 as a way to eliminate racial bias among their member unions. However, Roy Wilkins, executive secretary of the NAACP, speaking for the Leadership Conference on Civil Rights, said that he would like to see the bill strengthened. This plea was echoed by James Roosevelt (D-Calif.), son of the late Franklin D. Roosevelt. He urged the subcommittee to adopt the provisions of H.R. 405, a bill establishing an Equal Employment Opportunity Commission (EEOC), which had been approved earlier in the year by the House Education and Labor Committee with the support of five of its Republican members. This was the strong FEPC (renamed EEOC by Roosevelt's committee) demanded by the Leadership Conference on Civil Rights. But President Kennedy did not include it in his bill because he feared it was too controversial.

By August 2 Subcommittee No. 5 had completed 22 days of public hearings and compiled 1,742 printed pages of testimony. Chairman Celler announced that they would now go into private sessions to mark up the bill, the process by which it would be rewritten into its final form for consideration by the full Judiciary Committee.

In reality, however, Celler had been asked by President Kennedy to stall H.R. 7152 until his tax reform bill was voted out of the Ways and Means Committee. The tax bill had priority over civil rights for three reasons: (1) It had been in Ways and Means since January. (2) It was a highly contentious measure. This was not the traditional tax cut that congressmen usually embraced so fondly; rather, it was a radical approach—a planned series of annual deficits—that many conservatives feared would cause runaway inflation. The president wanted it badly, however, because he felt it would stimulate the economy and create more jobs. (3) Kennedy feared that the Southerners on the Ways and Means Committee would kill the tax bill, in retaliation, if H.R. 7152 got out of Subcommittee No. 5.

This fear was well-founded. Seven of the Ways and Means 15 Democrats, including its chairman, were from the South. They, together with the committee's 10 Republicans, formed a formidable conservative majority that Kennedy could not afford to alienate. The chairman, Wilbur Mills (D-Ark.), warned the president of this possibility. "If we are not careful. . ., we can get traded out of house and home on most any kind of legislation [that] comes up between now and the time the House acts on civil rights."

Kennedy attempted to placate the Southerner, upon whom he was dependent for passage of the tax bill. With soothing words, he implied that he did not care about H.R. 7152 and would not really fight for the bill: "I'm not worried about civil rights in the House. If it doesn't pass, it doesn't pass. I just thought we wanted a vote on civil rights."

Mills, wise to the wiles of presidents who sometimes had to carry water on both shoulders, merely repeated his warning: "These fellows will do anything. They'll make any kind of a trade just to try to stop it."

So Manny Celler and Bill McCulloch put H.R. 7152 under wraps. Celler, to avoid creating any news that might leak out and anger Ways and Means conservatives, restricted the first seven mark-up sessions, from August 14 to 27, to bland discussions; no amendments were proposed and no action taken. Meanwhile, McCulloch met secretly with Justice Department officials to work out a bill acceptable to them, to Celler, to GOP liberals, and to GOP conservatives.

By August 28 the House was preparing to go home for its Labor Day recess, and Subcommittee No. 5 was meeting for the last time that month. As the members of Congress arrived on the Hill that morning, they watched as more than 50,000 people milled below them on the lawns of the 180-acre Mall that stretches from the Capitol to the Lincoln Memorial. The massive lobbying demonstration known as the March on Washington for Jobs and Freedom was about to begin.

The evening before, people began arriving in the capital by plane, train, bus, and car for the biggest march in the city's history. Fifteen hundred and twelve chartered buses arrived from everywhere, a dozen people walked 237 miles from Brooklyn, and one man came from Chicago on roller skates. To maintain order, the District of Columbia provided 2,000 police, 2,000 national guardsmen, and 2,000 volunteer marshals. An additional 7,000 soldiers and marines were kept on ready-alert at Washington area military bases. But recalling the Bull Connor spectacle four months earlier, the Justice Department forbade use of police dogs.

Washington was edgy about the event. Throughout the summer the Kennedy administration had worried about potential danger points: provocation by whites, retaliation by blacks, and infiltration by Communists. The public was also apprehensive; a Gallup poll taken eight days earlier showed that 63 percent of the people were against the idea. And Bill McCulloch agreed with them. "They're not going to bluff me," he said at his August 24 press conference. "Doctors, lawyers, everybody could start marching, and there would be no end to it."

Actually, the march was a great stabilizing force during that summer of revolution, for by early July the black rebellion had become leaderless. The leaders were following, and the followers were leading. Martin Luther King and his nonviolent philosophy could not be everywhere. As he led 125,000 people in a peaceful march in Detroit, new demonstrations were breaking out like chicken pox: the Bronx, Chicago, Savannah, Charleston. And they were not all nonviolent. Other civil rights groups, irritated at the tremendous coverage given King by the media, competed for their own share of headlines and television time. The idea of one massive march drew them all together.

Masterminded from Harlem by veteran civil rights activist Bayard Rustin and by A. Philip Randolph, the march would bring 100,000 to 200,000 people to Washington. The job of getting them in town for one day and out by evening fell to a committee of civil rights organizations, union leaders, and church groups. Particularly crucial to the mood of the march were the religious groups with their emphasis on love and understanding.

24

In early summer there sprang up a new type of protester, as white ministers, priests, nuns, and rabbis began showing up to join the picket lines. When the president visited Europe in June, Pope Paul VI publicly expressed his concern for the American civil rights dilemma. And increasingly throughout the summer, declaring the movement as part of their mission in life, men and women of the cloth joined the struggle.

The Kennedy administration also joined in the planning for the August 28 event. It had every incentive for the march to succeed; failure, either through a poor turnout or violence, would dampen public and congressional support for Kennedy's civil rights bill.

There were no brass bands playing that day in Washington, D.C. There was soft singing and the sound of marching feet as almost a quarter of a million people, black and white, moved slowly down the Mall: Farm boots and hand-stitched loafers. March. Open-toed high heels, clergymen's oxfords, beach sandals, and worn-out track shoes. March, march. Across the grassy lawns of the majestic Mall, through the trees and around the reflecting pool, to the broad steps of the marble-columned Lincoln Memorial. The brooding statue of the Great Emancipator sat watching the awakened people of America come to gather at his feet.

By 2:00 P.M., when Camilla Williams opened the program with the National Anthem, a mammoth carpet of people surrounded the Lincoln Memorial and stretched almost to the Washington Monument. They were entertained by folksinger Joan Baez, the Peter, Paul, and Mary trio, and Bob Dylan, who led them in freedom songs. Author James Baldwin, singer Harry Belafonte, and actors Paul Newman, Charlton Heston, Marlon Brando, Burt Lancaster, and Sidney Poitier all made appearances. Finally, with A. Philip Randolph presiding, the speakers began. One by one, Randolph introduced the civil rights leaders. Though asked to limit their speeches to four minutes, most went longer.

It was late afternoon by the time gospel singer Mahalia Jackson finished singing "I Been 'Buked and I Been Scorned." The time had come: As Dr. Martin Luther King, Jr., walked to the podium, the crowd erupted into tumultuous applause. There were others who had labored in the civil rights vineyard longer than King. There were others who got along better with the president than King. There were others who knew how to lobby Congress more effectively than King. But there was no one who could put electricity into a crowd like Martin Luther King, the short, stocky man who in the hearts of his people towered above all others.

In his prepared speech, Dr. King noted that a hundred years had passed since Lincoln issued the Emancipation Proclamation. "One hundred years later," he said, "the life of the Negro is still sadly crippled by the manacles and the chains of discrimination. One hundred years later, the Negro lives on a lonely island of poverty in the midst of a vast ocean of material prosperity. One hundred years later, the Negro is still languishing in the corners of American society and finds himself an exile in his own land."

Then King began to improvise, piecing together parts of speeches that dated back to 1956. Swinging into the poetic rhythm of traditional Negro preaching, he stirred the people spread out before him into one clapping, crying, yearning mass.

"I have a dream today," he shouted.

"Tell us, tell us," implored the crowd.

"I have a dream today that my four little children will one day live in a nation where they will not be judged by the color of their skin but by the content of their character. I have a dream today."

"Tell us, tell us," they cried.

As Dr. King's voice rose and fell, President Kennedy, watching the speech on television, murmured admiringly, "That guy is really good."

When the tremors of King's oratory quieted, when the singing and the shouting and the clapping died down, when the several hundred thousand people drifted away through the trees and across the lawns, when the planes and trains and cars and buses whisked them out of town as quickly as they had come in, only then did official Washington relax from its edgy fear that the whole thing might turn into a riot.

It was about 5:00 P.M. when President Kennedy greeted the leaders of the march at the White House.

"I have a dream!" he said, smiling.

Then he ordered sandwiches and coffee from the kitchen when he discovered they had not eaten since breakfast. The 10 men included Martin Luther King, Walter Reuther, A. Philip Randolph, Whitney Young, executive director of the Urban League, and Roy Wilkins. They took this opportunity to lobby the president about strengthening H.R. 7152. Specifically, they urged him to back their efforts to beef up Title VII (Equal Employment) by adding the

FEPC-style provisions of James Roosevelt's H.R. 405, as well as a new title authorizing the Justice Department to intervene in cases of alleged discrimination. But Kennedy was frankly pessimistic about a stronger bill's chances. To show them how difficult it would be, he went through a detailed state-by-state analysis of House Democrats.

"Alabama, of course, none," he began. "Alaska, one. Arizona, you've got one sure and one doubtful. Arkansas, nothing. California, ah, all the Democrats are right." The president analyzed all 50 states, concluding, "We've got 158 to 160 Democrats." The other 60 votes, he pointed out, would have to come from the Republicans, and they "are hard to get."

"Congressman McClintock," said Kennedy, mispronouncing McCulloch's name, "indicated to the Department of Justice this week that he thought he could vote for our bill with some changes. He's the chief fellow. He won't vote for it unless he's got the green light from Halleck. If we can get him, we will get the 60 Republicans."

Then the president tried to discourage the civil rights leaders from pressing any further on strengthening Title VII (Equal Employment) by warning that McCulloch had said, "If I wanted to beat your bill, I would put FEPC in. And I would vote for it, and we would never pass it in the House." Kennedy concluded by saying, "I don't want the whole thing lost in the House."

"From the description you have made of the state of affairs in the House and Senate," said A. Philip Randolph, "it is going to take nothing less than a crusade to win approval of the civil rights measures. It is going to be a crusade that, I think, nobody but you can lead."

Lyndon Johnson interrupted, telling of the limitations to the power of a president. "He can plead and lead and persuade and even threaten Congress, but he can't run the Congress. This president can't get those 60 votes if he turns the White House upside down and he pleads on television an hour every day."

At the end of the hour-long meeting, the president thanked them for doing "a great job," and said, "You're very helpful to all of us." The civil rights leaders left town that night satisfied with the giant lobbying effort but disappointed by John Kennedy's caution. They realized, as *Time* magazine put it, "There would be no FEPC, no authorization for the Justice Department to step into every sort of civil rights case. Most frustrating of all, they knew that the public accommodations section of the administration's package was quite unlikely to pass the Senate.''

Also leaving Washington that evening were members of the House of Representatives, going home for the Labor Day recess. Even though 75 of them had joined in the march on Washington, realists among them knew that when they returned on September 10, there would be nothing but trouble for the civil rights bill. Many of the signs carried on the Mall that day said, ''We want our freedom—NOW.''

But the 535-headed creature that lived on Capitol Hill had a long history of turning tail on civil rights fights. ''Now'' might never come.

Two

Republicans to the Rescue

A N AUTUMN wind slapped at the American flags flying
above the House and Senate wings of the Capitol. It was
September 10, and the flags signified that the two chambers were
in session. Dry, cool breezes from the north had pushed the hot
August air out to sea and, with it, the sluggishness that had persisted all summer long on Capitol Hill. Congress was back in town
after the Labor Day recess, and the pace on the Hill was quick.
That morning the president's tax cut bill finally was approved, 17–8,
by the House Ways and Means Committee. With this roadblock
out of the way, Chairman of the House Judiciary Committee
Emanuel Celler prepared to move on the markup of Kennedy's civil
rights bill, which had been stalled in subcommittee since August 14.

As Celler headed from his office to the Judiciary Committee
room just down the hall, he carried absolute power in his vest pocket.
He was responsible to no one except his constituents. At 75, the
Brooklyn Democrat was at the peak of his career. Bald, bandy-
legged, and bespectacled Manny Celler was the second most senior
member of the House, serving his 41st year as congressman from
the Tenth Congressional District of New York. Son of a Democratic
district leader, Celler graduated from Columbia University Law
School before being elected to Congress in 1922. Seniority propelled
him to the chairmanship of the Judiciary Committee in 1949.

A master of words, well-grounded in the law, and always
knowledgeable about the subject at hand, Emanuel Celler was a
tenacious, strong-willed partisan. But behind his gruff exterior was
an innate gentleness that usually led him to treat committee members

with courtesy and tact. When committee meetings became overheated, the chairman often cooled things off by telling jokes, reciting poetry, or spinning anecdotes. An inveterate reader, Celler jotted down quotations from such historical figures as Moses, John Milton, and Lord Acton; when the occasion seemed appropriate he would slip one of these quotes into a speech he was giving. The chairman also loved music and would often go into Manhattan to spend an evening at the Metropolitan Opera, sometimes joined by his colleague from across the Hudson River, Peter Rodino. A tireless campaigner in election years, Manny Celler attracted large crowds of children who begged him to perform his legendary feats of magic; his favorite parlor trick was converting dinner napkins into rabbits.

There were, however, many people who believed that Celler was losing his touch, a victim of the generation gap. He was one of a band of 21 House committee chairmen, averaging 76.6 years in age, whose despotic ways were becoming distasteful to those inside Congress as well as to the country at large. As the congressional work load increased during the 1950s and early 1960s, he persisted in dividing his time between Washington and his thriving Brooklyn law practice, not noticing the changes that were taking place on Capitol Hill, not grasping the restlessness among junior members who wanted greater participation in the decision-making process. The chairman kept his own counsel, sharing his plans only with his two principal staff assistants, Bess Dick and Benjamin Zelenko. This sometimes irritated his fellow committee Democrats, who complained that "he never said what the bottom line was."

This tactic, common among Celler's fellow chairmen, produced a backlash among the younger liberal and moderate congressmen of both parties. Four years earlier the young Democrats had organized the Democratic Study Group (DSG), one of whose goals was to strip committee heads of much of their power. And the young Republicans, too, were starting to move in the same direction. The domineering elders were being challenged.

However, this day, as Emanuel Celler's slightly stooped figure moved down the hall of the gracious old Cannon Building, he was quite oblivious to the changing winds on Capitol Hill. Celler was determined to follow his own strategy, which had served him well during his committee's consideration of the 1957 and 1960 civil rights bills. He simply ignored a confidential letter he had received on August 13 from Deputy Attorney General Nicholas Katzenbach outlining tactics that the Kennedys wanted him to follow during the markup of H.R. 7152. With Subcommittee No. 5 his personal enclave, he planned to come out with a bill far stronger than President Kennedy's. It, then, would be used for "trading purposes" with the southern Democrats and conservative Republicans who sat on the full committee.

This approach served Celler in several ways. First, by bringing a strong bill out of subcommittee, he would maintain his credibility with the civil rights leaders who were demanding far-reaching legislation. Second, by bowing to the conservatives during the full committee markup, he would make them look effective in the eyes of their constituents and thereby retain their friendship. Third, although he would trade away a portion of the bill, he at least would be credited with bringing a decent civil rights measure—one that stood a chance of ultimate passage—out of his committee.

It was 2:30 P.M. when Manny Celler settled into his chair, ordered visitors from the room, directed that the doors be closed, gaveled the meeting to order, and started the long-delayed markup of H.R. 7152.

The markup of a bill in 1963 was a process in which Congress followed set rules. The committee or subcommittee had before it a working document, usually the president's bill. The clerk read it aloud, sentence by sentence. At this point individual members of Congress could work their will on administration bills: as each section was read, they could offer amendments (to add, revise, or delete language). Each amendment was discussed and voted on— by a voice vote, a show of hands, or a roll call. After all sections had been considered, the bill (as amended) was put to a final vote by the chairman. If this process began in the subcommittee, the bill, if approved, was reported to the full committee. The full committee, again in closed session, could accept the subcommittee measure in its entirety, completely reject it, amend it, or simply not act on it at all.

Celler announced that, as usual, minutes of the markup sessions would not be available to the press and that the record would contain only the voting results, not how each member voted. The reason for this traditional practice was usually explained to new aides by Bess Dick, the committee staff director. "You always have to give a member enough room to change his mind," she would say. "If you put down how he voted, he's stuck with it."

The chairman insisted that votes on H.R. 7152 and all other

actions taken within the room were to be kept confidential. Celler wanted secrecy on H.R. 7152 because Kennedy's tax bill would be coming up soon for a vote on the House floor. He did not want any information seeping from Subcommittee No. 5 that might upset the Southerners and jeopardize the tax measure.

He soon realized, however, that complete secrecy was impossible; hoards of reporters were camped outside the closed doors waiting to grab members as they emerged. The veteran NAACP lobbyist Clarence Mitchell was also anchored in the hall, anxious to pick up news from the inner sanctum. Until the tax bill had been voted on by the House, Celler would permit only minor, and relatively weak, amendments.

The administration was anxious to keep tabs on H.R. 7152 at this crucial time. So the suggestion was made that, because the bill had been spawned in the Justice Department, Burke Marshall and Nicholas Katzenbach should attend the markup sessions and help in the draft. This was a highly irregular request. The legislative branch of the government guards its power jealously and always is wary when the executive branch tries to look over its shoulder. Celler claimed that the Republicans on the committee objected. This was partly true; Bill McCulloch was not anxious to publicize his close working relationship with the Justice Department. But it was also a fact that Celler, like most chairmen, ruled his committee like a kingdom and would not share his scepter with anyone.

Unlike other chairmen, however, Celler seated the Democrats on his subcommittee to his left and the Republicans to his right. The reason was simple. The chairman was deaf in his right ear, and it might be handy on occasion not to hear a comment from the minority side of the table. Also handy, in some cases, were the rules. The Judiciary Committee actually had no rules in 1963, but if a member did something that Celler did not care for or agree with, he would state authoritatively that the member's actions were in violation of the committee rules.

And so Celler launched the markup of H.R. 7152, assuring the outnumbered Republicans of complete bipartisan harmony. He guaranteed that all votes on amendments would remain tentative until the subcommittee had thoroughly studied and analyzed the bill.

During the next two days the parliamentary procedure inched slowly forward line by line. Robert Kastenmeier moved to strengthen Title I (Voting Rights) by adding state and local elections to the provisions for federal elections. Emanuel Celler also moved to broaden Title I by accepting proof of a sixth-grade education as a qualification for voting in any state that required a literacy test. Bill McCulloch proposed adding a new title, which was taken from the bill he had introduced the previous January; it would direct the Bureau of the Census to obtain statistics about the race, color, and national origin of voters. And Celler introduced an amendment to make the Civil Rights Commission permanent. All amendments were accepted easily by the Republicans because, as the chairman had promised, they were only tentative.

Strangely enough, the subcommittee also weakened the Kennedy bill. Reflecting the fear of northern members, Bill McCulloch offered an amendment to delete from Title III (Public Education) the phrase "and racial imbalance." It would permit the commissioner of education, at the request of local school boards, to give technical and financial assistance for problems of desegregation but not of racial imbalance. In accepting this amendment, the subcommittee made the bill applicable to *de jure* (by law) school segregation in the South but not the *de facto* (by custom) segregation in the North. Southerners immediately charged that H.R. 7152 was aimed only at their section of the country. Bill McCulloch and Manny Celler realized that if the bill was to have any hope of passage, they had to make this end-justifying-the-means concession to northern members of Congress.

While Subcommittee No. 5 dissected H.R. 7152, schools across the nation opened. In the South many states were integrating their public schools for the first time, and for most, it was a peaceful step; Georgia, South Carolina, Texas, Tennessee, Maryland, and Florida quietly complied with federal court orders. But Governor George Wallace of Alabama, in keeping with his campaign promise of "segregation today, segregation tomorrow, segregation forever," moved state troopers into Tuskegee, Huntsville, Mobile, and Birmingham to stop schools from opening. Immediately, all five of Alabama's federal district judges issued an injunction prohibiting the troopers from obstructing court orders. The governor then replaced them with national guardsmen. President Kennedy countered by federalizing the National Guard and ordering the guard to withdraw from the schools. Finally, despite the governor, integration proceeded in Alabama.

But for every step forward, blacks paid a price. This time they paid with Sunday-school children. On the morning of September 15, five days after schools opened, a bomb exploded under the steps of the Sixteenth Street Baptist Church in Birmingham. Four little girls were killed, and twenty other youngsters were injured. When angry, rioting blacks took to the streets, police responded with shot guns and tanks, killing two more youngsters.

The nation was horrified. Senators and congressmen were deluged with mail and telephone calls demanding that something be done. The NAACP's Roy Wilkins, before leaving Washington to attend the funerals of the six children, held a press conference in which he pleaded, "The latest Birmingham outrage demonstrated the need of going beyond the present bill and enacting legislation that will eradicate the consuming poisons of racial discrimination from our national life at once."

The nation's lawmakers also responded. Historically, Congress always has been a passive body, stirring only when hit over its collective head with something too outrageous to ignore. The spring of 1963 was a good example. During the first four months of the year, veteran newsmen on Capitol Hill swore they had never seen the place so somnolent. Even an energetic liberal like Emanuel Celler seemed to be half asleep. By May 1, three months after Bill McCulloch had introduced his civil rights bill, Celler had not yet scheduled a single hearing on it nor on any of the other 88 similar bills piling up in his committee. But five days later, after Birmingham police chief Bull Connor turned attack dogs and fire hoses on school children, Celler announced that Subcommittee No. 5 would start hearings the next morning. And in mid-June when Medgar Evers, who had been invited to testify, was murdered a few hours after President Kennedy's speech, the Judiciary Committee chairman angrily challenged his subcommittee at its next meeting. "We must no longer palliate and ponder, quibble and quarrel," Celler had thundered. "We must pass stringent laws and pass them soon."

In mid-September, following the Birmingham bombing, the liberal Democrats on Subcommittee No. 5 vowed to put more muscle into the Kennedy civil rights bill. During the next week, they introduced three amendments. Byron Rogers offered an amendment to broaden the education title by authorizing the attorney general to intervene in cases where a person was denied access to any public facility—such as a park or library—operated by a state or one of its subdivisions. Manny Celler offered an amendment to add Title X, which permitted higher federal courts to review civil rights cases that were transferred to state courts by unsympathetic federal district judges. And Bob Kastenmeier offered an amendment to broaden

Title II to cover every form of business including private schools, law firms, and medical associations; excluded, however, were rooming houses with five units or less.

Bill McCulloch was shocked that the move to strengthen Title II, the most controversial section, came with Manny Celler's support. Only a few days earlier, McCulloch had finally worked out a compromise Title II with the Justice Department, a compromise that Celler had said he could support. McCulloch, a gentleman who believed that other gentlemen always kept their words, was angry and disappointed with his friend and chairman. He could not understand Celler's betrayal. However, remembering the chairman's assurance that the amendments were only tentative, he held out hope that Title II might be cut back before the bill was voted out of subcommittee.

On Wednesday, September 25, the strengthening reached a crescendo when the two amendments most desired by the Leadership Conference on Civil Rights were introduced. At Celler's request, Rogers offered a new and far-reaching Title III, which authorized the attorney general to initiate or intervene in civil suits, charging discrimination by state or local officials.

The second amendment, offered by Peter Rodino, was a tough new Title VIII. It established an Equal Employment Opportunity Commission with the power to (1) investigate any U.S. firm with 25 or more employees on charges of discrimination based on race, color, religion, or national origin and (2), after a hearing, order such practices stopped. This 30-page amendment was actually H.R. 405, the Equal Employment Opportunity bill, which had been approved by the House Education and Labor Committee. It would replace Kennedy's Title VII, a relatively weak employment section that dealt only with government contracts and relied on persuasion rather than the force of law.

Bill McCulloch was upset about these amendments, which he felt would make the bill all but impossible to pass on the House floor. But he still hoped that there would be time to reconsider them before the bill was voted out. As he emerged from the committee room, McCulloch told the crowd of newsmen that the public accommodations provisions were "so severe they threaten passage of civil rights legislation, not only in the Senate but even in the House. I am opposed to these unbelievably severe powers that would cover every business in Ohio that carries goods and services to the public."

McCulloch was seething. He and Celler had been comradesin-arms on the Judiciary Committee for 16 years, during which time McCulloch was profoundly influenced by the acute mind of the Brooklyn Democrat. In addition, they were friends; they and their wives often dined together when the House worked late, Manny entertaining them with his wit and fine story telling. Finally, both men shared a deep respect for the House of Representatives. It took all of Bill McCulloch's considerable self-control to keep from exploding.

Actually, Celler had been playing a little game with two factions since midsummer. On one side were McCulloch and the Justice Department, who, as agreed in Piqua, were constructing a bill that the Republicans could support. On the other side were the liberal Democrats and the civil rights lobbyists in the Leadership Conference, who wanted a stronger bill. Celler felt he had to try to please them all and, at the same time, follow his own scenario for getting a good bill out.

Earlier in the year, on July 26, James Farmer, national director of CORE, testified before Subcommittee No. 5 that he would like to see a strengthened section on voting, with state and local elections added to the bill.

The chairman gave him a stern lecture on legislative tactics, explaining, "That was left out deliberately, not on principle but on expediency. It would be very difficult to get the bill through, the whole package through, if we had such a provision."

Farmer, acknowledging the political problem, declared ruefully, "When we ask for one-half of a loaf, we get one-quarter of a loaf. We ought to ask for what we want and then fight for it."

Several days later they did just that. Having learned of the secret McCulloch–Justice Department meetings and fearing that Celler would cooperate with the moderate Republicans to give them less than the strong bill they wanted, some high-pressure advocates descended on the chairman's office. Clarence Mitchell, Joseph Rauh, Andrew Biemiller, Walter Fauntroy, Arnold Aronson, and others demanded a whole loaf. One participant told columnists Rowland Evans and Robert Novak that "they stomped Manny." Celler agreed to support a strong public accommodations section, recognition of a sixth-grade education as proof of literacy, and a requirement that school districts begin complying with the Supreme Court school decision by the end of the year. He publicly affirmed his commitment to a stronger bill on August 7 when, speaking to an NAACP convention at Washington's Statler-Hilton Hotel, he promised to add an FEPC provision and widen the attorney general's authority to sue.

But what the civil rights leaders did not know was that this cave-in was part of the chairman's plan to bring a strong bill out of subcommittee and then trade away those sections most objectionable to the southern Democrats and conservative Republicans on the full committee.

It had taken months, but Manny Celler's long-planned scheme was soon to be carried out. Two hours after McCulloch's statement to the press, the House passed the Kennedy tax cut bill. With this measure safely on its way to the Senate, the chairman shifted into high gear. It was time to move H.R. 7152 out of subcommittee.

Celler the diplomat became Celler the dictator. At the next subcommittee meeting, on October 1, the Republicans discovered a curious change in the atmosphere of room 346. Gone was the bipartisan harmony. Tentative decisions overnight had become permanent and unchangeable. GOP alternatives to titles and sections were rejected high-handedly. The minority members (including John Lindsay, who sat in as a nonvoting observer) were stunned as they reviewed what was now an irreversible bill. McCulloch sat silently. He had been betrayed twice.

The next morning Celler called for voice votes and announced triumphantly that H.R. 7152, as revised, was reported favorably to the full committee. It was a vastly strengthened bill.

Title I (Voting Rights) was expanded to cover all elections—federal, state, and local.

Title II (Public Accommodations) was extended to cover every form of business including private schools, law firms, and medical associations; owner-occupied boarding houses of five units or less were exempted.

Title III (Desegregation of Public Facilities) was new, authorizing the attorney general to initiate or intervene in civil suits on behalf of any individual who the Justice Department believed was denied his rights.

Title IV (Public Education) extended the power of the attorney general to institute action in cases of school desegregation as well as in cases of discrimination in other publicly operated or supported facilities. Technical and financial assistance could be offered in cases of desegregation but not racial imbalance.

Title V (Community Relations) was placed under the jurisdiction of the Commerce Department.

Title VI (Civil Rights Commission) made the commission permanent instead of extending it for four years.

Title VII (Federally Assisted Programs) gave the Justice Department added power to file suits where federal funds were extended to state and local governments.

Title VIII (Equal Employment Opportunity) established the commission by law, instead of having it exist at the president's discretion. EEOC was empowered to investigate charges of discrimination in all firms with 25 or more employees and issue judicially enforceable orders.

Title IX (Registration and Voting Statistics) was new, directing the Census Bureau to gather election data.

Title X (Judicial Intervention) was new, permitting higher federal courts to review civil rights cases transferred to state courts.

Title XI (Miscellaneous) provided for funds and protected the entire bill from being voided in case one of its sections was judged unconstitutional.

There was instant reaction to the subcommittee bill. Civil rights leaders were elated that it contained all their proposals. The Leadership Conference on Civil Rights, in its weekly bulletin, asked its member organizations to "write now! Urge the committee, with floods of communications, not to dilute the bill."

"It's a pail of garbage," snapped Bill McCulloch, his voice as brittle as dry leaves. He predicted that the bill would never make it on the House floor but, instead, would be recommitted to the Judiciary Committee.

"We had everything under control, and then he collapsed in the face of the liberals," charged Deputy Attorney General Nicholas Katzenbach of Celler, adding that his "spine was not Manny's strong point."

"Nicholas Katzenbach didn't know that the subcommittee bill was for the purpose of trading," explained Committee Staff Director Bess Dick. "So when it came out, he hit the ceiling."

Actually, Nicholas Katzenbach, while a smart lawyer and a tough tactician, did not have a great deal of experience passing legislation. Neither did his boss, the attorney general, whose expertise on the Hill was limited to investigative committees. They were unprepared for Celler's feint, even though he had hinted to Katzenbach that "the stronger the subcommittee bill, the stronger the final product." It was humiliating to the balding, bulky, 41-year-old deputy attorney general; he was the chief link between the White

House and Capitol Hill on H.R. 7152. During the summer and early fall, he had assured Larry O'Brien, in brief weekly memos, that everything was proceeding according to plan, and the president's political adviser forwarded this good news to the Oval Office.

O'Brien's September 23 memo to Kennedy stated, "Celler should have bill out of subcommittee this week. Anticipates ten days in full committee. Report it out by October 10."

Nicholas Katzenbach had been an Air Corps navigator during World War II, had spent 30 months as a prisoner of war, and was later a Rhodes scholar and then a professor of law at both Yale and the University of Chicago. He was not happy to be hoodwinked. Neither was Larry O'Brien, who was caught in the middle. But most unhappy of all was the president. He hardly recognized his bill.

John Kennedy was angry not only with Celler but also with Clarence Mitchell and the Leadership Conference on Civil Rights, which had been pressuring the subcommittee for a stronger bill. He felt they were unrealistic. In a meeting with the Reverend Eugene Carson Blake, a spokesman for the Leadership Conference, Kennedy asked heatedly if civil rights leaders had looked ahead to the coming fights over the bill in the conservative-dominated Rules Committee and on the House floor.

"Can Clarence Mitchell and the Leadership group deliver 3 Republicans on the Rules Committee and 60 Republicans on the House floor?" the president demanded. "McCulloch can deliver 60 Republicans. Without him it can't be done. McCulloch is mad now because he thinks that an agreement he had with us on the language of compromise has been thrown away by the subcommittee. So now he's sore. The question is, how many Republicans are you going to get? Once McCulloch is mad, then it ceases to be bipartisan. I'll go as far as I can go, but I think McCulloch has to come with us or otherwise it is an exercise in futility."

In addition to Bill McCulloch, the other 13 Republicans on the full Judiciary Committee were also on the warpath. Stung by Celler's high-handedness and vowing vengeance, they gathered in conference room H-202, a hideaway just off the House floor, three hours after the subcommittee passed the strong bill. With them was Charles Halleck (R-Ind.) their minority leader.

Florid-faced Charlie Halleck was a tough-talking "gut fighter," as he called himself, from rural Indiana, who gave no quarter to his political opponents and expected none in return. He was not one of John Kennedy's favorite Republicans. Before Kennedy had introduced his civil rights bill in June, he invited Halleck and Everett Dirksen (R-Ill.), Senate minority leader, to the White House to ask for their support. Dirksen had listened sympathetically. But Halleck, a hard-liner who enjoyed seeing the other party squirm, had not been so agreeable. "Why," he demanded later at a meeting of Republican leaders, "should the GOP bail out the administration?" Newsmen reported that he also relished the idea of Kennedy "on the hook over civil rights." Halleck, of course, indignantly denied it.

Charlie Halleck's favorite way of leading was to ask questions and listen. In this way he learned how his Republican members felt and was better able to get a bill that most nearly met their position. On civil rights he asked one Judiciary Committee member, "You're not in favor of this bill are you—coming from a state with no real problems in this connection?" To another he remarked, "Are you sure you really want to go this far? Do you think this is the right thing to do? Maybe, aren't you going a little too fast? Wouldn't it be better to take this in bites rather than get such a comprehensive legislative package together?" In posing these queries, Halleck was well aware that Senator Barry Goldwater, the leading Republican candidate for the 1964 presidential nomination, was openly appealing for southern support. He had been very surprised, therefore, at the strong feelings voiced by a majority of Judiciary Committee GOP members for more than a token bill.

This afternoon, however, the angry Republicans were united on just one thing: they would not be the scapegoats again. Bitter at Celler's partisanship, they told Halleck they had caught on to the chairman and would refuse to play his trading game; refuse to cooperate with the southern Democrats to cut the bill back; and, more to the point, refuse to get the blame for emasculating H.R. 7152.

Politicians, more often than not, are motivated less by what is right than by the desire to avoid wrong. This leads them either to do nothing or, if action must be taken, to band together and circle the wagons in defense. Halleck understood this completely.

"Well, this is the way it will be," he agreed, not at all unhappy. "Let them clean up their own bill."

The muscular new H.R. 7152 was to be formally presented to the full Judiciary Committee of the House of Representatives on Tuesday morning, October 8. While Chairman Emanuel Celler had easily controlled his hand-chosen subcommittee, this larger panel was a different matter. It was a prestigious body of 35 diverse men, all lawyers. There were 21 Democrats and 14 Republicans. But more importantly, they transcended their political parties to divide themselves into philosophical groups: 17 liberals, 8 conservative Southerners, 9 moderate-to-conservative Northerners, and 1 maverick.

It would take a master magician to pull a decent civil rights bill out of this polyglot mixture, but Emanuel Celler was confident he could do it. He was relying on a coalition of conservative Republicans and southern Democrats to trim back the subcommittee product. It had worked twice before, in the Eisenhower years, and would work again. The end result would be a reasonably good bill. Celler would not be blamed by the civil rights leaders for the cutbacks but, instead, would be proclaimed a hero by the press for having accomplished the clever sleight of hand.

At the start of the meeting, closed because it was still part of the markup process, each member was handed two documents. One was a 99-page Committee Print. The first 37 pages contained President Kennedy's original bill, which was crossed out, and the remaining 62 pages carried the "clean" version of the substitute. The second document was a Confidential Print showing how the changes were made in each section of the original bill. Celler explained that the subcommittee bill would be read title by title, at which time additional amendments could be offered. Then he read a general explanation of the bill and answered questions, confident that everything was proceeding according to his plan. The committee adjourned at noon, just in time to hear the bell calling the House into session.

If Manny Celler was pleased with himself, others were not. In his zeal the Brooklyn Democrat had made two fatal mistakes. First, Celler assumed that 1963 was just like 1957 and 1960, that the Republicans would consent to play the heavies in order to get a good bill out. But the two previous civil rights bills had come out during the administration of a Republican president who could be counted on to back his men. This time there was a Democratic president who might resort to politics-as-usual and blame the Republicans for messing up the bill.

Moreover, Celler failed to appreciate the difference between the 4 relatively new liberal Republicans on his committee—John Lindsay, William Cahill (N.J.), Clark MacGregor (Minn.), and Charles Mathias (Md.)—and the 10 older conservative Republicans. Whereas the older men had voted to cut back the previous bills, the younger men were as committed to civil rights as any liberal Democrat and would refuse to cut H.R. 7152 drastically.

Celler had lost touch. If he wanted the widest possible support, knowing what was ahead in the Senate, he should have gone for a big consensus victory. But instead he relied on his old heavy-handed strategy, unaware that changing times called for a delicate, sensitive approach.

A few moments after the House convened on October 8, three solemn men sat down in the office of the Speaker of the House of Representatives to discuss H.R. 7152 as it then existed. There was the Speaker, John McCormack, the gentle, elderly leader of the Democrats. There was Nicholas Katzenbach, the link with the White House. And there was Minority Leader Charles Halleck, who had requested the meeting in order to pass along the message that the Republicans would not do Celler's dirty work.

All three men agreed that the bill must be moderated. The Republicans, said Halleck, would cooperate by offering half of the amendments. But to protect themselves, they insisted that the rest of the amendments come from Democrats, "not from Southerners but from the liberal Democrats." Otherwise, he warned, the Republicans would reject all the weakening amendments and let the strong bill die of its own weight on the House floor.

This presented the Kennedy administration with a dilemma. Either they patched up the subcommittee bill so it could pass or the president got on the side of the liberals, supported the subcommittee version, and "threw the bill away." They would destroy the whole bill if they tried to amend it on the floor without the support of the Republican leadership.

Attorney General Robert Kennedy opted for patching up the bill. He decided that they must "get the Republicans and Democrats to agree on it on the floor and have that agreement made prior to the time it ever came to the floor."

The first step was getting Emanuel Celler to change his position. An angry Bobby Kennedy summoned the chairman to the Justice Department. It was not a pleasant meeting. The attorney general tore into Celler for not following the tactics that the Kennedys wanted him to use, tactics that had been spelled out in the letter from Nick Katzenbach that Manny received on August 13 and then promptly ignored.

"It wasn't a gratuitous lecture," Kennedy said later. "We'd lost him, and he wasn't giving any leadership. The reason I was as strong as I was, was that he was no good to us with his present posture."

The second step in the salvage operation was to make amends to Bill McCulloch. The Justice Department realized that the Ohioan had been burned by Celler's tactics. McCulloch was also angry because, in his quest for a moderate bill, he felt he had been put unfairly on the defensive by those who claimed he was taking the guts out of the civil rights bill. McCulloch was in the position, even if he trusted the Department of Justice, of having liberal Democrats stab him in the back. So Kennedy told Celler to arrange a meeting between McCulloch and the two Justice Department officials, Marshall and Katzenbach. Somehow, the two men would try to persuade the Ohio congressman to help them again. Celler, although privately fuming at the attorney general's cavalier treatment of him, followed orders and found his erstwhile partner willing to meet with Kennedy's emissaries. "Have I ever run from a cause?" was a question that Bill McCulloch had asked more than once during his political career.

When the two tireless negotiators arrived at McCulloch's office, hats in hand, they discovered, as before, that the congressman was a man of conscience, still open to their entreaties and willing to try once more. But as they might have anticipated, the country lawyer again had his price. This time he insisted on an ironclad guarantee that the Justice Department would make the Democrats support any changes that were made in the bill.

"It won't work," complained a group of liberal Democrats when they heard McCulloch's terms.

"Well, we've got to try it," Katzenbach replied, "because otherwise you can't get a civil rights bill."

While McCulloch, Celler, and the Justice Department began trimming the bill, Bobby Kennedy threw his weight behind William McCulloch. Determined to bolster McCulloch's confidence in the administration, Kennedy gave orders that no one in the White House or the Justice Department would take credit for the bill if it was successful. All statements would say, "Congressman McCulloch has done it... and Congressman Emanuel Celler." Bobby Kennedy, in effect, became Bill McCulloch's press aide.

The Republican members of the House Judiciary Committee, however, were still edgy, fearful that somehow they would still get the blame. Politicians instinctively position themselves on the safe side of a sticky issue. Congressmen cast scores of votes each year and always must know what they would say, in defense, in case a vote has to be explained. This often causes timidity because most congressmen are unwilling to speak out on an issue until public sentiment can be measured. And if they are conscious of being less than courageous, they can always rationalize, in all humility of course, that the country's best interest would be served if they were reelected.

So the Republicans, to protect themselves from getting the blame for the cutbacks in H.R. 7152, hit upon a marvelous idea. They would let Bobby Kennedy do the dirty work. He did not have to worry about getting reelected every 730 days. They devised the clever plan of innocently suggesting to Celler, who might be only too glad to comply, that the attorney general be invited back to the Hill to tell the Judiciary Committee what the administration thought of this new muscle-bound version of the president's bill. Even though the meeting would be closed, they were aware that Kennedy's critical comments would be leaked to the press, thus diverting criticism from them. Yes, they all happily agreed that shifting the blame to Kennedy was the best ploy.

The White House was fully aware of the fancy footwork on the part of the Republicans. John Kennedy was as knowledgeable about hardball politics as anybody in the country. Under his monogrammed shirt was the tough skin of a big-city pol. Weighing his options, the president decided that Bobby should accept the invitation. The attorney general did not fear tough jobs. He had, after all, dealt successfully with the governors of Mississippi and Alabama when they refused to integrate their state universities. He had pressured the balky Birmingham retailers when negotiator Burke Marshall needed him to provide a little last-minute convincing. Bobby was at his best when the chips were down.

The Cannon Building was again crowded with newsmen and spectators on October 15 when Attorney General Robert Kennedy arrived at 10:00 A.M. Looking solemn, he made his way to the large third-floor caucus room, which had been specially set up for the hearing. Since the Judiciary Committee was meeting in executive session, the room was closed to everyone except committee members and staff. In opening the meeting, Chairman Celler emphasized the bipartisan nature of civil rights legislation, a point reiterated a few moments later by Bill McCulloch. Celler then introduced Kennedy who, flanked by Nicholas Katzenbach and Burke Marshall, read a prepared statement that had been cleared in a meeting the previous

evening with the president and his political aides, Kenny O'Donnell and Larry O'Brien.

"I am here today," the attorney general began, "to support
the legislation which the President submitted.... I am pleased that
the subcommittee has recommended a print of H.R. 7152 which,
in many respects, closely follows the bill as introduced. Of course
the print, which I am here to discuss today, also makes a number
of changes and additions. I shall discuss the most important of these
changes in the hope that my comments will assist the committee
in arriving at what the President called 'the most responsible,
reasonable, and urgently needed solution.' "

Kennedy then went over the subcommittee bill, title by title,
and suggested changes already agreed to by McCulloch, Celler, and
the Justice Department. The attorney general was peppered with
questions and offered to return that afternoon for further inter-
rogation, providing there were no objections; committee meetings
were not usually held in the afternoon while the House was in
session.

As he emerged from the caucus room, the press descended on
the attorney general like locusts on an asparagus patch. Clamoring
for a usable quote, they thrust a dozen microphones in front of
his face. "What I want is a bill," Bobby Kennedy said with a thin
smile, "not an issue."

A few minutes later objection was raised in the House about
holding a Judiciary Committee meeting that afternoon, so the attorney general agreed to return the following morning. On Wednesday morning, Chairman Celler called the meeting to order and obe-
diently carried out step one in the Justice Department's scenario:
he changed his position.

"The urgency for bipartisan legislation at this session is so
strong that I intend to put aside my own feelings with respect to
the desirability of provisions in addition to those recommended by
the administration," said Celler. "I shall exert every effort toward
achieving a bill along the lines recommended by the administration
to be reported out of this committee within two weeks."

During both the morning and afternoon meetings (The House
did not conduct legislative business that day.), the attorney general
repeated his "bill, not an issue" theme. And he insisted that retreat
was necessary because, as he told Bob Kastenmeier, "I think the
vote on this bill is going to be very close." One Republican, James
Bromwell of Iowa, called Bobby Kennedy's two-day appearance

brilliant. "He used no notes," said Bromwell. "He had stacks of books in front of him and Katzenbach and Marshall behind him. He referred to neither. He had a complete grasp of the bill. Also, I was impressed with his forthrightness. There was no equivocation. He took full responsibility for the proposed cut backs."

But civil rights leaders were not so impressed. Clarence Mitchell stated, "There is no reason for this kind of sellout." CORE's James Farmer maintained that the president "thinks he has the Negro vote in the bag and . . . can back out on civil rights." On October 17 Arnold Aronson, acting on behalf of the Leadership Conference on Civil Rights, sent telegrams to the president, attorney general, and members of the House Judiciary Committee strongly disagreeing with Bobby Kennedy's proposals for softening the subcommittee bill. "To weaken the bill at this time," Aronson wrote, "would simply encourage civil unrest and heighten racial tensions. It would be an invitation for others to weaken the measure." In a newsletter sent the next day, the Leadership Conference described Kennedy's testimony as a blow and urged all member organizations to "send messages, telegrams, phone calls, and delegations to home offices."

President Kennedy had anticipated, just as the Republicans had, that there would be this outcry from civil rights leaders and that his administration would bear the brunt of the attack. To soften the criticism, Kennedy campaigned for press support for his position, before the attorney general's Judiciary Committee appearance.

A president has the same problem as other politicians: he does not want to reap the blame if he can help it. But unlike other politicians, he has access to vast media resources that can be used to influence public opinion. Starting on October 11, John Kennedy called in a number of powerful journalists, several of whom were also his close friends—syndicated columnists Joseph Alsop, Holmes Alexander, and Joseph Kraft; *New York Times* correspondent Anthony Lewis; *Newsweek's* Benjamin Bradlee; and newspaperman Charles Bartlett, godfather of the president's son John, Jr. And it was only natural that a man as intellectually nimble as Kennedy would not limit himself to being defensive about the cuts. He went on the offense to attack the "real liberals," as he called them, like Bob Kastenmeier and John Lindsay, who were pressing for stronger legislation that theoretically might be fine but, practically speaking, would be impossible to pass.

On Capitol Hill, meanwhile, Emanuel Celler was stalling the

Judiciary Committee while he, Bill McCulloch, and the Justice Department worked to moderate the bill. They agreed to apply Title I (Voting Rights) to federal elections only, as in Kennedy's original version. The scope of Title II (Public Accommodations) was reduced to conform to McCulloch's earlier demands—that retail stores and personal service firms not be covered. And they deleted Title III (Judicial Intervention) altogether. As soon as they were ready, Celler would schedule a showdown session to ram the amendments through.

Complying with Charles Halleck's demands that these changes be shared with nonsouthern Democrats, Manny Celler picked Chicago congressman Roland Libonati to introduce the Title I amendment. Libonati was a pudgy, 62-year-old product of Mayor Richard Daley's political machine, and in selecting him for this chore, Celler was looking for a loyalist who could be counted on to do what he was told. At the same time, the cagey Celler was also looking ahead to the coming debate on the House floor. He knew that Mayor Daley kept a tight rein on his nine Democratic congressmen, meeting with them each weekend to discuss legislation, and that the mayor's power to dispense patronage and to control the outcome of primary elections meant that the congressmen, as a matter of prudence, deferred to his judgment. With Libonati as his accomplice in the mission to tone down the bill, Celler not only complied with Halleck's demands, but he also might gain the support of the eight other Chicago congressmen, all liberals, during any future fight on the House floor.

Everything rolled along smoothly, according to the salvage plan, until the morning of October 10, when Libonati, as ordered, made his motion to cut back Title I. Because of a parliamentary problem, however, the committee did not have time to vote on Libonati's amendment before adjourning. And this, in turn, gave Bob Kastenmeier time to try to block the move.

Kastenmeier was a 39-year-old Democrat from Madison, Wisconsin, and one of the most liberal members of the House. He had originally strengthened Title I in the subcommittee, and he was understandably angered by this attempt to weaken it again. After the meeting he hurried to the office of William Dawson (D-Ill.), the senior member of the Chicago delegation and one of five black congressmen in the House.

"Bill," said Kastenmeier, "you know what the problem is. Libby wants to change the Voting Rights section to federal only.

47

You know what it means for a black in the South who only can...vote in federal elections and not...in local elections for the sheriff and others.''

"Don't worry," replied Dawson, "I will give him a call."

Dawson told Libonati that the move to water down Title I was not popular among the committee's liberal Democrats and would be a very unwise thing to do, and this started Libonati thinking. An appearance by Emanuel Celler a few days later on a CBS-TV news show did the rest. Celler, unable to resist the temptation to make himself look good, denied any connection with attempts to weaken the bill. At that point, the street-smart Libonati suspected that his slippery chairman was going to pin the blame on him. "Old Libby knows when he's been had," he confided to a colleague.

The morning of October 22 was cool and crisp on Capitol Hill. The hardwood trees in the plaza wove a vibrant canopy of scarlet and yellow and orange as members of the House Judiciary Committee gathered for the showdown session on H.R. 7152. A confident Emanuel Celler was prepared to deal with Libonati's pending amendment to remove state and local elections from Title I. And after that had been voted on, they would handle the other motions to soften the bill. In Celler's folder were amendments to create a new Title II and to delete Title III. Then, like a house of cards, the carefully crafted scenario crumbled.

"Mr. Chairman," Roland Libonati called out, "I move to withdraw my amendment!"

Manny Celler was caught unawares, and Libonati's motion carried by a voice vote. In one minute's time, the McCulloch-Celler-Justice Department plan, carefully constructed over two weeks, went out the window. Celler's bulldog face was a study in belligerency, and his freckled bald dome glistened under the bright chandeliers. Bill McCulloch sat back wearily, his usually smiling face cold and stern as he faced his third betrayal. Bob Kastenmeier looked pleased. Libonati looked stubborn. Everyone else looked on in confusion. Then, in the absence of any alternate plan, H.R. 7152 was tossed from conservative to liberal and back to conservative again.

William Tuck (D-Va.) suggested that the bill be sent back to subcommittee. Unhappy with that idea, Byron Rogers said if Tuck offered his suggestion as a formal motion, he would move that the subcommittee bill be reported favorably to the House, which would surely kill it. Tuck backed off. Next eight Southerners tried to send the bill back to subcommittee, a motion that was rejected 9–21.

Finally, Arch Moore (R-W.Va.), frustrated by the Machiavellian maneuvers and Celler's partisan handling of H.R. 7152 all along, spoke up. "Mr. Chairman," he said firmly, "I move we report the bill out favorably to the House."

Manny Celler was once again caught by surprise. This was the last thing in the world the chairman wanted to happen. If Moore prevailed, it was almost certain the bill would be defeated. On the part of Arch Moore, this reflected no grand design, but simply his frustration with Celler's manifest ineptness.

"The shame of our times," said Moore,

> is that the subject of civil rights has from the early days of the 88th Congress been made the butt of political opportunism.... The committee chairman was forced to label the subcommittee bill "drastic" irrespective of the fact that it was his bill. Amendments were offered and withdrawn. Signals were called and then missed. Coalitions [were] formed and then rejected. To attempt to enact civil rights legislation in the heavy handed and politically motivated manner that is presently being attempted is a disservice to the democratic process and to all citizens who want and expect effective legislation.

Celler was impaled on his own gaff. The motion, if adopted, would end the committee's control of the bill, in all probability condemning it to death in the Rules Committee, on the House floor, or in a Senate filibuster. Clearly, Arch Moore had the votes. Liberal Democrats, anxious to please the civil rightists, were only too happy to vote out a strong bill. Southern Democrats, who believed a strong bill would die on the House floor, were suddenly in favor. And the Republicans, feeling once again double-crossed by Libonati's refusal to follow orders, were willing to vote for the unpassable bill and to let Celler and the administration suffer the consequences.

The doomed chairman was literally saved by the bell. When the House bell rang at noon announcing the opening of the House's daily floor meeting, Celler's ally Jack Brooks hastily pointed out that the chamber was in session and, in accordance with House rules, all committee business must be suspended. A visibly relieved Celler quickly adjourned the committee until the next morning when, he announced, there would be a roll call on the Moore motion. But after several phone calls, Celler realized he did not have the votes, and the next day he wisely cancelled the meeting.

John Fitzgerald Kennedy, a navy man who never forgot his

salty language, was furious when informed of the chaos in the Judiciary Committee. He had relied on Manny Celler's 41 years of experience and had been assured by Larry O'Brien's memos that everything was going well. But suddenly and without warning, the bill was as good as dead.

Kennedy had no taste for the romance of a lost cause. As tough as any politician who ever paced the floor on election night, the president did not intend to lose either the civil rights bill or the next year's election. Quickly taking stock of the situation, he summoned the principals to the White House.

Early on the evening of October 23, a caravan of limousines rolled up to the diplomatic entrance, out of sight of the ever-present reporters working the west wing. Vice President Lyndon Johnson, House Speaker John McCormack, Majority Leader Carl Albert (D-Okla.), Minority Leader Charles Halleck, Minority Whip Les Arends (R-Ill.), Emanuel Celler, and William McCulloch gathered in the Cabinet Room and waited for the president. The attorney general and his ubiquitous aides, Nick Katzenbach and Burke Marshall, were nearby in case they were needed.

Like the parent of a child who had gone astray, John F. Kennedy strode irritatedly into the room. For the first time since he introduced his civil rights bill in June, the president took personal control of the legislation. Kennedy had never stayed in the House or Senate long enough to become chairman of a committee. The quintessential young-man-in-a-hurry, he had always been running for higher office, a fact that rankled many of the older congressmen and senators and might have contributed to his difficulties getting his programs through Congress. He had never been one of the good old boys of Capitol Hill.

But as a nuts-and-bolts, vote-counting politician, Kennedy had no peer. During the two-hour meeting he did much of the talking, citing the need for legislation that, unlike the subcommittee bill, would not run the risk of being defeated on the House floor or hung up by a Senate filibuster. Most important, he was anxious to get a compromise bill written and passed by the end of the year to avoid considering the controversial measure during 1964 when he would be running for reelection. "Let's get this bill," he urged, "agree on what we can agree on, and let's send it to the floor."

The Cabinet Room was a jumble of voices as the men argued back and forth about how the subcommittee bill could be trimmed. Then came the slow and deliberate midwestern tones of Bill

McCulloch. "Certainly I can't vote for the bill that came out of subcommittee," he said, adding in his wry, deliberate way that if he had a little time, "all the king's horses and all the king's men could put humpty-dumpty together again."

At these cryptic words the room quieted. The president and the others listened as the calm and logical congressman made a pitch for some Republican input into H.R. 7152. "When it comes to compromise," he reflected, "you know if the only compromise is between this abhorrent subcommittee bill and the administration bill, there hasn't been anything upon which we have a chance to compromise, that is, the minority. There may be some things, too, that we might want to compromise."

"What is it we can do with the various sections?" asked the president. "Let's go through them very quickly and see how far apart we are."

"I don't think we are too far apart," answered McCulloch.

Kennedy was delighted; that was exactly what he wanted to hear. Enthusiastically, he led a lengthy discussion of the bills and McCulloch's suggestions for compromise. Impatient for immediate action, he suggested, "Why don't we agree on this procedure? If we can get Nick, Manny, and Congressman McCulloch together in the morning, say about 9:00 or 9:30, let them come to an agreement."

McCulloch objected. "This preliminary work can't be done in an hour or two. I've got to have a little time for maneuvering and some help. I'm just a country guy who has to muddle along."

John Kennedy laughed heartily. He loved the political comraderie usually associated with smoke-filled backrooms. But throughout the long meeting he kept pressing to get the bill out of committee before the weekend.

"Goddammit, Mr. President," exploded Halleck, explaining why more time was needed to persuade the GOP members. "Our principal trouble over there has been the conviction, after Manny's subcommittee blew this thing up to beat hell, that the whole purpose of that was to put the Republicans in the position of emasculatin' the bill."

"And can I interrupt there, Charlie?" asked McCulloch. "And that I had been taken for a ride."

Finally, McCulloch, Celler, and Katzenbach agreed to meet at 10:30 the next morning to start work on a compromise bill. Celler suggested that he would be happy to have them meet in his office.

McCulloch turned it down. "As Charlie says, you have your arm around me too much now," he quipped to Celler. Instead, a neutral site, Nick Katzenbach's office, was chosen.

Kennedy, although not happy about the delay, was persuaded that Monday was the earliest possible date for a compromise bill. Celler said he would schedule a Judiciary Committee meeting for Tuesday, October 29, to try to defeat the Moore motion and railroad out the compromise. Realizing that the vote was sure to be close, the president bargained with Halleck.

"If we can get a majority of the Democrats who are willing to take the heat," suggested Kennedy, "and a majority of you fellows do, that's a reasonable position."

Halleck countered. "Let's let it set at seven on our side against the Moore motion." Then he thought about it for a moment. "We've got to take another reading," he hedged, promising that he would meet with "my guys" the next morning and call the president by noon to give him a count.

After the Republicans left the Cabinet Room, Vice President Johnson suggested that the president meet with the northern Democrats on the committee the next morning and explain that a compromise bill was being written. "You can say," Johnson told the president, "now listen, I've had some talks here, and here is going to be our position. Fellows, you can have this or we won't have a bill. It's up to you. Now please help me." Kennedy agreed.

After the meeting the president joined his wife, Jacqueline, and Ben and Tony Bradlee in the family quarters for dinner. Referring to his discussion with Halleck, Kennedy complained that "trying to touch Charlie is like trying to pick up a greased pig." He added, "It's a lousy bill as it now stands." A few minutes later Burke Marshall called and Kennedy asked him to resurrect some statements from civil rights leaders praising Kennedy's original version of H.R. 7152.

The next morning, following Johnson's advice, President Kennedy started lobbying the Democratic liberals on the Judiciary Committee to defeat the Moore motion. Kennedy called the 9:30 A.M. meeting despite warnings by Larry O'Brien that if it failed, the president's prestige would suffer. O'Brien mistrusted Bob Kastenmeier who, he felt, would talk to the press afterward and cast Kennedy's effort in the worst possible light. To ensure secrecy, the congressmen, headed by Emanuel Celler, arrived at the diplomatic entrance and took the elevator to the president's living quarters.

They met in the Yellow Oval Room, considered by many experts to be the most beautiful room in the White House. Three large windows overlook the fountains on the south lawn and, beyond them, the Washington Monument and Jefferson Memorial. Franklin D. Roosevelt had used the oval chamber as his private study. Jacqueline Kennedy turned it into an elegant 18th-century drawing room with antique French furniture and exquisite paintings. In truth, the politicians looked slightly out of place.

Kennedy, sitting in a rocking chair to ease his chronic back pain, told the men, "We want to pass something. We sympathize with what you've done but we can't pass the bill in its present form."

"We're with you, Mr. President," spoke George Senner (D-Ariz.). "We're going to stick with you." There was no rush to join Senner, however, for other than its original bill, the administration had no firm alternative to offer the liberals. So the half-hour meeting ended with what one participant characterized as "no immediate results."

After they had left, a bitter Bobby Kennedy remarked, "What my father said about businessmen [they're SOBs] applies to liberals. Some of these people would rather lose the whole bill and lose the legislation than make the kind of effort we wished. An awful lot of them...were in love with death."

Charlie Halleck, who had promised to call the president by noon to tell him how many Republican votes he could deliver to block the Moore motion, did not keep his promise. An overloaded calendar had kept Halleck busy until noon, when he finally met with the GOP members. He told them that he was getting "a lot of heat from the president. You'd better make up your minds. When you guys decide what you want, I'll take it down to the White House."

Bill McCulloch, realizing that the Republicans held the crucial votes, implored his colleagues to forget partisan politics and work with him for the good of the nation. McCulloch was not an arm twister; he believed in appealing to his colleagues' sense of right. "If you have one iota of compassion in your heart, and if you support the Constitution, you know there is only one thing to do," was one of his arguments.

The meeting ended with what Congressman James Bromwell described as a "restless agreement" to oppose the Moore motion in the hope that a feasible alternative could be worked out.

By 12:45 P.M. the president, waiting for Halleck's call, was getting edgy. He debated with Larry O'Brien about whether he should make the call himself, even though he felt somewhat inhibited about asking a favor of an opponent whom he had so often defeated on the House floor. Finally, Kennedy picked up the phone. "When we made that call to Charlie," confessed O'Brien, "the president of the United States and I figured we'd had it. He was ducking us."

"No such thing," Halleck reassured Kennedy. "Mr. President," he announced firmly, "we've got enough votes for you." Kennedy was elated. And according to Larry O'Brien, "We couldn't have been more pleased. It was a major, major breakthrough."

The president never could understand why the minority leader agreed to cooperate with him. Halleck's reason was simple; the same one that motivated many other conservatives to support civil rights legislation. He saw for himself that segregation robbed a man of his most precious possession, his self-esteem. According to Halleck,

> They couldn't understand that once in a while a guy does something because it's right. I had a few experiences. I had a black driver. We used to go down to Warm Springs, Virginia, to see friends. We'd stop at a little bit of a restaurant. I'd go in and ask if he could go in with the Hallecks. They said no but they would be glad to serve him in the car. The goddamned thing just didn't look right to me. Hell, I didn't do it for political advantage. The colored votes in my district didn't amount to a bottle of cold pee.

Bill McCulloch, meanwhile, was pursuing his own course. He had told Kennedy he needed "a little more time" because he realized that, before he could start compromising with the Democrats, he had to resolve the internal Republican differences, especially those between liberal John Lindsay and himself. If Lindsay and the three other GOP liberals on the committee did not have a bill they could support, they were sure to vote for the Moore motion. On Thursday McCulloch held a preliminary meeting with Manny Celler and Nick Katzenbach, and on Friday he made his approach to Lindsay. That morning he sent the Judiciary Committee minority staff counsel William Copenhaver to see Lindsay's aide Robert Kimball. Copenhaven asked Kimball what he thought Lindsay would accept in the way of a compromise. Kimball replied that he doubted Lindsay would go along with anything. "Not that we don't want a bill," said Bob Kimball. "Lindsay simply doesn't trust the administration to keep any kind of commitment."

"I know how you feel," Copenhaver persisted, "but can't we talk?" Kimball relented. "I'll go to Lindsay if you think this time there is a chance. I'll try to help, but only if that is the case."

Luckily, John Lindsay had attended Subcommittee No. 5's hearings and markup sessions as a nonvoting participant, taking the place of Bill Miller, chairman of the Republican National Committee. McCulloch had felt that Lindsay's views should be heard while H.R. 7152 was being amended. Consequently, the New Yorker now knew enough to help write a compromise measure.

Later that same Friday afternoon, Bob Kimball dropped into Bill McCulloch's Longworth Building office. The Ohio congressman, mentioning that he would be working long hours that weekend, asked Lindsay's aide where he could get in touch with him.

"I'll be in my office," replied Kimball. "That's good," smiled McCulloch, suggesting that he would call on him for assistance from time to time.

Bill McCulloch at this point was conducting a lone crusade, for most of the principals were out of town. Charlie Halleck had gone hunting in Minnesota and then home to Indiana. John Lindsay was in Richmond, Virginia, for a family wedding. Manny Celler had returned to his Brooklyn law office. And Arch Moore was back in West Virginia. But McCulloch had the telephone numbers where these and other key people could be reached.

Early on Saturday morning Bob Kimball found the Ohio congressman already in his office. That in itself was not unusual. A firm believer in the American work ethic, McCulloch worked from dawn to dusk and usually spent a good part of every weekend at his desk. Most of the time he worked on legislation, but occasionally he could be seen licking labels and sending infant information to new mothers in his district. He believed he should never ask anything of his staff that he would not do himself. This morning he exuded optimism because he had talked with Lindsay on the phone, and the Manhattan congressman had agreed to come to the Hill on Sunday afternoon.

John Lindsay, the handsome, tall, 42-year-old congressman from New York City was in his third term in Congress. A leader of the young Republican liberals, he was often irritated with the conservative leadership he found in the House of Representatives. But he liked Bill McCulloch and agreed with him that if they could work out their differences, it might just be possible to rescue H.R.

7152. Both had followers on the Judiciary Committee who shared their philosophies and probably could be persuaded to support the compromise.

That Sunday afternoon, McCulloch and Lindsay, along with aides Copenhaver and Kimball, went through the bill title by title. In some instances Bill McCulloch accepted the younger man's stronger views. But in other areas Lindsay deferred to his ranking member, feeling that McCulloch had gone quite far, especially in supporting a strong public accommodations section. And throughout, Kimball played devil's advocate, voicing arguments that were sure to be raised by the civil rights people like Joseph Rauh and Clarence Mitchell. When the gap between the Ohioan and the New Yorker was finally closed, the next step was to join with the administration and finish forging the new product. But secrecy was essential in order not to trip the alarm and send the Democratic liberals, the civil rights leaders, and the Southerners out with their shotguns. McCulloch called Katzenbach and they set up a clandestine meeting for the next morning at the Congressional Hotel.

After leaving Bill McCulloch's office, an exultant Lindsay remarked to Kimball, "I'm so proud that Bill has come so far. I can't desert him now. He has made a tremendous step toward a stronger bill."

The herculean efforts of McCulloch and Lindsay to resuscitate the president's bill, however, received a jolt the next morning. Republicans, both liberal and conservative, were disparaged in two of the nation's greatest newspapers. By a bit of bad timing, John Kennedy's campaign to get major journalists to write in support of his original bill climaxed and, unfortunately, resulted in some overkill.

In the *Washington Post,* Joseph Alsop wrote, "The vital civil rights bill is directly imperiled by the sorriest display to date of the endemic disease of American liberalism, which is the Liberals' fatal fondness of empty, competitive posturing."

But even more damaging to the delicate thread of bipartisanship that stretched between the White House and Charles Halleck was the *New York Times* article by Anthony Lewis.

> The key figure in the civil rights picture remains the House minority leader, Charles Halleck of Indiana. But as of tonight [October 27] no one seems to know what, if any bill he would agree to support. President Kennedy, who took a personal hand

in the fight last week by calling legislators to two White House meetings, may have another meeting with Committee Democrats tomorrow. But the real problem is still getting agreement with the Republicans. Mr. Halleck has been home duck-hunting this weekend. But the ranking GOP member of the Judiciary Committee, William M. McCulloch of Ohio, has been at work on the problem and has talked with administration representatives.

Charlie Halleck called Bill McCulloch early in the morning from Indiana. He had read the paper and was spouting earthy epithets at both Lewis and the administration, which he suspected of planting the story. McCulloch urged the minority leader to calm down, promising to get back to him later in the day after Halleck returned to Washington.

But when McCulloch joined Katzenbach, Marshall, Copenhaver, and Kimball at the Congressional Hotel, he, too, was furious. A patient man until provoked by what he considered ungentlemanly behavior, Bill McCulloch was scathing about the unfavorable press coverage given the Republicans that morning. Here they were risking their political lives on the president's ramparts to save his bill and, meanwhile, some of his friends were shooting them in the back. His anger vented, the congressman left the room and let the others get to work.

The four men swiftly and professionally fashioned a compromise bill, focusing more on principles than on specific language, which for each philosophical position had already been drafted. Most differences between the McCulloch-Lindsay "consensus" and the other two bills (original and subcommittee) were resolved in the direction of the McCulloch-Lindsay approach. On a few points, Katzenbach called Bobby Kennedy and the White House to get OKs. By lunchtime there were only a few details to work out, and those points were cleared in the afternoon by telephone between McCulloch and Katzenbach.

In turn, Bill McCulloch called Charles Halleck. Then, having received a green light from the minority leader and with Bob Kimball beside him to help, McCulloch spent the rest of the day on the phone with other committee Republicans; he guided, he explained, he entreated them to go along. He also called Arch Moore, but the West Virginia Republican refused to cooperate by withdrawing his motion to send the strong subcommittee bill to the House floor.

Meanwhile, a bank of Justice Department stenographers was commandeered to type the new 56-page measure, a compromise that was substantially stronger than the original H.R. 7152 but somewhat weaker than the subcommittee bill.

Title I (Voting Rights) was limited to federal elections only, and a three-judge federal court was permitted to hear voting rights cases if requested by the attorney general.

Title II (Public Accommodations) was reduced in its coverage to places of lodging, sports stadiums and arenas, theaters, restaurants, cafeterias, lunch counters, and gas stations. Retail stores and personal service firms, such as barbershops, were dropped.

Title III (Public Facilities) was retained, but the broad authority of the attorney general to initiate legal action was eliminated. Instead, the Justice Department could go to court only when suits alleging discrimination were filed by others or when it received a written complaint that segregation existed in a public facility owned and operated by a state or community and the aggrieved person was unable to file suit because of financial reasons or fear of personal harm.

Title IV (Public Education) was retained with no substantive changes, but it now specified that no official or court could issue an order to achieve racial balance.

Title V (Community Relations) was eliminated. New Title V (Civil Rights Commission) retained the permanent status of the commission. Added was a proposal contained in Congressman William Cramer's bill, H.R. 7115, authorizing the commission to investigate allegations of voting fraud.

Title VI (Federally Assisted Programs) was retained, but the right of departments and agencies to cut off assistance funds was reduced to federal grant, contract, and loan programs. The authority of the attorney general to file suits was eliminated.

Title VII (Equal Employment) was retained, but the commission's powers were limited to investigation and conciliation. Instead, a proposal by Congressman Robert Griffin (R-Mich.), Charles Goodell (R-N.Y.), and Albert Quie (R-Minn.) of the House Education and Labor Committee was incorporated requiring the commission, if it wished to compel action, to do so in a federal district court where both business and labor would be entitled to a trial.

Title VIII (Registration and Voting Statistics) was retained, but compilation was limited to those areas where the Civil Rights Commission requested information.

Title IX (Judicial Intervention) was retained without change.
Title X (Miscellaneous) was retained without change.

A summary of the compromise bill was hurriedly delivered to
the White House. At 4:00 P.M., in the Cabinet Room, the president pulled it out of his pocket and began his last-ditch effort to
persuade Judiciary Committee liberal Democrats not to vote for
the Moore motion, scheduled for the next morning. Kennedy read
the shortened version of the new bill, possibly leaving the impres-
sion that it was his own, announced that it had the support of Bill
McCulloch and Charlie Halleck, and asked which of the 13 men
sitting around the cabinet table could support it.

Kennedy needed 10 votes and knew that he could count on only
three men there: Manny Celler, George Senner, who had voiced
his support the previous Thursday in the Yellow Oval Room, and
Harold Donahue, an early Massachusetts ally of the president. A
fourth vote, that of hospitalized William St. Onge (Conn.), was
assured because St. Onge had given his proxy to Celler. And a fifth
probable vote was Jack Brooks, a longtime associate of Lyndon
Johnson. But in what figured to be a close vote the next morning,
the president knew he had to convert at least five of the remaining
nine men. But which five?

1. Bob Kastenmeier, the liberal Wisconsin congressman, remained adamant in his support for the subcommittee bill because
he felt the time was right and Congress should, as he put it, "strike
while the iron is hot." He felt it necessary "to create the greatest
pressure for a better bill, a strong bill."

2. Jacob Gilbert, from the Bronx, was even more liberal than
Kastenmeier. With his large number of Jewish, black, and Hispanic
constituents, Gilbert was one of only seven House members who,
for the past three years, had a zero score on *Congressional Quarterly
Almanac's* "conservative coalition" chart. He was certain to follow
the lead of Kastenmeier.

3. Byron Rogers, a Colorado representative whose southern
accent (he spent his youth in Texas and Oklahoma) belied his liberal
instincts, had worked diligently in the subcommittee to strengthen
the Kennedy bill. His second of Arch Moore's motion to vote out
the subcommittee bill clearly signaled what he would do the following morning.

4. Roland Libonati remained a problem. During the meeting,
when the president asked him if he would support the "package
which we got together with the Republicans which gives us about

everything we want," Libonati answered, "No." Shortly afterward Kennedy slipped away from the meeting to call Chicago mayor Richard Daley.

"Roland Libonati is sticking it right up us," said the president, "because he's standing with the extreme liberals who are gonna end up with no bill at all."

"He'll vote for it," exploded Daley. "He'll vote for any god-damned thing you want. I told him, 'Now lookit, I don't give a goddamn what it is, you vote for anything the president wants, and that is the way it will be.' "

"That'd be good," responded a still-skeptical Kennedy.

5. Don Edwards, of California, was the newest member of the committee. As a former naval gunnery officer and FBI agent, Edwards seemed an unlikely liberal, but liberal he was. "I had known Joe Rauh for a very long time," said Edwards. "I first met him when I joined the ADA. I would go to dinner at his home and swim in his pool on Sundays. Rauh and Clarence Mitchell were sort of helping me think in a subject that I knew very little about, and I trusted them." So Edwards had previously told the civil rights leaders that he would not yield.

Charles Daly, a fellow Californian and a member of Larry O'Brien's congressional liaison staff, had called Edwards several times before the meeting. "President Kennedy really wants you to give in on these one or two items," Daly had said.

"No, I can't," Edwards had replied.

"You mean you won't. The President of the United States has asked you to do this."

"I can't, and don't put pressure on me," said Edwards as he hung up.

6. Frank Chelf, of Kentucky, had voted against the 1957 and 1960 civil rights acts, but now, operating on the philosophy of "keeping everybody happy," he told President Kennedy that the compromise bill "had a right to be heard, debated, and acted upon." He assured Kennedy that he would vote the bill out of the Judiciary Committee but that he reserved the right to oppose all or portions of it during the House debate.

7. Peter Rodino, son of Italian immigrants, was a Celler confidant, often described by the chairman as his "right arm." But Rodino wanted a strong bill. "I don't think we should weaken the FEPC provision," he said. "If that were the case, I would bring an amendment to the floor."

"Now, come on Peter," said House Speaker John McCormack disapprovingly. But Kennedy interrupted in an accommodating tone, "No, Peter, we'll go along."

8. Herman Toll, a native of Kiev, Russia, was giving signs that he might desert the administration. But he, like Libonati, was a spoke in a big-city political machine, the Philadelphia organization presided over by Congressman William J. Green, Jr. And so, the president threatened Green that he would withdraw from the Philadelphia parade and $100-per-plate fund-raiser for Mayor James Tate, scheduled for October 30, if Toll stepped out of line. This was enough to keep Toll in place.

9. James Corman, the Los Angeles congressman, then in his third year as a House member, looked to Emanuel Celler for guidance. The former Marine Corps officer said, "I would do anything Manny wanted. I had total confidence in him. He had been there for well over forty years and I knew that he knew what he could do. Also, although I wasn't a very experienced legislator, I just knew if folks like Tuck were for something, I hadn't ought to vote for it no matter how good it sounded."

As the meeting ended, Chuck Daly came into the Cabinet Room and approached Corman. "Jim, we really need you on this."

"Ok," said Corman, who trusted Daly and figured he knew what he was talking about.

The White House felt they had four votes—Chelf, Rodino, Toll, and Corman—and remembering Libonati's change of mind, they could not be sure of him until all the votes were counted. To escape the press, the congressmen were hustled out through the Rose Garden, but Peter Rodino lingered behind to ask a favor of the president. Rodino's young son, Peter, Jr., had initiated a "little people to little people" letter-writing campaign whose purpose was to flood world leaders with mail urging them to take a position for peace and against the use of atomic weapons. Rodino asked if Kennedy would meet his son so that Peter could explain the project to him. The president replied that he would be delighted to see the boy and suggested that Rodino call his secretary, Mrs. Lincoln, who would set an appointment for after the president's forthcoming trip to Texas.

Later that evening, as lights burned brightly in the Justice Department, copies of the freshly printed compromise bill were put into large manila envelopes. A fleet of chauffeur-driven limousines fanned out through the darkened streets of Washington to deliver the mysterious packages to homes of Judiciary Committee members. By midnight all had received the anonymously written bill, and as a smiling Bill McCulloch had so thoughtfully pointed out to his coconspirators, no one could claim he had not seen it before it made its dramatic debut in the Judiciary Committee meeting the next morning.

During the night Bob Kimball received several telephone calls, one from William Higgs, Bob Kastenmeier's civil rights adviser. Higgs told Kimball that he felt it was so close that he did not know which way the vote would go in the morning. "It could go either way, by one or two votes," Higgs reported.

But the tide was slowly beginning to turn. At 8:00 Tuesday morning, Judiciary Committee members Jim Bromwell and Garner Shriver (R-Kans.) met for breakfast in the Longworth cafeteria. Bromwell respected Shriver and felt that since both came from the same type of midwestern state, neither with a large black population in his district, they could view the compromise bill objectively.

Shriver said he had decided to support the compromise bill. "The time was right and something was needed." Bromwell agreed. "The country had reached a turning point on a major social issue. Either it had to be dealt with in Congress or it would be dealt with elsewhere."

After breakfast they walked to a meeting of Judiciary Committee Republicans in Minority Whip Les Arend's office. Agreeing to support the compromise bill were Lindsay's three liberal colleagues, William Cahill, Charles Mathias, and Clark MacGregor. McCulloch carried William Miller's proxy in his pocket. These six votes, when added to Bromwell and Shriver, gave the president the Republican majority that Halleck had promised. For good measure, George Meader agreed to cast the ninth GOP ballot against the Moore motion but said he would oppose the compromise bill both in committee and on the House floor.

Then Charlie Halleck and Bill McCulloch drove down to the White House for a last-minute meeting with the president. Joining them were Vice President Lyndon Johnson, Majority Leader Carl Albert, Emanuel Celler, Nicholas Katzenbach, and Burke Marshall. Referring to Republican votes against the Moore motion, Halleck told Kennedy, "We've got at least seven and maybe another on our side."

"We've got nine," responded the president, "and we hope maybe Libonati will support us."

Sixteen votes were one short of the 17 needed to block the Moore motion. But Halleck had deliberately understated the Republican total; he wanted the Democrats to provide at least half of their members so that his Republicans would not get the blame for the defeat of the motion. His guarantee of 7 votes fulfilled his promise of delivering half the Republicans. Now he wanted to see if the president could produce his half, which would be 10.

"We have nine sure," repeated a nervous Kennedy, who always counted his votes carefully. "Libonati said he wouldn't and then later last night said he would. Assuming that his heart is still strong, we've got 10 and we'll be all right. Now," Kennedy paused for a moment, "he may blow it. In that case, we're in trouble." Turning to Halleck, the president asked, "Could you see if you can get an eighth if we need him? And if we don't, tell him to vote the other way."

"We'll try like hell," rasped Halleck grudgingly, who already had the extra vote in his pocket. He intimated that it would be tough but that, as a loyal opposition leader, he would go the extra mile to help the president. "I think he'd come along," finished the minority leader confidentially.

With that assurance, the president turned to Manny Celler, who recited step by step how he was going to ram things through the committee later that morning. Like a locker room before the big game, the air was filled with gratuitous advice, occasional expletives, overlapping talk, and bursts of laughter.

"I think we got a pretty good bill here," said Kennedy as the meeting ended. "We've got the FEPC that the Republicans—"

"Let's understand one thing, Mr. President," Halleck interrupted. "You know my concern about FEPC. And so I wouldn't want it understood here that when this gets out on the House floor that I support FEPC."

The president roared with laughter and needled Halleck for disavowing the section written by his own young GOP liberals. "That's the Republican FEPC," he chortled. "That's pretty good!" Halleck just sputtered.

Kennedy had him there. The "fair employment" language in Title VII had been written by the same three young congressmen, Robert Griffin, Charles Goodell, and Albert Quie, who had recently directed a successful plot to oust Charles Hoeven (R-Iowa), Halleck's conservative lieutenant, as chairman of the House Republican Conference and install Gerald R. Ford (Mich.) instead. This was intended as a warning to Halleck, who was sometimes accused of high-handedness by the younger Republicans. The minority leader got the message. If he cared about his future with the party, he would quietly bow to the demands for an FEPC title.

Emanuel Celler called the fateful Judiciary Committee meeting to order at 10:45 A.M. Of the 35 members, 3 were absent: William St. Onge, William Miller, and Michael Feighan (D-Ohio). Celler and McCulloch had the proxies for the first two. But Feighan, who was a delegate to an international immigration conference in Geneva, Switzerland, had a long-standing feud with Celler and refused to give the chairman his proxy. The magic number to block the Moore motion was 17, half the total. A motion is defeated on a tie vote.

No Broadway show was ever more carefully choreographed than the virtuoso performance in room 346 of the Cannon Building. The Kennedys wanted no miscues, muffed lines, or unexpected entries of villains on stage this time. Bill McCulloch was prepared to explain the compromise bill in exactly one minute. And William Foley, the committee's general counsel, had been up since dawn practicing reading the massive document at breakneck speed. But the Justice Department, skeptical of Manny Celler's ability to ad lib his starring role, had written a six-point script for the chairman to follow.

1. Take roll call on pending Moore motion (to report out the subcommittee bill).

2. Introduce compromise bill and read in its entirety as a single amendment.

3. Make brief explanation of bill by Celler and McCulloch— "not to yield for anything but a question, particularly not an amendment of any kind whatsoever."

4. Move previous question (that is, a call for a vote and an end to all discussion).

5. Take vote to accept compromise bill language as the new language of H.R. 7152.

6. Take final vote on H.R. 7152.

Celler followed the scenario, as rehearsed, point by point. First, he ordered a roll call on the pending Moore motion. Since, by tradition, majority members are called first, the Republicans had the luxury of waiting to see if President Kennedy fulfilled his part of the bargain by furnishing 10 Democrats. The president, with an assist from Manny Celler, delivered. The Democrats who voted against the motion were Celler, Chelf, Willis, Rodino, Donahue, Brooks,

Toll (a victim of throat cancer, who wrote his vote on paper), Corman, St. Onge, and Senner. Joining them were 9 Republicans, 2 more than Charlie Halleck had promised: McCulloch, Miller, Meader, Lindsay, Cahill, Shriver, MacGregor, Mathias, and Bromwell.

Once again Roland Libonati had changed his mind, voting for the Moore motion despite his commitment to the president the night before. The 10th Democratic vote came from a totally unexpected quarter—Ed Willis of Louisiana, a leading opponent of civil rights legislation. He was a close friend of Celler and McCulloch, often dining with them and their wives after committee or floor sessions. Willis was indebted to Celler for naming him chairman of three of the committee's seven permanent subcommittees. He repaid this favor by not joining those who voted for the Moore motion.

After the Moore motion was defeated, Celler read the first sentence of the subcommittee bill and moved to strike all the following language and insert the language of the new bill. William Cramer raised a point of order, claiming that the chairman's move was invalid since Celler had previously promised that the subcommittee bill would be open for amendment, title by title. But with the absolute power that a committee chairman so conveniently possessed, Celler ruled against Cramer's point of order; and a subsequent appeal by the Florida Republican was voted down by the committee, 22–11. The chorus line was right in step.

William Foley then began to read the 56-page bill, and by 11:30 A.M. he had completed 38 pages. But Foley, whose health had been weakened by recurring bouts with alcohol, started to lose his voice. He struggled manfully onward, finally whispering his way through the last 18 pages, and ending his heroic assignment at 11:52 A.M.

Third, Celler allowed himself one minute to explain the bill after which he yielded 60 seconds to McCulloch for the same purpose. Everything was right on cue.

Fourth, Peter Rodino moved the previous question which, if adopted, would prevent any more discussion on the new bill. It passed, 20–12. Now it was a race against time.

A vote to accept the language of the new bill as the official language of H.R. 7152 was ordered by Celler. The clock on the wall showed it was almost noon, and the southern-liberal bloc was ready to use the same adjournment tactic that Jack Brooks had used on October 22 to prevent a vote on the Moore motion. But Committee Staff Director Bess Dick, on Celler's instructions, raced like lightning through the roll call. As the bell rang announcing the opening of the House floor session, she triumphantly called out the last name. The compromise bill was accepted, 20-14.

Time had run out, and so the sixth step, a final vote on reporting the bill out of committee, was scheduled for that afternoon. But it would be a perfunctory epilogue. The curtain had just come down on the prize-winning play.

Bill Copenhaver and Judiciary Committee counsel Ben Zelenko drove down to the Justice Department to give the good news to the attorney general. As they entered Kennedy's office, the first question they heard was a barbed one. "How did Libonati vote?" demanded the attorney general.

Kennedy's ire at the hapless Chicagoan was caused by Libonati's disloyalty to the president, as well as his alleged underworld connections. According to *Mafia*, by Ed Reid, Libonati was ranked 41st in the Mafia's hierarchy in the United States. One of his staff members was Anthony Tisci, son-in-law of Chicago gangster Sam Giancana. Kennedy said no more, but he was known to be a strong subscriber to the Irish adage, "don't get mad, get even." Several weeks later, Libonati confided ruefully to a Republican colleague, "I have been told my political career is over."

Reactions to the new H.R. 7152 were predictably mixed. The president called it "a comprehensive and fair bill." The attorney general contended that if it had not been for the support and effort of Halleck and McCulloch, "the possibility of civil rights legislation in Congress would have been remote." He called the new bill "better...than the administration's in dealing with problems facing the nation." The Leadership Conference on Civil Rights deplored the defeat of the strong subcommittee bill and said that the new bill was "inadequate to meet the needs of 1963."

Arch Moore, reflecting the views of the unhappy losers on the Judiciary Committee who claimed they did not even get a chance to read the bill before it was rammed down their throats, decried "the mysterious origins of the compromise bill that appeared in the middle of the night." The southerners charged that it was "the greatest grasp for executive power conceived in the 20th century."

Shortly after the vote on the Moore motion, President Kennedy called to thank Charlie Halleck for his help. "You did a great job," said the elated president. "You really did what you said."

"I hated to overpromise down there, Mr. President," explained Halleck.

"Well, that was good," replied Kennedy. "Unfortunately, we didn't get Roland. Evidently that Cook County machine isn't as strong as we hear."

"You know," continued Halleck, "whenever I say something, I underestimate a little bit...and I don't get to be made out a liar."

"Yeah," agreed the president.

Then Halleck added, "I got a little trouble on my side, a lot of guys bitching. I ain't sure they'll make me leader again, but I don't give a damn." Kennedy chuckled.

Confirming Halleck's suspicions, someone placed an umbrella, a symbol of Neville Chamberlain's Munich "surrender" to Hitler, on the Republican leadership desk in the House that afternoon. And the next day 70 disgruntled GOP congressmen held a secret meeting to castigate Charlie Halleck and Bill McCulloch for permitting President Kennedy to escape political embarrassment. They had wanted a strong bill, with no chance of passage, to prevent the Democrats from fulfilling their promise of a civil rights bill before the 1964 election. And all agreed that Halleck should receive a stern warning against making any future deals with the Kennedys.

President Kennedy, too, was the target of backlash. On October 30, as he travelled the 13 miles from the Philadelphia International Airport to the downtown Bellevue Stratford Hotel, where he was to appear at a $250-per-head cocktail reception, Kennedy found most streets deserted, the poorest reception he had received in a metropolitan center since his election three years earlier. At the hotel he was greeted by pickets bearing signs reading "Kennedy—Why Compromise Equality?" The fund-raising dinner for Mayor James Tate at Convention Hall was only half-filled, although 10,000 free tickets had been distributed to party faithfuls.

This citizen reaction to Kennedy's civil rights efforts foretold of trouble ahead. The president had wanted to get H.R. 7152 through Congress by the end of the year so that any backlash would not intrude into the 1964 campaign. However, after all the rush to get the bill out of the Judiciary Committee, by mid-November it had not yet been sent to the Rules Committee, a step that would precede its appearance on the floor of the House. Now it was obvious that Congress could not possibly consider it this year. What Kennedy had feared was going to happen. Civil rights would haunt him for months to come.

So he resorted to the politician's time-honored practice of protecting his own turf. Democrats traditionally blame the country's problems on the Republicans. Republicans in turn cite the sins of the Democrats. Congress lambastes presidents. And presidents can always find fault with Congress, which was what President Kennedy now did. With both his tax cut bill and civil rights bill stalled on the Hill, he used the presidential podium to try to sell his programs to the American people in the hope that public pressure would spur the Congress to action.

On Thursday, November 14, John F. Kennedy held his 64th presidential press conference in the State Department auditorium. After almost three years in office, the youngest man to be elected president of the United States still had overwhelming style. The six-foot figure in the London-tailored suit still moved with a restless grace, the understated wit was still wry, and the Irish charm still magnetic. The president enjoyed the sparring with members of the press, whose worldliness made them some of his favorite people, and most newsmen felt the same way about him. That day the questioning inevitably got around to the civil rights bill.

> Q. Mr. President, it now seems unlikely that you will get either your tax bill or your civil rights bill in this session of Congress. Does that disturb you?
>
> A. Well, I think that the longer the delay, I think—yes, I think it is unfortunate. The fact of the matter is that both these bills should be passed. The tax bill has been before the Congress for nearly a year. The civil rights has been there for a much shorter time; it didn't go up until June. I am hopeful that the House will certainly act on that in the next month, maybe sooner.

And on Monday, November 18, even though the polls showed him extremely unpopular in the South, the president flew to Tampa, Florida, for the 47th annual meeting of the Florida Chamber of Commerce. With the courage of an Irish slugger who figured the best defense was a good offense, he appealed to the innate decency of the southern people. During the question and answer period this exchange took place:

> Q. What is the outlook for your civil rights program and, sir, why are you pushing it so vigorously?
>
> A. While I know that this program has not gotten great support here in Florida, I think you gentlemen should recognize the responsibility of the President of the United States. In this country, I carry out, execute, the laws of the United States. I also have the obligation of implementing the orders of the

courts of the United States. And I can assure you that whoever is President of the United States will do the same, because if he did not, he would begin to unwind this most extraordinary constitutional system of ours....

The Congress, of course, must make the final judgment. What the Congress passes, I will execute. We will know in the next two or three months what judgment the Congress will reach. But I believe that this is a matter that is going to be with us long after I have disappeared from the scene. No country has ever faced a more difficult problem than attempting to bring 10 percent of the population of a different color, educate them, give them a chance for a job, and give them a chance for a fair life. That is my objective and I think it is the objective of the United States as I have always understood it.

That evening the president flew back to Washington, but because of his late arrival, postponed his weekly Tuesday breakfast with Democratic congressional leaders until Wednesday morning. During the meal Kennedy was irritable and impatient with the slow progress of his legislative program. He reminded his guests that Congress had passed only 4 of 12 appropriations bills and that the end of the year was close at hand. "What are you doing up there?" he demanded.

His legislative leaders asked him to be patient, assuring him that progress was being made on the civil rights bill; it probably would be sent that week to the Rules Committee. But since its chairman, Howard W. Smith (D-Va.), was sure to sit on the bill, there would have to be some fast parliamentary maneuvering in order to get it out of his committee and onto the floor of the House.

That afternoon H.R. 7152, along with its accompanying committee report, was sent to the clerk of the House and then to the Rules Committee with Emanuel Celler's request for an early hearing. But if the arch-conservative Howard Smith heard Celler's appeal, he gave no sign of it. Smith's complete silence, as well as the fact that more than three weeks had passed since the Judiciary Committee had acted on the bill, seemed an ominous sign to many people on the Hill.

Congressman Don Edwards began to believe that there would not be a bill under Kennedy "or at least it would be a very, very difficult process. There just wasn't that kind of movement behind it. It was running out of gas again." Congressman Richard Bolling (D-Mo.) agreed and also feared that the fragile bipartisan coalition, forged largely by Bill McCulloch and dragging along a reluctant and suspicious Charlie Halleck, was heading toward a possible split.

The next morning, November 21, President and Mrs. Kennedy flew to San Antonio, where Kennedy hoped to heal an intraparty fight between the Texas liberals, led by Senator Ralph Yarborough, and the conservatives, led by Vice President Johnson and Governor John Connally. While Kennedy was away, Charlie Halleck responded to the president's criticism of Congress, which Kennedy had made at his press conference the preceding week. Halleck, mindful that some of his Republicans wanted him to get tough with Kennedy, resorted to politics-as-usual.

Halleck criticized the president "who had promised major civil rights legislation in 1961" for failing to keep his word. "It was not until June 19, 1963," Halleck charged, "that he submitted a civil rights program, only after the crises of demonstrations and violence forced his hand. Then he expected Congress to act in two months on a program he had delayed two and a half years."

John Fitzgerald Kennedy was never to reply—either humorously or heatedly—to Charlie Halleck's charges. At 1:00 P.M. in Dallas the next day, an assassin's bullet ended the life of the 46-year-old president who had so loved the give-and-take of political life. And on Capitol Hill, where he had served six years in the House and eight years in the Senate, the flags were slowly lowered to half-mast.

Three

Johnson Takes Charge

A S AIR FORCE ONE glided through twilight skies into Washington, D.C., it carried the bronze casket of John F. Kennedy as well as the newly inaugurated 36th president of the United States, Lyndon Baines Johnson. Johnson had taken the oath of office in the plane as it stood on the runway at Love Field, Dallas, just 98 minutes after John Kennedy died. Now the new president gathered the reins of government into his rancher's hands, sending word ahead that, as a first order of business, he wanted to meet that evening with congressional leaders of both political parties. Anticipating his arrival, tearful White House staffers laid out pencils and pads on the large oval table in the Cabinet Room and moved Johnson's chair around to the president's place.

It was dark at 6:00 P.M. when the presidential jet touched down. The floodlights at Andrews Air Force Base were dimmed and, like a ghost ship, the giant 707 moved slowly down the runway. The casket was lifted off first, and Mrs. Kennedy and members of the family accompanied it to Bethesda Naval Hospital. Then President and Mrs. Johnson deplaned and were met by leaders of Congress. Johnson was grave as he looked into the television cameras and spoke his first words to the country as chief executive.

"I will do my best," he said slowly in his prairie drawl. "That is all I can do. I ask for your help—and God's."

Then he was whisked away in a helicopter for the seven-minute ride to the White House. The new president stepped out on the south lawn and passed through the Rose Garden into the Oval Office, where John Kennedy's things had already been cleared from the desk. The room was no longer Kennedy's but neither was it yet Johnson's. He didn't linger. Instead, accompanied by his staff, he walked to his old vice presidential three-room suite in the Executive Office Building. First he called former presidents Truman and Eisenhower to discuss funeral plans. Then he ate dinner on a tray at his desk and started giving brisk orders between bites.

This was the old Lyndon Johnson, the one that Washington had known for 32 years: the 23-year-old country boy Lyndon from the hills of Texas, who came to town as secretary to Congressman Richard Kleberg (D-Tex.); the fast learner Lyndon, who gained enough political savvy in five years to win his own Texas seat in the House; and, finally, the miracle worker Lyndon, who won a Senate seat in 1948 by a mere 87 votes and referred to himself, with an embarrassed laugh, as "landslide Lyndon."

The new senator from Texas was often crude, frequently corny, and usually uncomfortable with anything more intellectual than a memo. However, in the art of getting along with the prima donnas of the Senate chamber, he had no equal. The ingratiating freshman was elected minority leader before he finished his first six-year term, and in 1954, when the Democrats won control of the Senate, he found himself at the age of 46 in the power-packed position of majority leader. He loved it, quickly proving to be one of the most effective Senate leaders in history. Using relentless drive, politicking skill, and 18-hour days, the tall Texan seemed to be everywhere—in the chamber, the caucusroom, the cloakrooms, and the corridors—charming, threatening, bluffing, pleading, and promising. His six-foot, three-inch, 205-pound frame towered over his colleagues as he engaged in what Senator Frank Lausche (D-Ohio) described as overt "nostril inspections"—clutching a senator's lapel and drawing him so close that the victim was forced to lean far backward, enabling the majority leader to peer up his nose.

Predictably, these hard-driving tactics also produced bitter enemies. Johnson was described as power-hungry, flamboyant, and cruel to his aides, a man who felt he was slipping if he didn't chew out someone at least once an hour. His staff churned in turmoil, with people constantly threatening to quit but usually staying—he was the most fascinating man in town. There was a certain mystique in working for him because this was where the action was. He got things done.

There was only one person in Washington more powerful than Lyndon Johnson during the late 1950s, and he lived in the White

House. So, at the end of Eisenhower's second term, Johnson decided to try for the presidency. But at the Democratic National Convention in Los Angeles, he saw the nomination go to his junior colleague in the Senate, John Kennedy, on the first ballot. Unbelievably and seemingly out of character, the Texan accepted the powerless second spot on the ticket. But, for whatever private reasons, Johnson kept the South in line for Kennedy, campaigning indefatigably from the back of a train as it wound slowly through the cotton fields and bayous and small sleepy towns of Dixie. With missionary zeal he held the people spellbound, speaking their language, assuring southern Baptists that Pope John XXIII would not come to live in Washington if the young Catholic senator from Massachusetts were elected president, urging them to continue to vote Democratic. Then, in typical LBJ fashion, he hedged his bet by getting the Texas legislature to pass a special law permitting him to run for both vice president and senator at the same time. Regardless of what happened to John Kennedy, Lyndon B. Johnson was sure of returning to Washington.

After Kennedy won, his vice president fully expected to play a major role in pushing the New Frontier program through the Congress he had so recently dominated. But to his utter astonishment, Lyndon Johnson discovered that his former colleagues did not want him. Many, in fact, were frankly relieved that they had slipped out of his grasp. When a proposal that the new vice president preside at all caucuses of Democratic senators received 17 nay votes, the crestfallen former majority leader allowed it to die. The rebuff should not have surprised him; the legislative branch has always been wary of the executive branch looking over its shoulder. But Johnson, naively, had not expected it. He next turned to the president, suggesting in a memorandum that John Kennedy turn over the national defense and outer space programs to him. Again, he should have known better. No president would ever give away a major portion of his power. Kennedy was merely amused and declined to reply. Finally, the frustrated Texan who thrived on taking charge realized that his main function was to serve tea and cookies to minor foreign dignitaries.

Lyndon Johnson was devastated. He took to the background and, according to Washington gossip, to the bottle. The rumors flew: John Kennedy found him increasingly irritable to have around in his moody, unhappy state; the vice president was paranoid about the attorney general, suspecting Bobby Kennedy of being his enemy, of using the press to humiliate him, and of plotting a "dump LBJ" move for 1964. The man was miserable and let everyone know it. "I don't have any budget, I don't have any power, I don't have anything," he complained to Hobart Taylor, Jr., executive vice president of the Committee on Equal Employment Opportunity. As was traditional, Kennedy had made the vice president head of the committee, hoping it would keep him busy. Johnson considered it a crumb, however, and continued to grieve, complaining to Larry O'Brien, "Larry, I really don't have anything going for me. They don't listen to me as they used to."

However, once he donned the mantle of the presidency, Johnson's lassitude disappeared in a burst of frenzied activity. At 3:00 A.M., less than 12 hours after being sworn into office, the 55-year-old Texan lay stretched out on his bed in his imposing Washington home, The Elms, busily outlining the agenda for his administration. One of his first decisions was to address a joint session of Congress on Wednesday, November 27, the day before Thanksgiving, and he told his aides to start preparing his speech. Then, after a few hours of sleep, he launched into a whirlwind of 20-hour days, keeping the machinery of government moving while the nation buried John F. Kennedy with all the pomp and pageantry that attends the death of a president in office.

On Saturday Lyndon Johnson arrived in the drizzling cold at the north portico of the White House, the first of many dignitaries to pay their last respects as the body of John F. Kennedy lay in state in the East Room, the flag-draped coffin closed. Then the president returned to his old office to meet with cabinet members, congressional leaders, and military chiefs far into the night.

On Sunday, to the one-hundred-steps-to-the-minute beat of muffled drums, a caisson drawn by six gray horses carried the casket slowly up Pennsylvania Avenue to the Capitol. Here was where John Kennedy had begun his political career, where he had launched his campaign for the presidency, and where he had both won and lost important battles with the legislative branch. Johnson watched as Congress bid farewell to its sometime-friend, sometime-foe. Then he went back to work tackling, among other things, his upcoming speech to Congress. Helping him with ideas were Kennedy speech writer Ted Sorensen, Harvard professor John Kenneth Galbraith, former aide Horace Busby, and Adlai Stevenson, U.S. ambassador to the United Nations. Stevenson said Congress should be urged to pass the civil rights bill as a memorial to the late president.

Sunday night, as a quarter of a million citizens filed into the Capitol rotunda to pay their respects before the candlelit coffin, Lyndon Johnson was on the phone, inviting civil rights leaders to the funeral the next morning. When Whitney Young, executive director of the Urban League, said he would have trouble making it on time, the president assured him that a White House car would be waiting at the airport. And later that evening Johnson called James Farmer, national director of CORE, who stated, "I was astounded. I'd never been called by a president before. It was impressive."

On Monday morning, in the crisp bright sunlight, the horse-drawn caisson brought the casket back to the White House. Then President and Mrs. Johnson joined a corps of world leaders who walked behind Mrs. Kennedy and the family as they escorted the caisson seven blocks to Saint Matthew's Cathedral. And finally, after Mass, there was the last journey across the Potomac River to the gently sloping hillside at Arlington Cemetery.

On Capitol Hill Senator Margaret Chase Smith (R-Maine) laid a single red rose on the back-row Senate desk that Jack Kennedy had once occupied. And Republican leaders declared a 30-day moratorium on political partisan rhetoric. But the business of the Republic had to continue and of prime importance were the two bills that were mired at the time of Kennedy's death: the tax cut and civil rights.

Lyndon Johnson's accession to the presidency concerned civil rights leaders. "Johnson was our enemy all of the years that he was Senate majority leader," said Arnold Aronson, secretary of the Leadership Conference on Civil Rights. While conceding that in 1957 Johnson steered the first civil rights bill through the Senate in nearly a century, Aronson bemoaned the fact that the deals made by the majority leader "cut the heart out of the bill.... We never regarded him as an ally at all."

Even as vice president, Johnson "very rarely helped when he could help," according to Bobby Kennedy. And while this indictment reflected the hostility between these two tough-minded politicians, it correctly portrayed the malaise brought on by the feeling of powerlessness that afflicted the Texan during his vice presidency.

At the end of the previous May, when John Kennedy had finally decided, at his brother's urging, to submit a strong civil rights bill to Congress, Lyndon Johnson's position on the subject was an enigma. In his May 30 Memorial Day address at the Gettysburg National Cemetery, Johnson had been eloquent in his plea for equal rights. "Until justice is blind to color," Johnson said, "until education is unaware of race, until opportunity is unconcerned with the color of men's skins, emancipation will be a proclamation but not a fact." However, two days later, when President Kennedy told key members of his administration about his decision, the vice president had been noncommittal. "No," Johnson muttered when Kennedy asked if he had anything to add to the discussion.

The vice president had adamantly opposed sending strong legislation up to Congress because, knowing Congress as he did, he believed it "wouldn't get passed and was impossible and would cause a lot of trouble and was the wrong thing to do." Instead, Johnson looked to the long-range goals of blacks, such as greater educational and employment opportunities, rather than to laws designed to meet immediate needs. He wanted to pass this advice along to Kennedy privately, and at the end of the June 1 meeting, he had asked Kenny O'Donnell, the appointments secretary, for 15 minutes alone with the president. However, as so often happened, Johnson and his request were ignored.

Consequently, at another meeting on June 3, when he listened to Kennedy telling the Democratic leaders of the House and Senate about his plans, the vice president had become more and more agitated. Johnson, the master strategist, was disturbed not so much by what he heard as by what he did not hear. There were no plans to smooth the way for the bill with Congress or the general public.

Should not Republican leaders, Johnson wondered to himself, be called in and made to promise in blood to support the legislation? In exchange they would share the credit for its success (or the blame if it failed). Should not Kennedy consult all of the country's important black leaders to assure them that the administration was unreservedly on their side in the struggle for civil rights? Should not the three living ex-presidents (Hoover, Truman, and Eisenhower) be asked to join in a declaration of support for the bill at the time of its introduction? And, finally, should not someone make sure that Majority Leader Mike Mansfield, who was out in Montana campaigning, would give his complete attention to getting the legislation enacted? Otherwise, it had no chance of passage. But when Kennedy asked Johnson for his comments, the vice president had dourly replied, "I pass."

Later that day the president told two of his aides to find out what was on the vice president's mind. When Assistant Attorney General Norbert A. Schlei dropped by Johnson's office in the

Capitol, the Texan told him that many things still had to be done if there was to be any hope of success. Regarding his silence at the White House meeting that morning, Johnson explained that he would have been the only person expressing opposition to the plan, and this might have created problems for the president with some of the legislators there. He had also realized that what was said was almost certain to be picked up by the press and possibly reported either as his opposition to the bill or as an attempt to kill it indirectly. However, as Schlei left his office, Johnson assured him that, whatever happened, he would do everything possible to help Kennedy get the bill passed.

Next, Ted Sorensen telephoned. Whenever Lyndon Johnson was depressed, which happened quite frequently since the inauguration, the melancholy Texan, with eyes and face mournful as a basset hound, engaged in rambling soliloquies punctuated only by an occasional sigh. He told Sorensen: "I think he [JFK] will be cut to pieces with this and I think he will be a sacrificial lamb. I think his program will be hurt if it's not killed. So I make a point, that you haven't done your homework on public sentiment, on legislative leaders, on the opposition party, and the legislation itself. I don't know who drafted it, I've never seen it. Hell, if the vice president doesn't know what's in it, how do you expect the others to know what's in it? You might want to talk to Mansfield...see what he thinks. I would sure get the Republicans in on the thing."

Johnson's blunt remarks were passed along to the Kennedys. They were "very wise," admitted Bobby. "We went around and saw all the congressmen and senators, and that delayed the sending of the legislation about 10 days."

After Kennedy's death, however, when Lyndon Johnson returned to Washington as the new president, he immediately dispelled any doubts about his commitment to H.R. 7152. "The first priority," Johnson told advisers Jack Valenti and Bill Moyers, "is passage of the civil rights act."

After John Kennedy had been laid to rest in Arlington, President Johnson met with the governors assembled in town for the funeral. Referring specifically to the civil rights bill, he asked both Republicans and Democrats to support it. Then, that evening, he called Dr. Martin Luther King, asking for his help and, in turn, pledging his support of all Kennedy's programs. Finally, late that night, Johnson got around to a memo from Horace Busby regarding the president's speech to Congress in two days. Busby had tried to work on it over the weekend in a "two-hour spurt" as Johnson had asked, but he couldn't do it. Instead, he delivered only a partial manuscript with the explanation, "It should be a tribute to Kennedy and I was not in that frame of mind. His death was too sudden."

The next evening, after dinner at The Elms, the president and his two old friends, Washington attorney Abe Fortas and Senator Hubert Humphrey (D-Minn.), put together a final version of the speech. Drawing from drafts submitted by Sorensen, Busby, Galbraith, and others, the men did a "clip and paste" job, aided by the president's 19-year-old, elder daughter, Lynda. Much of Stevenson's eloquent phraseology, including, at Humphrey's insistence, his concept of civil rights as a "Kennedy memorial," found its way into the final draft. They finished at 2:00 A.M.

Ten hours later, at 12:31 P.M., the doorkeeper of the House of Representatives, William M. (Fishbait) Miller, intoned his honey-accented introduction that traditionally opened a special session of Congress, "Mistah Speak-ah, the President of the United States." As the towering figure with its familiar loping gait strode down the center aisle, the members of the House and Senate welcomed him with a standing ovation. Lyndon B. Johnson had returned to the chamber where, 23 years earlier, he had begun his elective career. Among those assembled were 87 representatives who had served with Johnson in the House and 78 senators who were his colleagues in the upper chamber. Also present on the floor were the Supreme Court, the president's cabinet, the Joint Chiefs of Staff, and the entire diplomatic corps. Above them, in the packed galleries, watched Mrs. Johnson and the president's daughters, families of House and Senate members, spectators, members of the press, and the television cameras. Silent for a few moments after he reached the Speaker's rostrum, the president looked around at the historic room where so much United States history had been enacted. His tall frame was slightly bent; the gregarious smile was gone.

"All I have," he said softly and slowly, "I would have given gladly, not to be standing here today."

It was less than a week after John Kennedy's death. The new president sought not only to reassure the country during its hour of darkness but also to convey his determination to complete the unfinished business of the Kennedy administration. Johnson made his position on civil rights unequivocal:

This is our challenge—not to hesitate, not to pause, not to turn about and linger over this evil moment, but to continue on our course so that we may fulfill the destiny that history has set for us. Our most immediate tasks are here on this Hill.

First, no memorial oration or eulogy could more eloquently honor President Kennedy's memory than the earliest passage of the civil rights bill for which he fought so long. We have talked long enough in this country about equal rights. We have talked for one hundred years or more. It is time now to write the next chapter, and to write it in the books of law.

I urge you again, as I did in 1957 and again in 1960, to enact a civil rights law so that we can move forward to eliminate from this Nation any trace of discrimination and oppression that is based upon race or color. There could be no greater source of strength to this Nation both at home and abroad.

Clarion words aside, however, it would take all of Lyndon Johnson's renowned powers of persuasion to keep the frail H.R. 7152 alive on Capitol Hill. But if anyone could do it, it was he. The former Texas schoolteacher who had scolded the Kennedys for failing to do their homework before submitting the bill to Congress now began burning the midnight oil himself—contacting civil rights leaders to assure them he was on their side, lobbying special interest groups, maneuvering behind the scenes with key lawmakers, and appealing to the better nature of the American people.

On Tuesday, November 26, Lyndon Johnson moved into the Oval Office, occupied by all American presidents since William Howard Taft. Gone were the furnishings from John Kennedy's 34-month occupancy: the desk carved from the timbers of HMS Resolute (a gift from Queen Victoria in 1880 to President Rutherford B. Hayes), the naval prints, and the rocking chair. In their place were Johnson's mammoth green plastic-topped desk with its 18-button telephone console, a bust of Franklin D. Roosevelt, four television sets that let the president monitor the news simultaneously on all channels, and, hanging on a rack outside the office door, the Texan's big Stetson hat.

Since Lady Bird Johnson had told Jacqueline Kennedy to take as much time as she needed in moving out of the White House, the president, his wife, and their two teenage daughters still lived in their Spring Valley home, a three-story, 12-room brick and stucco Norman chateau, which had once belonged to the legendary

Washington party giver Perle Mesta. The presidential motorcade usually swung out through the big iron gates at 8:00 A.M. and didn't return until after midnight.

Lyndon Johnson was taking control of the government with the zest of a Texas rancher rounding up a scattered herd, using the telephone like a lasso, moving people through the Oval Office in droves, gulping meals on the run, and snatching a few hours sleep just before dawn back at The Elms. Thanksgiving Day, November 28, did not deter Johnson from his frenetic pace. Pausing only long enough to enjoy turkey dinner prepared by the family cook, the president continued his roundup, which now included the American public. In a nationwide television address that evening, again alluding to the need for effective civil rights legislation, he exhorted the people to

> renew our dedication to the ideals that are American. Let us pray for this divine wisdom in banishing from our land any injustice or intolerance or oppression to any of our fellow Americans whatever their opinion, whatever the color of their skins—for God made all of us, not some of us, in His image. All of us, not just some of us, are His children.

The next afternoon the president began a series of private meetings with civil rights leaders to prove that he was on their team. At 12:30 P.M. he met with Roy Wilkins, executive secretary of the NAACP. Three of Johnson's advisers had given him "talking points" to be raised with Wilkins. White House aide Lee White suggested that the president urge the NAACP executive and his fellow black leaders to restrain demonstrations and, instead, channel their energies into such areas as education and vocational training. Former United Press correspondent George Reedy, who came to the White House with Johnson after serving as his press aide, advised making it clear to Wilkins that the administration viewed him as *the* black leader and stressing how important it was that "Negro organizations do not spend all of their time popping off without knowing what they are doing." Legislative aide Larry O'Brien suggested that while it would be helpful if civil rights spokesmen contacted key Republicans in the House, "Negro groups as such don't have the broad-spread strength to get this done. Urge Wilkins to press religious leaders involved with the Leadership group."

Sitting with Roy Wilkins in the Oval Office, the dominating

president pulled his chair to within a few inches of Wilkins' knees, pointed his finger dramatically at the NAACP official, and emphasized that passage of H.R. 7152 depended on how civil rights activists handled themselves in the months ahead.

"I want that bill passed," Johnson declared, adding that he would aid in any way he could but would not lobby for it. As Wilkins related it, "In effect, what Johnson said was, 'You have the ball, now run with it.' "

Roy Wilkins did not really need such an urging. He had been running at full speed for months. On September 9 the NAACP, in a departure from past practices, had asked their members to get more involved in the political arena and "work actively for the defeat in the next election of those lawmakers who fail to support and vote for strong civil rights legislation." And in November, after the compromise bill was voted out of the Judiciary Committee, Wilkins had told all NAACP branches to contact their congressmen and "get them on record" as to how they stood on the bill. Civil rights lobbyists were starting to apply pressure, and as the bill moved toward the floors of the House and Senate, that pressure would increase.

On Monday morning, December 2, the president met with Whitney Young, who had worked with Johnson since 1961 when the vice president became head of Kennedy's Committee on Equal Employment Opportunity. The black leader did not doubt the new president's sincerity. "A magnolia accent doesn't always mean bigotry," observed Young optimistically, as he emerged from the White House.

The president's first weekly Tuesday breakfast with Democratic congressional leaders began promptly the next morning at 8:45. Lyndon and Lady Bird Johnson had long been known for their southern hospitality, and they carried this same largesse to the executive mansion. The breakfast menu included orange juice, poached or scrambled eggs, bacon, sausage, toast, sweet buns, jelly and jams, and coffee or tea. The president, however, talked nonstop, firing questions right and left about the logjam of legislation on the Hill, which included the two top-priority items, the tax cut and civil rights. And, unfortunately, he expected rapid-fire answers in return. This was such a dramatic change from the graceful style of John Kennedy that the legislators left the White House with symptoms of nervous indigestion.

One and a half hours later, Dr. Martin Luther King was shown into the Oval Office. As with earlier visits by civil rights officials, the president was well briefed by his staff. A memo from Lee White suggested that Johnson discuss (1) the practical difficulties inherent in moving legislation rapidly through Congress; (2) the role black leadership could play to ensure the bill's favorable reception on Capitol Hill by avoiding violence, as it did so effectively during the August 28 March on Washington; and (3) voter registration, employment, and the Civil Rights Commission.

The next morning, before leaving The Elms for the White House, the president looked up from his paper and asked an aide to "find out where George Meany lives and maybe he can drive down with me this morning." When he learned the AFL-CIO chief lived just a few miles away, Johnson had his 1961 Lincoln Continental limousine pick Meany up, and on the way downtown the two men discussed the civil rights bill. Meany promised to push for its support among his fellow union officials, with whom the president would be meeting later in the day. Johnson then breakfasted Senator Everett Dirksen, who assessed the prospects for passage of H.R. 7152, saying that the Senate "certainly would act on the bill early next year."

Shortly after the Senate minority leader left for the Capitol, the president met with James Farmer. The head of CORE, noting that Johnson was opposed to southern plans to delete the Public Accommodations section from H.R. 7152, asked him how he came to feel so strongly. The president related the story of how his cook for 21 years, Mrs. Zephyr Wright, demurred when asked to take the family beagle with her as she and her husband drove from Washington to the Johnson ranch in Texas. "Driving through the South is tough enough," said Mrs. Wright, "without having a dog to worry about."

"Well, that hurt me," the president said. "That almost brought me to tears and I realized how important public accommodations were, and was determined that if ever I had the chance, I was going to do something about it." This experience added Lyndon Johnson to the list of those who favored passage of H.R. 7152 because they had seen for themselves how segregation destroyed even the smallest decencies of life.

Later that afternoon Johnson met in the Rose Garden with 20 members of the executive council of the AFL-CIO. He read from a prepared text:

The tax bill must pass. Before Congress also is a civil rights bill.... The endless abrasions of delay, neglect and indifference have rubbed raw the national conscience. We have talked too long. We have done too little and all of it has come too late. You must help me make civil rights in America a reality. I commend this labor leadership for the enlightenment that you have shown in moving to abolish discrimination in labor's ranks. Even as I compliment you for your action, I ask you to hurry even faster.

Emerging from their session, labor leaders told reporters how impressed they were by the speed with which the new president had gotten down to business. Observing that Johnson had listened and taken notes, they conceded that what transpired was more than a mere "get acquainted" meeting, which many had expected.

Shortly after 5:00 P.M. the president delivered much the same message to 90 members of the Business Advisory Council. After a brief analysis of the economy, Johnson asked the business executives to work for passage of the administration's $11 billion tax cut bill. Then, turning to the subject of civil rights, he stated, "I appeal to you for your support of legislation that will help to destroy discrimination, that will help to promote equality, that will help to give opportunity to all American citizens, regardless of their race, regardless of their religion, regardless of the region in which they may live."

The next morning, Thursday, December 5, the president resumed his "taxi service." This time his passenger was Charlie Halleck, who lived just three and a half blocks away. Having arisen two hours earlier than usual, Halleck was waiting on the front steps when the presidential motorcade swooped to the curb to pick him up. Morning commuter traffic hastily pulled over as the entourage flew down Massachusetts Avenue. "It was quite a little trip," said the House minority leader, awed by the motorcycle escort, flashing lights, wailing sirens, and guns-at-the-ready Secret Service agents riding behind them in two heavily armored black limousines.

During the breakfast at the White House, which included "thick bacon—the kind he knew a fellow from Indiana would like," the two men talked principally about the scheduling of the civil rights bill. Later that morning Johnson conferred with A. Philip Randolph, president of the Brotherhood of Sleeping Car Porters, keeping in mind aide Lee White's suggestion about Randolph's "natural eloquence." "He can be put to good use," wrote White, "especially after leaving your office when he meets the press."

While the commander in chief was thus moving his troops into position on the legislative battlefield, he wisely kept one eye on his tough, well-entrenched enemy. By now, the fight over H.R. 7152 had taken on a deadly irony. It was Southerner against Southerner—Lyndon Johnson against Howard Smith, the 80-year-old segregationist chairman of the Rules Committee, who had wrapped his iron grip around H.R. 7152 two days before John Kennedy was killed and who planned to do everything in his power to keep it captive.

The Rules Committee, the most powerful committee of the House of Representatives, existed for the sole purpose of assuring an orderly flow of bills to the floor, granting each bill a "rule" under which it would be debated. But it could also kill a bill by simply refusing to grant it a rule.

Howard Worth Smith, nicknamed "Judge" after his brief tenure on the bench, epitomized all that was obsolete in lawmaking. A veteran of 33 years on the Hill, he had long been feared as the most powerful person in the House. Through the years the crusty, old southern conservative had imposed his will on the nation by stopping, delaying, or watering down progressive legislation in such fields as civil rights, labor, public housing, education, minimum wage, and medical care. John Kennedy had been well aware that, just as a filibuster would be the chief obstacle in the Senate, Smith would be his major problem in the House.

There were, however, several possible ways to wrestle H.R. 7152 from the Judge's tenacious grasp, and during the first two weeks of December, members of the House tried two of them.

1. Discharge Petition. House Rule 27 provides that 30 days after a bill has been favorably reported by a standing committee, any member can file a Discharge Petition, which, if signed by a majority of House members (218), relieves the Rules Committee from further consideration of that measure. This step, on behalf of H.R. 7152, was taken on December 9 by Emanuel Celler.

The problem was that without 50 to 60 Republican signatures, this device could not possibly succeed. Bill McCulloch, a stickler for propriety, felt that it struck at the heart of the committee system and was "very damaging to the bipartisan support of civil rights legislation." In a closed caucus of House Republicans, Charlie Halleck made it clear that he would not sign either, stating that since the Judiciary Committee had held no formal hearings on the compromise bill, it would not be good legislative procedure to debate it on the House floor before the Rules Committee held hearings. With McCulloch and Halleck firmly against the Discharge Petition, hopes quickly faded for the necessary Republican signatures.

2. Calendar Wednesday. Under House Rule 24, on Wednesdays the Speaker is permitted to call each committee in alphabetical order, and its chairman can order any bill already reported out of his committee to the floor. Then the House resolves itself into the Committee of the Whole to debate it for two hours. However, since the bill has to be disposed of by the end of the day, Calendar Wednesday is rarely tried because opponents can prevent a vote with delaying tactics. In the case of H.R. 7152, 11 committees would be called before the Judiciary Committee, 6 of which had southern chairmen who could preempt Celler by calling up their own bills.

The Republicans, however, were worried that their refusal to sign the Discharge Petition might be misconstrued as anticivil rights. Consequently, on December 11 they announced plans to use a parliamentary strategy designed to force the Speaker to initiate Calendar Wednesday that afternoon. Merely a quixotic bit of oneupsmanship designed to challenge and embarrass the Democrats, it, too, failed, when Majority Leader Carl Albert moved successfully to adjourn the House.

The Judge, meanwhile, was setting up his own defenses. Hoping that time would be on his side, he protested innocently to CBS-TV about the hectic scrambling on the Hill. "I just don't think we ought to be acting on this bill in the present state of hysteria," he drawled.

But in truth, it was the threatened use of a third maneuver that worried Smith the most. House Rule 11 specifies that any three members of a committee can request that their chairman call a meeting. If after three days the chairman has not scheduled one, a majority of the committee, by addressing a notice to the clerk of the House, can order a meeting on a specific time, date, and subject. Democratic members of the Rules Committee could provide at least five of the required eight signatures. The key to the three Republican signees was another Ohio conservative, Clarence Brown, Sr., who was acting behind the scenes, quietly forcing open Smith's hand.

Brown, a 70-year-old gruff and formidable newspaper publisher from the small town of Blanchester, Ohio, represented the district next to Bill McCulloch's. As the ranking minority congressman on the 15-member Rules Committee, he controlled five GOP votes. These, combined with the votes of five northern Democrats, were enough to force the meeting. In 1957 and 1960 Clarence Brown had used this threat to free the Eisenhower civil rights bills from Smith's hammerlock, but then he had been acting for a Republican president. This time it did not seem logical for the loyal GOP partisan to help the Democrats.

But while Brown was a staunch conservative, he shared Bill McCulloch's reverence for the Republican party's historic position on civil rights, a stance strengthened by the presence of two major black universities in his area—Wilberforce and Central State. In addition, one of the major stations on the underground railway, by which slaves escaped to Canada, was the town of Xenia in his district.

Clarence Brown had no desire to take Judge Smith's power away from him. They were old friends and had fought many battles as allies in the committee and on the House floor. Now nearing the ends of their long political careers, they were philosophically alike, except on this one issue. But the times called for action, not delay. So when the stout Ohioan dropped into Smith's office on December 4 to say, "I don't want to run over you, Judge, but...," the chairman knew the game was up. Brown, reluctantly or not, had the votes to force a meeting. Fearful of losing control over his committee, the old Southerner finally yielded on December 18, promising to start hearings on January 9. "I know something about the facts of life around here," Smith said mournfully, "and I know that many members want this bill considered. They could take it away from me, and they can do it any minute they want to."

Lyndon Johnson was delighted with the news. Things were falling into place for the master manipulator. He and his family had moved into the White House on December 7. His daily appointment schedule had been considerably trimmed from the initial flurry of meetings set up after he assumed the presidency; and Lady Bird, mindful that her husband had suffered a heart attack in 1955 shortly after he became Senate majority leader, was partially successful in getting him to take an afternoon swim in the White House pool, followed by a short nap. So now, with the executive branch of government firmly under control, Johnson could begin to court his old handmaiden, the United States Congress.

Supercharged with energy as always, he was the old elbow-massaging Lyndon who had not lost his touch during three years on the sidelines. A man who enjoyed human contact, Johnson needed (as he said) to "press palms and feel the flesh." In a receiving line the president was a whirlwind, using both hands simultaneously. As his right hand grapped the other person's, his left grasped the elbow, so that he wound up having possession of his startled guest's arm. In his Senate days this was known as "the laying on of hands" or, among his colleagues, "the treatment." During Johnson's first three weeks as president he applied "the treatment" to Capitol Hill leaders during private breakfasts and lunches. Then, whenever he had a moment to spare, he called members of the House and Senate on the telephone, surprising them by drawling casually, "This is Lyndon." And by mid-December he found time to appear unexpectedly on the Hill. Senate staffers found him joining the merriment at a Christmas party with Everett Dirksen and enjoying himself thoroughly at a surprise party for Senate majority leader Mike Mansfield.

One noon the president remembered it was the day he always used to lunch with the Texas Democratic congressional delegation. Impulsively he ordered his car, sped up Pennsylvania Avenue to the Capitol, strode into the Speaker's dining room, and jovially took his usual place next to the head of the table. During lunch he related the story that Sam Rayburn, the late Speaker of the House, liked to tell of the time he visited the White House shortly after Truman became president. "Harry," said Rayburn, "they'll try to put you behind a wall down here. There will be people that will surround you and cut you off from any idea but theirs. They'll try to make you think that the president is the smartest man in the world. And, Harry, you know he ain't and I know he ain't."

"And," finished Lyndon Johnson to boisterous laughter, "you all know he ain't."

Unlike John Kennedy, who visited the Capitol only on formal occasions, Johnson used the place like his own clubhouse, and he began to get action on long overdue bills. Nor was he afraid, when circumstances called for it, to get out the whip. By Saturday, December 21, many House members had already headed home for Christmas when a quarrel over the foreign aid appropriations conference report turned into a partison showdown. With the Democratic ranks thinned, Charlie Halleck chose that moment to oppose giving the president power to use U.S. credit to subsidize wheat sales to communist countries. In retaliation, an anonymous White House source accused Halleck of leading GOP isolationists in a move "to seize control of the Republican party and impose its will upon the foreign policy of the United States." On hearing this charge, the House minority leader reminded reporters that the Democrats would need all the cooperation they could get in 1964 to pass the civil rights bill.

President Johnson, with his prestige on the line, determined to display his mastery over Congress. He ignored Halleck's hint of Republican reprisals, and cancelling plans to fly to the ranch, he spent the entire Saturday afternoon on the telephone, rounding up missing Democrats and ordering them to return to the Capitol. Back they came—by plane, train, and snowbound highways. Cracking the whip in the old way, the president said he would keep the House in session until he had the report written to his satisfaction.

By Monday, House members were ready for a vote on the resolution to consider the conference report. But because it had not been on the Speaker's desk for the required 24 hours, it needed a two-thirds majority to pass. At 1:20 P.M. Larry O'Brien called the president with the bad news. "We lost the two-thirds vote, 202–105," he said.

"Well, I'll be damned," Johnson swore. "God Almighty. We lost the vote. I can't help it. . . . That means they go over an extra day."

By holding the House over until December 24, Johnson would make the members angry, but he also would need only a simple majority to win. He knew he had the votes, and so with victory assured for the next day, he impulsively decided to heal the wounds. "Bird," he shouted to his wife through the upstairs living quarters of the White House, "let's have Congress over tonight!"

With only a few hours' notice, the patient and understanding Lady Bird prepared for a lavish Christmas party. Yule logs, bourbon-laced eggnog, and expansive southern hospitality greeted more than 200 members of Congress who trooped over through the snow that evening. Even the irascible troublemaker Charlie Halleck came.

"Charlie," drawled the president with an angelic smile, "I'm sorry if anyone down here said anything ugly about you."

Then Johnson, a man of rough-hewn tastes, who thought nothing of grabbing chicken legs from a buffet table, wolfing down the meat while talking nonstop, and then stuffing the bones in his pocket, decided to make a little speech. Climbing on one of the delicate gold damask chairs in the State Dining Room, he effusively praised the members of Congress who, he said, "had labored through the vineyard and plowed through the snow." Then he finished by citing the time-honored creed of Capitol Hill: "We're Americans first. I hope we can disagree without being too disagreeable."

At 7:00 the next morning, the bleary-eyed lawmakers trudged through the snow one last time, some inebriated enough to attempt a rousing chorus of "God Rest Ye Merry, Gentlemen." By a vote of 189–158, the House gave the benevolent tyrant in the White House his victory. Then the exhausted members of Congress headed home, for good this time, and the Johnsons flew off to the ranch.

Thus staggered to an end the longest peacetime session of Congress in history. It was also one of the most tedious and least effective, running for 356 days and accomplishing little outside of the Senate ratification of the nuclear test ban treaty. Failing repeatedly to meet its own deadlines, Congress seemed to do the least on the measures that President Kennedy wanted the most.

John F. Kennedy, a widely admired man with enormous popularity, articulated great issues extremely well and came into office seemingly capable of pulling everything into his grasp. Yet he found himself increasingly ignored on Capitol Hill. An intellectual and witty man who was cool and unemotional in his personal relationships, Kennedy had never been a back-slapping "insider" on the Hill. The former senator had seemed, in fact, to use Congress as a springboard for the presidency. Further, the lawmakers owed him nothing, and this did not help ameliorate the usual antagonism between the White House and Congress. While the country got vicarious pleasure out of the elegant, almost regal Kennedy style, the politicians were not impressed.

But when the first session of the 88th Congress adjourned and members went back to their districts for Christmas, they found that their constituents had formed some strong opinions of their own. Mourning the murder of the charismatic young president, Americans turned their wrath on the body of stubborn old men who had denied him his requests. Congress found itself in trouble with the people who really counted—the people at home.

The year end *Newsweek* poll showed that, by nearly two to one, Americans registered a vote of no confidence in Congress, faulting it for consistently dragging its feet. Coming in for particular scorn were the southern Democrats and the powerful, petty, petulant committee chairmen. There was an emotional commitment to the late president and his program—the tax cut and civil rights bills— and a feeling that by passing them the country could partly atone for his death. Public support of the civil rights measure stood at a strong 62 percent. And in any showdown between President Johnson and the Congress, the people were likely to side with the president. Johnson's own popularity was at an amazingly high 79 percent.

So when the 88th Congress returned to Washington on January 7 for its second session, the members knew that things had changed. The battered H.R. 7152, which seemed to have a slim chance of survival just a short time ago, suddenly owned a new lease on life, thanks in large part to one poignant factor—the memory of John F. Kennedy.

No one knew this better than Howard Worth "Judge" Smith. On the rainy, humid morning of January 9, the tall, round-shouldered and rumpled figure of the octogenarian ambled through the corridors of the United States Capitol. A pungent cloud of tobacco smoke trailing behind him, he headed for his lair, Room H-313, the three-windowed committee room overlooking the Library of Congress, where his Rules Committee was to start hearings on the civil rights bill.

Operating behind a screen of southern courtesy that was as thick as his ever-present cigar or pipe smoke, the Judge had all the tricks of legislation tucked up his long sleeves and all the idiosyncrasies of the 435 members of the House tucked away in his spry mind. And while many people disagreed with Smith philosophically, few questioned his skills. "Every parliamentary ruse lies right at the tip of his long bony fingers," said *Newsweek* of the crafty lawmaker. Often, when he did not want to bring a bill out of his committee, the Judge would leave town and go to his 170-acre farm in Fauquier County, Virginia, to avoid calling a meeting. Early in 1957 he resorted to this tactic to delay consideration of President Eisenhower's civil rights proposal, insisting that he had to return home to inspect a barn that had burned down. "I knew Howard Smith would do most anything to block a civil rights bill," said Speaker Sam Rayburn upon hearing this excuse, "but I never knew he would resort to arson."

Just before President Kennedy's death, the Judge had announced that when H.R. 7152 reached his committee, he might have to take another one of his famous trips. But after the metamorphosis of the intervening six weeks, Smith realized that his Appomatox was at hand. In a conversation with Bob Kimball as the hearings were about to begin, the elderly Virginian bemoaned the fact that a man of his age had to lead the fight against civil rights legislation; he felt that it was the duty of the younger generation but noted bitterly that it did not seem to have a taste for battle. Finally admitting the likelihood that the bill would pass, he promised to do everything he could to stop it.

"You'll have to run over us; we know that, and we know we'll be run over," the Judge stated dejectedly. But he made it clear that in the process he wanted to review the legislation and give opponents a chance to be heard on the McCulloch-Justice Department compromise bill that had been railroaded out of the Judiciary Committee before anybody could say "boo." Smith had long been itching to bring Judiciary chairman Emanuel Celler to task.

Now the long-awaited public hearings on H.R. 7152 were about to begin. The small committee room, which could seat only 45 people comfortably, was overflowing with reporters. Peering over his glasses, the Judge announced in dirge-like tones that the 15-member Rules Committee would now consider "this nefarious bill."

Strictly speaking, the committee's job is to consider a resolution that establishes the rules of debate for each bill before it goes to the floor of the House. The resolution, prepared by the House parliamentarian, spells out (1) the exact number of hours for general debate; (2) the allocation of these hours; and (3) any restrictions on the introduction of amendments (for example, which ones might or might not be in order). If the committee votes for the resolution, it is then sent to the Speaker of the House, who schedules it for floor debate.

Actually, however, what transpires in the Rules Committee often amounts to a second hearing on the bill. Proponents and opponents can testify on the substance and merits of the measure, including the way it was handled in committee. Its authors appear first to plead that the bill be granted a rule, which means, in effect, a plea for its life.

Emanuel Celler was the leadoff witness. And like an older fraternity brother reprimanding a younger member who had broken the rules, Smith sternly quizzed Celler about the manner in which the compromise bill was handled in his committee. Manny Celler evaded the question by pleading that, while the present hearings were open to the public (including reporters), his own committee had acted in executive session, and it would be a betrayal of confidence to divulge what had happened.

Smith, a country lawyer who pretended not to know much, smiled guilelessly. Then he delivered a scholarly analysis of the bill, which he described as being "as full of booby traps as a dog is full of fleas." And finally he guided the unsuspecting Celler into a legal corner, where the Brooklynite began to contradict himself.

Rules Committee member Katherine St. George (R-N.Y.) told Smith, "You've got him pretty well tangled up."

"I didn't tangle him up," the Judge protested. "He tangled himself up. He just doesn't know what's in this bill." But he promised not to obstruct H.R. 7152. "All I want to do is dissect it," he said benignly.

The meeting adjourned at 4:05 P.M. with Manny Celler still in the witness chair, and he continued his testimony when hearings resumed the following Tuesday morning, January 14. Clarence Brown, ranking Republican on the committee, questioned the propriety of his ordering a vote on the compromise bill without any discussion of the 56-page document, paragraph by paragraph, which is traditional procedure.

Celler defended himself, arguing that discussion was unnecessary since all of the elements of the bill had been previously heard and examined. Then, chameleon-like, he displayed the politician's penchant for telling different audiences what he felt they wanted to hear. Previously, the pragmatic Celler had assured civil rights lobbyists that he opposed efforts to "gut" the strong subcommittee bill. But now, to the basically conservative Rules Committee, the Brooklyn lawmaker insisted that he had not supported parts of the subcommittee bill "which I felt were too drastic." Moreoever, he earnestly insisted that it "was not unanimously reported by the subcommittee.... I personally did not agree to all terms of the subcommittee bill."

Smith merely raised his bushy eyebrows at this unbelievable bit of news. But it would have been ungentlemanly to dispute the word of his fellow Democrat and fellow committee chairman, who hastened to assure the Rules Committee that he would not try to offer any strengthening amendments on the House floor but would simply "pass the bill as is." And on this conciliatory note, Celler's testimony ended.

Bill McCulloch was next, testifying the next morning. Using his favorite phrase, McCulloch began his three-page statement by describing H.R. 7152 as "comprehensive in scope but moderate in application." He concluded by admitting that there were some last-minute changes in the bill, "which were not fully debated in the Judiciary Committee. But the committee did spend months and months taking testimony and amending language on the principle [sic] titles, either as they now stand or in a closely related fashion."

The Judge gave McCulloch one of his penetrating looks and then pointedly asked him to tell the committee who actually wrote the compromise bill. The Ohio country lawyer, recognizing the cat-and-mouse intent behind the Virginia country lawyer's question, hesitated only a moment. His carefully considered response was both accurate and yet, to Chairman Smith, not quite completely candid.

"I assisted in writing this bill, staff people on the Judiciary Committee participated in redrafting this bill, [and] duly constituted and appointed and confirmed people in the Department of Justice helped write the bill, the same general people who often help in writing difficult and technical bills which are considered by the Judiciary Committee," Bill McCulloch explained fastidiously.

Then Smith, his voice dripping with sarcasm, asked how the ranking minority member had managed to obtain a "whole minute" to explain the complex 56-page bill to the Judiciary Committee just prior to its breathless vote. "Because of my receding red hair," McCulloch lobbed back lightly, his whimsical smile hovering around the corners of his mouth. Then he grew serious. "Really, I said so much about every item on this bill for months and months, more time for explanation would have been unnecessary."

Later McCulloch followed Celler's lead of appealing to the conservative nature of most Rules Committee members. He stated that he had originally opposed the strong subcommittee bill "because Meader's amendment [Equal Employment], incorporating Griffin's language, was defeated. The Griffin language was incorporated in the redraft. It insured an employer his day in Federal court." Bill McCulloch was not above using a little psychology to bolster his position.

As the day's session ended, two liberal Democrats on the Rules Committee paid tribute to Republican McCulloch for his major contribution to the struggle for civil rights legislation. "Without his effort," said Richard Bolling, "it is, I think, absolutely sure that there would be no bill before us." And Thomas P. O'Neill, Jr. (Mass.) joined in: "Without you, there would not have been a bill of this type before the committee."

Sitting through all nine days of open committee hearings were Bob Kimball and Bill Copenhaver, the Judiciary Committee aides who had helped write the compromise version of H.R. 7152. "The key guys to watch," said Kimball, "were Ed Willis and the Judge." On January 16 Willis, a Louisiana Democrat, bitterly attacked the bill in the Rules Committee, complaining about the way it had been rammed through Celler's committee. While Smith had strategic command of the southern forces, Willis, who was on the Judiciary Committee, would lead the floor fight. Traditionally, members of the committee that hears a bill are given priority on the House floor.

Kimball wrote down every question Chairman Smith asked of the 33 witnesses who appeared before his committee. "He was well scouted," reported Kimball, "but he had to be—he was such a master of surprise." Kimball and Copenhaver prepared answers to all of Smith's queries for Bill McCulloch and John Lindsay to use in case the questions were posed during floor debate. Both staff aides discovered that the Judge concentrated on Titles I and II and very little else. They concluded, therefore, that when the bill reached the floor, its opponents would direct their attack primarily against those two sections. "If they were unable to make any headway against Title I and II, the rest of the battle," Kimball predicted, "would be a formality. If they could win a quick victory on those two, they would press the fight further."

As the Rules Committee approached the end of its hearings, the president was busy getting his forces in line for the action on the House floor, which he saw coming soon. On Friday evening, January 17, Lyndon Johnson impulsively telephoned Roy Wilkins, James Farmer, Martin Luther King, Whitney Young, and A. Philip Randolph, inviting them to meet with him the next morning at the White House. All but Randolph were able to get to the executive mansion by 11:00 A.M. During their conference the president discussed the strategy on the bill. He also told them about his pending message to Congress, in which he planned to outline his proposals for coping with poverty.

Upon leaving the White House, the four civil rights leaders were immediately surrounded by the press. Martin Luther King spoke first, commenting that, in his opinion, the president's proposed poverty legislation was inextricably linked to the civil rights issue.

"Poverty is a problem that affects the whole nation in general, not the Negro in particular," King stated. Then he revealed that he and his three companions did not discuss with the president any compromises, either in the House or Senate, with respect to H.R. 7152. "We feel that this bill should not be watered down any further. We are not prepared to compromise in any form."

The next Tuesday, at his regular breakfast with Capitol Hill Democratic leaders, the president got the latest House of Representatives head count from Larry O'Brien. As of the previous day, 220 House members had pledged to support H.R. 7152, including its three most controversial titles—II (Public Accommodations), III (Judicial Intervention), and VII (Equal Employment). Two hundred and eighteen were needed to pass the bill, so victory seemed assured. But trying to learn from a politician how he will vote on a pending bill is a tenuous proposition at best. Many representatives and senators view controversial issues in much the same way as some people regard a suspected cancer; so long as the possible victim avoids the doctor, the malignancy does not exist. By not thinking about a bill on which he fears to take a stand, the congressman clings to the hope that it will simply "go away." Further, why take a public stand, which certainly will lose friends, on a vote that might never materialize? It was this congressional reticence that occasionally subjected Larry O'Brien to accusations by his critics of "misleading" headcounts.

One critic, NAACP lobbyist Clarence Mitchell, complained that O'Brien "counted" Democrats but only "estimated" Republicans. But, by the same token, Mitchell was considered by Assistant Attorney General Burke Marshall to be "unrealistic in the sense that he would accept and repeat, as fact, wrong information. He would accept a member at face value."

Another executive branch official told Congressman Charles Mathias that Mitchell and civil rights activist Joseph Rauh, Jr. "walk down a corridor and go into each office, and if they don't get bodily thrown out, they count it as favorable."

Whether or not Clarence Mitchell was always exact in his vote projections, civil rights supporters throughout the country regarded him as their principal lobbyist in the nation's capital. "But this would only work if Lyndon Johnson treated him so," observed Joe Rauh, and with this in mind, Rauh arranged for the president to meet with him and Mitchell on January 21 after the Capitol Hill leaders' breakfast.

As the two men, white liberal Joe Rauh and black lobbyist Clarence Mitchell, walked into the Oval Office, they had more in common than just their deep devotion to the cause of civil rights. Both were born in 1911. Both were attorneys. Both were connected with the Fair Employment Practice Committee: Rauh had drafted the order creating it in 1941; Mitchell was appointed to its panel in 1943. Both specialized in labor law after World War II—Rauh as counsel for the United Auto Workers and the Brotherhood of Sleeping Car Porters, Mitchell as labor secretary in the NAACP's New York office. Both became crusaders for equal rights legislation during the 1950s. Both were indefatigable fighters. But there the similarities ended.

Joe Rauh, the fast-talking, fast-walking, bespectacled lawyer with an ever-present bow tie, was dogmatic and relentlessly determined. Not easily forgiving, he sometimes alienated those with whom he dealt. "Rauh," said one ADA official who knew him well, "is resourceful in his arguments and knows the Constitution and the law. But, God, he doesn't give an inch." In fact, Rauh's early relationship with the president had been a stormy one, and it was Lyndon Johnson who had given in. The quintessential liberal, Rauh had always viewed Johnson as an "outsider," a thorn in the side of the "true believers" in progressive causes. When word reached the floor of the 1960 Democratic National Convention that Jack Kennedy selected Johnson as his running mate, Rauh had expressed disbelief, issuing bitter statements on national television. He was dissuaded only at the last moment by *Washington Post* publisher Philip L. Graham from placing Minnesota governor Orville Freeman's name in nomination for the vice presidency. But shortly after he became president, Johnson extended an olive branch to Rauh when, on December 8, he invited the civil rights activist to accompany him to New York on Air Force One to attend the Temple Emanu-el funeral services for former New York governor and senator Herbert H. Lehman. Several days later, Johnson apologized for any offense he may have given Rauh in the past and said he hoped they could work together toward common goals.

Clarence Mitchell, on the other hand, was softer in manner, less likely to offend the uncommitted. Yet he could be very persuasive and adamant. Mitchell was so familiar and well-liked a figure on Capitol Hill that he was sometimes referred to as the "101st senator." Joe Rauh and Clarence Mitchell were a good team.

President Johnson made it clear to the two men that he opposed any effort to strengthen H.R. 7152. This disappointed Rauh and Mitchell who, along with other Leadership Conference officials, had gone on record on November 4 in favor of pushing for strengthening amendments when the McCulloch-Justice Department compromise bill reached the House floor. But the president's other news was exactly what they wanted to hear: Johnson would not be intimidated by a filibuster when the bill reached the Senate.

"I don't care how long it takes," declared the president. "I don't care if the Senate doesn't do one other piece of business this year, you've got to keep this bill on the floor. You can tell Mansfield, you can tell anybody, the President of the United States doesn't care if this bill is there forever. We are not going to have anything else hit the Senate floor until this bill is passed."

Rauh and Mitchell were elated with this promise for, as Rauh noted happily, this would remove "the filibusterers' greatest weapon—that they could hold out until other needed legislation required the Senate to put aside the civil rights bill."

At the same time that this meeting was taking place, the Rules Committee was resuming its hearings for the week. During the next three days it heard testimony from 12 House members, including E. Y. Berry (R-S.Dak.), who wanted to offer his civil rights bill for Indians as an amendment to H.R. 7152. At the end of the January 23 meeting, Chairman Howard Smith announced that 26 witnesses still remained to be called, and so hearings would continue through January 30.

On Monday, January 27, Robert Kennedy returned from a 12-day diplomatic trip to Asia. President Johnson had sent the attorney general to Indonesia to try to settle a dispute between Indonesian president Achmed Sukarno and the neighboring Federation of Malaysia. More importantly, the trip was designed to provide therapy for the late president's brother.

From the time that John F. Kennedy's body was returned to Washington, Bobby had never left Jacqueline Kennedy's side, being there to steady her arm, accompanying her late at night to stand in the shadows of the great Capitol rotunda and watch as thousands filed silently by the bier, and returning with her to Arlington Cemetery long after the funeral was over to leave a simple bouquet of lilies-of-the-valley on the grave. And while the eyes of the nation were riveted on the dignified young widow, few noticed the terrible anguish in Robert Kennedy's eyes. "I thought they'd get one of us, but," he said, "I thought it would be me." The focal point in his life was gone—the brother whom he helped elect president, the brother to whom he was so close that they were referred to constantly as "The Kennedys," the brother whom he had persuaded to introduce a strong civil rights bill because it was morally right. With puffy face, untrimmed hair, and unfocused eyes, he paid scant attention to his job. And even though he and Lyndon Johnson had long been antagonistic, the president's innate sympathy for those in trouble now led him to try to divert the attorney general's mind.

The mission was a diplomatic success. Kennedy was able to obtain a cease-fire agreement between the leaders of the two nations, along with a promise to begin negotiations to resolve their border dispute. The trip was also a therapeutic success. While the attorney general had not been a force during the two previous months and did not lobby the House of Representatives on the civil rights bill after John Kennedy's death, now he returned to Washington determined to face the unfinished business of his brother's administration.

On January 28 and 29, the last two days of open hearings, 18 Southerners from seven states came before the Rules Committee to testify in opposition to H.R. 7152. In making their appearance, they did not necessarily hope to influence the outcome of the panel's decision; indeed, it was apparent that its decision was already made. Rather, like so many other legislators who testify before congressional committees, they used the opportunity to "go on record" on an issue of vital concern to their constituents and to ensure political protection in defending a lost cause. In the future these congressmen could claim, "Look, I fought to the bitter end for you, but our side just didn't have the votes."

By January 29 Chairman Smith had come to the end of his witnesses and the end of the line. He knew that the Republican members of Congress wanted to get the bill out on the House floor and finish debate on it before their traditional Lincoln's Birthday speeches on February 12. He also knew that, under the leadership of Clarence Brown, the five GOP members of the Rules Committee might join in one of their rare alliances with the five northern Democrats and strip him of the bill by supporting a motion requiring the committee to act upon H.R. 7152 by a certain date. Not wanting to lose control over his committee and with nothing left to try for the present, the Judge resignedly called for a vote the next day.

On January 30, Chairman Howard Worth Smith presided at the 10th and last Rules Committee hearing on H.R. 7152, which was held in executive (closed) session. First the committee accepted the motion for H.R. 980 (the civil rights bill for Indians) to be considered as an amendment. Then it was finally time to vote on Resolution 616, which set down the rules for the procedure of the bill on the House floor.

"The question is," the Judge's plaintive voice asked, "shall the resolution pass?"

The tally was 11–4, with only southern Democrats opposed. And with that vote, H.R. 7152 broke free, managing to escape a plot in Judge Smith's graveyard in which so much liberal legislation had been entombed in the past. The next day it would, at last, come face to face with the 435 members of the House of Representatives.

Four

Bipartisan House Victory

T HE LONG-AWAITED DRAMA in the House of Representatives
began precisely at 11:59 A.M. on Friday, January 31, 1964.
At that moment 75-year old John McCormack entered the venerable
chamber and slowly climbed the steps to the top of the three-tiered
Speaker's dais.

He paused. Before him was arrayed his beloved House in all
its splendor. Directly below him, at the middle tier rostrum used
by the reading clerk and all presidents of the United States when
addressing joint sessions of Congress, stood the chaplain, the
Reverend Bernard Braskamp. On the lowest tier, at a semicircular
desk, sat 11 clerks ready to record and administer the day's proceedings. In front of them stretched the empty floor area known
as the "well of the House," into which members descended to debate
from two lecterns. And beyond the well rose a semicircular am-
phitheater of 448 unmarked seats for the members, Republicans
on the left of the center aisle, Democrats on the right. Overhead
in the press gallery, newsmen from all over the world were poised
to record the highlights of the historic event. The galleries had been
packed since early morning, with the steady hum of some 600 quietly
chattering voices echoing through the cavernous hall. Among that
crowd were the familiar faces of those who had godfathered the
bill—Nicholas Katzenbach, Burke Marshall, Joe Rauh, and Clarence
Mitchell.

At the stroke of noon the Speaker rapped his gavel on the desk.
Immediately one bell rang in committee rooms and offices on the
House side of the Capitol, notifying congressmen that the House

was now in session. As silence descended on the chamber, Chaplain Braskamp appropriately drew from Gal. 5:10 for his invocation: "As we have therefore opportunity, let us do good unto all men."

After the prayer, Speaker McCormack recognized Majority Leader Carl Albert and James Roosevelt, who, in their one-minute speeches, paid tribute to the California congressman's late father, Franklin D. Roosevelt, on the anniversary of his birth, January 30, 1882. Following that, H. R. Gross (R-Iowa), termed by his admirers "the conscience of the House" and by his detractors "a gadfly," noted the absence of a quorum (half of the House, or 218 members). Carl Albert, seated at the Democratic leadership table, reached for a microphone and moved a call of the House. Three bells, signaling a quorum call, rang throughout the Hill. During the next 35 minutes some 400 representatives, many wearing white carnations in memory of President Roosevelt, trickled through the 13 double-door entrances. After the lengthy roll call, the clerk announced the presence of a quorum, and the House of Representatives was ready to take up the most far-reaching civil rights bill since the Emancipation Proclamation.

To novice observers in the gallery, House floor practices appear mystifying, if not chaotic. Yet they remain much the same as those conducted in 1789 by the First Congress, many of whose rules were borrowed directly from Great Britain's House of Commons. H.R. 7152 would go through the same six-step process followed by all bills that had preceded it through the years. The House would (1) pass a resolution setting the guidelines for consideration of the bill; (2) resolve itself into a Committee of the Whole to engage in general debate; (3) offer, consider, and take unrecorded votes on amendments; (4) resume sitting as the House to take recorded votes on any accepted amendments if one-fifth of the members request it; (5) permit a minority party member to offer a recommittal motion, enabling the minority to obtain a recorded vote on any defeated amendment; and (6) vote on final passage of the bill.

Step One began when the Speaker recognized Rules Committee member Ray Madden (D-Ind.).

"Mr. Speaker," Madden said in his Irish brogue, "by direction of the Committee on Rules, I call up House Resolution 616 and ask for its immediate consideration." Madden briefly described the contents of H.R. 7152 and its short but chaotic history. He then outlined the rules, as stated in House Resolution 616, under which the bill would be considered.

"The question is," asked the Speaker, "shall the resolution be adopted?"

To debate the resolution, the House was allotted one hour, divided equally between the Democrats and Republicans. Clarence Brown, speaking on behalf of the Rules Committee, gave credit to its members, who were passionately divided on the most controversial bill to go through the House in all his 25 years there.

"I want to say," said the Ohio Republican, who had been the key figure in getting Rules Committee chairman Howard Smith to release the bill, "that despite the differences of opinion that might have existed within the committee itself, as well as within the House, no member of the committee or of this body said or did anything that reacted adversely in any way upon the dignity of the House of Representatives or its committees."

"Will the gentleman yield?" asked the voice of Emanuel Celler.

Brown yielded the floor to Celler, who diplomatically complimented Judge Smith, saying he was "very grateful. . . to the Chairman of the Committee on Rules, the gentleman from Virginia, because he kept his word, he kept the faith. He said he would grant a rule, and a rule was granted."

Then Brown reclaimed the floor. "There has been an agreement made between the leadership on both sides of the aisle, and between those who are opponents and proponents of this legislation, that no move shall be made to shut off debate or to close debate on this bill, when it is being considered under the five-minute rule, until and unless every member of the House who may desire to do so will have the full opportunity to offer and to discuss any amendment that he may wish to submit for consideration. I also understand that every attempt will be made not to waste the time of Congress by unnecessary quorum calls or by filibustering tactics." He closed by appealing to the House membership for cooperation, so that "we can at least say to our grandchildren, we participated in one of the great debates in modern American history and we did it as statesmen and not as quarreling individuals."

"What is the rush?" It was a rhetorical question from the angular Mississippi Democrat, William Colmer. "I ask, Mr. Speaker, is all of this done out of fear? Is the Congress of the United States to yield to threats of further demonstrations by minority group leaders—blackmail, if you please?. . .To what end will this bring us? Is the Congress to comply by legislation with the demands and even riots of every organized minority group in the country?"

Colmer's complaint was the opening shot in the southern salvo against the bill. But the House, anxious to get on with the historic business at hand, passed Resolution 616 by an overwhelming voice vote. Step Two, general debate, was about to begin.

The Rules Committee had limited debate on H.R. 7152 to 10 hours equally divided between the two political parties. So now the floor leaders, New York's scrappy liberal Manny Celler and Ohio's courtly conservative Bill McCulloch, moved to their command posts, a pair of 20-foot-long committee tables on the House floor, one on the Democrat side and one on the Republican. Although both men had a combined total of 57 years of legislative experience, this was the highlight of their careers. And they had prepared well. Each was armed with a manual of several hundred pages, prepared by the Justice Department, containing a section-by-section analysis of the bill. For each title there was a reference to its history and its need, a summary of its provisions, a review of its scope and constitutionality, probable major objections, possible amendments and arguments in response to them, replies to the Judiciary Committee's minority report dealing with each section, and a rundown of equivalent state legislation. They also had copies of Bob Kimball's and Bill Copenhaver's suggested answers to questions posed by Judge Smith during the Rules Committee hearings. Although the two leaders retained overall command, they assigned members of the Judiciary Committee to explain and defend the various titles. In addition, eight Justice Department attorneys, specialists in each title, were standing by if trouble developed.

"Mr. Speaker," intoned Manny Celler, "I move that the House resolve itself into the Committee of the Whole House on the State of the Union for consideration of the bill, H.R. 7152."

Such a move—agreeing to act as a committee rather than as the House—was traditional when the House was to consider major legislation. According to rumor, this centuries-old practice originated out of fear of the English monarch. The House of Commons devised it as a means of getting the Speaker out of the chamber during debate; since he was the king's ally, the Speaker could be expected to report back to the monarch who was loyal and who was not. Disloyal members sometimes lost their heads.

When Celler's perfunctory motion was approved, another antiquated practice was observed. The mace, a three-foot-long ceremonial staff, which was modeled on the clubs used as weapons in the Middle Ages and which ultimately came to symbolize legislative authority, was removed from the House chamber. John McCormack stepped down from the Speaker's chair and handed the gavel to Eugene J. Keogh (D-N.Y.), who took over as chairman of the Committee of the Whole and immediately recognized Emanuel Celler.

As the squat, sturdy man stood at the Democratic committee table, piles of books and papers spread out before him, he was truly at home. Celler loved the drama of flowing oratory, the excitement of political debate, the thrill of creating history. His bald pate glistened under the bright lights, and his broad face glowed in satisfaction as the opening statements of debate resounded through the chamber in his raspy Brooklyn accent.

"We now have bestowed upon us a golden opportunity to do a great thing," orated Celler. Then, drawing on his vast stock of quotations, he reminded his listeners that "it was John Milton who said, 'Peace has her victories no less renowned than war.' "

> Mr. Chairman, what we are considering this day in effect is a bill of particulars on a petition in the language of our Constitution for a redress of grievances. The grievances are real and genuine, the proof is in, the gathering of evidence has gone on for over a century. The legislation before you seeks only to honor the constitutional guarantees of equality under the law for all. It bestows no preferences on any one group; what it does is to place into balance the scales of justice so that the living force of our Constitution shall apply to all people, not only to those who by accident of birth were born with white skins.... Both parties joined hands. We felt we represented a cause. We shunned a political issue. I am grateful to the ranking member of the Republican party on the Judiciary Committee, the gentleman from Ohio.... I pay tribute to him and his fellow Republicans who stood by him.

Bill McCulloch took the floor next. The day had special meaning for him since it was exactly one year before, on January 31, 1963, that he had introduced his own civil rights bill, parts of which were now incorporated into H.R. 7152. McCulloch's words carried none of Celler's flourishes. His speech was like himself—spare and forthright. Meticulous in his attention to the finer points of the law, he explained why a federal law was needed.

> I believe in the effective separation of powers and in a workable federal system, whereby State authority is not

needlessly usurped by a centralized government. But, I also believe that an obligation rests with the national government to see that the citizens of every state are treated equally without regard to their race or color or religion or national origin.

McCulloch then directed an answer to those members who had charged that H.R. 7152 was drafted out of fear.

No people can gain lasting liberty and equality by riot and demonstrations. Legislation under such threat is basically not legislation at all. In the long run, behavior of this type will lead to a total undermining of society, where equality and civil rights will mean nothing.... Not force or fear, then, but belief in the inherent equality of man induces me to support this legislation.

The members of the House listening to Bill McCulloch represented 435 pieces of the American jigsaw puzzle. They came from Moline, Little Rock, Bangor, Austin, Atlanta, Duluth, Tucson, Yakima, and Providence, and from places in between, places where immigrants from Ireland, Poland, China, France, Greece, Russia, England, Germany, and elsewhere had come to carve out a better life for themselves on the abundant continent. Himself an Ohioan of Scottish descent, McCulloch was deeply aware of the diversity of the men and women of the Congress. "One of the examples of America's greatness," McCulloch had told a reporter, "is that people from radically different backgrounds can find a common ground on great issues."

As he stood alone at the microphone, this moment culminated seven long months of work in a quest to find that common ground. Meeting early in the mornings with Justice Department officials, he had constructed a bill that Republicans could accept. Then, after Emanuel Celler almost killed H.R. 7152 with overzealousness, McCulloch revived it, rewrote it with the help of John Lindsay, and helped Celler ram it through the Judiciary Committee. Finally, he began a series of early morning, midday, and late night meetings with Republicans to reconcile their many differences of opinion. Neither a booming orator nor a back-room arm twister, McCulloch preferred to coax and cajole, believing that persuasion was better than force.

"The Constitution doesn't say that whites alone shall have our basic rights," he told them quietly, "but that we all shall have them."

A modest man, Bill McCulloch was not a dramatic crusader for civil rights. He did not march at the head of a column with banners flying. He simply did what he considered to be the right thing. But it was this deep moral conviction of a conservative like themselves that persuaded fence-sitting Republicans to follow him. Liberals like John Lindsay and Manny Celler could not have done it.

Now the planted seeds of conviction had borne fruit. Everyone conceded that H.R. 7152 had enough votes to pass the House. But in what form? The Southerners, as in the past, were armed with a sheath of weakening amendments that could gut the measure if the backers of the bill lacked the discipline to stay on the floor and vote against them. McCulloch, a gentleman to his fingertips, would have to be a ruthless dictator on the floor; his partner, Emanuel Celler, was already a master of the role. It was the only way the two of them could get H.R. 7152 through the House unscathed.

When Celler and McCulloch—described by the latter as "the Brooklyn street urchin and the Ohio plowboy"—had finished their opening statements, they allotted segments of debate time to members of their respective parties. General debate was scheduled to run through Friday and Saturday. Members from the South received half of the total time, and they immediately began their attack on the bill by charging that the federal government was being given the power to encroach upon individual freedom.

Ed Willis called it "the most drastic and far-reaching proposal and grab for power ever to be reported out of a committee of Congress in the history of our republic." William Tuck predicted that it "would confer upon the attorney general autocratic powers such as may befit a commisar of justice in a totalitarian country." And E. L. Forrester (D-Ga.) declared, "Never has such a bill come before Congress with the Congress knowing so little about it."

When Forrester's 15 minutes expired, McCulloch gave him an extra 5, which the Georgian considered not enough. "Could the gentleman give me a little more time?" asked Forrester. "I have not talked in a long time."

"Mr. Chairman," replied McCulloch lightly, "I am a generous man where money is not involved. I will consider the application when the time comes."

"Mr. Chairman," responded Forrester with condescending courtesy, "the gentleman is a wonderful man ordinarily. I feel somewhat as the Scriptures when it says, 'Father, forgive him for he knows not what he does.' "

Arguments both damning and praising the bill continued to resound through the packed chamber, only ceasing when the time for general debate finally ran out at 7:00 P.M. Saturday. The weary members agreed to convene at noon on Monday, February 3, when Step Three, the offering of amendments, would begin.

While the House had been thus engaged, Lyndon Johnson held his sixth press conference as president. Johnson did not particularly enjoy meeting with newsmen; he regarded them as his natural enemies and the event had none of the witty repartee that livened his predecessor's sparring matches with reporters. When asked whether he expected H.R. 7152 to face a filibuster in the Senate, which might ultimately weaken it, the president's answers were uncharacteristically brief.

"No," he said shortly, "I don't think it will be substantially trimmed. And, yes, I do expect a filibuster."

When told Saturday evening of Johnson's statement, Bill McCulloch complained that it fell short of the unequivocal assurance he had sought from the administration if the House "stuck its neck out" for a strong bill. The following afternoon, during his appearance with Senate minority leader Everett Dirksen on "Meet The Press," Charlie Halleck echoed McCulloch's fears. Halleck did not want the House left "holding the bag" if the Senate later emasculated the bill.

For the most part, however, the loquacious Charlie Halleck was strangely silent during the House debate. He made no statement either for or against the bill. Neither did he call a caucus so that H.R. 7152 could be explained by Bill McCulloch, John Lindsay, or other Judiciary Committee Republicans. Halleck's silence reflected the schism in the GOP between those members who viewed themselves as carrying on in the tradition of Lincoln and those who had few blacks in their districts and saw no reason to get involved in a fight that did not concern them. If a Republican conference had been called to discuss the bill, said Minority Whip Les Arends, "all we would do was tear ourselves apart."

Charlie Halleck's contribution was to remain neutral and simply press for adjournment by February 9 so that the Republican members could go home to make their Lincoln's Birthday speeches. And if the GOP liberals and moderates saw an incongruity in this approach, they were too busy trying to pass H.R. 7152 to make the observation.

"Bill McCulloch and I felt we would have to 'hang together'

to preserve the bill,'' observed John Lindsay, referring to the absence of any Republican party endorsement.

The third day of debate was Monday, February 3. When the House convened at noon, the clerk was ready to start Step Three, the offering of amendments. He would read the bill, Title by Title, line by line. After each Title was read, members could offer amendments to that section under the so-called five minute rule which limited the remarks of an amendment's sponsor, its proponents, and its opponents to five minutes each. Often in the past, when discussion dragged on interminably, the majority party spokesman asked for unanimous consent to end debate on a given amendment at a certain time. But in the case of H.R. 7152, a gentlemen's agreement was made between the northern liberals and southern conservatives; Celler would not attempt to cut off debate and, in return, the Southerners would not delay debate by asking for quorum calls whenever it appeared that less than 100 members were on the floor.

Step Three was the crucial part of the battle: whether H.R. 7152 retained its strength or was substantially weakened depended on the amendments. The problem was that in 1964 those votes were unrecorded. Consequently, because constituents did not know how or even if their congressman voted on amendments, some members often did not even bother to show up. As a result, a small but determined force could pass its own amendments, often changing a bill drastically.

The big job for Manny Celler and Bill McCulloch, then, was to keep their forces on the floor. They were helped by the fact that each vote could be dragged out for at least 10 minutes. First, the chairman called for a voice vote. Then, if an objection was heard, he called for a standing vote. Finally, if 20 members objected, he called for a teller vote, appointing two people—the amendment's sponsor and its principal opponent—to count heads as the yeas and nays walked up the center aisle.

To get members from their offices to the floor within those 10 minutes Celler and McCulloch set up a three-pronged whip system:

1. The Democratic Study Group (DSG) operated on the House floor. Composed of 120 liberal-to-moderate Democrats, the DSG replaced the regular majority whip, Southerner Hale Boggs (D-La.), with a ''buddy'' plan. Under the supervision of Frank Thompson (D-N.J.), 17 DSG members had responsibility for 6 to 8 congressmen. When a vote on an amendment seemed imminent,

Thompson would call the DSG office, which in turn would call the offices of the 17 whips. Those staffs would then call the congressmen on their lists, asking them to get to the floor, and would call them a second time if they had not appeared by the time the vote started.

2. O'Grady's Raiders patrolled the office building hallways. This was a squad of 25 volunteers, all with previous experience in labor union lobbying, headed by Jane O'Grady, lobbyist for the Amalgamated Clothing Workers of America. When the bells in the Cannon and Longworth buildings announced a teller vote, they hurried to congressional offices, making sure members got to the floor.

3. The Leadership Conference on Civil Rights watched from the galleries. Since writing in the galleries is forbidden, hundreds of volunteers each memorized the faces of several congressmen and watched to see who voted and who did not.

At noon on Monday, all was ready. Celler and McCulloch had agreed that if a proposed amendment did no violence to the bill or to the principles which underlay it, they would be flexible to preserve harmony among Judiciary Committee members and within the House itself. However, if substantive changes were sought, they would be intractable.

"Title I [Voting Rights]," called the clerk.

The first two amendments offered by the Southerners were defeated. The next two were constructive changes offered by southern Republicans Dick Poff (Va.) and Bill Cramer; since they felt they could not stop the bill, they decided to make it as good as possible. Poff's amendment granted to defendants the same rights as the attorney general to ask for a three-judge court to hear charges of voting rights violations. Cramer's included Puerto Rico within the bill's scope. Both were accepted by Celler and McCulloch without objection and adopted by the House.

The well-organized team was cranking out H.R. 7152 smoothly and efficiently. Four additional amendments were defeated, and backers of the bill began to relax, feeling that the job might not be so hard, after all. The teller vote on the last amendment, however, was surprisingly narrow, 117–124, and warned the two leaders not to get complacent. That night the DSG sent out a message to its whips to make sure "that every member is notified when he is needed on the floor to prevent emasculation of the bill."

Tuesday, February 4, was the fourth day of debate. The DSG warning worked. Three remaining southern amendments to Title I were decisively defeated.

"Title II [Public Accommodations]," read the clerk.

Surprisingly, the debate on Title II was noteworthy for its moderation, especially in view of the intense feelings public accommodations evoked. Late Tuesday afternoon, however, Judge Smith went beyond the bounds of propriety. Referring to the fact that a chiropodist whose office was in a hotel would be covered by Title II, he made a shrill outburst. "If I were cutting corns," he cried, "I would want to know whose feet I would have to be monkeying around with. I would want to know whether they smelled good or bad."

This offensive language, however, never appeared in the *Congressional Record*. Taking advantage of a House rule which permits members to revise their floor remarks, Smith simply removed the sentences from the official transcript of the proceedings.

The doughty old segregationist's next remarks came during debate over his amendment, which cleverly proposed that no one could be required to render labor or service without his own consent. "This amendment," explained Smith, "merely implements the 13th amendment, ...[which] provides that neither slavery nor involuntary servitude should exist in any place in the United States." A look of cunning crept across his face as he dared the civil rights backers to vote, in effect, for slavery by opposing his amendment. "See if you can vote against it," he shouted triumphantly. "I defy you to do it." They did, 107–149, and then adjourned. The fourth day of debate ended at 5:28 P.M.

Most Southerners, who had conceded privately that it was all over when H.R. 7152 slipped out of Judge Smith's grasp, now started disappearing from the floor. Their absence now was as striking as their presence had been formerly. In the past each southern state had its own whip, charged with insuring that members were on the floor to vote for issues dear to Dixie. But now the feeling of apathy was keeping most of them away. On Wednesday afternoon, after additional southern amendments to Title II were crushed, Edward Hébert (D-La.) looked forlornly at the empty seats around him, got up, and wondered aloud where his colleagues from the South were at such an important time. Only about 30 of the 96 Southerners were present.

"Let me pay you a tribute and a compliment," Hébert told the members of the DSG. "You are here on the job. I disagree with you but I respect you, and I admire your courage and your determination to be here and be counted."

The most sweeping civil rights bill in nearly a century was about to pass the House, and the Southerners were helpless. Only a few, like Judge Smith, still stood guard for the Old Confederacy. He sat slouched in his seat, one last card tucked up his long sleeve, waiting for the right moment to play it.

Hébert's comment about the missing Southerners came during consideration of northern conservative George Meader's amendment, which Bill McCulloch predicted would be the "biggest test" of the public accommodations title. Rejected when originally offered in the Judiciary Subcommittee, it would substantially limit the coverage of the bill to those hotels, motels, inns, restaurants, and gas stations immediately adjacent to interstate or primary highways. McCulloch chided Meader.

"He comes from Ann Arbor," the Ohioan told the House. "If that great Michigan football team was on its way to Miami to play that great school down there in Florida, and a Negro family were traveling with them and could not get service in Fort Lauderdale, Florida, what could be done? There is just no teeth in this amendment, and it should be defeated." It was, 68–153.

After that, it was a rout. Four other amendments to Title II were overcome by margins ranging from 81 to 92 votes. By the time Wednesday's floor session ended at 8:05 P.M., it was evident that, in three days of amendments, the enemies of H.R. 7152 had made no major changes in the bill.

A new problem, however, appeared the next day. Thursday, February 6, was the sixth day of debate, and now Manny Celler and Bill McCulloch, after being on their feet for eight and nine hours at a stretch, began to tire. Separated as they were at committee tables on different sides of the chamber, it was not surprising that signals got crossed and misunderstandings arose. Frictions were bound to occur between them, considering Celler's innate deviousness and McCulloch's sensitivity to slights. But both men magnanimously overlooked them; otherwise H.R. 7152 would be the victim.

"Title III [Public Facilities]," read the clerk.

Of the 10 amendments offered by Southerners to Title III, only one passed. This was a proposal by Dick Poff that provided for defendants' attorney fees to be included in the cost assessed the federal government when it lost a suit to desegregate public facilities. Manny Celler initially objected to the amendment and listened with surprise as Bill McCulloch endorsed it: "This might be an effective brake on district attorneys and assistant district attorneys who have motives not in accord with those of us who drafted this bill."

Celler looked over at McCulloch and acquiesced graciously. "I am always loath to differ—particularly in the consideration of the terms of this bill—with my distinguished colleague from Ohio. We have always been in tandem, as it were.... I shall yield to the wishes of the gentleman from Ohio and withdraw my objection and accept the amendment."

"Title IV [Public Education]," intoned the clerk. Of the eight amendments offered, six were rebuffed and two accepted by Celler and McCulloch.

"Title V [Civil Rights Commission]" was announced next.

One amendment offered by Southerner Ed Willis, a member of the Judiciary Committee, proposed that the commission not be required to investigate the "membership practices of any bona fide fraternal, religious, or civic organization which selects its membership." This was one occasion that illustrates the flexibility of Celler and McCulloch. Although they did not wholly approve of the amendment, neither did they think that it did violence to the bill. To preserve rapport among the Judiciary Committee members, they agreed to accept it. Celler responded for the pair.

"I am interested in getting this bill passed. I do not want to encourage so much opposition to the wording of a particular section that it might jeopardize the entire bill. I am a pragmatist. Although I may not be thoroughly in accord with this amendment, I believe it proper in order to get this matter expedited and get this bill passed and sent to the Senate, I would accept it and concur in the gentleman's wishes."

Staff members, however, were not always so pliable. Judiciary Committee counsel Ben Zelenko, sitting next to Celler at the committee table, was shocked to hear his chairman's concession. "I almost quit on the spot," he confessed. And before the vote was called, Zelenko raced up to the gallery to relate his dismay to Burke Marshall. But the assistant attorney general, appearing unconcerned, explained to the distraught counsel that occasionally "we have to give away things. After all, we have to deal with the Southerners tomorrow."

Next it was Bill McCulloch's turn to be surprised. An amendment by Byron Rogers restored the language of the original Kennedy bill by extending the life of the Civil Rights Commission only four years. And while McCulloch seemed to agree placidly, it was only a mask to hide his irritation with Celler and the Justice Department, who, he felt, had broken their agreement with him to make the commission a permanent body. Without debate, the House accepted the amendment.

By Thursday evening everyone was exhausted. It seemed that their repeated losses had completely drained the anti-civil rights members of their will to fight. Not a single objection was raised when Celler proposed cutting off debate on Title V at 9:15 P.M., a motion that normally would bring a flood of objections, especially since Clarence Brown had promised that debate would not be shut off. Wearily, the House defeated the last two amendments to Title V and prepared to adjourn for the night.

Minority Leader Charlie Halleck, sensing that the Southerners were finished and wanting to get his members away for their Lincoln's Birthday speeches, asked unanimous consent for the House to meet an hour earlier than usual for the next two days so that it could "wind up debate. . .on this coming Saturday evening." Then Halleck, who never believed in using a scalpel when a hatchet would do, threatened that if the Southerners refused to cooperate, he would retaliate by supporting motions to cut off debate.

Suddenly it was evident that some vestiges of southern spunk remained. Judge Smith rose in righteous anger to thunder that if Halleck did this "to suit somebody's convenience to get away from Washington next week, then as far as I am concerned some unpleasant things are liable to happen." Those unpleasant things would most likely be timeconsuming quorum calls and other delaying tactics, the only weapons that the Southerners had left. Smith effectively called Halleck's bluff; objections were raised to meeting any earlier. The sixth day of debate ended Thursday at 9:34 P.M., with agreement to convene at the usual hour of 12:00 noon the next day.

During six days of long hours, rambling debate, and tedious teller votes, there had been enough pro-civil rights congressmen on the House floor to protect the bill against attack. It was a victory for the three-pronged whip system. Many House members were frankly intimidated by the packed galleries. "All I could see was a sea of black faces," said one representative. "I couldn't tell, therefore, whether my constituent was there or not, so I didn't take any chances. I voted on all of the amendments." And in the words of their youthful leader, O'Grady's Raiders kept a "nagging presence" in the corridors of the Cannon and Longworth office buildings, constantly badgering congressional staffs as to the whereabouts of their members. If congressmen were located in their offices when an amendment was being voted on, "we still had to be sure that they actually got to the floor," said Arnold Mayer of the Meatcutters Union. So Mayer escorted the errant member from his office to the elevator, waiting there with him until its arrival. Those legislators who wandered beyond the boundaries of Capitol Hill, including one as far away as Europe, were traced by the Leadership Conference staff and urged to return.

The seventh day of debate began at noon on Friday, February 7. Five titles remained.

"Title VI [Federally Assisted programs]" called the clerk.

Oren Harris (D-Ark.) offered an amendment that would drastically weaken the section and remove all provisions for judicial review. While Bill McCulloch was in the rest room, Majority Whip Hale Boggs rose to support the amendment. Returning to the floor, McCulloch heard about the whip's action and immediately became suspicious. Boggs was not only a Democratic leader but also a close friend of Lyndon Johnson. McCulloch feared another betrayal was in the offing, such as had occurred the previous day when the permanent life of the Civil Rights Commission was reduced to four years. This looked like a last-minute effort by the Democrats to avoid a party-splitting filibuster in the Senate by compromising with their southern wing. McCulloch had seen this tactic work before, when the Civil Rights Act of 1957 was weakened.

"Look!" McCulloch's wife, Mabel, whispered to Roy Wilkins, who was sitting next to her in the gallery. "Bill's face is red. He's mad!"

McCulloch grabbed the microphone. "If we pick up this old provision which does not provide for judicial review," he announced angrily, "I regret to say that my individual support of the legislation will come to an end."

Shocked silence filled the House. The bipartisan coalition, a tenuous thread at times, was about to break. McCulloch, flaming from the neck up, stared straight ahead, fed up with being repeatedly betrayed each time he thought that he and the Democrats had a firm agreement. His startled colleagues, including Emanuel Celler, gave Bill McCulloch a long look and decided he meant it. The Democrats knew they had to have McCulloch's help to get any bill at all. Reacting to his threat, the House crushed Harris's amendment by a standing vote, 80–206. Not one Republican voted against McCulloch. It was his finest hour.

Catastrophe averted, H.R. 7152 trudged on. The seventh day

of debate ended at 8:20 P.M. with the House, in 10 minutes, defeating the last seven amendments to Title VI and then rebuffing southern objections to meeting at the earlier hour of 11:00 the next morning.

"Title VII [Equal Employment]," stated the clerk, as the Saturday session started.

Emanuel Celler immediately introduced 10 amendments designed to bring the Title, borrowed from the Education and Labor Committee, into technical conformity with the rest of H.R. 7152. After each amendment was submitted, Bill McCulloch arose, stated it was acceptable to the minority, and urged its adoption.

After one such concurrence, Jamie Whitten (D-Miss.) remarked that in 22 years in Congress, "I have never seen as close a relationship—almost without any difference whatever—between the Democratic leadership and the Republican leadership—between the gentleman from New York and the gentleman from Ohio." McCulloch replied that he was "pleased to march up the aisle...with any patriotic American who is a member of this body in support of a moral issue."

At one point, however, when the members were in the midst of debating Celler's second amendment, the plaintive voice of Judge Smith was raised in objection. "We were told," he complained, "that this legislation was perfect and it did not need any amendments.... We are confronted today with a series of amendments from members of the [Judiciary] committee, who have a preferential right to offer amendments, and who are being recognized while other members, who are not members of the committee, who would like to offer some meritorious amendments, are waiting. I have one and I have been waiting here a long time to get it before the Committee [of the Whole]."

Finally, after the rest of Celler's 10 "perfecting" amendments were accepted by voice vote, the old master of surprise got his chance to offer a "meritorious" amendment. It was the trump card he had been waiting so long to play. As he reached for a microphone, his wrinkled face couldn't help breaking into an expectant smile. "Mr. Chairman," he drawled, "I offer an amendment."

The clerk read the paper that Smith had given him. "After the word 'religion,' insert 'sex' on pages 68, 69, 70, and 71 of the bill."

The House erupted in shock as the full import of the amendment sank in. By adding the word "sex" to the list of discriminations (race, creed, color, and national origin) prohibited in employ-

115

ment, it would give all women—black and white—their first equal job rights with men. It would affect every employer, labor union, governmental body, and employment agency in the country. It would be one of the most radical civil rights amendments in U.S. history.

The Judge ambled down to the lectern in the well of the House and paused until the tumult died down. Peering innocently over his glasses at the confusion of his colleagues, he savored every delicious second. "Now, what harm can you do to this bill that was so perfect yesterday and so imperfect today?" he queried, his voice dripping honey.

It was a brilliant move by the arch foe of civil rights. Smith counted on the amendment passing and making H.R. 7152 so controversial that eventually it would be voted down either in the House or Senate. The cunning old Judge had warned Celler, during the Rules Committee hearings, that the bill was "as full of booby traps as a dog is full of fleas." And now he had proved it. If anything could kill the bill, he thought, this would.

To explain his "chivalrous" action, the Judge read extracts from a letter he said he had just recently received from a lady: " 'I suggest that you might also favor an amendment. . .to correct the present "imbalance" which exists between males and females in the United States. . . . The census of 1960 shows that we had 88,331,000 males living in this country and 90,992,000 females, which leaves the country with an "imbalance" of 2,661,000 females. I am sure you will agree that this is a grave injustice to womankind.' " Smith's point was that if all women could not get husbands, they at least should get jobs with equal pay.

"The time of the gentleman from Virginia has expired," intoned the chairman.

"Mr. Chairman," called Emanuel Celler loudly, "I rise in opposition to the amendment."

"Oh, no!" exclaimed the Judge, in mock horror.

Celler tried to pull H.R. 7152 out of the trap, pointing out that Smith's amendment would strike down many state laws that were enacted to protect females from hazardous work conditions. The Brooklyn Democrat wanted, first of all, to save the bill. But he also held a traditional, old-world view of the "weaker sex" and was concerned about the revolutionary changes this amendment would bring to his male-dominated world. People in the galleries, listening to the discussion between the 75-year-old Celler and the 80-year-old

Smith about the "biological differences" between men and women, couldn't help snickering.

Suddenly there arose, in a spontaneous spirit of sisterhood, a bipartisan coalition of five congresswomen—Frances P. Bolton (R-Ohio), Martha W. Griffiths (D-Mich.), Catherine May (R-Wash.), Edna F. Kelly (D-N.Y.), and Katherine St. George (R-N.Y.)—to support Smith's amendment.

"Mr. Chairman!" called Katherine St. George, speaking into one of the three microphones on the Republican side of the House.

"For what purpose does the gentlewoman from New York rise?" asked the chairman. When she replied that she rose in support of the amendment, the chairman granted her five minutes.

"I can think of nothing more logical than this amendment at this point," cried Congresswoman St. George, addressing her dumbfounded male colleagues. Women, she said, "do not need any special privileges. We outlast you—we outlive you—we nag you to death, . . . [but] we are entitled to this little crumb of equality. The addition of the little, terrifying word 's-e-x' will not hurt this legislation in any way."

Pandemonium reigned on the floor, where the men of the predominately male House of Representatives were self-righteously indignant at having to take this unexpected stand for or against women. Smith smiled triumphantly, Celler sputtered helplessly, and McCulloch discreetly remained silent. His silence during debate reflected what certainly was a no-win proposition. He really could not argue against the sex amendment on principle, and to speak against it to preserve the bill would be self-defeating because to do so would alienate most women in the country. Moreover, it was probably going to pass.

"168–133," announced the tellers. "We've won, we've won!" cried a lady in the gallery jubilantly.

Congressmen looked up in astonished disapproval. Outbursts by visitors were rare. One such disruption had occurred in 1954 when four Puerto Rican nationalists fired bullets into the Republican leadership table where Charlie Halleck was now sitting. The scars were still there. House attendants promptly ejected the deliriously happy woman. And the befuddled members of Congress, some of them wryly aware that things would never again be quite the same, went back to consider the suddenly bisexual H.R. 7152.

"But," declared George Meader, "Smith outsmarted himself. At this point there was no way you could sink the bill."

Actually, there was much poetic justice in the addition of the word *sex*. The first boatloads of blacks and women had come to America in 1619, 12 years after an all-male contingent had founded a colony at Jamestown, Virginia. Blacks were brought to till the soil. Women were brought to cook and sew and bear children. Now, both would have a chance to challenge the marketplace so long dominated by white males.

Suddenly a precursor of women's liberation, H.R. 7152 marched on. In short order, the still-reeling House accepted two more amendments, one preventing discrimination in job retraining programs and the other allowing church-related colleges or groups to hire employees on the basis of their religious beliefs. Four additional amendments were handily rejected.

Politicians throughout the years have been accused by cynics of taking a positive stand on little outside of "God" and "motherhood." Now Howard Smith's sex discrimination amendment allowed House members to demonstrate their support for motherhood. And John Ashbrook (R-Ohio) let them come out in favor of God by proposing that "It shall not be an unlawful employment practice for an employer to refuse to hire and employ any person because of said person's atheistic beliefs." Recognizing the political futility of opposing such an amendment, McCulloch said nothing while Celler spoke only seven words: "There is no need for your amendment." On a standing vote, Ashbrook and the Almighty carried the day, 137–98.

Although amendments to Title VII were still pending, it was now Saturday evening and the exhausted House voted to adjourn. Carl Albert moved that they convene on Monday, but the Republicans objected, wanting to meet on Sunday to get away for their week of Lincoln speeches. They were defeated, 220–175, and the eighth day of debate ended at 9:00 P.M.

The ninth day of debate began at 10:55 A.M., Monday, February 10. Emanuel Celler asked for and won unanimous consent that all debate on Title VII end at 1:00 P.M. In the next two and one-quarter hours, 26 amendments were offered, of which 22 were defeated. Each of the 4 accepted amendments was approved by Celler and McCulloch. One was a slight language change. Another increased by 25 the number of employees a firm must have before being subject to the law. The third included sexual discrimination (to conform to the Smith language contained in an earlier section). And the last, offered by William Colmer, stated that it shall not be unlawful to refuse employment to Communist party members. Regarding this last, James Roosevelt mirrored the views of most of his colleagues when he stated, "If we oppose this amendment, it would put [us] in company with Communists or pro-Communists. I do not think any member should be put in that light."

After all amendments to Title VII had been considered, E. Y. Berry offered as a new Title VIII his bill, H.R. 900—Equal Employment Opportunity for Indians through Industrial Development— to improve conditions among Indians on reservations and in other communities.

Manny Celler, weary after nine days on his feet, was unusually blunt in his opposition to the South Dakota Republican's amendment, which he said was "about as germane to a civil rights bill as an elephant is to a pussy cat. . . . pray tell me how in thunder an Indian reservation is relevant to a labor organization, or how financing Indian factories is relevant to discrimination on the grounds of race, color, national origin, or sex. If you approve this amendment you will approve a most gauche method of bringing bills before the House." The Judiciary Committee chairman, who had few, if any, Indians in his Brooklyn district, prevailed. Berry's amendment was rejected in a teller vote, 95–149.

The end was now in sight. At 4:00 P.M. Joe Rauh and Clarence Mitchell, sitting in the gallery, got a frantic signal from a 13-year-old boy, who had skipped school for the historic week to work as a volunteer. Upon hearing that the president had called the Leadership Conference office in the Congressional Hotel, trying to reach them, Rauh dashed to the nearest pay phone and called the White House.

"What are you fellows doing about the Senate?" demanded the impatient commander in chief, and he proceeded to bang out suggestions at rapid-fire speed. Fifteen minutes later Johnson called Roy Wilkins reminding him to get ready for the impending Senate battle.

"Title VIII [Registration and Voting Statistics]" was announced by the clerk, attracting a mere four amendments, all defeated.

"Title IX [Judicial Appeal]" followed, drawing only one amendment, also defeated.

It was close to 6:00 P.M. when Robert T. Ashmore, a South Carolina Judiciary Committee Democrat, offered a new Title X, establishing a Community Relations Service to aid local residents to resolve disputes arising out of alleged discrimination based on race, color, or national origin. This concept was similar to that first proposed in 1957 by Senate majority leader Lyndon Johnson, then embodied in Title V of John Kennedy's bill, and later dropped by the Judiciary Committee. Before Ashmore could explain his amendment, Celler intervened.

"Mr. Chairman," said Celler, anxious now to complete the bill that evening so the Republicans could leave, "the amendment is technical in nature and acceptable to me."

"The amendment is acceptable on this side," echoed Bill McCulloch.

This ready concurrence was a deliberate move by the two leaders to appease conservative House members by incorporating into the law a mechanism which, if effective, would greatly reduce federal involvement in local civil rights disputes. The new title was quickly adopted by voice vote.

After the House accepted Celler's routine motion to change the number of original Title X (Miscellaneous) to Title XI, eight amendments to Title XI were quickly defeated. Accepted, however, was an amendment offered by Charles Mathias stating that no provision of H.R. 7152 should be construed to preempt similar state laws.

"Are there any further amendments to Title XI?" asked Eugene Keogh, the chairman of the Committee of the Whole. "If not, under the rule, the Committee rises." With these words, the members ceased working as a committee and resumed sitting as the House. Keogh stepped down from the Speaker's chair and handed the gavel back to John McCormack. An aide carried the mace back to its usual resting place on the Speaker's dais. From the well of the House, Keogh spoke again: "The Committee, having had under consideration the bill, persuant to House Resolution 616, reported the bill back to the House with sundry amendments adopted by the Committee of the Whole."

It was now after 7:00 P.M., and the next two steps in the legislative process, in which debate was not permitted, were quickly dispatched by the tired, hungry lawmakers.

Under Step Four, the House could take recorded votes on any amendments accepted in the Committee of the Whole if one-fifth of the members request it. John Bell Williams (D-Miss.) attempted to obtain record votes on the Smith "sex" and Ashbrook "atheist" amendments, but he was unable to muster the necessary support from the House membership.

In Step Five, the House would permit a minority party member to offer a recommittal motion by which he could obtain, if he so chose, a recorded vote on any defeated amendment. Bill Cramer eschewed this option. Instead, he simply moved that "H.R. 7152 be recommitted to the Committee on the Judiciary." This was promptly downed by a voice vote.

At long last, it was time for Step Six. The final question was put by Speaker John McCormack to the weary House. "Shall the bill pass?" he asked.

Responding aye or nay as their names were called, the members had their final say. Supporting the bill were 152 Democrats and 138 Republicans. Opposing it were 96 Democrats (86 from the 11 states of the Confederacy) and 34 Republicans, including 10 from the South. In a vote that belied its stormy history, H.R. 7152 passed overwhelmingly.

"Two hundred and ninety to 130," announced the speaker.

And so ended a debate that *Newsweek* columnist Kenneth Crawford hailed as a "triumph in itself."

> Never since the Civil War had race relations been discussed in either branch of Congress with anything like the dignity and restraint of this performance. Scores of weakening amendments were beaten down by a coalition of northern Democrats and Republicans. What emerged was a stronger bill than Kennedy administration officials had thought feasible.

The bill which came out of the House on February 10 differed little from the one Bill McCulloch and his coconspirators had hammered out on the weekend of October 25. Of the 124 amendments offered (excluding amendments to amendments), only 34 were written into the bill. Most were technical revisions, including the 12 submitted by Emanuel Celler. Ironically, the only amendment adopted that Celler had vigorously opposed, the Smith "sex" clause, actually broadened and strengthened the bill, as did Bill Cramer's amendment to include Puerto Rico in the coverage. Three other amendments (to delete membership practices of fraternal, religious, and civic groups from Title V, and to exempt atheists and Communists from protection under Title VII) were not significant enough for Celler and McCulloch to risk all-out floor fights.

This extraordinary success can be credited primarily to the

ruthless efficiency of the three-prong whip system, which spotlighted individual congressmen, demanded their accountability, and prevented them from falling into their old habits of evading amendment votes. Those who failed to vote did so at their own peril. This psychological leverage produced large turnouts for standing and teller votes and gave the Celler-McCulloch team their outstanding victory.

A few minutes before the House adjourned at 8:24 P.M., Celler took the floor to pay tribute to Bill McCulloch. "I want to state that the result would not have been the way it was were it not for the wholehearted support and most earnest and dedicated cooperation of my distinguished colleague and counterpart on the Judiciary Committee, the gentleman from Ohio."

Speaking to reporters after leaving the chamber, Celler called the passage of the civil rights bill his greatest accomplishment during his 41-year legislative career. "I sort of feel like I climbed Mount Everest and I'm just pausing up there and looking around."

Celler descended from the Himalayan heights long enough to take a telephone call from Lyndon Johnson, who profusely thanked the chairman for steering through the House what the *Washington Post* termed "the most comprehensive civil rights bill in history." Also receiving congratulatory calls from the president that evening were Charles Halleck, James O'Hara (D-Mich.), Speaker John McCormack, James Corman, James Roosevelt, Eugene Keogh, Frank Thompson, Attorney General Robert Kennedy, Nicholas Katzenbach, and Peter Rodino. At home when the president called, Rodino said that Johnson "really moved in." The New Jersey Democrat also received a call from Bobby Kennedy, "but his tone was much more subdued," said Rodino.

A startling omission from the president's congratulatory list was the quiet Ohio congressman, without whose cooperation, as Emanuel Celler said in his victory statement to the press, "we could not have done anything." Johnson tried to rectify his political blunder with a telephone call to McCulloch at 6:55 the following evening. But he was too late, for the low-profile Republican, who was as sparing in his use of press releases as he was with his staff allowance, already had left with his wife, Mabel, for a well-earned vacation in Bermuda.

Not forgotten that Tuesday afternoon, however, were congressional staffs. Delivered to each of their offices were Equality Cookies (sugar cookies stamped with an equal sign), compliments of Jane

O'Grady, who had stayed up the entire night before to bake them. ''We had imposed on so many people and had been so 'naggy,' I just wanted to show our appreciation,'' said the leader of the successful corridor patrol operation.

The indomitable H.R. 7152, more muscular than ever after having survived nine days on the House floor, now headed over to the Senate, where a dreaded filibuster was waiting to either kill it or compromise the guts out of it.

Five

Senate Filibuster

THE WINDOWS of the Oval Office looked out on a Rose Garden blanketed with 10 inches of newly fallen snow on Tuesday afternoon, February 11. It had started coming down at about 8:30 the previous evening, and 250 city snowplows worked through the night to keep the streets open for traffic. This was Washington's third major snowstorm of the winter. It was enough to make Lyndon Johnson think longingly of his 5,000-acre ranch in warm, dry Texas.

This afternoon, however, the highly charged president had other things on his mind. Yesterday the House of Representatives had successfully passed H.R. 7152, the strongest civil rights bill in history. Next Monday, after the six-day Lincoln's Birthday recess, it would go to the Senate, where the Southerners were sure to launch their lengthy filibuster.

The filibuster is an infamous Senate weapon. Unlike the House, where floor action is governed by strict rules, the Senate has a hallowed tradition of unlimited debate. It was designed to foster leisured and scholarly discourse on great national issues, and often it does. But it also can be used less nobly to delay bills. By making prolonged speeches, introducing irrelevant material, and requesting nuisance quorum calls, a small but determined group of senators can prevent a bill they do not like from being acted upon, and the boycott can last for as long as they have the strength to keep talking.

Fear of a filibuster had prompted President Kennedy to start his civil rights bill in the House. He hoped that it would gather enough strength there to survive the inevitable Senate talkathon.

124

For there were only two ways to stop a filibuster and both took time: invoke cloture, a vote by two-thirds of the Senate to halt debate, or invoke fatigue and wear the filibusterers out.

Lyndon Johnson liked the second method. In 1960, as majority leader, he had scheduled round-the-clock sessions, forcing the Southerners to debate Eisenhower's civil rights bill 24 hours a day for nine days, until they finally agreed to let the Senate consider it. Now the president wanted the anticipated filibuster on H.R. 7152 handled in the same way, as he imperiously informed the five men gathered in his office: Attorney General Robert Kennedy, Nicholas Katzenbach, Burke Marshall, Larry O'Brien, and press secretary Pierre Salinger.

But Robert Kennedy and his aides knew that Johnson's technique had not worked as well as the president liked to think. It had not worn down the Southerners, who cleverly divided themselves into three teams, each talking for eight hours while the other two slept. Instead, the majority leader had exhausted his own forces and then, after failing to obtain cloture, had agreed to the filibusterers' demands for substantial concessions as their price for stopping debate. Similar bargaining by Johnson had produced the 1957 bill.

But this time there could be no compromise with the Southerners. The Justice Department had no alternative but to go for cloture since it was the only way it could keep its pledge to Bill McCulloch not to weaken H.R. 7152. And it fell to the tough, bald-headed, strong-jawed deputy attorney general, Nicholas Katzenbach, to explain this gently to the president.

"McCulloch insisted that he would support us, but not if we were bargaining the House against the Senate [as happened in 1957 and 1960]," explained Katzenbach. "I had to make a commitment to McCulloch that we would do everything possible in the Senate to get the same bill the House passed and that the administration would not remove one title of that bill as a deal in the Senate.... He wanted my personal word and that of President Kennedy."

Hell hath no fury like a president told that he cannot have his own way. The temperature outside was 28 degrees, but inside it was boiling hot as Lyndon Johnson insisted in colorful Texanese that his tyrant tactics would work. The Southerners were four years older now, he argued, and less likely to hold out; in addition, their leader, Richard B. Russell (D-Ga.), suffered from emphysema. Johnson knew how to sense pressure points and when to use them. As early as 1962, while presiding over the Senate as vice president, he had observed to Stewart L. Udall, secretary of interior, "The Southerners don't have the stamina they used to have."

And uppermost in the president's mind, now, was an early southern surrender. This was a marked departure from his offhand remark to Joe Rauh and Clarence Mitchell on January 21: "I don't care if the Senate doesn't do one other piece of business this year." Although he still accorded first priority to John Kennedy's unfinished agenda—to lose either the tax cut or civil rights bill would tarnish Johnson's leadership image—he was anxious to escape from the Kennedy shadow and stamp his own imprint on American society. Plans for his antipoverty program were well underway; on February 1 he had appointed Sargent Shriver, Peace Corps director and John Kennedy's brother-in-law, to head it. But unless H.R. 7152 cleared the Senate reasonably early, Congress would not have time to pass Great Society legislation before adjourning in the fall for the 1964 election campaign.

So for all these reasons, Lyndon Johnson was not happy about going for cloture nor convinced that it would work. He knew every facet of every senator better than most of their wives did, and for the life of him, he did not see where his forces were going to come up with the necessary 67 votes for cloture.

Cloture, or Rule 22, was adopted by the Senate on March 8, 1917, after what President Woodrow Wilson described as a "little group of willful men" had wrecked his proposal to arm U.S. merchant ships against German submarines. Specifically, it permitted 16 or more senators to file a petition with the clerk of the Senate against a bill or amendment. The petition had to be acted upon within two days of its submission, and then, if approved by two-thirds of those members present and voting, it limited debate to one hour per member, or a total of 100 hours. Of the 28 cloture votes taken since 1917, only 5 had succeeded. Tried 11 times on civil rights bills, it had failed 11 times.

Conservatives in particular were philosophically opposed to cutting off the Senate's historic right to unlimited debate. Many other senators were wary of imposing cloture on their colleagues since it might be invoked on them someday. Carl T. Hayden (D-Ariz.), who had been in the Senate since 1927, had never yet voted in favor of the controversial device.

There was only one slim chance that cloture could succeed this time, as the men in the Oval Office knew, and that lay with Minority

Leader Everett Dirksen. With 21 of the 67 Democrats coming from southern states, the administration needed support from at least 22 of the Senate's 33 Republicans. Dirksen was the key. But Johnson and his strategists were well aware that the wily minority leader, while generally supporting the concept of civil rights, was not in favor of either Title II (Public Accommodations) or Title VII (Equal Employment) in H.R. 7152. Getting Dirksen would be tough.

The meeting in the Oval Office ended with Johnson still haranguing against, and Katzenbach still arguing for, cloture. Two hours later, the predatory president grabbed the startled deputy attorney general by the arm at a White House diplomatic reception and, pulling two chairs together in the middle of the marble-floored entrance hall, continued his tirade, oblivious to the beribboned ambassadors and their exquisitely gowned wives milling around them.

When he finally found a chance to get in a couple of words, Nick Katzenbach reminded Johnson that many conservatives had voted for cloture in 1962 for the first time to halt a liberal filibuster of the communications satellite bill. The filibuster was broken and the bill passed. "So," he made his case, "their argument that they couldn't vote for cloture had disappeared." He then pulled a Senate roster from his coat pocket and, going over each name, showed the president that 58 senators could be counted upon to vote for cloture.

"Now where are you going to get the others?" demanded Johnson irritatedly, not in the least disturbed about being overheard by his guests. In the uninhibited world of Lyndon Johnson, there was no need for muted voices.

"Well, we've got to get 9 of these 14 to make it," admitted Katzenbach, pointing out the "possibles" on his list, most of whom were Republicans. As they went over each name, the deputy attorney general was more optimistic than Johnson, who could not forget his failure as majority leader to secure cloture on the 1960 bill. Nick Katzenbach closed his brief by pleading that, even if the president did not think they would succeed, he at least do nothing to upset their apple cart. "If you do anything publicly but indicate that we're going to get cloture on this bill, we can't *possibly* get cloture," Katzenbach cautioned. "The only way we can get it is for you, with your experience, to express absolute confidence publicly and privately that we're going to get cloture on this bill."

Sixteen blocks and a world away from Lyndon Johnson's White House, another man was also worried about a cloture vote on H.R. 7152. As he strode stoically to his ornate office, Senate Majority

Leader Michael Mansfield neither spoke nor looked as if he wanted
to. The plain man from Montana, who now ran the Senate, had
the demeanor of someone who had never slapped a back in his life.
A six-foot, 175-pound, taciturn pipe smoker who habitually wore
a look of long-suffering and was sometimes compared to St. Francis of Assisi, Mansfield was one of the most diffident leaders in
the 174-year history of the Senate. The poor Irish boy from the harsh
western plains, who did not get his high school diploma until he
was 30 years old, had no illusions about life. "Being a senator is
the best job in the world," he reflected, "but the leadership is a
headache."

Nothing could be further afield than the styles of Lyndon
Johnson and Mike Mansfield. The 60-year-old senator had been
the Democratic whip when Johnson was majority leader, but actually Mansfield held the post in name only. The flamboyant Texan had floor-managed all the major bills himself, acting as his own
chief lobbyist, strategist, parliamentarian, and whip. Then when
he became vice president, the Senate Democrats elected his quiet
deputy to lead them.

What a change. Spare in appearance and word, the former
Montana State University professor of history and political science
habitually responded to questions with a simple yes or no answer;
newsmen who interviewed him on "Meet the Press" claimed that
they had to prepare twice as many questions when he was on the
show. Also unlike Johnson, he tended to be quite inaccessible,
holding a somewhat parochial view of pressure groups—"if they're
not from Montana, I won't see them." And finally, the new majority leader was well known to be absolutely incorruptible.

"Mike was the most popular leader we ever had and yet he
wasn't a leader," observed Utah Democrat Frank (Ted) Moss. "He
would speak fervently in caucus on an issue when there was sharp
cleavage. He would get it all wrapped up, everybody in his hands,
then would say 'but you are the judges.' The whole thing would
collapse." Gale McGee (D-Wyo.) noted that "Mike didn't like to
shake down for votes.... He didn't like to lead. It was an uncomfortable thing for him. But Mike was so gracious and lovable that
he was the secret to getting all people of all faiths to finally come
together."

Not surprisingly, Mansfield had already decided not to become
intimately involved in the myriad details surrounding H.R. 7152's
odyssey through the Senate. By staying aloof from the day-to-day

discussion on the bill, Mansfield felt he could preserve his negotiating status. But in his own strong and deliberate way, he made two decisions that vitally affected the fate of H.R. 7152. The first was to appoint Hubert Humphrey as floor manager for the bill. The second was to stand up to Johnson and refuse to go along with his plan to wear out the Southerners by enforcing Rule 19, which limited each senator to two speeches during one "legislative day."

A "legislative day" was a senatorial oddity. Unlike the House, which almost always adjourned at the end of each work day, the Senate recessed, adjourning only after the matter before it had been concluded. This meant that a "legislative day" could extend over several days or weeks. If Rule 19 were enforced and if the Senate leadership extended the daily sessions well into the night, as Majority Leader Johnson had done in 1960, the Southerners, in the president's view, would soon be exhausted.

But Mansfield knew that there were obvious pitfalls to this approach. Could a single speech go on for 20 hours over a period of several days? What about amendments? Would a speech on an amendment be counted as one dealing with the bill itself, or would the two-speech rule also apply to each separate amendment? Kenneth Teasdale, assistant council to the Democratic Senate Policy Committee and a principal civil rights adviser to Mike Mansfield, opined that, under these circumstances, the filibuster could go on forever. "The two-speech rule will not work," Teasdale concluded. "The need is very simply for cloture."

On February 5, when Rabbi Richard Hirsch and a group of fellow rabbis met with Mansfield, they reminded him that the president and the Leadership Conference on Civil Rights both felt that enforcement of Rule 19, not cloture, was the appropriate route to follow in the Senate. "When Johnson was majority leader, he ran things the way he wanted them," snapped Mansfield. "Now I am majority leader and will run things the way I want them."

The Montana senator said he would eschew the round-the-clock exhaustion technique that Johnson had used in 1960 to try to break the filibuster, telling the rabbis that he was not going to be responsible for killing 86-year-old Carl Hayden or any other senator and pointing out succinctly that the all-night sessions had not worked. Mansfield was acutely aware that the 1957 and 1960 bills that Johnson rammed through the Senate covered only limited areas—mainly voting rights and school desegregation—and that they had few innards left in them by the time the Senate surgeons got finished. H.R. 7152 was a strong, husky bill that had emerged from the House with all its vital organs, including public accommodations, intact. Mansfield wanted it to emerge from the Senate in the same healthy state.

But privately, the majority leader remained pessimistic about the chances of getting cloture on a civil rights bill. This opinion was based on experience. In 1962 President Kennedy had introduced a relatively weak civil rights bill to abolish literacy tests as a prerequisite for voting. When a Senate coalition of conservative Republicans and southern Democrats filibustered, Mansfield tried cloture twice. After both attempts were defeated soundly, Kennedy's bill was removed from the Senate calendar. "You'll never get a civil rights bill with a Democratic president," Mike Mansfield had counseled Burke Marshall after this failure, pointing out that it would be impossible to get enough Republicans to vote for cloture.

Robert Kennedy confided to his aides that Mansfield, remembering this bitter defeat, told him that he probably would call for a cloture vote in March or April. If, as the majority leader expected, it was decisively beaten, he would try again. If the second effort failed, he would give away Title VII (Equal Employment) and try again. Kennedy objected strongly to this plan, insisting that Mansfield not call for cloture until he knew that they had the necessary 67 votes.

Bobby Kennedy won the argument, and he also turned out to be the surprised victor of the earlier jousting between Nick Katzenbach and President Johnson. When the president discovered that, in a rare test of wills, Mike Mansfield adamantly refused to use his exhaustion technique, he backed off completely and ceded authority for day-to-day operations on H.R. 7152 to the Justice Department, telling Mansfield not to do anything "that didn't have Bob's approval." Burke Marshall suspected that this sudden and uncharacteristically conciliatory Oval Office gesture was based on the fact that Johnson "didn't think we'd get the bill." The attorney general agreed.

"If I worked out the strategy," said Bobby Kennedy cynically, "then if he didn't obtain passage of the bill, he could always say he did what we suggested and didn't go off on his own."

Lyndon Johnson, then, would sidestep the blame if H.R. 7152 failed. The old master gambler still knew how to hedge his bets. And, indeed, the odds looked less and less favorable in the Senate, where only three things were certain: Majority Leader Mike

Mansfield would lead the fight for the bill, Richard Russell would lead the fight against it, and between them they would wage a tug-of-war for the political soul of Everett Dirksen.

This was how matters stood on Monday, February 17, as both 12:00 noon and H.R. 7152 arrived together at the tradition-loving, ego-preening Senate chamber. Where the more plebian 435-member House was cavernous, the exclusive 100-member Senate was clubby. Each member sat at a schoolroom desk on which rested relics of a bygone era: two tiny lacquered snuffboxes; a crystal shaker of blotting sand, which was used to dry the ink from quill pens; and, underneath, a polished brass cuspidor. The desks were arranged in four semicircular rows facing the dais, with Democrats on the left, Republicans to the right, senior members up front, and freshmen in the rear. And with a pride approaching pomposity, the inhabitants of this rarefied, mahogany and gold room treasured their reputation as the world's greatest deliberative body.

Immediately after Father Joseph J. Matutis, pastor of Saint Casimir's Church in New Haven, Connecticut, completed his invocation, Charles W. Hackney, Jr., a reading clerk of the House of Representatives, entered the Senate and bowed to the presiding officer. Traditionally, the vice president of the United States presided over the Senate; indeed, it was his only official duty. However, since the country was without a vice president until after the November elections, an acting president pro tempore was appointed for each day's session from the ranks of the Senate. In measured tones Hackney announced that the House had passed the civil rights bill. Then he gave the document to a page, who delivered it to the dais.

DURING ITS STAY in the Senate, H.R. 7152 would face the same eight parliamentary steps taken by every bill introduced in the chamber or received from the House. It would be (1) read for the first time; (2) read for the second time, unless an objection was heard; (3) assigned to a committee or, in rare instances, placed by majority vote directly on the Senate calendar to avoid a hostile committee chairman; (4) heard by the committee and, depending on the chairman, allowed to die or be acted upon; (5) put on the Senate calendar of pending bills; (6) scheduled for floor action, subject to majority consent; (7) debated with no time limits (amendments might be offered at any point, but only debated when called up by the sponsor); and (8) read for the third time and given a final vote.

Mike Mansfield arose from his desk in the front row and stated, "Mr. President, I request that House Bill 7152 be read the first time."

After the Senate legislative clerk read the bill by title only (all that was required), Mansfield declared, "Mr. President, I object to the second reading of the bill today."

The majority leader's action postponed Step Two for several days, which enabled him to retain control of the bill's course. Then he announced that he would shortly propose that H.R. 7152 be placed directly on the Senate calendar without first being referred to the Judiciary Committee. The chairman of that committee was James Eastland of Mississippi, who had been holding the Senate version of the original Kennedy bill hostage for the past eight months. Mansfield explained that while circumventing a committee was not usual, it also was not unprecedented. "And," he noted cryptically, "the reason for unusual procedures are too well known to require elaboration."

The solemn Montanan, ever considerate of his friends and foes alike, had alerted James Eastland before the session opened that he would make this move. Then, in his own grave style, Mansfield challenged his colleagues about the task that lay before them. "We hope in vain," he said, "if we hope that this issue can be put over safely to another tomorrow, to be dealt with by another generation of senators. The time is now. The crossroads is here in the Senate."

After deprecating his own role as majority leader ("no special or unique powers, no expert on the rules"), Mansfield then turned to his right and addressed the puckish looking, 68-year-old man with a scouring pad of curly gray hair atop his head who sat in the front row, center aisle desk on the Republican side of the chamber.

"I appeal to the distinguished minority leader, whose patriotism has always taken precedence over his partisanship, to join with me— and I know he will—in finding the Senate's best possible contribution at this time to the resolution of this grave national issue."

The minority leader arose, and in a moment the moist, mellifluous tones of Everett Dirksen filled the chamber, following in the oratorical footsteps of the Senate's legendary speakers—Henry Clay, Stephen Douglas, John Calhoun, Charles Sumner, and Daniel Webster.

"I trust," Dirksen intoned, "that the time will never come in my political career when the waters of partisanship will flow so swift and so deep as to obscure my estimate of the national interest.... I trust I can disenthrall myself from all bias, from all prejudice, from all irrelevancies, from all immaterial matters, and see clearly and cleanly what the issue is and then render an independent judgment.''

He then responded to James Farmer's veiled threat of the previous day that CORE members might picket the minority leader's office. ''When the day comes,'' Dirksen's cello tones deepened, ''that picketing, distress, duress, and coercion can push me from the rock of conviction, that is the day, Mr. President, that I shall gather up my toga and walk out of here and say that my usefulness in the Senate has come to an end.''

The senator from Illinois closed by assuring Mansfield that he would ''cooperate in every possible way, consonant always with the duty to make an independent judgment.... I expect to give this measure considered attention.... Already some amendments have occurred to me. I shall try to shape them. I shall try to put them in form. If I think they have merit, I shall offer them.''

As he intended, these words clearly cast Ev Dirksen in the role of the reasonable but firm opposition leader, an approach designed to reassure the conservative members of his flock who were not enthusiastic about the prospect of voting for a strong civil rights bill.

Richard Russell, the leader of the Southerners, sensed in Dirksen's remarks an opportunity to entice the minority leader into the southern camp, and he wasted no time in lavishing praise on him. ''I cannot refrain,'' said Russell, ''even if it does harm to the senator from Illinois, from expressing to him my great admiration for his political courage.... It gives one hope for the future of the Republic to see a man who has convictions and the courage to sustain them though it may endanger his seat in the Senate.''

And so, with graciousness all around, the battle began. After the Senate recessed, Clarence Mitchell called the NAACP's New York office with an optimistic report. ''Mansfield made a good speech in which he stressed the Senate's responsibility to act. Unfortunately, there was hanging over our heads the remarks of Jim Farmer yesterday in which he talked about picketing Dirksen. But, nevertheless, we are off to a good start.''

For the next week, however, H.R. 7152 was temporarily put on hold while the Senate dealt with the late President Kennedy's other legacy, the tax cut bill. In the interim, cloture talk permeated the Hill. In a meeting of Senate staffers and civil rights lobbyists,

William Welsh, aide to Senator Philip Hart (D-Mich.), argued that votes for cloture were available and rested with "Dirksen's group" and "Johnson's western colleagues." Joe Rauh disagreed, commenting that nothing could be done about the mountain states Democrats except hope that "even if they were feeling well, they would absent themselves at the time of the cloture vote." Others were more optimistic, pointing out that 14 of 21 western Democrats had cosponsored the original Kennedy bill.

On February 26, the tax cut bill was disposed of and Mike Mansfield immediately turned to H.R. 7152, taking Step Two in the parliamentary process by asking that the bill be read for the second time. Afterward, he moved, as promised nine days earlier, that the bill be placed directly on the Senate calendar instead of going to the southern-dominated Judiciary Committee. Thus, he skipped Steps Three and Four and went directly to Step Five, which required approval by a majority vote.

Richard Russell immediately objected on the grounds that this went against Senate rules. Surprisingly, he was joined by Wayne Morse (D-Ore.). Morse was a strong civil rights advocate, but he also believed that H.R. 7152 deserved a full committee hearing. "We would make a great mistake," he argued, "if we put this bill directly on the calendar and proceed to turn the Senate into a Committee of the Whole and debate it." He reasoned that the bill should be sent to the Judiciary Committee so that a record could be made of H.R. 7152 "as a historic document to which we can point as a basis for evidence on point after point that will be raised in the hearings."

Throughout the heated debate on Russell's appeal, Mike Mansfield and Everett Dirksen were repeatedly charged by their colleagues—with the utmost senatorial courtesy, of course—with inconsistency. To their mutual embarrassment, the charges were valid. Mansfield, who now wanted to put H.R. 7152 on the Senate calendar, had voted in 1957 (along with John Kennedy and Lyndon Johnson) to send Eisenhower's civil rights bill to committee. The majority leader lamely defended himself: "All I can say in extenuation is that consistency is not always a jewel, that times change, and that were I not the leader, perhaps I might still feel the same way—although I doubt it at the moment."

Everett Dirksen, who now wanted H.R. 7152 sent to the Judiciary Committee, had voted to put the 1957 bill directly on the calendar. He offered two reasons for his turnabout. First, the Senate

Judiciary Committee, in hearing President Kennedy's bill for 13 days the previous fall, had listened only to the testimony of Attorney General Robert Kennedy. Second, the Senate Committee had never considered Title VII (Equal Employment), which was not contained in the original Kennedy bill, having been added "in a somewhat frivolous fashion" by the House Judiciary Committee. Dirksen agreed to support a move "to limit the time and have the Senate mandate the Judiciary Committee to send the bill back by a given date, either with or without recommendations." However, he urged the Senate to avoid the indictment that it had gone before the people with a measure they had not actually studied, "except to hear the government's case from the lips of the attorney general."

Mike Mansfield finally won his tactical point, 54–37, with 20 Republicans deserting Dirksen. And so H.R. 7152 was placed on the calendar of bills awaiting Senate action.

Mansfield, however, then made an unexpected move. With the bill safely on the calendar, yet having to be again delayed for a week or so while the Senate considered another bill, he figured he could afford a throwaway gesture to placate Morse and perhaps pick up votes for cloture from Alaska's Ernest Gruening and other liberal Democrats who believed that normal committee procedures should be followed. The majority leader requested unanimous consent that H.R. 7152 be "referred to the Judiciary Committee with instructions to report back, without recommendation or amendment, to the Senate not later than noon, Wednesday, March 4." It was a well-intentioned feint that, unfortunately, simply stirred up trouble.

There was consternation in the galleries, where Clarence Mitchell, who earlier that day had warned Mansfield that the NAACP would consider such a move "as betrayal," watched in dismay. And anger filled the bill's supporters on the floor, where Jacob Javits immediately shouted, "I object," effectively blocking the move. Although a Republican, Javits was one of the chamber's most liberal senators. "Javits," observed his GOP colleague from Kansas, James B. Pearson, "had the best mind of anyone in the Senate. He was involved in an enormous range of subjects. But he had a unique capacity of making some members mad by just saying 'good morning' to them. He made Mike Mansfield turn purple."

It had been a perplexing day in the Senate. As they were leaving the chamber at the end of the session, the secretary for the Senate majority, Frank Valeo, asked George D. Aiken (R-Vt.) why 20 of 28 Republicans had voted with Mansfield and against the wishes of their own leader to put the bill on the calendar. Aiken's answer revealed much about the unpredictability of the Senate as well as about the power of the quiet man from Montana: "Because that's what Mike wanted."

Step Six, a vote to bring H.R. 7152 to the floor, would follow Senate debate on the farm bill. Both President Johnson and Mike Mansfield had originally opposed this scheduling, but Majority Whip Hubert Humphrey had convinced them of the serious economic consequences if Congress failed to pass the farm bill before the March 1 planting deadline. Reminding them that the wheat provisions in the bill involved the interest of several senators, including Mansfield, Ted Moss, Frank Church (D-Idaho), George McGovern (D-S.Dak.), and Gaylord Nelson (D-Wis.), Humphrey also hoped to use the farm bill in getting some advance concessions on H.R. 7152 from the Southerners; he would help them get what they wanted on cotton if they would give him a little cooperation on the civil rights bill.

There was no doubt that Mike Mansfield had made the right choice in appointing Hubert Humphrey floor manager for H.R. 7152. Humphrey's strengths were in areas where Mansfield did not excell—communicating with people, encouraging outside sources, and orchestrating a giant grass-roots effort. In addition, he knew the bill and was concerned about the subject. Humphrey had long been a champion of the black people. Sixteen years earlier, when he was mayor of Minneapolis, he had aroused the 1948 Democratic National Convention to accept the cause of civil rights. Leading the fight, he fractured the party but got a strong civil rights plank passed. "The time has come," he had cried to the convention, "for the Democratic party to get out of the shadow of states' rights and walk forthrightly into the bright sunshine of human rights."

And now, learning that he was to manage the floor fight for H.R. 7152, Hubert Humphrey literally talked to himself about his future role. "I made up my mind early," he said, "that I would keep my patience. I would not lose my temper and...if I could do nothing else, I would try to preserve a reasonable degree of good nature and fair play in the Senate...with a degree of respect and friendship." Humphrey also decided that the bill's backers would take the offensive on the Senate floor to prevent the Southerners from getting all the headlines. And finally, he planned to avoid around-the-clock sessions but, instead, make them "long enough to be disagreeable so that the senators would recognize that their time was being frittered away." However, the senator from Minnesota knew that this would be the most difficult legislative assignment of his career. He refused to guess how long it would take, and he talked to newsmen of a spiritually exhausting struggle with a lot of strain on personal friendships. As with most people, Humphrey liked to be liked. But, he also admitted, "before this is over, I'll be everybody's SOB. It can't be helped."

Humphrey, a perpetual-motion machine, had long been a familiar sight as he dashed down the Senate corridors, pockets bulging with scribbled, unanswered phone messages and arms filled with stacks of books and papers, talking a mile a minute, and always, to no one's surprise, arriving late. Stories of his boundless energy and endless optimism were constantly surfacing around town. Senator George McGovern, who lived next door to the Humphreys in the Washington suburb of Chevy Chase, Maryland, was not surprised to see him sweeping out the garage after midnight or to hear him humming happily at 2:00 A.M. while washing down kitchen walls—all to burn up surplus energy.

Talking buoyed him. "Humphrey has more answers than there are problems," noted a Capitol Hill wit. One day, ill with the flu and running a temperature of 102 degrees, the senator was supposed to address a meeting at a Washington hotel. He intended to show up only for a minute and wave, but instead he started talking and, after 45 minutes, announced to the crowd that he felt "just great!"

"There is something in the water that makes people from Minnesota talk too much," observed Lyndon Johnson, who could churn out a few words himself.

More than 30 years before, on his first visit to the nation's capital, the recent Phi Beta Kappa college graduate had written home to his young wife, Muriel Buck Humphrey:

> Maybe I seem foolish to have such vain hopes and plans. But, Bucky, I can see how, some day, if you and I just apply ourselves and make up our minds to work for bigger things, how we can some day live here in Washington and probably be in government, politics, or service. I intend to set my aim at Congress.

Now the effervescent Humphrey applied himself as floor manager for H.R. 7152 with all the organizational talents at his command. During the next week, he set up a bipartisan team similar to that which had worked so well under Celler and McCulloch, in the House. Minority Whip Thomas Kuchel (R-Calif.) had been named by Everett Dirksen as the Republican floor manager, and he was a natural choice. Kuchel was a self-proclaimed progressive in the style of the late California senator Hiram Johnson, whom he was fond of quoting in his speeches. As a youth Kuchel developed an extensive vocabulary by reading to his blind father, who owned, published, and edited the *Anaheim Gazette*. Later, as a young attorney, he became a protégé of California governor Earl Warren and, in 1952, Warren appointed him to serve the remainder of Richard Nixon's Senate term when Nixon was elected vice president. Tommy Kuchel possessed the temperament to bridge the philosophical gap between the Senate's liberal and conservative Republicans, and he had an excellent working relationship with Minority Leader Everett Dirksen, who looked on him almost as a son.

The newly formed Humphrey-Kuchel team huddled in a long strategy session with Clarence Mitchell and Joe Rauh on Friday, February 28. The four men had to iron out some differences of opinion if they were going to operate smoothly together. One difference concerned the two-speech rule. Rauh wanted it enforced, believing that the Southerners could not carry on the debate physically since their average age was 65. Humphrey disagreed. And Mitchell counseled that they be permitted to talk without resorting to the rule, quoting Johnson, who had said some months earlier, "let them talk until summer."

Kuchel argued against the Senate permitting any committee meetings while the civil rights bill was being debated. "It won't bother me if the committees do not meet," remarked the minority whip. "This should be a show. Let them [the senators] sit in their offices and answer quorum calls. They have nothing else to do."

Stressing that the Leadership Conference opposed weakening the bill, Clarence Mitchell recommended that any proposed amendments be brought to McCulloch and Celler before being introduced. Humphrey agreed, emphasizing that a constant working relationship with the two House members was essential. And Kuchel promised to work closely with Humphrey, while maintaining an open and fair relationship with Everett Dirksen, whom he liked and admired.

"Dirksen," reported Kuchel, "told me the other day that he wanted to rethink the bill." Humphrey replied, "I told Dirksen that it is not Hubert H. Humphrey that can pass this bill; it boils down to what he does." Then, turning to Mitchell, the majority whip added, "Dirksen doesn't want somebody picketing him," a pointed reference to the recent demonstrations against him by civil rights groups in Illinois.

As the meeting ended Humphrey cautioned, "We need faith and perserverance. Senator Russell runs a war of nerves. He will yell Benedict Arnold, traitor, and lynch law. He is like the French general who always said, 'Attack, Attack, Attack.' If he were on a bear hunt, he would let the rabbits out of the cage and have the hounds chase them. He doesn't want us to get bear."

And so the new team was launched. But in addition to legislative details, they had to contend with Washington gossip, which, during the past month, had Lyndon Johnson making a deal with the Southerners—southern backing on the tax cut for his own concessions on civil rights. Suspicions came quite naturally since, as Senate majority leader, Johnson had employed just such tactics. One of his most skillful manipulations brought out the 1957 civil rights bill. But those on both political sides of the Senate aisle categorically denied that the president had agreed to any compromise on H.R. 7152.

"Not a scintilla of evidence," allowed Everett Dirksen.

"Not a shred of truth," echoed Hubert Humphrey.

On the contrary, Lyndon Johnson had every reason to go for a strong bill; it would embellish his national image. In his Saturday, February 29, press conference, the president scotched rumors of a compromise. "I am in favor of it passing the Senate exactly in its present form," he said. "So far as this administration is concerned, its position is firm and we stand on the House bill."

On the Sunday, March 1, television program "Face the Nation,"southern leader Richard Russell also doubted that any compromise on H.R. 7152 was possible. After castigating the bill, the Georgia Democrat explained why diluting it in the Senate would be difficult. "President Kennedy could have lost this bill completely, or in large part, and not one of those who were affected directly by it would have held it against President Kennedy. . . . I think President Johnson feels if he loses any substantial part of it, that it will cast all of his statements of support for it in doubt as to their sincerity. . . . That really makes it a much more difficult position as to any possible compromise than there would have been had President Kennedy not met his tragic fate."

The Senate passed the farm bill on Friday, March 6, and immediately Mike Mansfield announced that H.R. 7152 would be called up the next Monday. Hubert Humphrey was ready, as he pointed out enthusiastically that Sunday on the NBC television show "Meet the Press." "I believe we can win this time," he told the panel, "because there is a time in the affairs of men and nations when an idea comes to fruition. I really believe the American public recognizes the need for civil rights legislation."

Lawrence Spivak, the program's moderator, again raised the specter of a rumored compromise. "Nonsense," snorted Humphrey. "There's no truth to it at all.... There will be no wheels and no deals and no compromise that will in any way fundamentally affect or alter this bill."

May Craig, columnist for the *Portland* (Maine) *Press Herald,* who had championed Judge Smith's antisex discrimination provision of H.R. 7152 (it already had become known as the "May Craig" amendment), asked whether it would be retained by the Senate. The senator smiled. "I think we can accept that provision and it is a workable one."

After the program went off the air Lyndon and Lady Bird Johnson called Humphrey at the television station to congratulate him on his performance. Then, dispensing with the amenities, the president chided the majority whip about the role he would assume the next day. It was a pep talk in LBJ's own unique, challenging style.

"You have got this opportunity now, Hubert, but you liberals will never deliver. You don't know the rules of the Senate, and you liberals will be off making speeches when they ought to be present in the Senate. I know you've got a great opportunity here, but I'm afraid it's going to fall between the boards."

Hubert Humphrey's reaction was exactly what the president had hoped. "He sized me up," Humphrey thought to himself. "He knows very well that I would say, 'Damn you, I'll show you.' "

The next morning Humphrey held a final strategy session with Clarence Mitchell, Andy Biemiller, Joe Rauh, Jack Conway, Deputy Assistant Attorney General Joe Dolan, and three Senate staff aides. In the past it had been the Southerners who were always well organized. This time, however, the civil rights forces were knit into a smoothly operating team. And the majority whip promised that in the days ahead he would use every method available to win the fight.

"The House bill is a good bill," he asserted. "In fact. there is so much good with it that it is hard to tamper with it." Then, as if to make sure his meaning was clear, Humphrey added that House leaders had warned him, "if the Senate messes around with it too much, there won't be any bill." After Clarence Mitchell argued that Bill McCulloch was flexible about changes to improve the bill, the senator cautioned, "The newspaper fellows like to start controversy. I am saying what Kuchel said the other day: we will take a look at amendments but that is down the line."

Clarence Mitchell wondered aloud whether one of the Leadership Conference lobbyists could attend some of the daily Humphrey-Kuchel team meetings. "Keep it small," said Humphrey, "but if one of you attends, that is okay. The meetings will be in the morning a half hour before the session begins. If you meet twice a week with me and Kuchel, that should be enough." Mitchell agreed to sit in on Mondays and Thursdays with the two Senate leaders, their staffs, and Nicholas Katzenbach.

The Southerners held their own last caucus that morning in Richard Russell's office, pledging to conduct a "last ditch" fight against H.R. 7152. First they would stage a lengthy debate—"for a week or more"—on Mike Mansfield's motion to schedule the bill. To accomplish this, Russell would have to prevent Mansfield from taking Step Six during the "morning hour," a two-hour period at the start of each legislative day set aside for consideration of routine business. Senate Rule 7 provided that, to schedule a bill for floor action without debate, the motion must be made during the second hour. Russell's first task, therefore, was to kill two hours. For such a master of Senate talkathons, that should not be too hard.

At noon on Monday, March 9, one long ring of the bell on the Senate side of Capitol Hill announced that the Senate was now in session. "Eternal God...empower us and sustain us, as with strength unequal to our tasks, we face the call of the world's great need," prayed Chaplain Frederick Brown Harris.

A few minutes later, Richard Russell rose and launched the southern attack, objecting to the majority leader's routine motion to dispense with the reading of the previous day's journal. "I trust the clerk will read the Journal slowly and clearly enough for all members of the Senate to understand it," Russell drawled with a sly wink at Humphrey.

The filibuster was on. After the clerk had used up almost an hour, the Georgia senator was on his feet again with an amendment to the journal. It turned into a lengthy Russell monologue, during which John Sparkman (D-Ala.) dozed at his desk, a handful of other senators sat glassy-eyed, and Everett Dirksen skipped up to the press gallery to sit cross-legged on a table and swap stories with his friends in the media. There was no telling how long the Southerners would keep the talkathon going. But the administration feared they would make somebody pay before they turned it off. The price could either be Title II (Public Accommodations) or Title VII (Equal Employment).

In fact, if Dick Russell had his way there would be no bill at all. He already had made that clear when he told the press, "I see no room for compromise on our part. We are preparing for a battle to the last ditch—to the death." And now on the floor he denounced it bitterly. "Mr. President, this measure not only is the strongest measure of its kind to be proposed since Reconstruction, . . . it is much more drastic than any bill ever presented even during the days of Reconstruction. And I state unhesitatingly that no member of the Reconstruction Congress, no matter how radical, would have dared to present a proposal that would have given such vast governmental control over free enterprise in this country so as to commence the process of socialism."

Two hours and five minutes later, Richard Russell sat down. The glass of water on his desk was untouched. He did, however, suck on two lozenges while he alternately read his remarks and presented them extemporaneously. After he finished, the Georgia Democrat turned to the clerk and politely inquired whether the "morning hour" was over. The clerk advised him that it had been concluded at 2:00 P.M., and therefore, any motion to schedule a bill was not automatic but debatable.

When Mansfield finally reclaimed the floor, his unanimous consent request to proceed with consideration of H.R. 7152 met with objection from J. Lister Hill (D-Ala.). This required Mansfield to move that the Senate make H.R. 7152 its pending business. Then, inasmuch as that motion was debatable, the Southerners could spend "a week or more" as they had promised, arguing the point.

Recognizing this inevitability, Mike Mansfield, before making his motion, pleaded that "the issue of civil rights can wait no longer in the Senate. The country, private groups throughout the country, the House of Representatives, and the president have faced this issue squarely and have taken a great deal of action within the limits of their capacity. Now it is the time and the turn of the Senate."

Hubert Humphrey echoed the majority leader's appeal. "The issue before us," Humphrey stated, "is a national issue." He then introduced the theme that he planned to pursue during the days ahead. "It...is above all a moral issue, and not merely a political issue." Not ruling out a suggestion made by Jacob Javits earlier that afternoon that the Senate be forced into all-night sessions to break the coming filibuster, the majority whip observed that they "would do well in the greatest deliberative body in the world, the great U.S. Senate, to follow the pattern of the dignified, responsible, articulate debate that was conducted in the House of Representatives. The House had its finest hour."

Disregarding such predictable pleas, the Southerners took up their "extended debate," as they liked to call it, with relish. Actually, all members (including liberals) filibuster when it suits their purposes. They are the stuff that Senate legend is made of. In 1908 Robert LaFollette, Sr., (R-Wis.) orated for 18 hours and 23 minutes. Strom Thurmond (D-S.C.) held the all-time Senate record with an uninterrupted 24-hour, 18 minute speech during consideration of the 1957 civil rights bill. And in 1935 Huey Long (D-La.) rambled on for 15½ hours about the delights of "potlikker" and corn pones, finally giving up because his colleagues denied him a "gentleman's quorum" so he could go to the men's room.

That afternoon and the next and the next and the next stretched on as, hour after drowsy hour, the Southerners, who always did have a way with words, talked on. Their soft, melodious voices resounded beautifully throughout the Senate chamber and the word around Washington was that they planned to keep on with all this speechifying until doomsday, or at least until Congress adjourned for the Republican National Convention in July.

The Humphrey-Kuchel bipartisan team, meanwhile, continued to get into combat shape for the anticipated long floor battle. On March 10, Humphrey informed his colleagues that a new system was devised to bring members "to the chamber quickly to respond to quorum calls." Calling quorums when less than 51 senators were on the floor had long been a favorite device of the southern members. Not only did frequent quorum calls kill time, but they also gave filibusterers some rest while the clerk called the roll of 100 names. Dick Russell had already divided his rebel forces into three platoons—headed by Lister Hill, Allen Ellender (D-La.), and John Stennis (D-Miss.)—to conduct such a delaying operation. To meet the challenge, Humphrey appointed six Democrats—Frank

Church, Edward Kennedy (Mass.), Thomas J. McIntyre (N.H.), Patrick McNamara (Mich.), Gaylord Nelson, and Edmund Muskie (Maine)—each of whom was expected to produce four to six colleagues on the floor as soon as possible after the two bells denoting a live quorum had rung. And on the other side of the aisle, Tommy Kuchel was to provide 16 Republicans. A special telephone communications system was installed in senators' offices to speed up the operation, and Pauline Moore, chief clerk and counsel of the Senate, would coordinate the calls. In addition, all members were to give her their schedule of dates, through May 18, when they would not be in Washington.

Daily meetings of the team went smoothly. Each morning the two floor managers, their staffs, and Justice Department officials reviewed plans for the day; on Monday and Thursday Clarence Mitchell and other Leadership Conference officials joined them. And every evening the senators' staffs met from 5:30 to 6:00 to follow up on details.

Early each morning the "Bipartisan Civil Rights Newsletter" was printed on an AFL-CIO mimeograph machine that Andy Biemiller donated. Designed to keep senators abreast of the latest developments in the debate, the paper first appeared on March 10 and highlighted such items as the quorum scoreboard, the daily floor schedule, and the current parliamentary situation. Also included were reprints of editorials and rebuttals of anticivil rights arguments given on the senate floor.

"Who writes these mysterious messages," demanded an indignant John Stennis on March 12, "which come to Senators before the *Congressional Record* reaches them, and in them attempt to refute arguments made on the floor of the Senate?"

"The newsletter," retorted the majority whip proudly, "is the product of the distinguished senator from California [Mr. Kuchel] and the senator from Minnesota [Mr. Humphrey] and their staffs. It is paid for by the Senate, out of the funds we have available to operate our offices. My legislative assistant works on it. Senator Kuchel's legislative assistant works on it."

That afternoon A. Willis Robertson (D-Va.) held the floor for two hours, during which time he punctuated his remarks by waving a small confederate flag. After he finished, he presented the flag to Humphrey. Accepting it in the friendly manner he was determined to follow, Humphrey commended Robertson for his "eloquence, great knowledge of history and law, and his wonderful, gracious, gentlemanly qualities and his consideration.'' Referring to the flag, the majority whip said that it represented the "bravery and courage and conviction of which the senator spoke earlier today.''

On March 16 Richard Russell revived an old idea—a $1.5 billion plan to distribute blacks equally among the 50 states. (Blacks constituted 42 percent of the population in Mississippi but only 0.1 percent in Vermont and North Dakota.) And on St. Patrick's Day, J. Strom Thurmond, wearing a green carnation in his lapel, commanded the floor for 5 hours and 40 minutes. An aide stopped Senator John Sherman Cooper in the corridor. "I am worried about Strom's health," he said. "Would you go in to check to see if he is all right?" The Kentucky Republican brought back word that the South Carolinian felt fine.

By now citizens groups were becoming actively involved. The most vigorous opposition to H.R. 7152 came from the Coordinating Committee for Fundamental American Freedoms, Inc., chaired by William Loeb, the arch-conservative publisher of the *Manchester* (N.H.) *Union Leader*. The organization's secretary was John C. Satterfield, a Yazoo City, Mississippi, attorney and a former president of the American Bar Association. With offices in the Carroll Arms Hotel near the two Senate office buildings, the coordinating committee operated on a $260,000 budget, supported largely by contributions from the Mississippi Sovereignty Commission, which, in turn, was financed by the state of Mississippi.

A full-page advertisement with the headline BILLION DOLLAR BLACKJACK—THE CIVIL RIGHTS BILL was inserted in 200 newspapers throughout the country. Charging that H.R. 7152 was the "Socialists' omnibus bill," the coordinating committee's advertisement began to generate considerable anti-civil rights mail. Senators Kenneth Keating (R-N.Y.) and Philip Hart told Clarence Mitchell that they had received a large influx of opposition letters. Roman Hruska (R-Neb.) reported that 40 percent of his communications were inspired by the coordinating committee, Frank Church said that he was receiving 200 letters a week against the House-passed bill, and mail to midwestern and Rocky Mountain senators ran as high as 10-1 against.

Thomas Kuchel's aide Steve Horn, in a chat with Jack Steele of the Scripps-Howard Washington bureau, stated that their civil rights mail was going four to one against the bill, largely because of the newspaper advertisement. Bill McCulloch, too, was becoming increasingly worried. He confided to John Lindsay's assistant Bob Kimball that if a vote were to occur now in the House on civil rights, supporters would lose 25 percent of those who voted for H.R. 7152 on February 10.

On March 18 Senator Humphrey took the floor to denounce the advertisement as a "reprehensible lie." "It is not a Socialist bill," argued the majority whip. "Who is the Socialist, Mr. President? Was it the minority leader of the House of Representatives [Mr. Halleck] who voted for it? Was it the distinguished representative from the state of Ohio [Mr. McCulloch] who voted for it?"

"Hubert's speech knocked a home run," averred Tommy Kuchel during a bipartisan team meeting.

On March 19 the Senate's two principal civil rights antagonists—Hubert Humphrey and Richard Russell—engaged in face-to-face debate on NBC's "Today Show." Throughout the program the Georgian's coughing attacks revealed the lung illness which afflicted him. Nervously twirling his thumbs, the balding Russell told interviewer Martin Agronsky that the Southerners were "not closing the door to compromise," although he had rejected the idea entirely only 10 days earlier.

"As we go along in this debate," responded a conciliatory Humphrey, "if opposing forces make adjustments in their position, we are reasonable men."

This hint of compromise from the majority whip fueled the concerns of those who felt that he would eventually get enough votes for cloture but would have to make concessions to get them. That afternoon during their bipartisan staff meeting, Steve Horn good-naturedly chided Humphrey's aide John Stewart by threatening to remove Senator Kuchel's name from a memorandum that the Humphrey-Kuchel forces were issuing later in the day. "Our friends would never understand why we were associated with such a conservative," Horn told Stewart.

On Monday, March 23, it was still the "Legislative Day of Monday, March 9" in the United States Senate, and the Southerners, fresh as daisies, were still talking. Although they had indicated to Mike Mansfield that they would not filibuster very long on his motion to take up the bill—probably not more than four or five days—those statements had been made just to keep the majority leader from ordering longer sessions.

It had taken the House of Representatives only nine days to debate, amend, and pass the bill. But the Senate already had taken two weeks just debating a motion on whether to consider it. Finally Humphrey had had enough. That evening he carried out his "long enough to be disagreeable" plan by holding the members in session until 10:15. And the next day Wayne Morse applied another turn of the screw when he announced that he would object to any committee hearings being held while H.R. 7152 was before the Senate. "I do not believe," said Morse, "any other business should be transacted by the Senate until the matter of delivering the Constitution of the United States to the Negroes of America, for the first time in our history, is finally settled by the Congress."

Each evening after the Senate had concluded its session, Clarence Mitchell summarized the day's events in longhand and then had his notes typed up for distribution. Occasionally, he also wrote details in numbered letters to Roy Wilkins in New York. Despite his earlier optimism, Mitchell was now disturbed by the scarcity of pro-civil rights mail. In his March 24 "Senate Letter Number Two" to Wilkins, he suggested that the NAACP secretary try to get "wheelbarrow loads of mail in. In fact, if you have the time to do it, why not fill a wheelbarrow with bona fide letters, get some outstanding civil rights supporters, and have a picture taken for publication.... In any event, please, please, please, give us a snowstorm of mail to senators *no matter whether they are for the bill or on the fence.*"

At last, on the eve of the Easter recess, the Southerners yielded. Holding a caucus, they decided, 7–5, to allow the Mansfield motion to come up for a vote. On March 26, in a subdued Senate chamber, the motion to permit the Senate to consider H.R. 7152 passed, 67–17, opposed only by the southern Democrats. The civil rights bill was now the pending business of the Senate.

"A battle has been lost," admitted Richard Russell, and then he warned ominously, "We shall now begin to fight the war."

Now, however, the bill's backers disagreed on the next move. Wayne Morse moved that "H.R. 7152 be referred to the Committee on the Judiciary, with instructions to report it back to the Senate not later than April 8, 1964." He maintained that this was the best way to prepare for cloture. Glancing up at the civil rights advocates in the gallery, he cautioned them, "You will not get a civil rights bill until cloture is invoked. The senior senator from Oregon is only seeking a procedure which, in his judgment, will enhance our prospects of invoking cloture."

Everett Dirksen joined Morse, arguing that the way to attain a strong civil rights bill was to "follow a procedure that will stand up to the test in the light of destiny."

Reversing his February 26 position, Mike Mansfield strongly disagreed, feeling that the delay would only hurt H.R. 7152 and the country. But he also feared that the committee chairmen would turn against him, hostile to a move which would deny a committee the right to hear testimony and to mark up legislation. Therefore, in opposing Wayne Morse's motion, he stressed the perils involved in sending the bill to segregationist Jim Eastland's Judiciary Committee. On its return from the committee, Mansfield warned, H.R. 7152 "will not come before the Senate at once. It will go on the calendar, as any other bill which might be reported from committee. It will have no privileged status. It will no longer be, as it is now, the pending business of the Senate. It will be on the list, subject to being motioned up all over again.... For how many days after, then, will we have to repeat the ordeal of the last two and a half weeks in order to make H.R. 7152 once again the pending business?"

Mansfield moved to table the Morse motion. Again the majority leader won, but this time by a much closer margin, 50–34, with Everett Dirksen and eight other Republicans joining 25 Democrats in opposition. Then, gratefully, the weary Senate adjourned for the Easter weekend. But any rest would be brief. When they returned on Monday, they would face a fierce filibuster—this time on the bill itself—that could be stopped only by cloture. And cloture—two-thirds of those members present and voting—had never been successful on a civil rights bill.

Hubert Humphrey, to get the crucial 22 to 28 Republican votes needed for success, would have to heed the words of Lyndon Johnson. Even though the president had vowed to stay in the background, he couldn't resist pulling Humphrey aside at the White House–congressional leaders breakfast on February 18 and giving him some unsolicited advice.

"The bill can't pass unless you get Ev Dirksen," confided Johnson. "You and I are going to get Ev. It's going to take time. We're going to get him. You make up your mind now that you've got to spend time with Ev Dirksen. You've got to let him have a piece of the action. He's got to look good all the time. Don't let those bomb throwers, now, talk you out of seeing Dirksen. You get in there to see Dirksen. You drink with Dirksen! You talk with Dirksen! You listen to Dirksen!"

Six

Dirksen's Conversion

EARLY EASTER MONDAY five inches of snow surprised the city of Washington, D.C. Morning commuter traffic skidded to a massive halt, and the traditional White House Easter egg hunt was postponed until the next day. But the paralysis that hit the nation's capital did not deter CBS News. It set up its cameras on the Senate steps to begin five-a-day television reports on the progress of the civil rights bill.

Fred Friendly, president of CBS News, had decided to provide frequent television (9:00 A.M.., 12:24 P.M., 3:24 P.M., 6:30 P.M., and 11:00 P.M.) and radio (10:00 A.M., 12:00 M., 2:00 P.M., and 6:00 P.M.) reports to its network affiliates. In announcing this extended coverage, Friendly noted:

> The pending civil rights debate and the anticipated filibuster in the Senate gives every indication of becoming one of the most important running news stories of the decade. It warrants continuing coverage in the same manner we have dealt with the space shots and with primary elections. The fact that cameras and microphones will not be permitted access to the Senate floor does not affect our responsibility of reporting the debate and filibuster as completely as possible.

Correspondent Roger Mudd, fearful that his assignment could end up as a "gimmicky flagpole-sitting stunt," told Friendly that "there

149

would be no trickiness. It will be straight reporting with all sides being heard.''

As Mudd and his first interview guest, Senator Hubert Horatio Humphrey, emerged from the entrance under the Senate steps for the telecast, the majority whip looked in amazement at how much snow had fallen since he arrived at the Capitol. ''I'll have to get my coat,'' said the shivering Humphrey.

But there was little time before they were due to go on the air, so William Small, chief of the CBS News Washington bureau, took off his raincoat and gave it to the senator. ''It was several sizes too big,'' stated Small, ''but we promised to keep a tight shot on him— and did.''

At noon, as the Senate began its historic debate on the civil rights bill, Lee Metcalf (D-Mont.) assumed the president's chair— ''a peerless order-keeper,'' wrote columnist Mary McGrory, ''who learned it from Sam Rayburn.'' On top of Hubert Humphrey's and Tommy Kuchel's desks were copies of the Justice Department's huge briefing books, similar to those provided two months earlier to Emanuel Celler and Bill McCulloch.

When Hubert Humphrey arose to open debate, the Senate galleries were packed to the walls, but the floor of the dignified chamber was almost deserted. The world's greatest deliberative body consisted of a half-dozen members sitting at their desks reading reports and signing letters while Humphrey, a compulsive talker who was good for 250 words a minute, tore enthusiastically into his 55-page speech, on the margins of which he had scribbled last-minute thoughts.

''We will join you in debating this bill,'' he challenged his southern colleagues. ''Will you join us in voting on H.R. 7152 after the debate has been concluded? Will you permit the Senate, and in a sense the nation, to come to grips with these issues and decide them one way or the other?''

As the man with the bulging middle and the rumpled suit held the floor with his usual great length and great eloquence for three and a half hours, Senate observers knew that more was riding on the passage of H.R. 7152 than just victory for civil rights, even as this was paramount for the long-time liberal senator from Minnesota. It was an open secret that Hubert Humphrey wanted to be vice president. He had been a two-time loser in the political fast lane, edged out for vice president in 1956 when Adlai Stevenson gave the choice to the convention, elbowed aside in the 1960 primaries by the sprinting Jack Kennedy. But now Humphrey was the front-runner for the vice presidential nomination, in spite of some growing grass-roots movements backing Robert Kennedy for the spot. Victory in the civil rights battle could send the 52-year-old senator to the Democratic National Convention in August with enough momentum to be picked as Lyndon Johnson's running mate in the fall. And so his fierce ambitions for himself and for his country fueled his oratorical fire.

His co-floor manager Tommy Kuchel did not possess Humphrey's ardor, but he did share his deep conviction. The liberal Republican from California took the floor next, explaining the bill, title by title, and publicly expressing his zealous but unrealistic hope that it be strengthened on the Senate floor. Kuchel, a man of fewer words than his Democrat partner, ended his one-and-three-quarters-hour speech by anticipating that "this issue should not be a partisan fight; it should be, and is, an American fight."

Everett Dirksen, seated like a meditating monk at his front-row desk, was uncharacteristically quiet that day, and his silence was noted by those on both sides of the bill who hoped to snare his support. Dirksen was not an easy target. The mercurial Illinois senator with the unruly thatch of gray hair had acquired a variety of epithets during his 29-year congressional career. To many he was the Wizard of Ooze, a reference to the mellifluous speaking tones he had developed by marinating his tonsils daily with a mixture of Pond's cold cream and water, which he gargled and swallowed. ("It keeps my pipes lubricated," he said.) But to Richard Russell and other critics, he was Old Doctor Snake Oil, a reference to the slipperiness with which he eased his way through issues. And the press corps, recalling Dirksen's World War I service as a field artillery balloon observer operating 1,000 feet above German lines, termed him "the high flyer." "If he could live through that," mused *New York Herald Tribune* reporter Andrew Glass, "he could live through anything."

Despite his sometimes overblown rhetoric and farcical antics, Everett Dirksen was a master of the legislative process. "He was a legislator's legislator, one of the few real legislators in the Senate," observed Kuchel's aide Steve Horn. "He knew and mastered the rules. He knew what was in each bill. He took them home with him each evening." According to Senator Carl T. Curtis (R-Neb.),

Dirksen was a superb leader in getting divergent factions together to get something done. When there was a division of opinion between Republican factions, unlike Senator Knowland [Dirksen's predecessor as senate minority leader], he would never get involved siding with one group. He would try to work it out. He was very fair in dealing with people. He wasn't tricky at all. Senators Javits and Case didn't classify Dirksen as a hard-shelled conservative they couldn't deal with. I was as conservative as any, and I didn't think of Everett Dirksen as a flaming liberal. He had talents of leadership.

And Everett Dirksen, unlike Mike Mansfield, loved being a leader. "One hundred diverse personalities in the U.S. Senate," he soliloquized, "O great God, what an amazing and dissonant one hundred personalities they are. What an amazing thing it is somehow to harmonize them. What a job it is."

But Ev Dirksen's doubts about H.R. 7152 were well known. After the opening of debate on Monday, when he walked to his minority leader's office just 33 paces from the Senate floor, Dirksen told reporters that there were as many as a dozen amendments needed for Title VII (Equal Employment) before he could support the bill. Newsmen were also aware that the junior senator from Illinois had reservations about Title II (Public Accommodations). And these two titles comprised the heart of the bill.

Everett Dirksen's disputes with H.R. 7152 went back almost to the beginning of the bill. On the morning of June 11, 1963, when he and Charles Halleck had gone to the White House to meet with President Kennedy, the two Republican leaders arrived in the middle of Kennedy's tense confrontation with Governor George Wallace, who was "standing in the schoolhouse door" to bar two black students from entering the University of Alabama.

Kennedy met with Dirksen and Halleck to tell them of his decision to send a strong civil rights bill to Congress in the near future. While John Kennedy expected little from the highly partisan and irascible Charlie Halleck, he felt sure that Ev Dirksen would be, at least, a willing listener. Dirksen was genuinely fond of his former Senate colleague from Massachusetts and continued to call him Jack after Kennedy moved into the White House and became Mr. President to others on the Hill.

According to Robert Baker, Dirksen had been "a fantastic help to the Kennedy administration, and Kennedy knows it." Dirksen's friendship was reciprocated by Kennedy. During the senator's campaign for reelection in 1962, much to the consternation of Democratic political leaders, the president pointedly offered little help to Dirksen's Democratic opponent, Congressman Sidney B. Yates. On another occasion, Kennedy appointed a federal judge who had Dirksen's strong backing, despite the objections of Cook County's Democratic chairman Richard J. Daley.

But that morning neither Dirksen nor Halleck committed himself to support Kennedy's legislation. And they, like almost everyone else in Washington, were surprised by the president's televised announcement that evening that he was sending a strong bill up to Congress.

Dirksen's civil rights stand at that time was ambivalent. In 1957 and 1960 he had been instrumental in helping Lyndon Johnson get Eisenhower's two bills passed. However, during his 1962 reelection campaign, Dirksen felt unfairly treated by Illinois blacks, who accused him of being unsympathetic to their cause and gave him only 20.1 percent of the votes cast in Chicago's five black wards.

Regardless, President Kennedy was aware from the start that the colorful senator from Illinois was the key to getting the bill through the Senate. As minority leader, Dirksen controlled the Republican votes that would be needed to invoke cloture against the inevitable filibuster. As Robert Kennedy said, it would have to be "Senator Dirksen, nobody else. He was the one who was important." Therefore, when President Kennedy met on June 14 with the attorney general, Burke Marshall, Larry O'Brien, National Security Adviser McGeorge Bundy, speech writer Ted Sorensen, and appointments secretary Kenny O'Donnell to shape the final form of the legislation, the second item on the list of tactics was "How great a price should the administration pay for Senator Dirksen's cosponsorship?"

In view of the minority leader's importance, the president's men decided to bring him in from the start, and he was given a copy of the legislative draft to study over the weekend. But on Monday, June 17, in a meeting with the president and bipartisan congressional leaders, Dirksen told Kennedy that he had studied the bill and could not support any strong employment provision. The president assured him that the subject would be treated in a separate bill, and it was. It turned out, however, that the minority leader had other doubts as well. When he met the next morning in his office with members of the White House staff, Justice Department officials, and bipartisan Senate leaders, Ev Dirksen said he could support the bill except for the public accommodations section. Consequently, when Kennedy's bill came up to the Hill on June 19, Dirksen and Mansfield cosponsored it as S.1750, which contained all the provisions except for Title II (Public Accommodations). Title II was introduced as a separate bill by Mansfield and Warren Magnuson (D-Wash.).

During the months when H.R. 7152 battled its way through the House of Representatives, Dirksen had been watching, warily, both the bill and the rising racial tensions. There was no one, as columnist Kenneth Crawford put it, who "gauges the velocity of the political wind with a wetter finger." But Dirksen's serious side sometimes was obscured by his clownish eccentricities. During the frequent joint press conferences he held with Charlie Halleck—irreverently dubbed by newsmen the "Ev and Charlie Show"—the pair roasted the Democrats with theatrical flair.

Privately, Dirksen kept his own counsel, but publicly, he discouraged those who hoped he might succumb to future Johnson-Humphrey blandishments. During the February 20 "Ev and Charlie" press conference, the Senate minority leader expressed concern about H.R. 7152's public accommodations section and also stated, "I have an objection to the FEPC provision as it now stands. I've always had an open mind, and I always feel free to come along with alternatives and substitutes that are infinitely more to my liking."

When the bill reached the Senate in mid-February, Dirksen, who liked to express his thoughts in culinary terms, said he decided to just "sort of let the thing simmer and jell" for a while. Then during March, while the Southerners filibustered on the motion to consider it, he commandeered three lawyers from the Senate Judiciary Committee staff and assigned them to pick H.R. 7152 apart to see if it could be made more appetizing to the arch-conservatives in the GOP.

Meanwhile, the minority leader put his thoughts together. Like Manny Celler, Dirksen had a penchant for making notes and filing them away for future reference. His notebook bulged with observations on such disparate subjects as hunger, pure food, suffrage, income taxation, civil service, child labor, direct election of senators, the eight-hour work day, and poll taxes. On February 26 he penned his thoughts on H.R. 7152. Alluding to Bill McCulloch's description of the Subcommittee No. 5 bill as a "pail of garbage," Dirksen wrote that the House-passed version was "not salvage [sic] or gar-

154

bage but can be improved.... I have been and still am studying every aspect of Title II of this bill and I will have a substitute for this Title which I will present later." Under the heading Impatience, Dirksen wrote: "If this measure is the most important in several generations, is it not time to show patience and do a workmanlike job?" In dealing with the subject of Threats, he observed: "How worthy can we be as a deliberative body if threats of demonstrations and taking to the streets moves us to hurried and careless craftsmanship?"

Dirksen, however, was not the only one putting his thoughts into writing. On March 18 Hubert Humphrey wrote a memorandum to President Johnson outlining his assessment of the minority leader, and suggesting how he should be approached during the course of the debate. "Senator Dirksen," Humphrey wrote,

> is a man in his later years, probably not intending to serve another term in the Senate, one who is, therefore, not open to direct pressure on the civil rights bill or any other bill. He is increasingly concerned, I believe, about his historical role, about his place in history. He is a brilliant, gifted man, who somehow slipped off the track and wound up with the image of a clown—"The Ev and Charlie Show" routine, for example. In actual fact, he is a skillful, imaginative, and patriotic man, to whom an appeal can be made subtly to win his place in history as a real decision maker on the Civil Rights bill.
>
> The best way to [handle] Dirksen is to have people express confidence in him, to say they believe him to be a patriot, that they believe him to be a man dedicated to right and justice, and they believe that he will use his great power and influence to secure passage of the bipartisan bill passed by the House.

Actually, Everett Dirksen did not have too many options open to him. No one realized this better than Larry O'Brien, the Massachusetts political pro who advised Presidents Kennedy and Johnson. Among the advisers who met in the Oval Office on February 11, O'Brien was the most confident regarding Dirksen's future actions on H.R. 7152. "Ev Dirksen didn't have any alternative at all," O'Brien concluded. "The reality was that it was no longer a situation of total dependence on Ev Dirksen."

Statistics backed O'Brien up. There was mounting public support for H.R. 7152. A February Harris poll showed 68 percent favoring the House-passed bill. The Gallup survey, released on February 2, gave a 61 percent approval rating, contrasted with 49 percent in June 1963.

In addition Dirksen would confront extreme pressure from Bill McCulloch and his House Republican colleagues to keep intact the lower chamber's bill. The senator from Illinois was not oblivious to McCulloch's February 7 threat that he would withdraw his support from H.R. 7152 if it were amended to his dissatisfaction. Moreover, to preserve the integrity of the Justice Department, Robert Kennedy and his staff had no alternative but to support McCulloch's demands.

Finally, the emotionalism generated by the burgeoning civil rights controversy represented a potentially serious threat to 1964 Republican presidential and congressional candidates if the GOP mishandled the issue in the Senate. Dirksen, consequently, faced the task of neutralizing civil rights as a political factor in the November elections. The GOP would suffer if it took an opposing role in the Senate, and the minority leader certainly realized how much better it would be, not only for the Republican Party, but for the country as a whole, to have a bipartisan approach to the issue. In political terms, if H.R. 7152 passed Congress with substantial GOP support, urban state Republicans, such as Javits, Keating, Case (N.J.), Scott (Pa.), and Kuchel, could claim credit and rightfully seek campaign endorsements from black organizations. In rural states where the black voter turnout was neglible, Republican senators who voted for both cloture and the bill would be spared the opposition of the relatively small band of civil rights activists and, at the same time, by remaining silent about their role in the bill's passage, could avoid offending their more conservative constituents. And if, by chance, a backlash should occur after H.R. 7152 became law, President Johnson and the Democratic-controlled Congress, not the Republicans, would shoulder the blame.

On the afternoon of March 30, when Hubert Humphrey and Tommy Kuchel had finished presenting the case for the bill, they turned the floor over to their bipartisan team captains. Each title would be thoroughly explained by a member from each party in order to establish a proper record since the bill had not been heard in committee on the Senate side. This would take several weeks. Then the stage would be turned over to the opposition, who would probably talk until mid-May or June. No one really expected the garrulous Southerners to wear themselves out. The hope was that they would exhaust the patience of enough undecided Republicans and western Democrats to produce the necessary votes for cloture. The administration's strategy was simple—debate and wait.

But somewhere along the line, as Humphrey knew, pressure would have to be applied. The daily sessions would be drawn out until the one-third of the Senate up for re-election that fall would be anxious to get out campaigning. "The whole thing is timing," he concluded. "We've got to hold on until the pain is miserable, till it's really agony."

Off Capitol Hill, the strategy on H.R. 7152 was equally simple—pray and wait. The Leadership Conference on Civil Rights representing 74 organizations, held a large day-long meeting on Wednesday, April 1, to coordinate their plans for the coming months. The 80 civil rights leaders agreed that one hour before the Senate opened each day, a prominent clergyman would sponsor a daily prayer service in the Lutheran Church of the Reformation on Capitol Hill. B'nai B'rith Women announced that they would set aside April 6 as "wire for rights day." The Students Speak for Civil Rights organization scheduled daily rallies in the Sylvan Theater, located at the base of the Washington Monument, April 27 through May 2.

Enthusiasm was in the air. "Let's face it," declared Joe Rauh, "we have a bill now which is beyond our wildest dreams." But the upbeat mood of the day was personified in Hubert Humphrey, who exuberantly pronounced, "I am so conditioned morally, physically, psychologically, the fight can go on for 10 years and I won't run out of steam."

In the Senate, meanwhile, the almost empty chamber echoed with the dry, lengthy explanations of H.R. 7152's complex provisions. All this, however, hardly constituted high drama, and most senators were elsewhere. This became a serious problem, for the favorite southern harassing tactic was mischievously "suggesting the absence of a quorum" and then sitting back while the leadership frantically tried to round up the necessary 51 bodies. Actually, the Senate had always been a rather dilatory place. It took the first Senate 33 days to muster a quorum in 1789, and things had not improved much since. But in the case of the civil rights bill, failure to get enough members to conduct Senate business meant not only an overnight recess but a symbolic defeat as well. On Thursday it was 22 minutes before they found a majority, and on Friday the search dragged on for more than an hour.

Saturday, April 4, was a disaster. Only 39 members (23 Democrats and 16 Republicans) responded to the quorum call. Forty-four of the absentees were civil rights supporters, and three of them—John Pastore (D-R.I.), Edward Long (D-Mo.), and Magnuson—were captains of Hubert Humphrey's team. So the Senate, for the first time in nearly two years, was forced to recess. Where were they all? the furious Humphrey demanded. A quick check found Scoop Jackson (D-Wash.) in his home state dedicating a new forest service laboratory. Clinton Anderson (D-N.M.) was in Albuquerque meeting with an Indian organization. And Utah's Ted Moss was at the annual conference of the Mormon Church in Salt Lake City. Politics had taken them home, but it was the angry majority whip who got them back. Humphrey fired off curt telegrams to the missing Democrats, demanding confirmation of their receipt by return wire. Then he sat down with the returned truants, handed them a list of scheduled sessions through mid-May, and told them to either be present or be prepared to be scolded publicly.

"The only way we can lose the civil rights fight is not to have a quorum when we need it," Humphrey lectured them, pointing out that the battle would be won not on oratory but on organization and the staying power to endure and finally break the southern filibuster.

The president, on the other hand, gave the appearance of being quite relaxed about the whole Senate scene. During his press conference on Saturday, when asked to comment on the progress of the civil rights bill, he drawled, "I do not want to set any time limit because it is something over which I have no control. I don't think anyone can speculate." But, in fact, time was an ally of the president, a truth of which he was well aware.

At 10:00 A.M. on Monday, April 6, as the Senate began its fifth week of debate on H.R. 7152, Roger Mudd huddled in a drizzling rain on the east front Capitol steps interviewing arriving senators in the clammy morning air while inside, on the almost deserted Senate floor, the team captains were still defining the bill line by line. Lobbying efforts against H.R. 7152 appeared to be waning. Mail deliveries to Senate members showed a dramatic turnaround, with Phil Hart's office, for example, logging 204 letters in favor of the bill the previous week and only 90 against. And confirming this trend, John Synon, director of the Coordinating Committee for Fundamental American Freedoms, which had placed the "Blackjack" newspaper ad, admitted morosely, "We've shot our wad."

Sitting at his desk in the minority leader's ornate office, Everett Dirksen added another page of reflections to his notebook. The April

6 entry considered, in his cryptic style, possible factors favoring cloture:

1. Faced with log-jam legislation.
2. 1964 an election year. Members will want some time to campaign.
3. July 13, 1964—Republican Convention—Hope it not necessary to dispose of unfinished business after convention.
4. Factor of weariness.
5. Group pressures—emotionalism.

Dirksen knew that ahead of him lay the toughest job of his long career. He recognized that the country had to resolve the racial injustices accumulated from 350 years of neglect. And he realized, as Bill McCulloch had realized in the House, that he was the key in the Senate. If the conservatives had a bill they could support, they would eventually vote for cloture. But it would be extremely tough for Dirksen to produce a bill that not only would please the diehard conservatives and the ultraliberals in the Senate, but would pass inspection by the House as well. For if H.R. 7152 managed to get through the Senate unscathed, it still had to go back to the House for approval before being signed into law by the president.

It would take a master magician to pull it off. First, the minority leader would have to appear genuinely troubled by the omnibus bill and to be looking for ways to weaken it drastically. Then, privately, he would have to carefully amend the bill enough to make it seem like a Republican measure, so that the undecided conservatives could support it, but, at the same time, not weaken it so much that it would lose McCulloch's support. Finally, as a midwestern conservative himself, he would have to endorse the new product so strongly that some of his colleagues, who were fearful of criticism back home, could lean on him like a crutch. It was a job for a man who was good at sleight of hand.

Dirksen made his first move on April 7. Meeting with his fellow GOP senators at the weekly Tuesday luncheon hosted by the Senate Republican Policy Committee to discuss pending legislation, Dirksen placed on the table a surprise package of 40 amendments dealing with Title VII (Equal Employment). He explained that this was the fruit of his month-long research with his legal staff of constitutional experts. The chairman of the luncheon, Bourke B. Hickenlooper (Iowa), was pleased with these weakening changes since he and other GOP conservatives had long been grousing over what they considered the too-powerful role of the federal government in Title VII.

Ev Dirksen also had been unhappy, to some degree, because Illinois had strong laws in this area, and he was concerned that the bill might usurp the state's jurisdiction. The amendments were only discussed informally, however, with concrete action to take place at a Republican caucus on Thursday morning. And later, at a press conference, Dirksen emphasized that the proposed alterations were his views only, not those of the Republican party. "This is a vulnerable section," he said, and then added for good measure, "I'd like to strike it altogether."

GOP moderates and liberals were furious when they heard their minority leader's statement and were waiting for him at the Thursday morning Republican caucus. The spirited shouting in the mahogany-paneled room reflected the widely divergent philosophical differences within the ranks of the party. Of the 33 Republicans, 21 (including Dirksen) could be classified as conservatives, only 5 as moderates, and 7 (including Kuchel) as liberals. Dirksen's 40 amendments were tossed back and forth heatedly, while Chairman Leverett Saltonstall (Mass.) strove to maintain order. Margaret Chase Smith fought to retain the "sex" amendment, which, she pointed out, had been incorporated in the House bill with the help of Republican congresswomen. Finally, after two hours and 20 minutes, the quarreling colleagues adjourned with no agreement on any issue. But Dirksen had accomplished his main purpose—testing the Republican waters.

Afterward, he told the press corps that he was trying to make Title VII as "palatable as possible" and, therefore, might see many of his 40 changes "go down the drain." But he felt that "the remaining residue will help get this passed. My position is negotiable."

The Democrats got first-hand news of the GOP fracas when Tommy Kuchel ducked out of the meeting and hurried to his co-floor manager's office. Sitting in the office with Humphrey were Burke Marshall, Joe Rauh, Clarence Mitchell, Steve Horn, and the legislative assistants to Humphrey, Clark, and Magnuson. The response to the news varied.

Humphrey advised the group to "follow the course of not being openly antagonistic to Dirksen. The Republicans must carry the fight. Let the Republicans argue it out with their own leader. Dirksen told me that if he did not get support, then he would retreat."

Steve Horn said that he and his boss, Senator Kuchel, theorized that "Dirksen will go through his public acting process, take a licking, and then be with us." To Humphrey's aide he inquired,

"How many Democratic votes do you have to defeat Dirksen's gutting amendments?" John Stewart replied that his count showed 35 to 40 Democratic votes available. "Then we've got him," gloated Horn.

As the meeting ended, a poignant drama was unfolding on the Senate floor—Edward Kennedy was delivering his maiden speech. Seated in the front row of the Senate gallery were the senator's wife, Joan, his brother Robert, and the attorney general's wife, Ethel. Noticeably nervous as he began his talk, the Massachusetts Democrat explained that he had intended to make his initial floor address on the issues affecting industry and commerce in his home state.

"But," said Ted Kennedy, "I could not follow this debate for the last four weeks—I could not see this issue envelop the emotions and the conscience of the nation—without changing my mind.... As a young man, I wanted to see an America where everyone can make his contribution, where a man will be measured not by the color of his skin but by the content of his character." The junior senator closed his remarks with a reference to his late brother, but as he did so, his voice broke. Joan Kennedy dabbed tears from her eyes as she watched her husband struggling to continue. "My brother was the first president of the United States to state publicly that segregation was morally wrong. His heart and soul are in this bill." As Kennedy sat down, five senators went over to his back-row desk to congratulate him.

On Friday southern speeches attacking H.R. 7152 were interrupted so that the Senate could discuss the Cherry Blossom Festival. The weather had warmed enough that the blossoms of the trees around the Tidal Basin had emerged to their full, delicate pink bloom. The Senate agreed to have a quorum call at 10:00 the next morning so that senators who wanted to could leave to attend the traditional Cherry Blossom Parade. Senator Olin D. Johnston (D-S.C.) announced that immediately after Saturday's quorum call, Sam Ervin (D-N.C.) would take the floor.

"I shall be present," announced Hubert Humphrey. "It is a difficult choice to make between the princess of the Cherry Blossom Festival and the legal tidbits that we will receive from the great senior senator from North Carolina, but, difficult as the choice is, and adding the factor of duty, I shall be present."

"Good," said Johnston.

"Do I take prunes or South Carolina peaches?" quipped Everett Dirksen.

"On the present occasion, if I was the senator, tomorrow morning I believe I would take peaches," laughed Humphrey.

At 10:00 A.M. on Monday, April 13, as the Senate began its sixth week of debate on H.R. 7152, it was overcast and windy on Capitol Hill as Roger Mudd reported from the east front steps. The lengthy explanations of the bill were completed, the Southerners had resumed their filibustering with a flourish, and Hubert Humphrey gleefully reported that he had talked Ev Dirksen down from 40 amendments to 15.

Humphrey was holding the daily morning bipartisan team meeting in his majority whip's office, a veritable war room with organization charts, duty rosters, and progress calendars. And the senator from Minnesota was effusively optimistic about going for a cloture vote on May 15 or 20. "I will try to find the maximum number of votes we can get," he said. "We will wait until the people are anxious. That means after the first week in May."

Humphrey then expressed the need for a "barrage of propaganda." He felt that while "people may disagree on the substance of the bill, how can they disagree on the right to vote? It is outrageous that the business of government is held back because some people cannot vote. We need the right to vote not just in Mississippi, but also in the Senate of the United States."

That afternoon the major league baseball season opened at D.C. Stadium with Lyndon Johnson vigorously throwing out the first ball for the Washington Senators–California Angels game. He was surrounded by 17 hooky-playing members of the U.S. Senate, including Mike Mansfield, Hubert Humphrey, and Everett Dirksen, while back on the Capitol steps a Gone Fishing sign hung behind Roger Mudd's cameras. Then, suddenly, at the end of the third inning, the public address system blared out a cheerless announcement. "Attention please! All senators must report back to the Senate for a quorum call."

In response to this unsportsmanlike gambit, the pro-civil rights lawmakers scrambled from their seats and hurried unhappily out to their waiting limousines for the one-mile dash to the Capitol. A smiling Richard Russell never moved from his seat in the stadium.

The next day John McClellan (D-Ark.) decided to have some fun at the expense of his former colleague from Texas and resurrected a speech that Lyndon Johnson had made as a freshman senator in 1949. In opposing the Fair Employment Practices Commission, Johnson had said, "Such a law would necessitate a system of federal police officers such as we have never before seen," adding that he hoped "the Senate will never be called upon to entertain seriously any such proposal again."

There was no answering salvo from the Oval Office, at least none that could be repeated in polite company. But there were some complaints from a few of the northern senators who were getting weary of endless Saturday and dinnertime quorum calls. The words "let's try cloture and see what happens" began to be heard.

Cloture, and how to achieve it, once again dominated the conversation at the Thursday morning, April 16, bipartisan team meeting. Joe Rauh gave his standard speech, "The Leadership Conference is united in thinking that a cloture discussion is unwise. Public discussion of cloture leads to talk of compromise with the Dirksen amendments. There should be no cloture [attempt] until the votes are counted. We had that pledge from Hubert in this room." Several of the others present suggested that the best method was to have "exhaustion precede cloture." But Humphrey rejected it:

> Unless we are ready to move in our clothes and our shavers and turn the Senate into a dormitory—which Mansfield won't have—we have to do something else. The president grabbed me by the shoulder and damned near broke my arm. He said, "I'd run the show around the clock." That was three weeks ago. I told the president he is grabbing the wrong arm. I have the Senate wives calling me right now, asking "Why can't the senator be home now?" They add, "The place isn't being run intelligently." Even though I'm pushing for longer hours, the president continues to ask, "What about the pay bill? What about poverty? What about food stamps?"... We aren't going to sell out. If we do, it will be for a hell of a price.

That afternoon Everett Dirksen took the Senate floor to offer his anticipated amendments to Title VII (Equal Employment). At the urging of moderate and liberal Republicans and Hubert Humphrey as well, he had reduced his original 40 changes down to 10. "These 10 amendments," explained Cornelius Kennedy, his legal assistant, "were for educational purposes." Since, in effect, they were designed to test the waters, Dirksen announced that he "would not call them up yet." (An amendment, although introduced, can not be considered by the Senate until its author "calls it up," that is, formally asks for its consideration.) He also added that a "mysterious 11th amendment," as the press termed it, dealing with the enforcement powers of the Equal Employment Opportunity Commission, would be introduced at a later date.

But another person had also played a role in scaling down Dirksen's 40 amendments. Two days earlier Bill McCulloch had walked over from the House wing of the Capitol and paid a courtesy call on the Senate minority leader. Wherever he went, including the campaign trail, McCulloch usually arrived without much fanfare. There was no large staff, no advance men distributing position papers, no flood of press releases. Bill McCulloch carried everything he needed in his head.

People would look up and there he was, a soft spoken average-looking gentleman, so unfailingly pleasant and considerate that one almost did not notice the fine mind and resolute will. It was only when one started talking with McCulloch, and saw past the twinkling eyes and the little smile under the reddish mustache, that one discovered the tough and stubborn man who lived within.

As the melodramatic Dirksen and the matter-of-fact McCulloch sat down to talk business it was quickly evident why the Ohioan had come to call. Dirksen had not checked with him before making public his amendments, and McCulloch could not possibly go along with two of his proposals. The first would remove the Equal Employment Opportunity Commission's authority to file suits. And the second would let the state preempt the federal government when both had similar employment discrimination statutes. Consistent with McCulloch's commitment to basic constitutional principles, he sought to maintain a balance of individual freedom, state responsibility, and federal action. Dirksen was subtly reminded that in the end his amendments would have to pass McCulloch's inspection.

Sunday, April 19, saw the most dramatic moment yet on behalf of the beleaguered civil rights bill. Trios of Catholic, Protestant, and Jewish seminarians began a 24-hour-a-day vigil at the Lincoln Memorial that would continue until H.R. 7152 cleared the Senate. Theology students from 75 seminaries throughout the country came to Washington to pray in shifts around the clock at the memorial. The nation's capital had never before seen this kind of lobbying.

Hubert Humphrey had confided to Joe Rauh and Clarence Mitchell some weeks earlier, "The secret of passing the bill is the prayer groups." The active participation of church groups in the lobbying effort stemmed from the Leadership Conference's August

164

8, 1963, decision to broaden the base of involvement in central, southwestern, and far western states where labor unions and black organizations, such as the NAACP, had few members. Detailed plans were evolved in Lincoln, Nebraska, on September 13, when representatives from Catholic, Protestant, and Jewish faiths met to discuss civil rights strategy.

"This was the first time," said James Hamilton of the National Council of Churches, "that I ever recalled seeing Catholic nuns away from the convents for more than a few days. There was an agreement among religious groups that this was a priority issue and other things had to be laid aside."

In dealing with the Senate, church spokesmen, working through the Leadership Conference, decided on several strategies. First, newsletters would be sent to church members throughout the country urging them to contact their senators. Second, in some areas local ministers were asked to find out which of their parishoners might be influential with their senator because of previous campaign contributions or political support. This was new for church groups, which in the past had not engaged in purely political lobbying. Third, the National Council of Churches, the U.S. Catholic Conference, and the Jewish community planned for different clergy and lay groups to meet almost daily with their senators. There would be briefing sessions in the morning at the Lutheran Church of the Reformation on East Capitol Street, two blocks from the Senate office buildings, after which each group would visit with its two senators.

The presence of the clergy in the nation's capital and the moral tone which they gave to the debate were beginning to place the anti-civil rights forces on the defensive. On March 1, when Richard Russell had appeared on "Face the Nation," he lashed out at what he and his followers correctly perceived as a growing threat to their claim on the public conscience. "There never has been as effective [a] lobby maintained in the city of Washington as there is today," remonstrated the senior senator from Georgia. "We have a number of well meaning citizens, particularly men of the cloth, who are here."

One hundred additional churchmen descended on the city on March 17. Catholic, Protestant, and Jewish lobbyists met with Hubert Humphrey and laid plans for a major interdenominational convocation to be held at Georgetown University on April 28. However, the church officials were cautioned to keep sight of their

165

ultimate goal: passage of legislation, not condemnation of those who disagreed. Humphrey asked them not to question the motives of those who might oppose H.R. 7152.

On Monday, April 20, the seventh week of debate was starting. Roger Mudd's TV reports from the Capitol steps now showed a superimposed clock ticking off the hours, minutes, and seconds. Inside, the rhetoric rambled on as the Southerners neared the 37-day record for civil rights filibustering.

On Tuesday, Everett Dirksen had his 11th amendment ready. At his joint news conference with Charles Halleck that morning, he told reporters that he would present the amendment on the floor that afternoon, after which he would come to the Senate press room and "get my accustomed cup of tea from Joe Wilk [the press gallery attendant] and then submit myself to your tender mercies."

After the Senate convened at 10:00 A.M., Hubert Humphrey proposed holding a "morning hour" so that business other than H.R. 7152 could be discussed. During this hour, members would be able to introduce bills, resolutions, and petitions, with statements not to exceed three minutes per member. After Humphrey's proposal was adopted without objection, Dirksen arose and stated, "I now present the 11th amendment, which deals entirely with enforcement [under Title VII]. At this time, I will not attempt to state an explanation of the amendment; that will come later when I call it up." Dirksen's amendment, in brief, restricted the time in which the attorney general could file discrimination charges once proceedings had begun under existing state law or local ordinance.

By mid-afternoon 35 amendments, including Dirksen's 11, had been introduced, but none had been called up for debate. This meant that for 20 days the discussion had focused on one issue: the bill itself. This gave proponents of H.R. 7152 an advantage by permitting them, as Humphrey had planned, to remain on the offensive.

Suddenly, the Southerners switched tactics. Herman Talmadge (D-Ga.) sent an amendment to the desk and asked that "it be read and made the pending business." He proposed that, under Title XI, anyone charged with willfully disobeying a court decree requiring compliance with an antidiscrimination order be entitled, upon demand, to a trial by jury. Talmadge's move did two things. It narrowed the debate to one question: the right of trial by jury. And it placed civil rights supporters in the difficult position of explaining why, in the case of contempt of court, the defendant should not be granted a jury trial.

166

Senator Talmadge argued that a jury trial "is indeed a basic and fundamental civil right.... It was wrested by our British forebears from King John at Runnymede in 1215. Since that time, the right of trial by jury in all Anglo-Saxon jurisdictions has been held to be a sacred privilege of personal liberty." Wayne Morse, in reply, made the obvious point, "With a southern jury, prosecution for contempt would become meaningless because convictions could not be obtained."

When Kenneth Keating asked Talmadge whether he intended to press for a vote that day, the Georgian stated that he would not, to which Willis Robertson added, "I believe the Senate can look forward to a considerable elucidation of what is involved."

But while the jury trial amendment was being argued loudly, another far more important conversation was being held in low tones. Hubert Humphrey, heeding the president's advice about seeing Dirksen and talking with Dirksen and listening to Dirksen, regularly came over to the Republican side of the Senate and dropped into a chair next to the minority leader's desk. There he would pass the time of day in a pleasant fashion, just being a friend and, incidentally, a friend in whom one could confide if one felt so moved. The strategy seemed to pay off that afternoon, when Everett Dirksen, having decided the time was right, turned to his Democratic colleague and, in a lengthy monologue, poured out his soul. In recognizing his key role in the historic event approaching, Dirksen conceded that H.R. 7152 was a good bill and that it would be passed. He realized it was his duty to lend his weight to the measure, and to that end, he had only one more amendment in mind, a minor one to Title II.

Hubert Humphrey was delighted. He predicted enthusiastically that this would be a great opportunity for the minority leader because, by playing the role of statesman, he would be credited with saving the civil rights bill. Dirksen then tested the firmness of the administration. He suggested that a cloture vote might not be needed after all. He sensed that the Southerners were wearing out and, if so, he might be able to avoid the herculean task of producing those 25 necessary Republican votes. Humphrey firmly disagreed, arguing that the southern forces needed the cloture vote to end the filibuster because it was a good way for them to get themselves off the hook. Dirksen, convinced that the administration was firm about going for cloture, conceded that Humphrey had a good point but urged him not to insist on Rule 19—limiting senators to two speeches apiece—which had been a subject of heated discussion on the floor the previous day. Dirksen contended that their colleagues from the South were about to collapse anyway and, therefore, the Humphrey-Kuchel forces should not further irritate or embarrass them. Instead, he suggested that the filibusterers be reminded from time to time that the rule did exist and could be enforced.

That afternoon the Southerners talked past the old 37-day record for civil rights filibustering. A weary Richard Russell, in an off-the-record chat with NAACP's Clarence Mitchell, admitted that "the jig was up." The Georgia Democrat explained himself by saying that there was no hope of gaining a compromise from Lyndon Johnson, something he felt might have been possible if John F. Kennedy were still alive.

Everett Dirksen still had this fact about Johnson to learn. The minority leader had decided that his route to statesmanship took him right by Lyndon Johnson's door. What better way to bring out H.R. 7152 than to make a deal with the master wheeler-dealer himself? So at the White House the next morning, Dirksen broached the subject. The president had asked Democratic and Republican congressional leaders to come for breakfast to be briefed on another problem, America's growing military commitment in Vietnam. Afterward, Dirksen took Johnson aside and suggested that they talk about the civil rights bill. The president agreed to see the minority leader the following Wednesday afternoon, April 29.

But if by this time, Everett Dirksen was ready to talk business with the president, Mike Mansfield was equally ready to talk business with Dirksen. They had long been close friends and respectful opponents, with Dirksen coming to Mansfield's defense several times against Democratic malcontents. In 1962, when Wayne Morse decried Mansfield as a leader and obliquely accused him of lying, Dirksen jumped to his feet and, in a rebuke rare on the Senate floor, commanded Morse to sit down. And in 1963, when Thomas Dodd, in an acrimonious speech, questioned Mansfield's abilities, Dirksen suggested that Dodd had been drinking too much and was emotionally unstable. Mansfield valued the minority leader's friendship and considered him an invaluable ally in running the Senate.

On Thursday, April 23, Mansfield mulled over Dirksen's current position on H.R. 7152. With the majority leader in his office were Hubert Humphrey, Robert Kennedy, Nick Katzenbach, Burke Marshall, Secretary of the Senate Democrats Frank Valeo, and Larry O'Brien's aide Mike Manatos. They felt the Senate would ultimately

ℒℷcept Herman Talmadge's jury trial amendment. So it would be smart to get together with Dirksen and work out a substitute amendment that would be more acceptable to the bill's supporters. Mansfield picked up the phone and called him.

Minutes later, when Ev Dirksen walked into Mansfield's office to join the Democrats, an important step was taken along the thorny path to a good civil rights bill. Dirksen agreed, after hearing the arguments in favor of compromise, to cosponsor a substitute amendment with Mansfield. And with that settled, they zeroed in on Dirksen's 11th amendment. After much discussion, the minority leader consented to retain the Equal Employment Opportunity Commission's right to file suit, and Nick Katzenbach offered to prepare new language, which he would work out with Hubert Humphrey and Cliff Case.

As he left Mansfield's office, a beaming Bobby Kennedy said, "I think we will be able to work something out that is satisfactory." "Splendid," exclaimed Hubert Humphrey. "I think things are looking great." "It was a most productive meeting," observed Mike Manatos in a memo to Larry O'Brien. And Mansfield's aide Charlie Ferris believed that with the minority leader "now engaged, the time had become ripe to think about cloture."

The next day Dirksen submitted the Mansfield-Dirksen substitute jury trial amendment to the Senate. It provided that, at the judge's discretion, a person accused of criminal contempt of court could be tried with or without a jury. If, however, there was no jury, the total fine could not exceed $300 and the total length of imprisonment could not exceed 30 days. Dirksen asked for its immediate consideration, and consequently, it replaced the Talmadge amendment as the pending business before the Senate.

When asked his view of the substitute amendment, Dick Russell scoffed that it was "just a mustard plaster on a cancer." When Lyndon Johnson was asked the same question by newsmen, he protested innocence of what was happening on the Hill. The jury trial question, he said, "is a matter for the senators who are considering it, and the counsel of the Justice Department and the attorney general, who are examining those amendments as they are proposed. I haven't seen it. All I know is what I read in the paper."

Behind the scenes it was a different story. The president, whose clarion battle cry was a deafening roar of "get it done," impatiently received regular progress reports and just as impatiently swore at the meager messages they contained. "How are you doing?" he demanded, when the Senate leaders came down for their weekly Tuesday breakfasts. Johnson's get-things-done-now style made the White House breakfasts so much like battlefield briefings that often his guests left without knowing whether they ate or not.

But in spite of the president's pique, things seemed to be inching forward, and by the end of the week, there was growing optimism among the bipartisan leaders that cloture could be attained. Encouraged by a Harris poll that showed 70 percent supporting the bill and 63 percent favoring limiting debate, Hubert Humphrey told "Face the Nation" panelists on Sunday, April 26, that despite Senator Engle's (D-Calif.) operation for a brain tumor on Friday, they were just four or five votes short.

On Monday morning, April 27, as the Senate started the eighth week of debate, the weather was cloudy and the temperature was 62 degrees. The divinity students were praying around the clock at the Lincoln Memorial, and Roger Mudd was as much a tourist attraction as the Washington Monument. On the Senate floor the Southerners were slowing down but showing no sign of quitting, and cloture got another boost, this time from a conservative Republican, Gordon L. Allott (Colo.).

Reflecting the growing restlessness among his colleagues, Allott stated in a floor speech that "senators have the right and the duty, at some point, to bring debate on this subject to a conclusion.... I am willing to stand upon what I believe the Senate should do after it has had reasonable time in which to debate the bill. I think the time to act is now."

Everett Dirksen felt the same way. He told his fellow Republicans at their weekly policy luncheon on Tuesday that he planned to give the Southerners "one week's notice" on the jury trial amendment and that if it had not been voted on by the next Tuesday, May 5, he would file a cloture petition. And later he told the press corps that "this isn't a bluff. I can count. There was an amazing consensus in the policy luncheon that the time had come to move off dead center."

That evening at Georgetown University, 5,000 church leaders overflowed McDonough Gymnasium into nearby Gaston Hall, where loudspeakers were set up, to rally in support of H.R. 7152. Among those packed into the gym were the two Senate floor leaders, Hubert Humphrey and Tommy Kuchel, as well as New York's senators, Jacob Javits and Kenneth Keating. On the platform were the Catholic Archbishop of Baltimore, Lawrence J. Shehan, Rabbi

Uri Miller of Baltimore, and the Reverend Eugene Carson Blake, whose speech was the highlight of the evening. The Protestant clergyman, frequently interrupted by applause, said that in order to pass the civil rights bill they must convert the "unconverted" and "uncommitted." And for most, as Jim Hamilton said, "the evening was an emotional high."

The next morning, however, spirits were low in the Humphrey-Kuchel team meeting. In spite of Humphrey's earlier declaration that he would never get tired or discouraged, the daily strategy sessions were starting to be interspersed with outbursts of temper as time was flying by and they were still no closer to cloture. The big question facing the leadership was whether to seek cloture on just the jury trial amendment or on the entire bill. Humphrey declared that while Dirksen wanted to try for cloture on the jury trial amendment, he was against it for either the amendment or the whole bill because, as he pointed out, "we don't have enough votes."

Katzenbach stated that Ev Dirksen was the key. Indicating that many "substantive" problems had been worked out, the deputy attorney general felt that Dirksen could produce up to one-third of the votes needed for cloture.

"Let's not kid ourselves," retorted the perenially angry Joe Clark (D-Pa.), "This has become the Dirksen bill! I deplore it but that's it."

"I've said this since the beginning," Humphrey pointed out.

While Dirksen was being so heatedly discussed on Capitol Hill, he was merrily on his way to the White House to meet with the president. Talking with reporters before he left, the minority leader gave a preview of what he intended to say to Johnson. "You say you want the House bill without any change," he planned to tell the president. "Well, in my humble opinion, you are not going to get it. Now it's your play. What do you have to say?" If Johnson accepted his invitation to strike a bargain, the senator told the press that he believed he could deliver 22 or 25 votes for cloture.

But the scenario did not work quite that way. Dirksen had taken the president a little gift—an alarm clock commemorating the 100th anniversary of the LaSalle, Illinois, firm that manufactured the Big Ben timepiece. After dispensing with this pleasantry, the senator turned to the serious business at hand. But to his complete astonishment, he found old compromiser Lyndon Johnson in a strangely uncompromising mood. There was to be no deal on H.R. 7152. Instead, Johnson threw the ball right back to the minority leader.

Somewhat taken aback, Dirksen had to tell newsmen that he and Johnson had barely touched on the subject of civil rights.

The plain truth was that Dirksen had been outmaneuvered by Hubert Humphrey. The majority whip had gone to the White House the day before and, after waiting for two hours, managed to see the president, delaying a scheduled National Security Council meeting. Presidential adviser McGeorge Bundy accused Humphrey of "holding us up."

"You're goddam right," replied the Minnesotan spiritedly. "He needs me more than he needs you." Fearful that Johnson might succumb to Dirksen's supplications the next day, Humphrey assured the president that "victory was in sight" and pleaded with him to "lay down the law" with those who wanted to weaken the bill. And Lyndon Johnson, in spite of all his trading instincts, went along.

On the Hill that Wednesday afternoon it was becoming evident that, as so often happened in the Senate, everyone was all talked out but no one knew how to stop. The Southerners caucused at 2:30 P.M. and, after 75 minutes of impassioned arguing, could not agree on whether to allow the Senate to hold a vote on the jury trial amendment. Afterward Dick Russell strode into Ev Dirksen's office to tell him of the impasse. In the best Senate tradition of comradeship, the two men went arm-in-arm into Mike Mansfield's office. Finally, after 20 minutes, they parted amicably with, also in the best Senate tradition, nothing settled.

At this point the backstage maneuvering grew more critical and the need for secrecy more important. From now on, therefore, the lobbyists from the Leadership Conference were to be kept in the dark about what was going on. And as the Monday and Thursday morning sessions took on the appearance of mock meetings, Clarence Mitchell and his allies guessed that they were being excluded from the real decisionmaking and grew increasingly restless. Hubert Humphrey felt that including them would have invited chaos.

The stonewalling began at the Thursday, April 30, bipartisan team meeting. To keep the discussion away from relevant issues, Humphrey turned to Mitchell with a question about round-the-clock sessions. "What should we do, Clarence? Let's put it on the table."

"I'm going to put it on the table with 'all deliberate speed'," retorted Mitchell. "I went through Lyndon Johnson's all-night sessions [in 1960]. He knew where every absentee was, and he did not call them in."

"Every senator is ready to come in," soothed Humphrey.

"We could maybe deliver 51 of them within 30 years," snapped Mitchell. "Hubert, I am very fond of you. My authority is you, Hubert. The missing ingredient is to compel the attendance of the absentees. Our troops can be worn out unless we bring in the missing senators." The NAACP executive's proposal that the Senate sergeant at arms should be ordered to arrest absent senators and escort them to the chamber was deftly sidetracked by Humphrey and Kuchel. They suggested, instead, that the National Council of Churches' "nationwide program to contact the errant brothers" be expanded and improved.

The deadlock on the jury trial amendment was finally broken on Friday afternoon, May 1, when Mike Mansfield and Everett Dirksen huddled together on the Senate floor and got Dick Russell to agree to Wednesday, May 6, as the date for the vote. Earlier that afternoon, however, things had become more complicated. Thruston Morton (R-Ky.) had introduced a "perfecting" amendment to the original Talmadge proposal and asked that it be called up for immediate consideration. This, then, replaced the Mansfield-Dirksen amendment as the pending business of the Senate. So the first vote on May 6 would be on Morton's proposal and then on any other perfecting amendments (to the Talmadge amendment) that might be called up.

Another deadlock was also broken that afternoon. Ever since Dirksen had signaled his willingness to contribute to the success of the bill, Humphrey had been hounding him daily to negotiate. "Well, Dirk," Humphrey would say, "when do you think we ought to meet and talk over some of your amendments?" Dirksen would reply, "Well, just give us a couple more days. It isn't the time yet."

Having learned two days earlier that the president was not going to make any deals, Dirksen decided it was time to talk with Humphrey and company. That afternoon he invited a select bipartisan group of senators, as well as Justice Department lawyers, to a private meeting in his office the following Tuesday morning.

On Monday, May 4, as the Senate began its ninth week of debate, the weather was cloudy. The divinity students were in their 16th day of 24-hour vigils at the Lincoln Memorial, and Roger Mudd stood in front of his CBS cameras for the 151st time.

Five senators were present in the chamber as George Smathers (D-Fla.) held the floor when suddenly, in the gallery, there was an inpassioned outburst. "How can you say you are protecting the black man if only five are here?" shouted a 26-year-old black man,

Kenneth Washington. "I thought this was America, the land of the free. This involves 20,000,000 people!" Guards hustled him off while Smathers never missed a word in his speech nor even looked up.

Early on Tuesday, before their meeting with Dirksen, Mike Mansfield and Hubert Humphrey, along with Carl Hayden, the Senate's president pro tempore, had their weekly breakfast with the president. But in addition to the usual bacon and eggs, Hayden found there was something new to chew on. Johnson had decided that since the Senate action was so sluggish, it was time for him to do a little arm twisting. Since 1948 the 87-year-old Hayden had been pushing for congressional approval of the Central Arizona Water Project, which was designed to bring urgently needed water from California to Phoenix and Tucson through an elaborate system of dams, pumping plants, aqueducts, and canals. The president suggested that if Hayden voted for cloture, Johnson would help the Arizona Water Project. Such a trade-off posed great difficulties for the Arizona senator for, like many lawmakers from sparsely populated states, he felt that the filibuster was the only protection they had against the demands of the larger states. Consequently, he had never voted for cloture. In addition, Hayden had a personal reason for his views. In 1911 the Senate had filibustered to keep President William Howard Taft and a Republican Congress from merging the Arizona and New Mexico territories into one state, which would have resulted in the election of two GOP senators. As Hayden observed, "I never would have been here but for the right to filibuster. I think it's a good procedure."

The president did not push, but just left the suggestion on the table. After breakfast Mansfield and Humphrey were driven back to the Capitol for the meeting with Dirksen. Joining them were Robert Kennedy, Nick Katzenbach, Tommy Kuchel, Warren Magnuson, Bourke Hickenlooper, George Aiken, and members of the senators' staffs. The fate of H.R. 7152 was about to be decided. If the bill had to be redrafted, the chore would fall to Dirksen's and Mansfield's legal advisers, along with Nick Katzenbach and Burke Marshall. At the Illinois senator's side, therefore, was his legal counsel—Cornelius Kennedy, Clyde Flynn, and Bernard Waters (nicknamed Dirksen's Bombers by the press). The Democrats had a two-member legal contingent, Kenneth Teasdale and Charles Ferris.

After the men seated themselves at the long conference table, Dirksen sprang another of his little surprises. Instead of only 1 more amendment, as he had promised, he submitted 40, divided into three categories: Track A—technical; Track B—semitechnical; and Track C—substantive. Agreement was reached that morning on the technical changes, and it was decided that the B and C amendments would be taken up the next morning. Tommy Kuchel was as astounded as the Democrats by Dirksen's unexpected move and later expressed to his aide Steve Horn his disgust at his wily leader's slowdown.

The next day the president held a news conference on the south lawn of the White House, attended by families of Washington reporters. He expressed the hope that Congress would pass H.R. 7152 by the end of May or early June "and then we can go on with our food stamp programs in the Senate, our poverty program, our Appalachia bill, and our medical aid bill. I think the people of the country are entitled to have a vote on these important measures." If the Senate failed to act on the civil rights bill in sufficient time to permit consideration of his Great Society proposals, Johnson intimated he would call a special session of Congress after the national conventions and before the fall elections. "The people's business must come first," he declared.

That day Lyndon Johnson also started working on another vote for cloture. In a memorandum to the White House, Mike Mansfield reported that they were still three or four votes short. Then he suggested that it might be wise to gain the goodwill of Bourke Hickenlooper, who, at that point, was unhappy with the administration for rejecting Horace Smith as ambassador to the Philippines. Mansfield said that the White House might show deference to Hickenlooper by seeking his advice on matters unrelated to civil rights, such as Latin America policy (a subject in which the Iowan was well versed). If Hickenlooper could be won over, the memo argued, he might carry with him Senators Curtis, Pearson, Hruska, and Karl E. Mundt (R-S.D.). That afternoon a note was sent from presidential aide Lee White to Mansfield saying that the president had sent Secretary of State Dean Rusk to see Hickenlooper that day "as per your memorandum."

All that day, in Everett Dirksen's conference room, his amendments were carefully analyzed. It was purely exploratory, however, because the Democrats had decided that there would be no final agreement with Dirksen until a quid pro quo—the minority leader's agreement to work actively for cloture—had been obtained. But all was not harmony among the Republicans either. During the morning session Hickenlooper referred to Dirksen as a softie and indicated that the minority leader "did not speak for the senator from Iowa." He also cast doubt on the number of votes Dirksen could actually get for cloture.

In the afternoon only the Justice Department officials and Senate staffers worked on the amendments. And in a memorandum to Larry O'Brien, Mike Manatos described Nick Katzenbach's reactions to the first two days of negotiations:

> Katzenbach tells me that the meetings in Senator Dirksen's office on the package civil rights amendments approach go much better in the afternoon sessions when the staff technicians and Katzenbach meet. Apparently the morning sessions are devoted to leadership meetings which Nick indicates are mostly consumed with educational pursuits. He indicates it is surprising to note the lack of real understanding of the civil rights bill and the effects amendments proposed would have on it.
>
> Katzenbach feels the attitude is most encouraging as it applies to Dirksen and his group. He has meetings scheduled again (for Thursday) which gives him hope that progress is being made.

Progress was definitely not being made on the Senate floor that day, however, as Mike Mansfield and Hubert Humphrey were losing control of their troops. The usually deserted chamber was crowded as members gathered for the first real action in nearly six weeks, a vote on the jury trial amendments. In a surprisingly narrow setback, Thruston Morton's southern-backed perfecting amendment was defeated only by a 45–45 tie vote. And on the next vote, a routine motion to table the amendment so that it would not be brought up again, Mansfield and Humphrey were defeated, 44–47.

What had happened to the supposedly strong Humphrey-Kuchel bipartisan forces? The two whips discovered that they lost one vote when the usually affable Ted Moss became angry at Mike Mansfield for failing to call him in time for the vote on the Morton amendment. So Moss joined the opposition on the tabling motion. On such slender threads, booby traps are sprung.

Subsequently, when the Morton amendment was brought to a vote for the second time, a mollified Moss supported Mansfield to defeat it, 45–46. But the closeness of the vote and the lack of discipline among his forces caused Humphrey to postpone a roll call on the Mansfield-Dirksen amendment. It looked as though the

Democratic leadership was not only frittering its time away but also mismanaging things as well.

The next morning at the bipartisan team meeting, Humphrey explained why he postponed the vote. "It is terribly important to get a bigger vote on the Mansfield-Dirksen than on the Morton amendment. I told [Dirksen] the first test is on the Mansfield-Dirksen amendment. If the leaders backed up by their deputies can't produce, then we are in trouble. If we can produce 64 votes, then we are okay. But if we only secure 49 votes, then we have had it."

After the meeting, Humphrey, Clark, and Katzenbach joined the other negotiators for a third day of wrestling with amendments to H.R. 7152 in Dirksen's conference room. During the morning the minority leader objected to the phrase "massive resistance" as a suitable description of violations punishable under Title II (Public Accommodations). "Dirksen," said his legal assistant, Neil Kennedy, "felt that the bill should be a self-enforcing piece of legislation and [that] an offense should be clearly described and the judicial action automatic."

A major breakthrough occurred at the staff meeting that afternoon when Clyde Flynn suggested that the words "pattern or practice" be substituted for "massive resistance." During a break in the discussion, Charlie Ferris called Burke Marshall at the Justice Department and asked him what he thought of Flynn's proposal. "Jump at it, Charlie. That's marvelous," replied the assistant attorney general.

Acceptance of this terminology "was the key to any Senate compromise," concluded Neil Kennedy. And so, with agreement on the amendments in sight, Tom Kuchel approached Hubert Humphrey about the possibility of setting Friday, May 22, as the date for a cloture vote. "Tommy," responded a discouraged Humphrey, "I'm talking out of both sides of my mouth." Humphrey did not believe that any action could be secured before the first week in June and admitted that he was talking about an earlier date "just to keep the civil rights groups in line."

Earlier that day, the president had received a memo from Stewart Udall regarding Johnson's discussion of the Arizona Water Project with Carl Hayden at Tuesday's breakfast. "The reports I get from Senator Hayden's staff," the interior secretary wrote,

> indicate that your gambit on cloture with the Senator...was very persuasive. From a tactical standpoint I think it would be wise for you to defer your decision on the Hayden-Brown

[waterway] proposal *until after the vote on cloture.*
You are, of course, fully aware of the effect which a Hayden vote for cloture would have. Some of the Senators tell me that he will carry several other votes with him, such as the two Nevada senators.

Following the president's instructions, Udall, a former congressman from Arizona, already had begun talking to western senators, with whom he was close, about voting for cloture. "I couldn't argue with them that they were wrong in principle," Udall said, "but I did suggest that they should make an exception in this case." Udall's words, of course, were not lost on those western senators who were interested in securing funds for dams, waterways, national parks, and other Interior projects.

Friday, May 8, was the fourth day of negotiations in Dirksen's suite. The only unresolved issue concerning Title II was whether the attorney general would have the right, as in the House bill, to file court suits when local and state governments were allegedly discriminating. Justice Department spokesmen argued that they could not solve the problem if they had to wait until a lot of grievances were filed by individuals in order for a "pattern or practice" to be established.

That same day two of the main antagonists in the civil rights battle carried the fight into the heartland of the South. President Lyndon Johnson, in addressing members of the Georgia legislature at a breakfast in Atlanta's Dinkler Plaza Hotel, declared: "In our search for justice, you have a sure and faithful guide—the Constitution of the United States. Because the Constitution requires it, and because justice demands it, we must protect the constitutional rights of all our people. The rights of no single American are truly secure until the rights of all Americans are secure." The greatest applause from the approximately 1700 guests that morning, however, went to the president's daughter Lynda, who stated that her heart had been in Georgia for years, "because of my beloved friend Senator Dick Russell who helped raise me."

After breakfast the Johnson presidential motorcade wound for 15 miles through Georgia's capital while an enthusiastic crowd of 500,000 lined the streets. But elsewhere in Atlanta Dick Russell, speaking to the Georgia Junior Chamber of Commerce, painted a gloomy picture for his anti-civil rights followers. "I must, in candor," said the senator, "tell you that we do not have the votes to prevent passage of the bill, and the outcome is uncertain."

178

On Saturday, May 9, after his return from the South, Lyndon Johnson held the 18th press conference of his presidency. When asked his view of cloture, the president again feigned ignorance. "Since I left the Senate and the majority leader's position," he said convincingly,

> I have taken the position that there is one majority leader. If you have more than that, you get confused and frustrated and get into great difficulties.... As president, I don't try to involve myself in the procedure of the Senate. I think Senator Mansfield and Senator Humphrey are much closer to the situation than I am. I am not trying to dodge you. I just don't know.

But only a few days later, the president received a memo from Mike Manatos urging Johnson once again to make it clear to Carl Hayden that the Central Arizona Water Project was contingent on Hayden's vote on civil rights. Manatos also suggested that whatever arrangements the president worked out with the Arizona senator be cleared with Tommy Kuchel, whose state of California also would be involved in any waterway. In this way, noted Manatos, "you would not only be getting Hayden's vote but also giving recognition to a Republican who is working his heart out for us on civil rights."

On Monday, May 11, as the Senate began its 10th week of debate, Washington was at its most beautiful as the pinks and whites of the azaleas and dogwoods bloomed. The divinity students were at their most devotional as they maintained a 24-hour vigil at the Lincoln Memorial and Roger Mudd was at his most resourceful as he thought of fresh questions to ask about the interminable impasse. Hubert Humphrey was at his most scolding as his long-stretched patience finally snapped.

The next day the Senate would tie the longest previous filibuster in history—a two-month talkfest in 1846 on the Oregon bill, by which the United States was to end its agreement with England on joint occupancy of the Oregon territory. Humphrey put the blame for the current impasse not on the Southerners, whose opposition was expected, but on those senators who professed to support civil rights but who refused to shut off the debate with cloture. That afternoon in a press conference, he scathingly rebuked them, "The whole procedure is disgusting," he shouted. "All that is being accomplished here is a display of adult delinquency."

At the White House breakfast the next morning, the president was furious when a discouraged Mike Mansfield told him that progress on H.R. 7152 was "nil." Lyndon Johnson always considered Congress a workshop for getting things done rather than a forum for debating great issues. Abstract ideas bored him. But as a brilliant tactician, he could always figure out how to use people, how to manipulate them into doing what he wanted. So now Johnson demanded that the Senate go into all-night sessions. Mansfield and Humphrey stood their ground, disagreed with him, and then braced themselves for what they knew was coming. This president could be ravagingly cruel; he knew every vulgar word in the book and how best to use them. And now in plain language he told both men what he thought of their ability to run the United States Senate.

Embarrassed and stung, they maintained their composure and finally eased out the White House door after murmuring some meek words of praise for Johnson's recent "forthright explanations" of the bill, which, they told him, helped the public better understand the measure and the Senate's approach to it. Then they hurried gratefully back to the Hill to let the president cool off while they said a few prayers that their approach would eventually produce cloture. They would not enjoy seeing him again if they failed.

In spite of Johnson's tirade, Humphrey was sporting his old effervescence that afternoon when he met with the bipartisan team leaders. "What we did yesterday is paying off," he maintained, conducting a lengthy member-by-member analysis that indicated they now had 55 sure votes for cloture and eight possibles, including Dirksen, George Aiken, Frank Carlson (R-Kan.), Jack Miller (R-Iowa), Jim Pearson, Norris Cotton (R-N.H.), Edward V. Long, and Frank Lausche. "Perhaps," surmised Humphrey, "the president can help in the case of Walters [D-Tenn.], Hayden, Byrd of West Virginia, Bible [D-Nev.], Cannon [D-Nev.], and maybe Fulbright [D-Ark.]."

But while Mike Mansfield was dourly pessimistic and Hubert Humphrey doggedly optimistic, Everett Dirksen was exuding great confidence. Leaving the weekly Republican policy luncheon, the minority leader told the press that there were GOP senators talking cloture who would not have countenanced it a week earlier. "There is a feeling the time has come for action, and we've just about gotten there," said the buoyant Dirksen.

That afternoon, however, the long-suffering Mike Mansfield showed a rare display of temper. Irked about a southern caucus that morning, in which the Southerners had refused to allow the Senate to act on the still-pending Mansfield-Dirksen jury trial amendment, Mansfield felt that Dick Russell had broken his pledge to allow a vote that week. "We are witnessing a travesty on the legislative process. The majority is being told what it can and cannot do."

Hubert Humphrey jumped into the fray next. While stating that he had no personal wish to go "around the clock," he asked the members to examine their consciences. Were they fulfilling their constitutional responsibilities, he asked, by denying the Senate the right to vote on legislation guaranteeing equal protection of the law to all Americans?

That evening, in retaliation against the Southerners' stubbornness, Mansfield stretched out the session until 12:18 A.M. At this evidence that the leadership might use Lyndon Johnson's exhaustion technique, the press asked Dick Russell for his reaction. "That doesn't scare us," scoffed Russell. "We're ready for it."

Adding to the short tempers was another factor—the Senate found itself taking orders from, of all places, the House. "Perhaps never before in Senate history," wrote columnists Rowland Evans and Robert Novak, "has a handful of minority party congressmen in the House held such a whip hand over the Senate." To some senators, annoyed with McCulloch's insistence that there be no substantive changes in the bill without his approval, McCulloch became known as the czar of the Senate. "We must go to him on bended knee with an amendment and say to him, 'will you accept this?'" charged Joe Clark. "If he says no, we dare not make the change." Kenneth Keating voiced a similar complaint, telling black civil rights leaders that any proposed amendment first had to be rushed over to the House for McCulloch's examination and approval. Jack Miller lamented that "if the Senate can't make any changes in the bill, the Senate might as well be abolished." And Dick Russell observed that "one note of consistency that has permeated discussion of possible amendments to the pending bill is that nothing must be done that would not be completely acceptable to Mr. McCulloch. In my first 31 years of service in the Senate, it was entirely kosher for the Senate to pass a bill that differed from the version approved in the other body. But we now find that the name of the game is 'Clear It with Mr. McCulloch—Don't Have a Conference.'"

On Wednesday morning the fifth negotiating session with Everett Dirksen was scheduled for 10:30. Beforehand, a small group—Hubert Humphrey, Robert Kennedy, Joe Clark, Larry

O'Brien, and Frank Valeo—met at 9:30 A.M. in Mike Mansfield's office to get their signals straight. The men had finally come around to the position that Larry O'Brien had held since early February—that Ev Dirksen had no alternative but to support cloture, and that he needed the Democrats as much as they needed him. Therefore, they decided to not give way so easily on any more of his demands; instead they would hang tough.

Dirksen was ready, as always, with some helpful suggestions. First, he said that if an understanding was reached that day, he would like to see the new language mimeographed and sent to all senators. Next, he suggested that the Republicans and Democrats should each caucus with their members to get agreements on the new package. And finally, he felt that the Senate should vote on cloture title by title. Humphrey strongly objected to the last point, stipulating that there must be only one vote for cloture on the entire bill; otherwise there was no use talking any further. Dirksen backed down.

Then Bobby Kennedy zeroed in on the final areas of disagreement. He persuaded Dirksen to discard the idea of a new Title XII that would define the attorney general's powers to handle any resistance to the act. Instead, Kennedy got him to agree to the "pattern and practice" language to Titles II (Public Accommodations) and VII (Equal Employment).

Next, Kennedy got the minority leader to concede that, in Title II, the commission be granted specific authority to recommend that the attorney general take direct enforcement action. Both sides agreed to Karl Mundt's amendment excluding Indian jewelrymakers from the provisions of the bill, which was Mundt's price for cloture.

Finally, the attorney general came down hard on Dirksen's strong objection to the voting fraud provision of Title V (Civil Rights Commission). Kennedy, while agreeing that it did not belong in the bill, explained that he had promised Bill McCulloch to keep it there and so, as Kennedy noted, "it stayed in." Burke Marshall observed that throughout the negotiations, "Robert Kennedy was the lawyer for Bill McCulloch. That's essentially what happened."

While Bobby Kennedy was hitting Dirksen from one side, Joe Clark came at him from the other. By prearrangement with Humphrey, Joe Clark was "hard-nosed." At one point he stalked out of the conference room, pretending disgust with a proposal to modify Title VII. "It's a goddam sellout," shouted the Pennsylvanian as he slammed the door. Turning to Dirksen, Humphrey pleaded, "See what pressure I'm up against? I can't concede any more on this point."

The strategy worked. The remaining differences melted away, and a spirit of harmony engulfed the negotiators. It was a happy trio that emerged victoriously at the end of the long day.

"We have a good agreement," Dirksen announced triumphantly to the press. "The bill is perfectly satisfactory to me," declared the grinning attorney general. "And to me, too," echoed Hubert Humphrey. "We have done nothing to injure the objectives of the bill."

The Leadership Conference representatives, however, were noncommittal. Joe Rauh complained strongly that they had not had an opportunity to see the amendments that Humphrey had accepted. Therefore, said Rauh, they would reserve judgment until they had examined the revisions firsthand.

By the next day, however, reactions were more positive. Nick Katzenbach explained the changes to Emanuel Celler and Bill McCulloch, after which he told Humphrey, "[McCulloch and Celler] are OK, but they won't make any public statements until the Senate has acted." Later that day McCulloch again came over from the House to spend an hour with Dirksen and gave him his word that the package was acceptable. Privately, Joe Rauh and Arnold Aronson, after seeing the amendments, were pleased. "I thought it would be a lot worse," said Rauh, who confided to Humphrey that if the bill passed the Senate as rewritten, "it would be a great victory for civil rights." Aronson agreed, "It was a much stronger bill than we expected." And Jacob Javits, reassuring his liberal colleagues, Democrat and Republican alike, rejoiced that "no title has been emasculated, and the fundamental structure of the bill remains the same."

One group, however, had not been heard from. The Senate's conservative Republicans were suspiciously quiet. And on Friday, when Nick Katzenbach was chatting with Kenneth Keating and a group of Senate staffers, he was asked the key question. "What happens if Dirksen shows the Republican conference the amendments and nobody changes his mind on cloture?" Katzenbach replied, "Marshall and I will cut our throats. [But] I can't believe that Dirksen would go as far as he did unless he is able to produce the votes."

On Monday, May 18, the Senate swung into its 12th week of debate. The day before had marked the 10th anniversary of the

Supreme Court school desegregation decision and was declared a national day of prayer by Catholic youth organizations throughout the country. Inside the Senate the Southerners were still talking; outside Roger Mudd was still interviewing. And 200 clergymen from 41 states descended on the Capitol to see their senators. They were led by Woodrow Wilson's grandson, the Very Reverend Francis Sayre, dean of the Washington Cathedral.

On Tuesday morning senators from both parties gathered in their respective caucus rooms to review the Dirksen amendments to H.R. 7152. They had, the day before, received copies of the 70-page mimeographed document, which showed the original bill with proposed new language underlined and omissions bracketed.

The Democrats met in the old Supreme Court chamber, a small marble-columned hall where the Senate sat until 1860 and which was then occupied by the Supreme Court until 1935. A gilded eagle from Daniel Webster's day looked down on the room as Hubert Humphrey held the floor for most of the meeting, going over the revisions with 49 members of his party. As expected, the southern senators, who had held their own caucus earlier, were ready with objections. Dick Russell exclaimed that Dirksen's amendments made the bill even more obnoxious—"a punitive expedition into the South. It is clearer than ever that this bill is directed at the South and no other part of the country." Sam Ervin doubted that the law could be enforced, comparing it with the Volstead Act of the Prohibition era. Also, as expected, the liberals, while not approving of the compromises with Dirksen, had nowhere else to turn. Joe Clark planned to support the agreement, saying, "It is a good compromise that ought to be accepted." Phil Hart pointed out that the basic question to be answered was "Can I, in all good conscience, support these changes?" The Michigan senator affirmed that he could. Finally, with nonsouthern Democrats expressing no general opposition, Mike Mansfield closed the meeting by praising Hubert Humphrey at great length for his steadfastness.

Twenty-seven Republicans caucused in S-207, the large conference room near the Senate chamber, with Everett Dirksen, assisted by Neil Kennedy, going over 10 of the 11 titles. It was not a placid meeting. The dignified old room was filled with a cacophony of voices raising questions and objections and doubts. Harshest by far was the strident voice of Bourke Hickenlooper, the conservative party elder who openly resented what he considered to be his leader's cavalier high-handedness. The fissure in the Republican ranks, first detected when Hickenlooper criticized Dirksen as a "softie" during the May 6 negotiating session, widened when the senior senator from Iowa stated that it was not until now that he realized how great the powers of the attorney general would be under the bill. "It's a gargantuan thing," Hickenlooper ranted.

Full-scale mutiny under Hickenlooper's leadership suddenly loomed. It was time for action; any good leader could see that. Everett Dirksen, like Martin Luther King a year earlier at Birmingham, knew instinctively that the moment had come for a dramatic incident. The minister had reached for the school children and sent them into battle. The minority leader reached for religion.

It was a newly converted Everett Dirksen who called reporters into his office after the GOP caucus. Open-mouthed, newsmen listened as the senator from Illinois sermonized with evangelistic fervor about the moral basis for the bill. Culling from the wealth of quotations in his notebook, Dirksen likened the inevitability of the passage of H.R. 7152 to a phrase that he said Victor Hugo had written in his diary on the night he died.

"No army is stronger," he quoted, "than an idea whose time has come."

While no diary of Hugo (1802–85) had ever been found and while Dirksen, at various times, attributed the phrase to Disraeli and others, the minority leader's zeal was not at all deterred. (The quote, in fact, comes from Hugo's *Histoire d'un crime*.)

"Today the challenge is here!" Dirksen cried. "It is inescapable. It is time to deal with it!" Gesturing toward the Senate chamber, he finished with a magnificent flourish, "No one on that floor is going to stop this. It is going to happen!" Everett McKinley Dirksen had become the Saint Paul of the civil rights movement. It was his greatest role.

Like a thunderbolt from out of the blue, the minority leader's emergence as a crusader for civil rights was totally unexpected by a majority of those who had followed the course of H.R. 7152 through Congress. Roger Mudd noted that most of his colleagues in the press gallery viewed the junior senator from Illinois as a major opponent of the bill. "Thus," he said, "we were all surprised when he gave his 'time has come' speech." To Ted Moss, Ev Dirksen had been "carrying out on the surface his function as the opposition leader." So Moss, like many of his fellow senators, was unaware of Dirksen's behind-the-scene role on behalf of the bill. For Clarence Mitchell, as he wrote in his 11th letter to Roy Wilkins, the minority leader's apparent change came as a "dramatic development." And Senator Hugh Scott observed that "when Dirksen turned around, he turned around all the way in a very dramatic fashion."

Actually, Dirksen's conversion was no conversion at all. It was simply the last scene in a script whose ending he had written several months before. Because of the divergence in his party, Dirksen lacked the flexibility to effect any significant change in the House-approved bill. To keep peace in both philosophical camps, he had to bring out old H.R. 7152 *in disguise*—which, to maintain liberal support, would retain the substance of the original measure, but rewritten in a way that would assuage the conservatives. It was precisely this kind of document that Dirksen presented his followers on the morning of May 19. That noon, his Sermon on the Mount, in which he trumpeted to the nation that "the time has come," wrung down the curtain on his three-month-long drama.

During the remainder of the week, the Republicans followed their leader, holding caucus after caucus to iron out their differences over the proposed revisions to H.R. 7152. At their second meeting, on Wednesday, Dirksen discussed Title VII (Equal Employment), allowing ample time for analysis of each of its sections. Although the minority leader felt that many doubts had been settled by his amendment to give state agencies original jurisdiction in the handling of employment discrimination complaints, Bourke Hickenlooper again complained, telling reporters that he left the meeting with "serious reservations" about the title. Immediately, speculation arose among the press corps as to what effect Hickenlooper's attitude might have on other Republican conservatives such as Norris Cotton.

As 22 GOP senators gathered on Friday for their third conference, they were armed with three pages of proposed changes that had been drafted in response to points raised during the first two meetings. Various new amendments to the first five titles were discussed, and in several instances the staff was asked to undertake a more detailed study to clear up additional points of disagreement. They also questioned whether the revised H.R. 7152 should be introduced in the Senate as a new bill, as a substitute to the House-passed measure, or as an amendment "in the nature of a substitute." They agreed, however, that whichever procedure was followed, it should be sponsored jointly by Mansfield, Dirksen, Humphrey, and Kuchel. A fourth caucus was scheduled for the following Monday morning.

On Monday, May 25, as the Senate staggered into its 12th week of debate, the temperature was 75 degrees and there was a 15-mile-an-hour wind on Capitol Hill. Roger Mudd was now broadcasting from the sidewalk across from the Capitol. (He was moved from the east front steps after southern senators complained that the crowds he was attracting blocked the entrance to the building.) The divinity students were in their 864th hour at the Lincoln Memorial; the Southerners were still holding the Senate floor; and Republican senators, gathering for their fourth caucus, were discussing Dwight D. Eisenhower's "A Personal Statement," which had appeared on page one of the *New York Herald Tribune* that morning.

"Right now," wrote the former president, "the nation's most critical domestic challenge involves man's relations to his government and also to his neighbor—the issue of civil rights. The Republican Party was born of a crusading concern for human dignity; it retains that concern today." Eisenhower pointed out that as members of the party of Lincoln, "we Republicans have a particular obligation to be vigorous in the furtherance of civil rights. In this critical area, I have been especially proud of the dramatic leadership given by Republicans in Congress these past two years."

During two conferences that lasted all day, Everett Dirksen led 20 recalcitrant Republicans down the twisting path toward consensus. He discussed, argued, pleaded, promised, and compromised until, finally, as the fifth caucus ended late that afternoon, it began to appear that the minority leader, by keeping his feet in both camps, had achieved what many thought impossible.

"I think we have consensus," said John Sherman Cooper in wonderment. "I believe that consensus has been arrived at," parroted Jacob Javits.

Lyndon Johnson, meanwhile, was busily twisting a few more arms. On Tuesday morning, Howard Cannon, at the president's request, came to the Oval Office. Cannon, a highly decorated World War II pilot who evaded capture for 42 days after being shot down behind the German lines in Holland, was ending his first term in the Senate. When he had arrived in Washington in 1959 as a newly elected senator from Nevada, majority leader Lyndon Johnson had befriended him, placing him on the Armed Services Committee and on Johnson's own Science-Aerospace Committee. Now Cannon's old friend asked him for his vote on cloture. "It wasn't a sell type meeting," Cannon conceded. "He didn't push as hard on this as he did on other things." But Johnson did stress the importance of making progress in the civil rights area and of Cannon's vote on cloture.

The president used a similarly low-key approach several days later in a telephone call to J. Howard Edmondson, a lame duck who had been defeated in the recent Oklahoma Democratic primary. Johnson had discretely helped Edmondson during the election by announcing several presidential appointments the senator had recommended. "But Johnson did not mention this during his conversation with Howard," said Edmondson's administrative assistant, John Criswell. "Nor was there any specific overtures of a trade or a quid pro quo. The president argued the case for cloture on its merits. He sought to persuade Howard that he should vote for it for the good of the country."

On Tuesday Hubert Humphrey, in keeping with his long-held plan to make Everett Dirksen the hero of the civil rights epic, gave the minority leader the honor of introducing the revised version of H.R. 7152. The press immediately labeled the 74-page document the "Dirksen substitute." In his remarks to the Senate, the minority leader observed:

> As a result of various conferences and by the process of give and take, we have at long last fashioned what we think is a workable bill. . . . I believe this is a salable piece of work, one that is infinitely better than what came to us from the House. . . . Frankly, I believe it is a good measure and would take us well down the road and will prove to be fair, equitable, and easy of administration.

Dirksen finished by pointing out that the Senate had been considering the bill for 64 days; then he threw down the gauntlet for cloture. "We have now reached the point where there must be action."

Hubert Humphrey had the job of explaining the basic differences between the House-passed bill and the Dirksen substitute. The new version, said Humphrey, was an improvement because it included a provision for local and state authorities to seek compliance with the law, wherever possible, through voluntary methods; then through the law if the voluntary methods fail. "If voluntary methods and local enforcement should both fail," continued the majority whip, "we then have the authority to seek compliance with the law through action by the federal government in the courts of law. This is a commonsense and just balance of federal and state responsibility."

Humphrey pointed out that the principal changes were to be found in Titles II, V, VI, and VII. "In each of them, and particularly in Titles II and VII, local and state responsibilities are emphasized, not merely local and state rights." Two of the three controversial provisions adopted by the House during floor consideration of H.R. 7152—the "sex" and "Communist" amendments—were retained. The "atheist" amendment, opposed by the American Civil Liberties Union, was dropped. Added to Title IX (Judicial Appeal) was a provision designed to appeal to Republicans' historical ties to the 14th Amendment by permitting the attorney general to intervene in cases filed by those seeking protection of this amendment.

An angry Dick Russell rose to castigate Everett Dirksen for his role in forging the document.

> Unless I am badly fooled, he has killed off a rapidly growing Republican Party in the South, at least so far as his party's prospects in the presidential campaign are concerned.... The bill now has been stripped of any pretense.... It stands as purely a sectional bill. As one who lives in the South, as one who has never been ashamed of being a Southerner, and as one who believes that the people in the South are as good citizens as people anywhere else in the country, I resent this political foray.

Reactions to the Dirksen substitute, among civil rights advocates, were good. The Justice Department, in a memorandum to the president, noted that while "many changes have been made in the bill, most of them are designed simply to clarify what was already understood to be the meaning of the text." The Leadership Conference of Civil Rights took a similar view in a bulletin to member organizations: "Coverage in all the titles is essentially what it was in H.R. 7152 as it passed the House, and the enforcement provisions are still intact." And Clark MacGregor, who helped draft the House measure as a member of the Judiciary Committee, commented that Dirksen

> basically agreed with us but he felt he had to put his stamp of authority on a lot of little niggling amendments that really didn't amount to much, so that the bill would come into law as a Dirksen bill and, more importantly, that he would be perceived as pouring the healing salve on the whole controversy. He did that very well. In other words, he would be perceived as making substantial changes in the bill and, on analysis, most of the amendments didn't amount to much.

189

On Monday, June 1, as the Senate blearily faced its 13th week of debate on H.R. 7152, hot summer weather had descended on Washington. Members of the Senate returned to the chamber after a three-day Memorial Day recess. Mike Mansfield announced that a cloture petition would be filed the next Saturday, with the vote occurring one hour after the Senate convened on Tuesday, June 9. One of the main reasons for delay was to wait until after the June 2 primaries. The California contest was crucial because it would bring to a climax the Barry Goldwater–Nelson Rockefeller battle for the Republican presidential nomination. This would let the pro-Goldwater senators, such as Carl Curtis, escape the embarrassment of taking a stand against their presidential candidate colleague, who was openly opposed to cloture.

That afternoon Dick Russell, without giving Mike Mansfield more than 20 minutes' notice, announced that he felt the time had come to vote on some of the pending jury trial amendments. At a meeting in Mansfield's office later that day, the majority leader decided to avoid a vote and "bull through this week for the scheduled cloture vote on June 9." Mike Mansfield and Hubert Humphrey would have to operate for the time being without their new partner, however, for Everett Dirksen took ill and went to his Virginia farm for a few days of rest.

For the rest of that first week in June, the Senate floor sessions were dominated by pro-civil rights senators explaining the Dirksen revisions. Dick Russell continued to press for a vote on the jury trial amendments, but Mike Mansfield stalled, saying that the need to educate the membership about the changes made it "impossible to get any votes this week."

On Thursday, seeing his own delaying tactics used against him, Russell accused Mansfield of conducting a "counter filibuster" and plaintively inquired, "Why does he wish to go over until next week?" Hubert Humphrey conceded privately, "Simply because we need more time to nail down those cloture votes."

An important step in this direction occurred that Thursday when Jack Miller, the conservative Iowa Republican, announced his support for the cloture motion. Miller had been the target of intense church lobbying. "The largest church in Iowa [is] the Methodist church," he remarked. "The Methodist ministers and lay leaders were very, very strong for this bill. . .and other church groups, too,. . .the Catholics, the Presbyterians, and the Jewish groups." But perhaps the most decisive influence of all was the Archbishop of Dubuque, the Very Reverend James J. Byrne, who urged Miller, a Catholic and former Notre Dame University law professor, to support cloture and the bill. This coincided with Miller's own philosophy that "we ought to bend over backward to make up for what happened over the past hundred years. So I felt I was on strong grounds."

When Everett Dirksen returned to his office on Friday, he discovered an uprising among his troops and informed Humphrey that suddenly the prospects for cloture did not look so good. At a rump meeting that morning, Bourke Hickenlooper led the 20 GOP conservatives in finding fault with H.R. 7152. Norris Cotton grumbled that Dirksen's substitute was written without giving him and others much of a chance to get their own amendments included. His charge was echoed by Roman Hruska. The disgruntled Republicans insisted that before there could be a vote on cloture, they be allowed to propose their own amendments.

Some of Hickenlooper's colleagues attributed his rebellion to his jealousy of Dirksen. "He tended to be a choleric and explosive type," said Hugh Scott. "He had been in the Senate longer than Dirksen, so Hickenlooper had seniority over him. He was a very prideful person. Certainly all the public attention and glory was going to Dirksen." Seniority undoubtedly played a major part in the differences between the minority leader and the Iowa conservative. Hickenlooper, said Jim Pearson, belonged to the "seniority-is-everything school," which demanded that junior senators, even those in the leadership, defer to their elders. As Jack Miller noted, "Bourke had the feeling that without talking to a number of his older colleagues, like himself, Everett had the tendency to run off and sit down with Hubert and sort of take over as representing the Republicans in the Senate without having done perhaps as much coordination as he might have.... To the average observer there was no friction, but in the corridors and cloakroom there were comments which indicated [otherwise]."

That afternoon Hickenlooper made his thrust. First, he proposed that Mike Mansfield move the cloture vote from Tuesday to Wednesday, June 10, because many of the senators would be attending the governors' conference in Cleveland on Monday. After Mansfield agreed to change the date, Hickenlooper asked unanimous consent to vote on three new amendments on Tuesday: Thruston Morton's revised jury trial amendment, Norris Cotton's proposal to restrict coverage of Title VII (Equal Employment) to employers of 100 or more, and his own amendment to delete all provisions of the bill relating to assistance for desegregating public schools. There was instant panic on both sides of the issue, with neither Northerners nor Southerners knowing quite how to react. If Mansfield, Humphrey, or Dirksen objected, Hickenlooper and his followers might retaliate by voting against cloture. If Russell objected, he might suffer the opposite fate. Dick Russell quickly suggested that they defer deciding on the motion until the next day, giving the rival teams time to figure out what to do.

Later that evening, despite this new monkey wrench in the works, Clarence Mitchell sent an optimistic telegram to Roy Wilkins:

> Our latest count is 64 votes. Prospects for the additional two look good [he assumed that bed-ridden Senator Engle would be absent]. As of now the two additional votes should come from among the following: Democrats: Bible (Nev.), Edmondson (Okla.), Gore (Tenn.), Hayden (Ariz), Walters (Tenn.), and Yarborough (Tex.), Republicans: Bennett (Utah), Curtis (Neb.), Hruska (Neb.), Williams (Del.), and Young (N.D.).

Overnight both sides decided that their best reaction to Hickenlooper was no reaction at all. After the Senate was called to order on Saturday, the senior senator from Iowa again offered his motion: that three amendments, after four hours of debate on each, be voted on Tuesday, June 9, the day before the cloture vote. No objection was raised.

As a matter of fact, the overnight delay had given Hubert Humphrey a chance to do some fast nocturnal bargaining. In exchange for agreeing to consider the new amendments, he extracted cloture commitments from Karl Mundt, Roman Hruska, and Norris Cotton. "I knew if Hruska would join us, so would Curtis," said Humphrey. Hruska's promise was not unexpected; he had served with Everett Dirksen on the Judiciary Committee and was the minority leader's closest Senate crony. Each evening he would drop by Dirksen's office for a convivial drink. "He was to Everett Dirksen," observed Charlie Ferris, "what Hubert Humphrey was to Mike Mansfield." It seemed unlikely, then, that Hruska would sever this bond by voting against his old friend on such a major issue.

Nick Katzenbach had often joined Dirksen and Hruska during their cocktail hour, using the occasion to engage in a little sociable negotiating. It proved to be a somewhat dubious tactic. "I would get Everett Dirksen's agreement in the evening over bourbon," commented the deputy attorney general, "but by the next morning he had forgotten it. I almost ruined my liver in the process."

On Saturday morning Dick Russell chided Hubert Humphrey for being unfair. While Humphrey had agreed to Hickenlooper's request, he had failed to cooperate with Russell earlier in the week when Russell wanted to vote on one or more of the pending jury trial amendments. "Well, Dick," replied the majority whip candidly, "you haven't any votes to give us for cloture and these fellows do."

The showdown was approaching. After 13 weeks and some four million words of the longest filibuster in history, it was almost time for the Senate to face itself and the American people. But there was now more at stake than the bill itself. While most senators and a majority of the American people favored passage of H.R. 7152, the Senate had for so long been incapable of acting. This impotency raised serious doubts among many people about the relevancy of the United States Senate in mid-twentieth-century America. At issue, therefore, was not only whether civil rights would be secured for all Americans but whether the Senate was, indeed, the "world's greatest deliberative body" or merely a withered legislative limb.

Seven

Triumph in the Senate

HIGH NOON on Capitol Hill was warm, humid, and teeming with tourists on Monday, June 8. As 56 senators gathered in their cool chamber to answer the opening quorum call, their minds were not only on the approaching cloture vote but also on two other events that had occurred over the weekend. The Bureau of Labor Statistics had announced the jobless rate in May had declined to 5.1 percent of the work force, a five-year low. This vindicated those senators who had voted for the tax cut in March, which economists generally agreed produced the drop in unemployment. On a gloomier note, however, two U.S. aircraft had been shot down over Laos on two successive days. This was additional evidence that the administration's policies in Southeast Asia were threatening to engulf the United States in a much wider scale military operation than was originally foreseen.

Shortly after the Senate convened, the acting president pro tempore, Lee Metcalf, recognized Mike Mansfield. As the majority leader rose at his desk, he was, as usual, emotionless. The press often criticized Mansfield for his passive style of leadership, but the chiding never bothered him; he was very secure in his role. The senator from Montana was a great believer in letting issues play themselves out. There was a time to wait and a time to act. The time to act on cloture had arrived.

"Mr. President," stated the majority leader, "I send to the desk a motion on House bill 7152. 'We, the undersigned Senators, in accordance with the provisions of Rule XXII of the Standing

Rules of the Senate, hereby move to bring to a close the debate on the bill [H.R. 7152].' '' The cloture motion that Mansfield presented was signed by 27 Democrats and 11 Republicans and would be voted upon at 10:00 Wednesday morning, after the Senate waited the required two days. In the meantime, the Senate planned to debate and vote on three amendments—offered by Senators Morton, Cotton, and Hickenlooper—which the latter insisted be heard. The rest of Monday afternoon was spent discussing the Morton amendment. In a memo to Larry O'Brien for use at the White House–congressional leaders' breakfast the next morning, Nick Katzenbach predicted a close vote on the Morton and Cotton amendments and the defeat of the Hickenlooper amendment.

The president's Tuesday began with a note from his secretary, Juanita Roberts: "22 years ago today you were flying the [World War II] mission over New Guinea." During breakfast O'Brien told Johnson of Mike Manatos's cloture "head count." O'Brien's chief Senate operative showed 42 Democrats (including Hayden, if needed) and 23 Republicans "for" cloture. That meant they had 65 of the 67 votes needed. The two additional votes would have to come out of the "probables" or "possibles." Edmondson and Walters were listed as "probable Democrats," Yarborough as a "possible Democrat," and Bennett, Curtis, Hickenlooper, Jordan (Idaho), Mechem (N. Mex.), Williams, and Young (N.Dak.) as "possible Republicans."

When the Senate convened at 10:00 A.M. Tuesday, its first order of business was a vote on the Morton amendment, which provided that all defendants in criminal contempt cases would be entitled to a trial by jury, except in those cases involving Title I (Voting Rights). It carried by a 51–48 margin. (Only terminally ill Clair Engle was not in the chamber to vote.) The Hickenlooper amendment, which sought to delete the authority of the commissioner of education to finance technical and training assistance in the preparation, adoption, and implementation of school desegregation plans, was rejected 40–56. The Cotton amendment, which increased to 100 the number of employees a firm must have before it would be subjected to the provisions of Title VII (Equal Employment), was handily defeated, 34–63. This cleared away all business for the cloture vote the next morning.

The last gasp of the filibuster began at 7:38 P.M., when Robert Byrd stood up at his desk and began to read an 800-page speech explaining why the Senate should not invoke cloture. Byrd, a former member of the Ku Klux Klan, had stated in a December 7, 1963, letter to the newly installed President Lyndon Johnson that he opposed H.R. 7152 because it "impinges upon the civil and constitutional rights of white people." Reminding Johnson of the 1960 presidential primary—"I stood with you when the going was rough in West Virginia and I was subject to scorn and ridicule"—Byrd had asked the president for his help. "There are those who would now curry your favor but who have never shown any interest in you and very little interest in me before the tragic event [Kennedy's death]." Members of the Senate realized that Byrd would probably talk all night.

As the Senate settled in for the anticipated all-night session, Hubert Humphrey felt confident enough to leave the Capitol for a relaxed dinner at the nearby Monocle Restaurant with reporter Andrew Glass of the *New York Herald Tribune*. Humphrey confided to Glass that he had one vote, including Clair Engle, to spare for cloture. He conveyed this same information to the president when Johnson telephoned him from the White House at 7:30 P.M.

"We have the votes," Humphrey reported enthusiastically. Johnson said he hoped so but still expected difficulty. The whip assured him that things looked good. And later that evening, when Humphrey learned that John Williams and Bourke Hickenlooper planned to support cloture, he called the president back to tell him that the two additional votes all but guaranteed victory.

Hubert Humphrey stayed up all night preparing for the morning's vote. More than an hour before the session was scheduled to start, his office was crowded with reporters and wire service representatives, all anxious for any final comments. His friend Cecil E. Newman, editor of a black weekly, *The Saint Paul Recorder,* observed that Humphrey, despite his lack of sleep, was his usual "exuberant, optimistic, bouncy self." At 9:00 A.M. they shared a pitcher of orange juice, with the whip raising his glass in a toast.

Then Humphrey made three last-minute calls to Ralph Yarborough, Howard Cannon, and Howard Edmondson to try to clinch their votes. Although Cannon and Edmondson had been previously contacted by the president, the ill feeling between Yarborough and Johnson precluded any direct communication between these two Texas politicians. "I didn't need to be told by them how to vote," stated Yarborough. "My philosophy on civil rights was set long before Lyndon B. Johnson and Hubert Humphrey entered the picture. I looked upon them as young men."

Humphrey left his office to go to the floor. On his way out, hearing of Carl Curtis's decision to support cloture, he handed Phil Hart a note bearing the number 69. Curtis had been influenced by his fellow Nebraskan, Roman Hruska, a confidant of Everett Dirksen. "Although there often was rivalry between senators from the same state, Roman and I got along well together," said Curtis. In the field of tax legislation, Hruska would seek guidance from Curtis, a member of the Finance Committee. On judiciary matters, for which he admittedly had little time for study, Curtis looked to Hruska. "He was my lawyer on the Judiciary Committee," Curtis remarked.

While Robert Byrd had been filibustering the night away, Everett Dirksen went home to Broad Run Farms in Sterling, Virginia, 32 miles from the Capitol. He and his wife, Louella, stayed up late that evening while he put the finishing touches on the 12-page speech he planned to deliver in the morning. The minority leader arose at 5:00 A.M. and, after a light breakfast, went out to his garden to clip some long-stemmed roses to take to the office. Leaving the farm shortly after 8:00 A.M. in his chauffeur-driven limousine, Dirksen arrived at the Senate just as Byrd was completing his marathon address of 14 hours and 13 minutes, the longest in the entire debate. It ended at 9:51 A.M., just 9 minutes before the Senate was scheduled to convene for the historic vote on H.R. 7152.

Precisely at 10:00 A.M. on Wednesday, June 10 (still the legislative day of March 30, 1964), Lee Metcalf called the Senate to order. One hundred and fifty standees, including many House members, lined the walls of the Senate chamber. The galleries were packed, although only six blacks were in the audience, including Cecil Newman and Clarence Mitchell, seated in the second row. Mike Mansfield delivered a short speech and then read a lengthy letter from a 29-year-old Montana constituent, a mother of four children. "I am only one person, one woman," she wrote. "I wish there was something I could do to help. The only way I know how to start is to educate my children that justice and freedom and ambition are not merely privileges, but their birthrights."

After Mansfield had consumed 12½ minutes, the chair recognized Richard Russell. "Mr. President," said the Georgian,

> those of us who have opposed this bill have done so from a profound conviction that the bill not only is contrary to the spirit of the Constitution of the United States, but also violates the letter of the Constitution.

We have opposed it because the broad abdication of power and authority by the legislative branch that it provides would destroy forever the doctrine of separation of powers. This great doctrine was devised by our forefathers as a bulwark against tyranny; and over the years it has protected our liberties and way of life.

During his 30-minute speech, Russell's demeanor, said Cecil Newman, "lacked the fire of conviction which had marked his former contests against rights bills. . . . It seemed to us as we listened to the venerable segregationist that we were witnessing the end of an era."

Mike Mansfield then yielded two minutes to Hubert Humphrey. Wearing a red rose in his lapel, the majority whip suggested that, by their votes, members of the Senate would "make that dream of full freedom, full justice, and full citizenship for every American a reality. . . and it will be remembered until the ending of the world."

Then it was Everett Dirksen's turn. First he introduced a new substitute package containing the provisions of the Morton amendment, which the Senate had adopted the previous day. Then he spoke for 15 minutes in a low, even tone, making no attempt at his customary oratorical flourishes. As he talked, it was evident that the minority leader did not feel well. Actually, he had been plagued for some time with ill health, including a peptic ulcer that flared up now and then, requiring hospitalization. He always kept a supply of medicine in his Senate desk. But now, the ordeal of driving himself through 14-, 15-, and 16-hour days to fulfill his historic mission had taken its toll. As he stood at his desk, his face was pale and deeply etched, the high-spirited glow gone. Twice he gulped pills handed him by a page.

"There are many reasons," he said quietly, "why cloture should be invoked and a good civil rights measure enacted." He then repeated his favorite vignette but changed the phraseology from that of his May 19 press conference. "It is said that on the night he died, Victor Hugo wrote in his diary substantially this sentiment: 'Stronger than all the armies is an idea whose time has come.' The time has come for equality of opportunity in sharing in government, in education, and in employment. It must not be stayed or denied." Culling from his bulging notebook, he cited other landmark legislation, such as the pure food and drugs law, creation of the civil service system, the eight-hour workday, the direct election of senators, and women's right to vote—all of which ultimately became law because their "time had come."

"The time of the senator from Illinois has expired. All time has expired," announced Lee Metcalf at 11:00 A.M.

As Everett Dirksen sat down at his front row desk, Hubert Humphrey crossed the aisle and extended his hand in congratulations. Then, after a quorum was established, Metcalf stated the long-awaited words. "The chair submits to the Senate, without debate, the question: Is it the sense of the Senate that the debate shall be brought to a close? The Secretary will call the roll."

As the Secretary of the Senate Felton M. Johnston called the role, each member kept his own tally sheet. So did many spectators, in violation of Senate rules. But no one stopped them. Standing out in the 100-degree temperature with a chart in his hand, CBS's Roger Mudd, receiving a telephone replay from the Senate press gallery, announced on the air each vote as it was cast.

When Johnston reached the name "Engle," the California senator, who had been pushed into the chamber only minutes earlier in a wheelchair and was desperately ill from the advanced stages of cancer, failed to respond. There was a painfully moving moment of silence. Finally, Clair Engle, unable to speak, feebly lifted his left hand three times and pointed toward his eye.

"I guess that means aye," murmured the clerk. He recorded Engle accordingly, while tears stood in other eyes throughout the Senate. The roll call continued. By 11:15 A.M., 66 votes had been cast for cloture.

"Williams," called the clerk.

"Aye," called the senator from Delaware.

It was the 67th vote. A sigh of relief resounded throughout the chamber. Raising his arms over his head, Hubert Humphrey looked up into the gallery and winked while reporters in the reserved press section scattered to telephone the results to their home offices. After four additional senators voted in favor of cloture, Carl Hayden, who had not responded when his name was called the first time, emerged from the cloakroom, cane in hand. Hayden had been prepared to support cloture if his vote was needed, but he was absolved from breaking his long-standing tradition when Mike Mansfield gave him the good news. "It's all right, Carl," said Mansfield. "We're in." The dean of the Senate then voted no.

The final tally was 71–29, 4 more than the required two-thirds.

And so, after 534 hours, 1 minute, and 51 seconds, the longest filibuster in the history of the United States Senate was broken. The final count announced by the chair showed 44 Democrats and 27 Republicans voting for cloture with 23 Democrats—20 from the South—and only 6 Republicans opposed. It was only the sixth time cloture had been invoked, the first time in 12 attempts for a civil rights measure. Vital to this success were western Democrats and conservative Republicans who previously had been listed as "doubtful."

Lyndon Johnson won over Howard Edmondson and Howard Cannon. Mike Mansfield and Hubert Humphrey, without the help of direct presidential pleading, received critical support from four other key western Democrats—Clinton Anderson, Ernest Gruening, E. L. Bartlett, and A. S. Monroney—who Joe Rauh, on February 14, had facetiously hoped would "absent themselves" during the cloture vote. Anderson, secretary of agriculture under Harry Truman, voted for the fourth time in four years in favor of a civil rights cloture, as did Ernest Gruening. But Gruening, a nonpracticing physician who had been editor of the *Nation* and the *New York Post*, and his Alaska colleague, E. L. Bartlett, had created considerable concern because they had opposed cloture on the communications bill in 1962. Bartlett, in addition, had voted twice that year against cloture on the literacy bill. But Lyndon Johnson's response to the Good Friday, March 27, Alaska earthquake, which claimed 115 lives and $311 million in property damage, removed any doubts as to how Gruening and Bartlett would vote on cloture this time. After the president had made Air Force Two available to the two senators and requested $50 million in Emergency Relief and another $22.5 million in Transitional Grants for Alaska, Gruening told Humphrey on May 13, "I am prepared, before long, to vote for cloture."

A. S. (Mike) Monroney of Oklahoma was not a great admirer of Lyndon Johnson, openly opposing his 1961 quest to preside over the Democratic senatorial caucus. He also had voted against all three civil rights cloture motions in 1960 and 1962. But, explained his legislative assistant, Mary Ann Miller, by 1964, after constant hounding by Larry O'Brien, Monroney had concluded "that his anti-cloture position would have to give way in favor of cloture on behalf of civil rights."

Alan Bible, who had been listed as a "possible" in Clarence Mitchell's June 5 telegram, proved a disappointment. But Bible had a personal stake in the continued effectiveness of the filibuster; he viewed it as the best bet for stopping antigambling legislation, which, if passed by Congress, would threaten the livelihood of many of his Nevada constituents.

The other 12 "Johnson western colleagues" (as they were described on February 14 by Phil Hart's legislative assistant, Bill Welsh) were less worrisome to Mansfield and Humphrey. None had a 1963 ADA Liberal Quotient Rating of less than 65 percent (nine were over 80 percent). All had cosponsored John Kennedy's 1963 proposal with its public accommodations section. While several were troubled by voting for cloture—"They made a 'thing' out of it back home," said Gale McGee—the protracted debate ultimately provided them with the rationale for supporting it. Each could explain, as Ted Moss did, that "I favored full debate, but in the long run the majority had to prevail." When the roll call ended, Humphrey's tally sheet showed that he had succeeded in corralling 19 of 21 western Democratic votes for cloture (including Mansfield), thus breeching the long-standing western–southern coalition in which the South often received western votes in exchange for southern support on western water projects.

Lyndon Johnson, Robert Kennedy, Mike Mansfield, and Hubert Humphrey realized from the outset that the geographically divided Senate Democrats would fall short of producing cloture by more than 20 votes. They knew, therefore, that the remaining support had to be provided by at least 23 to 25 of the Senate's 33 Republicans. The key, as the administration and Senate Democratic leaders so clearly foresaw, was Everett Dirksen. This, explained Hubert Humphrey, is why "I courted Dirksen almost as persistently as I did Muriel. I was told by Democrats a number of times that Dirksen was stealing the show, that I should be out in front. I knew if I tried to push myself any more than I did, that the bill would fail. Dirksen had the right to be out in front, and I gave him every opportunity to do so...."

Dirksen's concern was not with the GOP's 12 liberal-to-moderate senators. As expected, they all voted for cloture. But for cloture to succeed, he would have to snare at least 11 of his 20 conservative Republican colleagues. When the roll call ended, 14 had voted with him. In bringing these conservatives into his camp, the minority leader pursued two tactics.

First, while not diluting the federal enforcement powers of H.R. 7152, Dirksen was able, during the early May negotiating sessions, to redirect the bill's focus in a way that placated the states' rights instincts of his more conservative flock. Twenty states already had enacted both public accommodations and equal employment opportunity laws, while another dozen had adopted either one or the other. To Republicans who came from these states, Dirksen argued that passage of H.R. 7152 would not impose on their constituents any civil rights restrictions that did not already exist in their respective jurisdictions. He also reminded them that the package provided for federal intervention in alleged instances of discrimination only after local and state remedies had been exhausted. This appeal helped gain cloture votes from 16 of the 17 GOP senators from states that had both public accommodations and fair employment statutes. Eight of the 10 Republicans who represented states with either one or the other law also supported cloture.

Second, Dirksen recognized that politicians often defend their positions by pointing to others who have taken a similar stand. The minority leader therefore used his reputation as a conservative to provide a needed crutch for those colleagues who otherwise might have found it difficult to explain their vote for cloture. "I supported civil rights legislation personally," said J. Caleb Boggs (R-Del.), "but there was a lot of opposition to the bill in my state. Dirksen was a wonderful leader. He was able to understand our problems and operated in such a way that it made it easier for me to vote for cloture."

Obviously, external factors contributed to Dirksen's success in obtaining 27 Republican votes for cloture. As he himself stated on the Senate floor that morning, civil rights "has been the living faith of our party. Do we forsake this article of faith, now that equality's time has come or do we stand up for it and insure the survival of our party and its ultimate victory?"

Further, many Republican senators felt strongly about racial discrimination, often because of personal experience. John Williams, regarded by many as the "watchdog of the treasury," was upset to learn that a group of Delaware students, on their way to Washington to visit his office, was denied service at a restaurant because blacks were in the party. "That's wrong," he told Carl Curtis, and despite the problem it might cause him among his conservative constituents, he cast his vote for cloture.

Dirksen also benefited from the natural ability of all politicians to sniff the winds of shifting public opinion. A Gallup poll conducted during the period May 22–27 showed that 65 percent of nonsouthern voters would support congressional candidates who took a strong stand in favor of civil rights. When coupled with a massive outpouring of personal concern regarding the issue—in May, Kenneth Keating received 31,762 letters in favor of H.R. 7152 and only 1,292 against, a pattern similar to that observed in other Senate offices—the sentiments reflected by this survey could not be easily ignored.

Complementing this letter-writing deluge was the "influential citizen" strategy undertaken by the church groups. Milton Young, who previously had heard very little about civil rights from his North Dakota constituents, suddenly received numerous contacts from his churchgoing people. Church lobbyists prevailed upon the pastor of Omaha's First Methodist Church to ask one of his parishoners, a prominent banker, to contact Carl Curtis. A supporter of Curtis in past elections, the banker urged the Nebraska senator to vote for cloture. "Inasmuch as the pastor was not used to going to the banker for favors and the banker was not used to going to senators on a social issue, we couldn't write a script for such an approach," said Jim Hamilton of the National Council of Churches. "At that level, it had to be based on friendship."

Finally, the interminable debate had become a source of embarrassment to many Republicans. As Frank Valeo commented, "The last thing a senator wants is to have the Senate look foolish.... Cloture was the only answer." Thus, Norris Cotton, who believed that H.R. 7152 struck "at the heart of free government," voted nevertheless for cloture. He stated that he had "no appetite to explain back home why, after twelve weeks, I would help to defer action on this bill."

To Dick Russell, however, Lyndon Johnson had "more to do with [cloture's] success than any other man." Johnson's role was comparable to the field commander whose headquarters was a thousand miles from the battlefield: while coordinating strategy, he was far removed from the firing line. But the president's outspokenness and public advocacy constantly kept civil rights before the country as a burning moral issue. Despite being anxious to get on with his Great Society program, Johnson allowed the Senate to operate uninterruptedly for several months without considering other major legislation. This was a key ingredient in breaking the filibuster. Moreover, his refusal to compromise and his constant pressure on Hubert Humphrey to remain firm prevented the Southerners from trading the filibuster for a weakened bill.

After the momentous cloture vote, the victors had no time to pause and rejoice. The battle on the Senate floor continued. With the Senate operating now under cloture, the rules allowed each member to speak for up to an hour, for a maximum of 100 hours, before the final vote on the bill. Immediately, the Southerners launched their postcloture fight. And Hubert Humphrey, bone tired from having been up all night and groggy with the mental fatigue that inevitably follows a great triumph, suddenly realized that he was not prepared to fend off the continuing southern raids on the bill.

At the time of the cloture vote, Russell Long's (D-La.) perfecting amendment to the Talmadge jury trial proposal was the pending order of business. Following cloture, however, Long withdrew his amendment, after which Sam Ervin called up his own amendment prohibiting the bill from putting a person "twice in jeopardy for the same act or omission." In effect, Ervin's amendment would preclude the United States government from trying a defendant (a restaurant owner, for example), for violating a federal public accommodations law if that person had been acquitted in a sympathetic state court for the same transgression. "Adoption of this amendment would have gutted the bill," commented John Stewart.

After the roll call on the Ervin amendment, the acting president, on the advice of the clerk, announced its defeat, 47–48. This prompted Herman Talmadge to withdraw his amendment. A recalculation, however, showed that the Ervin amendment had been approved, 49–48. But since Talmadge's amendment, to which Ervin's was attached, had been withdrawn, Ervin's proposal became moot. This meant that the new Dirksen substitute bill became the pending business of the Senate. Therefore, any of the 560 previously introduced amendments that were eligible to be called up before the 100-hour time limit expired would be directed to the leadership-approved Dirksen bill. After the first amendment—Dick Russell's provision that November 15, 1965, be made the effective date of Title II—had been defeated, 40–59, Mike Mansfield felt it was time to "regroup, rethink, and recollect." At 12:14 P.M. the Senate recessed for a few hours.

As a disheartened Russell left the chamber, he was joined by Clarence Mitchell, who, in a conciliatory gesture, walked with the defeated gladiator to his Senate office. During their conversation Russell praised Hubert Humphrey for his fairness, his willingness to permit opponents of H.R. 7152 to have their say, and his refusal to use parliamentary tactics that might have embarrassed southern senators. Russell told Mitchell that without the lengthy floor fight which, thanks to Humphrey's patience, he and others were able to wage, the bill would not be enforceable in the South. But, he felt, having seen their senators defeated in a fair legislative battle, Southerners would now accept Congress's verdict and abide by the law which would soon be enacted. Russell emphasized this point in letters to his constituents. "It is the law of the Senate and we must abide by it," he wrote to Frank H. Williams of Columbus, Georgia. And in other communications he urged Georgians "to refrain from violence in dealing with this act."

Dick Russell had not deceived himself about defeat; he saw it coming. The Senate's youngest member when he took the oath of office on January 12, 1933, he spent 31 of his 66 years in its vaulted chambers. Before coming to Washington, Russell had memorized the Constitution, the Declaration of Independence, and all of the Senate's rules. Armed with this knowledge, he soon became the chamber's most skilled parliamentarian, floor managing New Deal legislation that created the Rural Electrification Administration, the Farmers Home Administration, and the school lunch program. Of his former senate colleague, Harry Truman once said, "Dick Russell had ability, integrity, and honesty. He was one of the best-informed men in the Senate and perhaps the best-informed on the agricultural situation in the nation. [He] was always able to present any problem in a clear and straightforward manner so that everyone understood it.... I believe that if Russell had been from Indiana or Missouri or Kentucky, he may very well have been President of the United States."

Chairman of the Armed Services Committee and a member of the powerful Appropriations and Democratic Steering committees, Russell was the unofficial leader of the southern caucus, which was composed of senators representing the 11 states of the Confederacy. In these "insider" positions, he influenced committee assignments, and without his support, no Democrat could be elected party whip or floor leader. Consequently, Dick Russell had been the first person Lyndon Johnson contacted after the 1952 electoral defeat of Ernest W. McFarland (D-Ariz.), the senate majority leader. On January 3, 1953, with Russell's early endorsement, the lanky Texan was named Senate minority leader in the Republican-controlled 83d Congress. During his two years as minority leader and six years as majority leader, Johnson rarely made a move without first consulting his Georgia mentor.

Although, according to Lady Bird Johnson, Dick Russell "was not a man you could be intimate with—he was a loner," the Georgian developed a close friendship with the Texas senator and his family. A frequent dinner guest at The Elms, the southern bachelor was affectionately called "Uncle Dick" by the Johnsons' two daughters. But it was the Senate to whom he was married, and sports and history were his hobbies. A friend of baseball's legendary "Georgia Peach," Ty Cobb, Russell frequently attended Washington Senators' baseball games and could recite from memory the batting average of each player. And according to his colleagues, he had a most remarkable knowledge of Civil War history.

A few hours after Lyndon Johnson returned to Washington after John Kennedy's death on November 22, 1963, the new president called his former Senate sponsor and, during their conversation, poured out all the terrible details of the assassination. Three days later Russell came to lunch at the White House, and on Sunday, January 12, he spent the day with the Johnsons at Camp David, amazing them with his descriptions of what had occurred in the surrounding Maryland countryside during the Civil War. During the next two weeks, by presidential request, the two old friends met five times at the White House. Clearly, whenever Lyndon Johnson discussed civil rights strategy with his advisers, one of his major concerns was to promote passage of H.R. 7152 without at the same time alienating his loyal counselor, Dick Russell.

After the Senate had recessed, Hubert Humphrey wearily returned to his office, where he was greeted by Eugene McCarthy (D-Minn.), Roy Wilkins, and later Clarence Mitchell. Humphrey gave his tally sheets to a staff member with a note: "Since I am sure that cloture will be of historic importance, here are the key amendment roll calls prior to cloture and the cloture roll call. Keep for history. HH." Next, he posed before a battery of cameras and fielded questions from members of the press who swarmed into his office. After the informal news conference, Humphrey made his way to the Senate television studio to face NBC news cameras. Then it was back to his office for a victory luncheon.

Immediately afterward Humphrey met with his floor captains, Senate staff, Justice Department officials, and Leadership Conference spokesmen to discuss the Ervin amendment, which wrongly had been declared defeated. The honorable thing would be to let Ervin offer it again and to have the Senate leadership accept it. It was agreed that the Justice Department would modify the language to make it amenable to both sides. Then the tireless whip returned to the chamber for the resumption of the floor session at 3:00 P.M., when the Senate considered and defeated, 25-69, Albert Gore's amendment to strike out Title VI (Federally Assisted Programs). Finally, amid pleas by southern senators of "let us go home," Humphrey moved that the Senate recess at 5:15 P.M. until 10:00 the next morning.

At 9:00 A.M., an hour before the Senate was to convene, the Democratic and Republican leaders met in Mike Mansfield's office to review and approve the Justice Department's revision of the Ervin amendment. Unlike its predecessor, which applied the "double jeopardy" standard to trials under both federal and state laws, the revised version prohibited putting a person "twice in jeopardy under the laws of the United States." They then decided to oppose all future amendments unless they were minor and had been agreed upon by the leaders of both parties. And since there was no specific order in which they would be called up, the only course would be to decide on them, one by one, as each came before the Senate.

During the Senate session that morning, the compromise Ervin amendment was accepted, 80-16. Thereafter, the Southerners suffered 11 straight roll call defeats, and Humphrey's legislative assistant, John Stewart, declared that the "steamroller had picked up speed. Richard Russell was discouraged and there was no real sense of organization among the Southerners—they had no particular plan of strategy."

However, on June 11, the leadership did accept five amendments, one by Russell Long and four by Jack Miller. "I wanted to perfect, not change, the substance of the bill," said Miller. "My amendments were consistent with the philosophy of the bill and would minimize any controversy which might later arise in the courts. Hubert Humphrey accepted them, for he knew I wanted to help, not hinder, the bill."

Stewart attributed Humphrey's willingness to accept Miller's amendments to the whip's natural inclination "to look for accommodation. He had an instinctual sense or desire to look for a common ground." But many, including Dirksen, felt that Jack Miller was extremely picayune. "Oh, Hubert," scoffed the minority leader, "we can't accept those. These are just cheese parings." Soon Miller, with his typewriter at his side in the cloakroom, became known as the "human comma machine."

On Friday, June 12, Everett Dirksen received a letter from Roy

Wilkins, which was both an apology and an expression of admiration from the NAACP executive:

> Let me be the first to admit that I was in error in estimating your preliminary announcements and moves. From my position, I must still regard any genuine palliation of the traditional Southern reliance on the sacredness of state action in Negro civil rights matters as an untenable move.
>
> But there were certain realities which had to be taken into account in advancing this legislation to a vote. Out of your long experience you devised an approach which seemed to you to offer a chance for success. The resounding vote of 71–29 on June 10 to shut off debate tended mightily to reinforce your judgment and to vindicate your procedure.
>
> Your leadership of the Republican party in the Senate at this turning point will become a significant part of the history of this century.

The rout of the opponents of H.R. 7152 continued that day. After taking time out to hear a brief address by Dr. Ludwig Erhard, chancellor of the Federal Republic of Germany, the Senate turned down 11 amendments while accepting another of Jack Miller's and one offered by Wallace Bennett. On Saturday, June 13, nine more proposed changes were defeated, although three sponsored by Russell Long, Karl Mundt, and John Tower (R-Tex.) were approved.

As senators returned to their offices on Monday morning, June 15, to begin what the leadership expected would be a final week of consideration of H.R. 7152, Lyndon Johnson fulfilled a presidential commitment made on October 28, 1963, to an influential member of the House Judiciary Committee. At 11:30 A.M. Congressman Peter Rodino, his wife, and his son, Peter, Jr., were escorted into the Cabinet Room, where almost eight months earlier John Kennedy had told the boy's father to "call Evelyn Lincoln" for an appointment after Kennedy's return from Texas. After the president beckoned them into the Oval Office for the customary picture-taking ceremonies, he dismissed Representative and Mrs. Rodino, explaining that "this is Peter junior's meeting." Then Johnson listened with interest as the boy told him about his "little people to little people" peace campaign, which he hoped might help end the nuclear arms race.

On the Hill that day the Senate leaders concluded that, like the House proponents of H.R. 7152, they could not wage a battle on two fronts, defending the bill from assaults designed to weaken it while simultaneously committing themselves to a fight to strengthen it. Thus the bipartisan team captains announced in a news release: "To expedite the remaining consideration of the bill, we who have been designated captains of the various titles of the bill have agreed to relinquish all of the strengthening amendments which we have proposed."

During Monday's session the Southerners batted zero, losing on all 14 roll calls, only one of which received over 30 votes. By the end of the day, Dick Russell, John Stennis, and Lister Hill were ready to end the fight. "Once cloture was invoked," commented Jim Pearson, "Dick Russell fell back in a Marquis of Queensbury attitude and accepted the decision." But to the irritation of Russell, Stennis, and Hill, who would do nothing to bring disrepute to their revered Senate, three other Southerners—Strom Thurmond, Sam Ervin, and Russell Long—were determined to continue. During a conversation with Hubert Humphrey, Lister Hill apologized, "This is extremely embarrassing."

Irked by the decision of the three southern members to prolong the agony, Mike Mansfield decided to keep the Senate in session beyond midnight the next day, hoping that a sufficient number of their disgruntled colleagues could persuade the trio to give up the hopeless struggle. Thus, on June 16, the Senate was kept working for over 13 hours (from 11:00 A.M. Tuesday until 12:01 A.M. Wednesday), which resulted in the most roll calls (34) ever taken in the Senate on one day; the defeat of all amendments (33); and the weakened resolve of Thurmond, Ervin, and Long to continue.

Karl Mundt, in a statement on the Senate floor, explained that he and most of the other members voted no 34 consecutive times "because there has been very little discussion of the amendments in connection with their presentation. So when there is any doubt, it is usually a safe parliamentary procedure to vote nay."

As the session dragged on into the late evening hours, John Stewart noticed that the "senators began to get well oiled by frequent visits to their hideaways around the Capitol." This led to several scenes, which were more appropriate for an *opéra bouffe* than for the "world's greatest deliberative body." At one point Russell Long offered an amendment, which seemed to violate the implicit understanding with the leaders that, in return for their acceptance of several of his earlier proposed revisions to the Dirksen substitute, he would limit his future ones.

Gesticulating wildly, Everett Dirksen rushed up to the Louisianan, shouting, "God damn you, Russell, you've broken our agreement. Why, you've welshed on our deal!"

Long looked horrified. But after the minority leader had calmed down, he and Long were soon seen striding about the Senate floor, arm in arm. Later Dirksen dashed madly about the chamber trying to locate Peter Dominick (R-Colo.) and Edwin L. Mechem, who had voted in favor of adjourning. Since this was against the leadership policy, Dirksen found Dominick, grabbed him, and made him change his vote. Then he dispatched a page to retrieve Mechem from the cloakroom. When the culprit appeared on the floor, Dirksen marched him down to the well of the Senate and ordered, "Okay, now vote."

Wednesday, June 17, brought both happiness and heartbreak to Hubert Humphrey. That morning, in negotiations, Strom Thurmond and Sam Ervin both promised him to limit the number of amendments they would call up; this assured the third reading of H.R. 7152 that afternoon and final passage no later than Friday evening, June 19. Tempering this good news, however, was a message Humphrey received in mid-afternoon from his wife, Muriel, that a biopsy on their son, Robert, revealed a malignant tumor in a lymph node on the right side of his neck. An operation on the 20-year-old was scheduled at Minneapolis's Saint Barnabas Hospital on the following Tuesday, June 23. Realizing that, under the circumstances, it would be difficult for him to concentrate on the floor proceedings, Humphrey nevertheless decided to remain in Washington until the civil rights bill cleared the Senate.

During Wednesday's 10-hour and 26-minute session, 22 amendments were offered to the Dirksen substitute. One, a "fraternity" proposal by Russell Long, was accepted by voice vote. The other 21 were defeated. The most critical vote came when Sam Ervin's motion to delete a section of Title VII (Equal Employment) was narrowly rejected, 47–51.

Sensing that the end was near, several southern senators took the opportunity to use up what remained of the one hour allotted to them under Rule 22. Spessard Holland (D-Fla.) spoke for 30 minutes, James Eastland for 41 minutes, and Lister Hill for 43.

After Strom Thurmond's final amendment had been crushed, 20–73, the presiding officer, Thomas J. McIntyre, with no further amendments in the offing, ordered the vote on the Dirksen-Mansfield-Humphrey-Kuchel substitute. Before the secretary began the roll call, Hubert Humphrey reminded his colleagues that the Morton amendment, which had been inserted in Dirksen's June 10 package, applied only to Titles II through VII, not to Title I. Then, in what was almost an anticlimax, the substitute passed, 76–18, supported by 46 Democrats and 30 Republicans. Now only one vote remained: final passage of H.R. 7152.

At 9:34 P.M. Mike Mansfield took the floor and suggested that the Senate recess until Thursday morning. "We have been under quite a strain for some time.... Take it easy and go home and get a good night's sleep," advised the majority leader. He then announced that closing arguments would be made on Thursday and Friday, with the final vote probably coming on Friday, June 19.

As the Thursday session began, Richard Russell still had 19 of the 60 minutes available to him under Rule 22. As he opened the debate that morning, the Georgia Democrat conceded that he and his sympathizers had

> used every weapon available. We have sought to appeal to the sense of fairness and justice of the members of this body. Finding that the ears of our colleagues were closed and a majority had already signed in blood to "follow the leaders," we undertook to go over their heads and appeal to the American people....
>
> Until we were gagged, we made no secret of the fact that we were undertaking to speak in detail and at length in an effort to get the message across to the American people. We did not deceive anyone as to our purposes....

"The time of the senator from Georgia has expired," said the acting president pro tempore, Ted Kennedy.

"I express the hope that those who are keeping the time will apply the same rules to others which they have applied to me," Dick Russell angrily exclaimed, believing himself the victim of a double standard. Russell noted that on June 17, Hubert Humphrey had yielded himself one minute to deliver a statement "that could not have been made even by the late Senator Tobey of New Hampshire in less than five minutes." Then the senator from Georgia inquired of Kennedy the actual amount of time with which the majority whip was charged on that occasion.

"The senator from Minnesota," declared the late president's brother, "was charged with nine minutes."

"I am glad to hear that," replied Russell facetiously, "because if the senator had been charged with all the time he actually used, we shall not hear from him any further." With that, his final words on the civil rights bill, Russell took his seat with tears welling in his eyes.

The June 18 debate, in the words of the Leadership Conference bulletin, "sounded like the death scene arias of an interminable opera.... In the end, with all hope gone of weakening the bill, the Southerners simply poured out their anger." John McClellan (D-Ark.) called the Dirksen substitute the "most ill-conceived, deceptive, and iniquitous legislation that ever engaged the serious consideration of the Congress of the United States." Strom Thurmond repeated a complaint frequently voiced by southern critics of H.R. 7152: "[it] is so drafted as to concentrate the major impact of its atrocious provisions on the southern states, while containing safeguards against the interference against the de facto type of segregation practiced in nonsouthern states, particularly in large population centers in the North."

Until June 18 the Republican party, thanks to the leadership of such conservatives as Bill McCulloch, Charlie Halleck, and Everett Dirksen, had projected a pro-civil rights image to the American electorate. "It is now clear," said Jacob Javits in a brief floor statement, "that the mainstream of my party is [in] support of this bill." And in a two-minute speech, Tommy Kuchel saluted Everett Dirksen "as the driving, unremitting, courageous senator who has, once again, rendered enormous service to the Republic, and the cause of free men. As a result our heterogeneous American society may look forward to better days."

The public's perception of a party's ideology, however, is usually formed not by an individual senator's or congressman's philosophy or by the sum total of their views; rather, it is predicated upon the more widely heralded statements of the party's presidential candidates (and ultimately, of course, upon the positions taken by those elected to the nation's highest office). In one afternoon, therefore, Senator Barry Goldwater, assured of the Republican presidential nomination after his California primary victory, negated the GOP civil rights posture that the Republicans in Congress had so assiduously established during the previous year.

In a short floor speech on June 18, the silver-haired former Phoenix department store executive, while professing his opposition to "discrimination of any sort," announced his intention to vote against H.R. 7152. "My basic objection to this measure...is constitutional. To give genuine effect to the prohibitions of this bill," said Goldwater,

> will require the creation of a federal police force of mammoth proportions. It also bids fair to result in the development of an "informer" psychology in great areas of our national life— neighbors spying on neighbors, workers spying on workers, businessmen spying on businessmen—where those citizens for selfish and narrow purposes will have ample inducement to do so. These, the Federal police force and an "informer" psychology, are the hallmarks of the police state and landmarks in the destruction of a free society....
>
> If my vote is misconstrued, let it be, and let me suffer its consequences.

The real fear among Republicans in Congress was that the "consequences" would not be limited to Goldwater on November 3 but would affect the entire party. Reflecting this concern was Jacob Javits. When Goldwater relinquished the floor, the New York Republican, seated next to him, reproached him. "Barry, this is a dreadful mistake," Javits said.

Carl Curtis, who had been appointed the Arizona senator's floor manager for the forthcoming GOP convention, declined to suggest how Goldwater should vote on H.R. 7152. But the Nebraskan secretly believed that both Goldwater's and the party's interests would be best served if the retired air force general expressed his objections to the measure and then announced, reluctantly, he would vote for it. In so doing, Curtis reasoned, Goldwater would retain the favor of his supporters but not alienate others.

Before Goldwater's speech Everett Dirksen had privately counseled the party's probable standard-bearer about his vote on the bill. "He did not twist my arm or attempt to influence my decision," related the Arizonan. Rather, the minority leader discussed the vote in terms of the larger issues—the effect it would have that fall on Goldwater's presidential candidacy and upon the Republican ticket generally. "But he didn't convince me," declared Goldwater.

As the Senate met on Friday, June 19, the first order of business was Albert Gore's motion to recommit the bill to the Judiciary Committee. Gore, one of the Senate's few southern moderates, could be counted on to support most liberal issues. But faced with a strenuous reelection campaign in the coming fall, Gore did what politicians seeking a "way out" often do: he attacked one provision of the bill, announcing that it was so repugnant that he could not support H.R. 7152 unless it was removed. He moved that the bill be recommitted to the Judiciary Committee with instructions to report it back to the Senate with language prohibiting the federal government from cutting off any school aid funds unless a school district had violated a district court order. After a short debate, his motion was rejected, 25–74.

After the Gore vote, Hubert Humphrey made his last floor speech on behalf of H.R. 7152.

> Mr. President, 83 days ago the Senate began consideration of the Civil Rights Act of 1964 [the title had been amended to reflect the change in the calendar]. The longest debate in the history of this body is now about to conclude with the passage of this measure.
>
> These have been difficult and demanding days. I doubt whether any senator can recall a bill which so tested our attitudes of justice and equity, our abilities as legislators, our sense of fairness as individuals, and our loyalty to the Senate as an institution of democratic government. In these historic circumstances, it seems necessary to ask the question: Have we fully met our responsibilities in this time of testing?
>
> I will consent to this measure, because for the first time in recent history the Congress of the United States will say in clear and unmistakable terms: "There is no room for second-class citizenship in our country." Let no one doubt the historical significance of this ringing affirmation which we now deliver to the Nation and to the world.

Humphrey concluded his remarks with the admonition, "As we enact the Civil Rights Act of 1964, then, let us be exalted but not exultant. Let us mark this occasion with sober rejoicing, and not with shouts of victory."

Then Mike Mansfield took the floor. During the early months of the filibuster, his role had been one of oversight, as he intended, rather than of day-to-day participation. This changed in May, however, when he became upset with Dick Russell for twice blocking votes on the jury trial amendment after Mansfield had announced that they would be held. "We had to get Mike angry to get him involved," observed Humphrey. After the Russell incidents, "Mike became much more involved."

In making the closing presentation on behalf of the Democratic leadership, Mansfield extolled Everett Dirksen—"this is his finest

hour''; Hubert Humphrey, who "has performed herculean feats";
Tommy Kuchel, "who filled the job of floor leader for the
Republicans"; and the bipartisan floor captains, "who made the
major speeches to explain and defend in detail the particular titles,
and served long hours on the floor." Mansfield ended with a tribute
to John F. Kennedy, who exactly one year before had submitted
his civil rights bill to Congress: "This, indeed, is his moment, as
well as the Senate's."

Everett Dirksen had the final word. "On occasion a number
of the 'boys' up in the gallery have asked me, 'how have you become
a crusader in this cause?' It is a fair question, and it deserves a fair
answer. I am involved in mankind," said the minority leader,

> and whatever the skin, we are all involved in mankind. Equality
> of opportunity must prevail if we are to complete the cove-
> nant that we have made with the people, and if we are to honor
> the pledges we have made when we held up our hands to take
> an oath to defend the laws and carry out the Constitution of
> the United States....
>   There is a moral basis for our case....
>   So, Mr. President, I commend this bill to the Senate, and
> in its wisdom I trust that in bountiful measure it will prevail.

Then, in a last dramatic gesture, Dirksen declared, "I am prepared
to vote."

The legislative clerk called the roll. The only surprise was Clair
Engle's appearance, again in a wheelchair and again with a mute
gesture toward his eye, to cast his last vote as a United States senator.
At 7:40 P.M., amid sustained applause in the galleries, the clerk an-
nounced that H.R. 7152, as substituted by the Mansfield-Dirksen-
Humphrey-Kuchel amendment, had passed, 73–27.

Forty-six Democrats and 27 Republicans voted aye, while 21
Democrats and six Republicans, including Barry Goldwater,
answered nay. Four senators who had opposed cloture—Bennett,
Bible, Hayden, and Young—voted for the bill. Two who had supported cloture—Cotton and Hickenlooper—voted against it. The
Dirksen substitute, the press's shorthand title for the bipartisan
amendment package, escaped unharmed between the time cloture
was adopted on June 10 and the moment of passage nine days later.
Of the 117 amendments considered during this period (excluding
the Dirksen substitute itself), only 11 minor revisions were adopted
by the Senate, all except the Ervin amendment on voice vote.

Lyndon Johnson was in San Francisco on June 19 to speak

at a Democratic fund-raising dinner. When he received news of the Senate's approval of H.R. 7152, he hailed it as a "major step toward equal opportunities for all Americans. I congratulate senators of both parties who worked to make passage possible. I look forward to the day, which will not be long forthcoming, when the bill becomes law." Much to his relief, Johnson was about to discharge faithfully the second of his two Kennedy legacies, the civil rights bill. Then he could concentrate his tremendous energies on his own agenda—the legislative bundle comprising his Great Society program—which had remained, until that day, on the Senate back burner.

If June 10, the date of cloture, belonged to Everett Dirksen, June 19 was Hubert Humphrey's day. "[It] was one of the landmarks of my life," declared the majority whip. Typical of the praise he received was the comment of Ted Moss. "I marvelled at the way he handled the bill's opponents all through the sharp debate. He always kept his ebullient manner and would talk with the Southerners. He was always genial and friendly, thus keeping the debate from becoming vicious. But there was no hiding what he wanted and where he wanted a senator to go. He was astute in the parliamentary process and his own nose counts. He knew what he needed." In the minds of many of Washington's political observers, Humphrey's performance propelled him as the favorite to receive Lyndon Johnson's blessing as the Democratic party 1964 vice presidential nominee.

Immediately after the Senate vote, Hubert Humphrey, who had lost 20 pounds during the lengthy debate (partially because of a weight-losing contest with Gaylord Nelson), walked out on the east front steps of the Capitol to receive the cheers of a throng that had waited patiently for word of the Senate's action. An hour later, several thousand people were still encircling the Senate wing, applauding and congratulating senators as they emerged from the Capitol. Three hours later, when Humphrey finally departed, a lingering crowd of several hundred people gave him a rousing send-off. "Never in my 15 years in the Senate," he marveled, "nor in the memory of senators with a far longer period of service than mine, had there been anything like it. The public was involved in that legislative battle in a way that was unique."

By this time it was too late for Humphrey to fly back to Minnesota, so he had a late evening dinner at Paul Young's restaurant with his legislative assistant, John Stewart, of whom he said, "His role was absolutely critical.... The civil rights bill of 1964 would not have been the same without him." But at a time which should have been an occasion for rejoicing, the usual Hubert Humphrey buoyancy was missing. Early the next morning he was to return to Minneapolis to be with his son, Robert, until his cancer surgery the following week. Humphrey described his mood as being "torn between the pride of victory and the pain of tragedy."

Tragedy also struck two other senators that night as Ted Kennedy and Birch Bayh (D-Ind.) flew by private plane to New England. They had been scheduled to address the Massachusetts Democratic Convention in Springfield that evening, but they delayed their departure until the final roll call on H.R. 7152. Caught in fog and a thunderstorm while approaching Barnes Airport in Westfield, Massachusetts, their light plane plunged into an apple orchard, killing the pilot and a member of Kennedy's staff. Bayh and his wife escaped with minor injuries, but Kennedy, dragged from the plane by the Indiana senator, sustained serious injuries that left him immobilized in Cooley Dickinson Hospital.

Earlier that day, the 76th and final edition of the leadership's daily "Bipartisan Civil Rights Newsletter" had hit Capitol Hill. With puckish pride, its editors announced its demise.

> Joining the legions of other small rural dailies, we cease publication with our thanks to those who helped produce it. Oratory and rhetoric will be found in the [Congressional] *Record* in sufficient quantity to please nearly anyone. Suffice it to say here that the job was done. We have a good bill. We still have a Senate, and we have miles to go before we sleep, and miles to go before we sleep.

And sure enough, around the last bend in the road ahead waited one more adversary, the redoubtable old Howard "Judge" Smith, who, with his band of conservatives on the House Rules Committee, was poised for the final chance to trip H.R. 7152.

Eight

The Bill Becomes Law

MANNY CELLER, the "Brooklyn street urchin," and Bill McCulloch, the "Ohio plowboy," were waiting when H.R. 7152 returned to the House.

Shortly after the opening quorum call on Monday, June 22, a clerk of the Senate strode down the maroon-carpeted center aisle of the House of Representatives, paused in the well, and bowed ceremoniously to Speaker John McCormack. "A message from the Senate," he proclaimed in trumpet tones.

The message was that the civil rights bill was back home after its hazardous trip to the other side of the Capitol, not too much the worse for its four-month stay. Indeed, some pundits held that since the upper chamber had emphasized the role the states should play in implementing the bill, it was actually improved. And while Manny Celler and Bill McCulloch would not agree totally with that opinion and could have nitpicked at the revised version, they gave it their immediate approval. In a joint press release, issued the previous Friday, they stated their reasons:

> Not all the amendments are to our liking. However, we believe that none of the amendments do serious violence to the purpose of the bill. We are of a mind that a conference could fatally delay enactment of this measure. We believe that the House membership will take the same position.

Avoiding a conference between the two chambers had been a Celler-McCulloch strategy all along. Since the Senate's negotiators

218

would be members of James Eastland's Judiciary Committee, in whose jurisdiction H.R. 7152 technically lay, prospects for any agreement among the conferees would be dim. If, in fact, a conference report should finally emerge, it would probably be subjected to another long Senate filibuster. This was one reason why Bill McCulloch insisted that the Justice Department honor its pledge not to allow the Senate to weaken the bill. Furthermore, by June 22, time was growing short. Faced with two national conventions, the Republicans' in San Francisco on July 13 and the Democrats' in Atlantic City on August 24, the traditional Independence Day and Labor Day recesses, and an early October adjournment for electioneering, the 88th Congress had only 10 more work weeks in which to complete its business.

House acceptance of the Senate bill, however, was not without its own problems because normal procedure called for it to go back to the Rules Committee, where it would face another bout with Chairman Howard "Judge" Smith. In a June 18 memo to President Johnson, Larry O'Brien listed the difficulties: "We must assume that Howard Smith will delay as long as possible on granting a rule [for floor consideration of House concurrence], and that he can parade witnesses through for several weeks unless we move to cut him off." He could be cut off in two ways.

The bill could be brought to the floor under "suspension of the rules." Using this procedure, the Speaker would refer H.R. 7152 to the Judiciary Committee and Celler would bring it directly to the floor, bypassing the Rules Committee. Suspension of the rules was designed as a timesaver to permit rapid consideration of the many noncontroversial bills favorably reported by standing committees. But to keep committee chairmen from abusing it by putting "sleepers" (controversial bills brought to the floor quietly and with little advance notice) on the suspension calendar, the shortcut contained some qualifications: only 40 minutes of debate were allowed, no amendments were permitted, and a two-thirds majority was required for passage.

McCulloch originally leaned toward suspension of the rules. However, since it was permitted only on the first and third Mondays of each month, they would have to wait until July 6 to use it. Charlie Halleck, meanwhile, was impatient to adjourn by July 4 so that the Republicans would have time to prepare for their July 13 convention. In addition, McCulloch and Celler were not absolutely sure they would get the two-thirds vote on the resolution. That left only the second option open.

They could force a hearing of the Rules Committee. Under House rules, any three members of the committee could file a request for a meeting. If the chairman failed to heed this request within seven calendar days, including three legislative days, eight members of the panel could write to the clerk of the House, calling for a meeting on a specific day. House rules required the chairman to comply.

Manny Celler and Bill McCulloch, remembering the Judge's ability to spring surprises, laid their plans carefully. On June 22, immediately after the Senate clerk announced the return of the bill, Celler arose and requested "unanimous consent to take from the Speaker's table the bill (H.R. 7152), with Senate amendment thereto, and agree to the Senate amendment."

"Is there objection to the request of the gentleman from New York?" Speaker John McCormack inquired.

"I object," called out William Colmer.

"Object," shouted John Bell Williams.

"Mr. Speaker, I object," chimed in James Haley (D-Fla.).

"Object," chorused Joe Waggoner (D-La.).

Anticipating the action of the Southerners, who all jumped to their feet in unison, Celler and McCulloch had prepared a resolution "to provide for the Concurrence of the House of Representatives to the Senate amendment to H.R. 7152," which Manny Celler dropped in the hopper, a wooden box attached to the lowest tier of the Speaker's dais. House Resolution 789 was immediately referred by Speaker McCormack to the Rules Committee, where, after waiting for the required three days, it would be up to the liberal members of Judge Smith's committee to force his hand.

Wednesday being the third day, Dick Bolling and two committee colleagues filed a formal request for the Judge to hear House Resolution 789. Smith, aware that his committee might embarrass him by forcing him to hold hearings if he did not comply, reluctantly scheduled them to start on the last day possible, June 30, intending to draw out testimony for several days. Committee insurgents, however, secretly made their own plans to finish all work in one afternoon.

On the morning of June 30, the mutinous members moved quickly. Immediately after the chairman gaveled the meeting to order at 10:30 A.M., Ray Madden informed him that a majority of the committee wanted to wind up all testimony by 5:00 P.M. so they could go into closed session and report a rule to the floor that afternoon. Smith, not deigning to comment on the threat but simply peering impassively over his glasses at Madden, called Manny Celler as the first witness.

"The Senate," declared Celler, "has made changes in our handiwork. These changes are not lethal. They do not do serious violence to the bill. They may not be to my personal liking, but I think the country can live with them. As you know, gentlemen," he continued, "politics is the art of the possible.... Acceptance of the amendments is a reasonable price, I believe, to pay to avoid a conference of both houses, which might renew lengthy debate, open up old sores, again encourage bitter controversy, the wounding of sectional pride, and searing of personal sensibilities."

After Manny Celler completed a 30-minute explanation of the Senate changes, Judge Smith called, as the next witness, Bill McCulloch. The Ohioan, in order to save time, submitted his remarks for the record instead of reading them. But during the question period, Smith's smouldering hostility toward McCulloch flared out. "I understand you were one of the architects of the Senate bill," the Judge began innocently, alluding to the "King of the Hill" label that senators and the press had bestowed on the Piqua congressman.

"I had some consultation with some senators on the bill," conceded McCulloch carefully. "I had some conferences with some of the senators who had no little part in drafting the amendments and approving the amendments which have been so thoroughly described."

"I know one thing," observed Smith. "You were very firm about amendments."

"That is right."

"We had an amendment," the Judge lashed out with the anger that had been building since February, "that was agreed to by the Democrats, an amendment of mine that I was about to offer. The coalition between the Democratic leadership and the Republican leadership had it so that no amendment could be adopted without your agreement."

House bells, denoting a quorum call, sounded at that moment, interrupting Smith's public scolding. The Ohio country lawyer was spared the full wrath of the Virginia country lawyer, who had been waiting four months to avenge his honor.

When the Rules Committee returned at 1:30, the insurgents started carrying out their plan to end hearings that day. Ray Madden moved that they hear all witnesses until 5:00 and then go into executive session. Judge Smith pointed out that the committee could act on this motion only in closed session. Madden proposed that the committee do so; the motion carried, 6–4; and the room was cleared of all spectators. Behind closed doors the beleaguered chairman argued that ending open hearings that afternoon would deny members, including four from the Judiciary Committee, an opportunity to be heard. Madden countered that the bill had been before the Congress for so many months that additional testimony was unnecessary. The committee voted on Madden's motion and, overriding its chairman 7–4, agreed to end all testimony at 5:00 P.M.

Reopening the doors at 1:50, Rules Committee members finished questioning McCulloch. Next they heard the testimony of four southern members, Edwin Willis, William Cramer, Richard Poff, and William Dorn (D-S.C.), who all opposed H.R. 7152. Promptly at 5:00 P.M. they went into executive session.

In private, Bolling moved that H. Res. 789 be granted a rule, specifying one hour of floor debate, and that it be reported immediately to the House. The motion carried, 10–5. Voting aye were the five northern Democrats, Texas Democrat John Young, and four Republicans—Clarence Brown, Katherine St. George, John Anderson (Ill.), and Dave Martin. Voting nay were the four southern Democrats and H. Allen Smith (R-Calif.).

Emboldened by this success, the rebellious members proceeded to do what Smith always knew and feared they could do—they took the committee away from him. A coup was as rash a move as it was rarely attempted.

Dick Bolling, in a skit obviously rehearsed, moved that Ray Madden report the rule to the House, a responsibility traditionally reserved for the chairman. Bolling explained that a House rule provided that if the chairman was opposed to a bill, the right to offer the rule went to someone else on the committee who favored the measure. Then, as if on cue, Madden replied that he would be happy to handle the resolution.

Southern members of the committee protested vehemently. William Colmer said that he had been on the Rules Committee for more than 20 years and had never witnessed anything like this revolt. "If Martin Luther King were chairman of this committee and I was opposed to his position, I would do nothing to take the chair away from him and slap him in the face."

The victim of the overthrow, Judge Smith, shook his head sadly and recalled that he had served on the committee for more than three decades. "I have never in all that experience...heard any member of this committee make the motion made by the gentleman from Missouri today."

Clarence Brown, the ranking Republican member, was torn between conflicting motives. While he wished to maintain his friendship and close working relationship with Smith, he also was under considerable pressure from his GOP colleagues to bring H. Res. 789 to the floor in time to let the House begin its recess before July 6. Brown, therefore, felt compelled to explain why, despite his fondness for the chairman, he would vote in support of Bolling's motion.

> I don't like to vote for any motion that takes away from the chairman any of his prerogatives.... But he would probably use every parliamentary tactic to delay as long as he could final action by the House on this legislation.... We have a Party Convention scheduled for the thirteenth of July in San Francisco.... Any delay even in the next week would not only inconvenience [us] but would mean that many could not meet their commitments to the Party.

Brown then joined John Anderson and six Democrats in support of the Bolling motion, assigning Madden the responsibility for managing the resolution on the House floor. Opposed was the same quintet that had voted against the motion to approve the rule.

The incorrigible Judge Smith, partly out of pique and partly as a last-ditch effort to let the opponents of H.R. 7152 put all their fears and forebodings into the *Congressional Record*, tried one final delay tactic. Turning the gavel over to his second-in-command, William Colmer, Smith moved that floor debate be extended to four hours. His motion was defeated, 5–8. Undaunted, he requested three hours. This, too, was rejected, 6–7. His third effort, asking for two hours, was objected to by Tip O'Neill and regretfully ruled out of order by Colmer. The Judge had gone down swinging.

The next day, on the House floor, the anger of the Southerners was expressed in a strident speech by Joe Waggoner. He complained that a "packed" Rules Committee "ran roughshod over the distinguished chairman." Waggoner called "unprecedented" the panel's action naming a member other than the chairman to handle a Rules Committee resolution on the floor, charging that the committee majority "allowed only a single day of gagged hearing, then railroaded the bill to this floor of the House with only one hour allowed to read and discuss more than 80 Senate amendments."

The following day, July 2, exactly one year since Burke Marshall's hurried trip to Piqua, Ohio, to get Bill McCulloch's support for H.R. 7152, saw the final scene in the long civil rights drama. Shortly after the House convened, Speaker John McCormack recognized Ray Madden. "Mr. Speaker," Madden stated, "by direction of the Committee on Rules, I call up House Resolution 789 and ask for its immediate consideration."

The clerk then read the short resolution that called for House concurrence with Senate amendments to H.R. 7152. After a quorum call, Madden announced he would allocate 30 minutes of the one-hour debate to Clarence Brown and another 15 minutes to Howard Smith.

In opening the debate, Madden, anticipating criticism, defended the Rules Committee's swift consideration of H. Res. 789. "Our only task on Tuesday was to hear the testimony of Chairman Celler [and] the gentleman from Ohio [Mr. McCulloch], and [to hear] other members of the Judiciary Committee explain the changes made by the other body to our House bill." Madden emphasized that "the bill has been considered by both bodies a total of approximately 114 days. If unnecessary delays, stalling tactics, and filibuster were eliminated, this bill could have been disposed of in one-tenth of the time and also have given every member of both bodies ample opportunity to be heard." In explaining why the Rules Committee prohibited Smith from handling the resolution, Madden declared that "the majority of our members decided it was time to call a termination to the shenanigans and delays to which the progress of this legislation has been a victim."

Clarence Brown used only 90 seconds of his 30 minutes to explain his dislike "for this method of legislating," while granting that "it had been used before," Brown, referring to the great public demand for civil rights legislation, concluded that "voting on the issue today, instead of a few days from now, can in no way change the final result. For that reason, rather reluctantly perhaps, I am supporting this method of bringing this matter before the House today."

Judge Smith's final monologue against H.R. 7152 was an impassioned bemoaning that "under the exercise of raw, brutal power of the majority of both the Democrats and the Republicans, the opponents of the civil rights bill on this side are given only 15 minutes to debate a bill that has never been before the Judiciary Committee of the House or before the House itself before today. But the bell has tolled. In a few minutes you will vote on this monstrous instrument of oppression upon all of the American people." As Smith yielded the floor the southern members applauded. And Emanuel Celler, reflecting the genteel traditions under which the House operated, stepped over to the last defender of the Old South and shook his hand.

Clarence Brown then yielded the balance of his time to William McCulloch, who, using his favorite characterization of the House bill, reminded his colleagues that it was "comprehensive in scope yet moderate in application, subject to effective judicial and administrative safeguards." He described the Senate measure as also "comprehensive in scope, with the individual states clothed with more authority and responsibility in the enforcement of the legislation than when it [the bill] left the House. In short, the bill comes back to the House tempered to and softened by the sober judgment of the members of the other body, yes, even by the wishes of the people."

"To my colleagues in the Congress," Bill McCulloch said in closing, "as well as to people everywhere who believe in equality under the law, who support the Constitution, and who love liberty not only for themselves but for others as well, the civil rights bill now before us for final consideration is in accordance with the best traditions of America."

"Mr. Speaker," John Lindsay spoke up, "I wish to express my appreciation to the distinguished gentleman from Ohio.... The country and the Congress owe him a debt of gratitude."

As Bill McCulloch sat quietly, the House rose in a rare standing ovation, a tribute to his leadership in helping steer H.R. 7152 through the treacherous crosscurrents of Congress. Acknowledging the appluase, McCulloch stated, "Mr. Speaker, I shall try to paraphrase a sentence of that great Englishman Sir Winston Churchill. ...: Never have so many of such ability worked so hard, and so effectively, for which so few received the credit."

The next speaker, Atlanta's Democratic representative Charles Weltner, expressed the sentiments of the New South when he announced that after voting against the bill in February, he intended to support it now. "I will add my voice," he said, "to those who seek reasoned and conciliatory adjustment to a new reality."

Ray Madden then yielded the remaining six minutes to Emanuel Celler. The Brooklyn Democrat, using much the same language he employed during his Rules Committee appearance two days earlier, assured the House that the Senate's amendments were not lethal and did no serious violence to the purpose of the bill and that "the country can live with them." He then outlined the substance of the changes made by the Senate. In concluding, Celler again drew from his bulky file of quotations. "I hope that we will have an overwhelming vote for this bill . . . so that it can be said the Congress hearkens unto the voice of Leviticus, 'proclaiming liberty throughout the land to all the inhabitants thereof.' "

Again the House rose in a standing ovation. The first man on his feet, leading the applause for Celler, was his chief rival Judge Smith. Then the House voted on House Resolution 789—to concur in Senate amendments to H.R. 7152. Celler's wish for an overwhelming vote was granted. Calling out aye were 153 Democrats and 136 Republicans; voting nay were 91 Democrats (88 from the South) and 35 Republicans; 20 members did not vote.

"Two hundred and eighty-nine to 126" announced Speaker John McCormack.

After McCormack had signed the official copy of H.R. 7152, it was carried ceremoniously to the Senate by a clerk of the House, who announced the word to the upper chamber. There the Senate's president pro tempore, Carl Hayden, put his signature on the document, and Thruston Morton, who was holding the floor at the time, yielded to Jacob Javits.

"Mr. President," cried the elated New Yorker, "we have just heard the historic announcement to the Senate that the House has passed finally the civil rights bill, the most momentous piece of legislation, in my judgment, which has come out of the Senate since the declaration of World War II."

Hubert Humphrey then took the floor to exclaim, "The act which has just been passed by the House . . . is not only one of the most important pieces of legislation of our time, but it has had amazing bipartisan support. . . . I salute the members of the House and the Senate. I believe we have performed a noble public service."

The bill was almost law; only one ceremony remained. At 6:00 that evening a large delegation of members from the House of Representatives and almost all the members of the Senate, except the Southerners, began arriving at the White House. Joining them in the gold and white East Room, where seven months earlier the body of John F. Kennedy had lain in state, were senior officials of the Justice Department and the nation's leading civil rights spokesmen including Martin Luther King, James Farmer, Roy

Wilkins, Whitney Young, A. Philip Randolph, Clarence Mitchell, and Walter Fauntroy.

Three immense chandeliers cast a warm glow over the elegant room, the largest in the executive mansion, traditionally the scene of splendid and solemn events—balls and receptions, weddings and funerals. Now it was ready for another historic moment. A desk had been placed in the center of the room, and on it rested two microphones, 72 pens, and the official red-bordered copy of H.R. 7152, which had been rushed to the White House from Capitol Hill in the late afternoon.

This poor, pulled apart, and plucky H.R. 7152 had, against all odds, not only survived but thrived. It was a better and stronger bill than John Kennedy would ever have dared send up to Congress.

Over the time of one year and 13 days, the 535-headed cantankerous creature, Congress, had been brought to heel by a succession of whip-wielding masters: Bill McCulloch, Hubert Humphrey, Manny Celler, Bobby Kennedy, Everett Dirksen, Clarence Mitchell, Nick Katzenbach, Tommy Kuchel, Burke Marshall, Mike Mansfield, Joe Rauh, Larry O'Brien, and countless others. But as the principals walked into the room, all was not harmony. Jealousies and rivalries continued; prerogatives and pride were flaunted. Some had the gaunt look that lingers after a grueling campaign. Exalted but drained, they all took seats facing the desk and waited for the arrival of the president of the United States.

At 6:45 P.M. the television lights were turned on as Lyndon Johnson strode into the room, nodded to acknowledge the applause, and sat down at the desk. In a slow, measured cadence, he delivered a 1000-word address to the nation:

> I am about to sign into law the Civil Rights Act of 1964. I want to take this occasion to talk to you about what the law means to every American. We believe that all men are created equal. Yet many are denied equal treatment. We believe that all men have certain unalienable rights. Yet many Americans do not enjoy these rights. We believe that all men are entitled to the blessings of liberty. Yet millions are being deprived of those blessings—not because of their own failures, but because of the color of their skin.... But it cannot continue. Our Constitution, the foundation of our Republic, forbids it. Morality forbids it. And the law I will sign tonight forbids it. Its purpose is not to punish. Its purpose is not to divide, but to end divisions—divisions which have lasted too long. Its purpose is national, not regional. Its purpose is to promote a more

abiding commitment to freedom, a more constant pursuit of justice, and a deeper respect for human dignity. We will achieve these goals because most Americans are law-abiding citizens who want to do what is right.

After finishing his remarks, the president reached for the first of the pens and, on the bottom of the last page of the bill, signed "Lyndon B. Johnson • approved, July 2, 1964 • Washington, D.C." Lady Bird Johnson came to his side and kissed him. He smiled and kissed her back. Then the guests swarmed around his desk offering congratulations. Johnson used the remaining 71 pens to sign additional copies of the bill, handing the pens as mementos to those who had worked so hard to pass the measure. When Hubert Humphrey, always thinking of history, asked the president for the manuscript from which he had read his remarks as a keepsake, they discovered that it had disappeared from the desk. Evidently another, faster-moving history buff was there that evening.

While the photographers took their customary bill-signing pictures, the men, both black and white, posed happily with the president. The smiles of the civil rights leaders, in particular, were ecstatic. The new law contained all the provisions they had wanted, but hardly dared hope for, on this date one year earlier, when the Leadership Conference on Civil Rights met in New York City to coordinate lobbying for the Kennedy bill.

After the signing ceremonies were over, the guests started drifting away. Climbing in his car to go home to dinner was the man of simple nobility and kindness who had played the pivotal role in passing H.R. 7152. While Bill McCulloch was optimistic about the possibility of lessening racial conflict—"turmoil is a sign of birth as well as decay"—he also believed that the problems between the races would not easily disappear.

The man from Piqua, Ohio, was just beginning to feel some of the criticism from back home. His house was picketed; he suffered uncomplimentary epithets; abuse came from quarters he least expected. He did not like to talk about it.

Although McCulloch recognized the problem—"How do you tear hatred and suspicion out of the heart of a man?"—he realized that "no statutory law can completely end discrimination. Intelligent work and vigilance by members of all races will be required for many years before discrimination completely disappears." On the House floor, a few hours before H.R. 7152 became law, Bill McCulloch issued a cautionary note. "To create hope of immediate and complete success can only promote conflict and result in brooding despair," he warned.

The Civil Rights Act of 1964 was not the opening chord of the Hallelujah Chorus. It was not the answer to all prayers of all black people. It would not bring instant economic good times. It was not the end of fear and mistrust and hate between the races. It was only a beginning...

All this will not be finished in the first hundred days.
Nor will it be finished in the first thousand days,
nor in the lifetime of this Administration,
nor even perhaps in our lifetime on this planet.
But let us begin.

John Fitzgerald Kennedy
Inaugural address
January 20, 1961

Conclusion

A ND SO ENDED the nation's longest debate, one that had nagged the country's conscience since the First Congress met on March 4, 1789. There are several reasons why it took the legislative branch 175 years to make racial discrimination illegal by finally enforcing, through statute, that which had been guaranteed by the Constitution.

The first reason rests with the Constitution itself. Mindful of the arbitrary power wielded by King George III, delegates attending the 1787 constitutional convention in Philadelphia drafted a document that sought to prevent domination by any branch of government and to protect the interests of both large and small states. With its emphasis on prevention, this system of checks and balances placed a premium on governmental inaction.

Second, part of the fault lay in a Congress whose structure almost assured, from the outset, chronic philosophical indiscipline. Unlike most organizations, Congress operates without any external or internal accountability. Products and services offered by business firms face the test of the marketplace. Even the executive branch, in the person of the president, is accountable to the public for its actions: citizens have the opportunity to vote for or against the chief executive when he seeks reelection. Congress per se is not on the ballot. Instead, in any given election, individual voters can select only one percent of the Senate and less than one-fourth of one percent of the House of Representatives. Ironically, many of those seeking membership in these two bodies attempt to advance their cause by, in effect, "running against Congress."

Like other enterprises, Congress possesses a leadership framework. But whereas subordinates in corporate America are accountable to their superiors, representatives and senators are responsible not to their leaders but to those back home who sent them to Congress. And while corporate executives can exact control over their employees through promise of reward or threat of punishment, congressional officials have no such authority. They can reward a few loyal members with choice committee spots or trips abroad. But the ultimate punishment, dismissal from Congress, can be exacted only by a member's constituents. And this is unlikely to happen because an independently minded congressman—impervious to the demands of the president and legislative leaders—is highly attractive to voters. In addition, the power to oust uncooperative committee chairmen or committee members lies not with the leaders but with the party members themselves, meeting in caucus. And party members are unlikely to take action against one of their own. Consequently, a maverick has little to fear in the way of internal reprisal. And if he stays in Congress long enough, he can expect to move up the committee ladder until ultimately he becomes its chairman and a power in his own right. This explains why, in 1963–64, 24 southern committee chairmen could be arrayed against the civil rights program endorsed by House and Senate leaders.

A third contribution to congressional inertia is the members' understandable instinct for survival. While motivation differs with individual legislators, all share one common goal—reelection. Elected initially because they were leaders of the people at home, most congressmen become followers of the people at home when they get to Washington. This metamorphosis is in keeping with the age-old formula for political success: keep the folks back home happy; don't get them mad; don't give them anything to shoot at. For incumbents, this involves a dual approach: whenever possible, avoid or oppose proposals that may offend a significant number of constituents (In 1964 this effectively muted the 52.4 percent of black Americans who lived in the South, where politicians dared not offend the white majority by appearing "soft on niggers."); do not take positions that require lengthy explanations to voters, who are notorious for their short attention spans ("The best vote," said a northern Democrat, "is the one you don't have to explain."). Throughout the years this collective antipathy toward controversy, aided by presidential recognition that to promote such legislation would be fruitless, has kept many politically embarrassing bills off the House and Senate calendars.

The interplay of these three factors favors the status quo, with major legislative action occurring only when there is a strong national consensus spurred by domestic or international crises, public fear, or citizen outrage. Several such examples happened during the previous three decades. Congress passed radical New Deal economic reforms in 1933 to combat widespread unemployment, bank failures, and farm foreclosures; the first peacetime draft in 1940 when World War II threatened; a Declaration of war less than 24 hours after the bombing of Pearl Harbor; the Charter of the United Nations and the Bretton Woods Arrangement Act (establishing the International Monetary Fund and the World Bank) in 1945 to create institutions to forestall future world wars and global depressions; $400 million in aid to Greece and Turkey in 1947, and the North Atlantic Treaty Organization in 1949, in response to cold war fears; and the massive National Defense Education Act in reaction to near hysteria over the Soviet Union's 1957 *Sputnik* launch.

In 1963–64, five forces, absent from previous civil rights movements, came together and spawned an outpouring of citizen support that resulted in what was hailed by many as one of the most important pieces of legislation ever enacted by Congress.

First, by 1963 blacks throughout America, as Martin Luther King explained, decided the time for effective civil rights legislation had finally arrived. They were disappointed with both political parties and, especially, with President Kennedy for not keeping his 1960 campaign promises. They felt that the 1954 Supreme Court desegregation decision, which had held out such great promise, had, instead, "been heeded with all due deliberate delay." And finally, one hundred years had passed since the Emancipation Proclamation with no profound effect on their plight, while in the previous two decades more than 34 African nations "had risen from colonial bondage." With Congress deaf to their pleas for equal justice, black Americans took their case to the streets.

Second, protest, which had been localized in the past, was widespread. Beginning with Birmingham, demonstrations quickly spread to 800 cities in all parts of the country by the end of 1963. This gave the issue of civil rights national, not just regional, visibility.

Third, the protesters' cause was abetted by the excesses of those who opposed their demands. While demonstrations can call attention to grievances (much the same as temper tantrums), they do not necessarily beget sympathy. Thus, in 1963, civil rights leaders ran the risk of antagonizing the country's white majority. Because most protests were peaceful, this did not occur. Instead, the violence was perpetrated by civil rights opponents. As it happened, Bull Connor's use of dogs and firehoses to subdue youngsters who turned the other cheek, the ambush of Medgar Evers, the bombing and murder of six Birmingham children—all came at critical times during congressional consideration of H.R. 7152.

Fourth, civil rights leaders successfully exploited these grisly incidents to attract support to their cause. For example, Andrew Young, field commander of the Birmingham operation, was very conscious of the media. "We saw this, frankly, as 'educational TV'," Young observed. "We had three minutes on the national news that is worth about $100,000 a minute. The demonstrations were designed to get a message across to the nation and to the world, so we knew pretty specifically what we were trying to do [each day]." Young's tactics worked. The television clips of peaceful demonstrators being brutalized pricked the conscience of millions who, until then, had little, if any, contact with blacks and their problems. For these Americans, the issue suddenly developed moral dimensions.

Fifth, the decision of the Leadership Conference on Civil Rights to frame H.R. 7152 in moral terms and to activate religious leaders in states with small black populations was critical to the success of the bill, especially in the Senate. Although citizen concern produced a deluge of pro-civil rights communications during the summer and fall of 1963, public interest in any given issue usually wanes with time. The persistent flow of mail and personal visits from religious groups created pressures on central and western state senators that they had never felt before. And nothing is more difficult for a legislator to resist than a holy crusade led by clergy of all faiths and made up of a large body of articulate followers. Who could argue that it was moral to deprive black Americans of their constitutional rights or to assault them for demonstrating for equal justice? Thus, opponents of civil rights legislation were effectively silenced by being placed on the wrong side of what the American people generally perceived as a moral issue. It was this new public climate that ultimately enabled the president and Congress to act without fear of electoral retribution throughout most of the country.

An accidental beneficiary of the 1963 black revolt was another large group that had been subjected to gross job discrimination—

America's female employees. Their coverage in H.R. 7152 did not come about through strenuous lobbying by women's groups; it was the result of a deliberate ploy by foes of the bill to scuttle it. But once Judge Smith added the word "sex" to Title VII, he created a broad, new constituency that successfully worked for retention of the sex protection clause as well as for Senate passage of the measure.

When the white majority joined the nation's black minority and women's organizations in demanding an end to discrimination, the congressmen who gathered in the East Room on July 2 were provided the national consensus that enabled them to secure enactment of strong civil rights legislation. A syndicated *Congressional Quarterly* article appearing in the *Milwaukee Journal* on the morning that the Senate passed H.R. 7152 speculated that had Richard Russell been willing to compromise at an early stage of the debate, he could have gained considerable concessions from the leadership, especially before the time of Dirksen's "conversion." This was highly unlikely, as Russell himself admitted on several occasions. Politicians, in submitting their records to the electorate, certainly like to point to their accomplishments, but they also want to avoid any exposure to blame. By the time H.R. 7152 reached the Senate, it was politically untouchable; leaders of neither party could afford to be charged with complicity in weakening it.

Everett Dirksen, for example, who seemed to reverse himself on the more controversial provisions of the House-approved measure, was not reacting to a heaven-sent message; he was following a carefully staged scenario designed to respond to the forces that made a strong bill inevitable: public opinion, the intractability of Bill McCulloch, the need to eliminate civil rights as an issue in the 1964 presidential and congressional campaigns.

Robert Kennedy, to whom President Johnson had entrusted the responsibility for helping Mike Mansfield and Hubert Humphrey move H.R. 7152 through the Senate, had his and the Justice Department's credibility to maintain—a solemn promise not to run out on Bill McCulloch by permitting the bill to be gutted in the Senate. Furthermore, Kennedy had a deep personal commitment to the House-approved bill. It was he who first saw its moral need and then convinced his doubting brother. To have agreed to emasculate the strongest civil rights bill in history, which John F. Kennedy had brought to life, would have denigrated the historical legacy of the nation's 35th president.

Finally, even before H.R. 7152 cleared the House, Lyndon Johnson made it clear, both publicly and privately, that he opposed weakening the bill in exchange for an early end to any southern filibuster. To have done otherwise would have raised doubts within the liberal community about his commitment to civil rights, and Johnson coveted this support. Further, it would have cast the president as the spoiler of John Kennedy's civil rights program (even though many, including Dick Russell, believed that Kennedy, concerned about losing the South in 1964, might have accepted a weaker bill had he lived). Johnson himself conceded that he had no other choice but to work for a strong bill. "I knew that if I didn't get out in front of this issue," he mused, "they [the liberals] would get me. They'd throw my background against me, they'd use it to prove that I was incapable of bringing unity to the land I have loved so much.... I couldn't let that happen. I had to produce a civil rights bill that was even stronger than the one they'd have gotten if Kennedy had lived. Without this, I'd be dead before I could even begin."

Although giving ardent public support to the Civil Rights Act of 1964, Lyndon Johnson was forced to keep his "private dickering," as *Newsweek* noted, to a minimum. Throughout the lengthy Senate debate, even as late as his telephone call to Hubert Humphrey on the eve of the cloture vote, the president was not at all certain that cloture could be attained. Thus, as Bobby Kennedy explained, by remaining the detached field commander, Johnson was in a position to fix blame on his corps leaders—the attorney general, Mansfield, and Humphrey—if they failed to achieve victory.

Three other elements combined to limit Lyndon Johnson's personal intercession to only three senators. The cloture issue, observed Charlie Ferris, "was of such high visibility and such maximum effort in the Senate and among outside groups that there were very few stones unturned. Everyone was being squeezed from every source and Lyndon Johnson was very aware of this..., that we were getting all of the milk out of the buffalos up there. So it was one of the few times where every stone was being turned and the White House was aware of this." For this reason, added Frank Valeo, "There was a tacit understanding that the president would 'lay off.' " For Johnson to have engaged in large-scale "arm-twisting" on a national issue that "surmounted all of these small things would have cheapened the process," said Valeo.

The fact that cloture, if it was to succeed, depended on wide

Republican support further prevented Johnson's direct intervention. Extensive face-to-face persuasion might have suggested to GOP senators that H.R. 7152 was a "Johnson" bill rather than a bipartisan measure. Instead, the objective, as the president told Hubert Humphrey, was to "get" Dirksen. After that, it was up to Dirksen to "get" the GOP votes.

Lyndon Johnson also wished to avoid affronting his former patron, Dick Russell. Much of the president's lobbying efforts, therefore, were conducted in the impersonal environment of the public arena, which would enable Russell and his fellow Southerners, who had constituted Johnson's base of support when he was in the Senate, to walk away from defeat with dignity. But Johnson's deep affection for Russell was not all; the president knew that he would need the Georgian's backing when the Senate began considering the antipoverty proposals, which mattered even more to Johnson than the civil rights bill. To unduly antagonize Russell at this point would prove counterproductive in the long run.

The *Milwaukee Journal* surmised in its June 19 article that had Senator Russell allowed more voting on amendments before cloture, several weakening ones might have carried. Even Hubert Humphrey could not understand why the anti-civil rights forces had permitted so few votes. "It seemed to me," reasoned the majority whip, "they lost their sense of direction and really had no plan other than what they used to have when filibusters succeeded." Both Humphrey and the newspaper correspondent, in their analyses, ignored the fact that a winning coach does not discard a previously successful strategy. In 1960 Dick Russell succeeded in weakening the Eisenhower civil rights bill *after* cloture had failed. Then he outdid himself in 1962 when, after two unsuccessful cloture attempts, the Senate leadership removed John Kennedy's literacy proposal from the calendar altogether. Thus, in 1964, as was true in 1960 and 1962, the magic number for Russell was 34, not 51. He hoped, therefore, that he could muster once again the necessary 12 or 13 nonsouthern votes to defeat cloture. But whether he could attract 30 members, in addition to his southern followers, to support weakening amendments *before* a cloture vote was highly speculative.

Richard Russell's doubts about his ability to achieve a majority on any given issue deepened on March 26, when he was decisively defeated on two procedural votes (despite Dirksen's support of the Morse motion), and again on May 6, when the amendment that had the greatest chance of success, Thruston Morton's jury trial proposal, twice failed to pass. Russell privately feared that further losses would result in the erosion of possible northern anticloture votes. Instead, he held out "in the hope that some development might extricate us from an all but impossible position." As the senator explained in a May 1, 1964, telegram to a constituent, W. H. McKenzie, "We have no intention of accepting a compromise. We are making an effort to delay a cloture petition past the Indiana and Maryland primaries." Russell hoped that the development he was seeking would come in the form of a backlash vote in support of George Wallace, who was running as a presidential candidate in the Indiana and Maryland Democratic primaries. Wallace, in fact, did unexpectedly well in both states, getting 29.9 percent of the vote in Indiana and 42 percent in Maryland. But the message never reached the Senate. Instead, civil rights supporters took heart in Charlie Halleck's 39,871–9,325 margin in Indiana's Republican primary ("I voted for the civil rights bill and I survived," boasted Halleck.) and J. Glenn Beall's two-to-one victory over James P. Gleason in Maryland's GOP primary. "Wallace won't affect the final vote on this bill," Everett Dirksen had commented. "On that you can stake the next two tea crops in China." In the final analysis, Russell failed because he did not anticipate the determination of the president and the Senate leadership to suspend all other business until the filibuster had run its course.

July 2, 1964, was a day of jubilation for those who had worked unceasingly during the previous 12 months. But H.R. 7152, admittedly, had its deficiencies. It was not all-inclusive in its protection of civil rights: blacks still could be barred from participating in certain state and local elections and could be refused service by small retail establishments; discrimination in the sale or rental of housing was not addressed. That future efforts would be made to close these loopholes was strongly suggested by the Leadership Conference, which, in the heading of its final newsletter, declared "Last MEMO—in this series, anyway."

The Civil Rights Act of 1964 was exactly what its title suggested: it guaranteed equal political, social, and economic *rights* to all Americans. But holding out the right to a better life for minorities does not guarantee attainment of that better life. Nor could the act erase three and one-half centuries of dehumanization. The effects of constant humiliation, substandard education, inadequate technical, professional, and managerial training could not be overcome by the stroke of the president's pen on a parchment handed him by Congress. It would be unreasonable, therefore, to assume that black Americans, in a society whose economic rewards are derived from acquired skills, could achieve overnight the same standard of living as white Americans, who had a 350-year head start. To translate newly won rights into a better life would require time, national patience, a willingness by minorities to pursue the educational and training opportunities now open to them, and, most of all, constant vigilance by those charged with enforcing the law to ensure that these opportunities are maintained. In the meantime, compensatory programs, such as those proposed by Lyndon Johnson in his Great Society package, would have to be pursued to relieve the economic inequality fostered by centuries of discrimination.

The principal value of the Civil Rights Act of 1964, "the value above all others," said Roy Wilkins to delegates attending the NAACP's 55th annual convention, "is the recognition finally—by the Congress of the United States—that the Negro is a constitutional citizen." Without this fundamental right, the pursuit of happiness through political, social, and economic progress could not begin.

Appendix

Major Provisions
of the
Civil Rights Act of 1964

Public Law 88-352

Title I. Voting Rights

Prohibited denial of the right to vote in national elections because of race, color, religion, or national origin (*state and local election coverage deleted in McCulloch-Justice Department compromise*)*; made a sixth-grade education a presumption of literacy; required all literacy tests to be in writing; made provisions of the act applicable to Puerto Rico (*Cramer floor amendment*); permitted a three-judge federal court to hear voting rights cases if requested by the attorney general (*McCulloch–Justice Department compromise*) or the defendant (*Poff floor amendment*).

Title II. Injunctive Relief against Discrimination in Places of Public Accommodation

Prohibited discrimination on the basis of race, color, religion, or national origin in motels, inns, hotels, rooming houses (except owner-occupied residences of five units or less), restaurants, cafeterias, lunch counters, soda fountains, motion picture houses, theaters, concert halls, sports arenas, stadiums, gasoline stations; specifically exempted private clubs and omitted from coverage retail stores and personal services, such as physicians, barber shops, and small places of amusement, except when operating in covered public accommodations (*McCulloch–Justice Department compromise*).

Authorized aggrieved individuals to file suit in federal court to seek relief against discriminatory practices; permitted the attorney general to intervene in such suit or to initiate a civil action when a pattern or practice of discrimination is believed to exist (*Dirksen substitute*).

Established procedures whereby grievances would be considered initially by local or state authorities (*Dirksen substitute*).

Title III. Desegregation of Public Facilities (*Rogers subcommittee amendment*).

Authorized the Justice Department to file suits to desegregate state or locally owned or operated public facilities, such as parks, upon receipt of written complaint of aggrieved individuals who, in the opinion of the attorney general, are financially unable to undertake legal proceedings or face personal dangers if they do so.

Title IV. Desegregation of Public Education

Permitted the U.S. Office of Education, upon request of local school boards, to give technical and financial assistance for the planning or implementation of desegregation programs, but not in cases of racial imbalance (*McCulloch subcommittee amendment*).

Authorized the Justice Department to file suit to desegregate public schools or colleges upon receipt of written complaint of aggrieved individuals who, in the opinion of the attorney general, are unable to undertake such a suit (attorney general must notify school board prior to initiating the suit to give local authorities time to remedy the situation); specified that nothing in the title shall empower any official or court to issue an order to achieve racial balance (*McCulloch–Justice Department compromise*).

Title V. Commission on Civil Rights

Extended the life of the commission through January 31, 1969 (*Rogers floor amendment*).

Authorized commission to serve as a national clearinghouse for civil rights information; permitted commission to investigate alleged vote frauds (*Cramer provision in McCulloch–Justice Department compromise*).

Prohibited the commission from investigating membership practices of fraternal or religious organizations, private clubs, college fraternities and sororities (*Willis floor amendment*).

Title VI. Nondiscrimination in Federally Assisted Programs.

Prohibited discrimination on basis of race, color, or national origin in the conduct of any federally financed programs; authorized federal agencies, upon failure to achieve voluntary compliance from fund recipient, to terminate funding; decision of agency to terminate assistance subject to judicial review.

Title VII. Equal Employment Opportunity (*Rodino subcommittee amendment*)

Prohibited discrimination by firms with 25 or more employees (as of July 1968) on the basis of race, color, religion, sex (*Smith floor amendment*), and national origin in the hiring and classification of employees; declared it not unlawful to apply different standards on basis of bona fide seniority or merit system agreements; made it illegal for unions to discriminate on the basis of race, color, religion, sex, or national origin in their membership practices; gave preferential treatment to Indian-operated enterprises on or near reservations (*Mundt provision in Dirksen substitute*); excluded Communists from coverage (*Colmer floor amendment*).

Created a five-member Equal Employment Opportunity Commission with the authority to investigate written charges of discriminatory employment practices; established procedures whereby commission would seek to resolve grievances through mediation but, upon its failure to do so, would refer them to state or local authorities for resolution (*Dirksen substitute*); if voluntary compliance not secured 60 days thereafter, aggrieved parties permitted to file suit in federal court where both plaintiff and defendant can request jury (*Griffin-Goodell-Quie provision in McCulloch–Justice Department compromise*); authorized court to permit attorney general to intervene in such suits; empowered attorney general to file suit whenever a pattern or practice of employment discrimination is believed to exist (*Dirksen substitute*).

Title VIII. Registration and Voting Statistics (*McCulloch subcommittee amendment*)

Directed the Bureau of the Census to gather registration and voting statistics based on race, color, and national origin for primary and general elections for the House of Representatives held since January 1, 1960, in districts designated by the Commission on Civil Rights.

Title IX. Intervention and Procedure after Remand of Civil Rights Cases (*Celler subcommittee amendment*)

Made reviewable in federal appeals courts the decisions of

federal district court judges to remand civil rights cases to state courts.

Permitted the attorney general to intervene in suits filed by those alleging violation of their rights under the 14th Amendment (*Dirksen substitute*).

Title X. Establishment of Community Relations Service (*Ashmore floor amendment*)

Established within the Department of Commerce a Community Relations Service to help states and communities resolve disputes alleging discriminatory practices based on aggrieved party's race, color, or national origin.

Title XI. Miscellaneous

Permitted jury trials upon demand in any criminal contempt cases arising under the act, except voting rights, with sentences limited to a maximum of six months imprisonment and a $1,000 fine (*revised Morton floor amendment*); prohibited individuals from being subject to both criminal prosecution and criminal contempt proceedings for the same act (*revised Ervin floor amendment*); specified that it was not the purpose of the act to preempt state laws except those that were inconsistent with intent of the legislation (*Mathias floor amendment*); authorized appropriations to implement the act.

---

*Changes made by Congress are inserted in parentheses and set in italics.

Notes

DSGC   Democratic Study Group (DSG) Collection, Manuscript Division, Library of Congress, Washington, D.C.

ECC   Emanuel Celler Collection, Manuscript Division, Library of Congress, Washington, D.C.

EMDC   Everett M. Dirksen Collection, Everett McKinley Dirksen Congressional Leadership Research Center, Pekin, Illinois

HHHC   Hubert H. Humphrey Collection, Minnesota Historical Society, Public Affairs Center, St. Paul, Minnesota

JFKC   John F. Kennedy Collection, John F. Kennedy Library, Boston, Massachusetts

LBJC   Lyndon B. Johnson Collection, Lyndon Baines Johnson Library, University of Texas, Austin, Texas

LCCRC   Leadership Conference on Civil Rights Collection, Manuscript Division, Library of Congress, Washington, D.C.

NAACPC   National Association for the Advancement of Colored People (NAACP) Collection, Manuscript Division, Library of Congress, Washington, D.C.

RBRC   Richard B. Russell Collection, Richard B. Russell Library, University of Georgia, Athens, Georgia

RFKC   Robert F. Kennedy Collection, John F. Kennedy Library, Boston, Massachusetts

WMMC   William M. McCulloch Collection, Ohio Northern University Law School Library, Ada, Ohio

WMFP   William McCulloch Family Papers; scrapbooks in the possession of Mrs. William M. McCulloch (some newspaper clippings without dates or page numbers)

WRC   Walter Rybeck Collection; collection of *Dayton Daily News* articles written by Rybeck while covering the Civil Rights Act of 1964 (some clippings without page numbers)

Preface

vii   Justice, observed Alexander Hamilton: Robert M. Hutchins, ed., "The Federalist, No. 51," in *Great Books of the Western World,* vol. 43, *American State Papers* (Chicago: Encyclopedia Britannica, Inc., 1952), 164.

viii   "a historic achievement": *Washington Star,* July 3, 1964, A4.

Introduction

xi   "sold us twenty negars": Peter M. Bergman, *The Chronological History of the Negro in America* (New York: Harper & Row, 1969), 10.

xi   "He [King George III]": Thomas Fleming, *The Man from Monticello: An Intimate Life of Thomas Jefferson* (New York: William Morrow & Co., 1969), 65.

xii   "three-fifths of a person": Originally in Article I, Section 2(3) of the U.S. Constitution.

xiii   "A crust of bread": Paul Laurence Dunbar, *The Complete Poems of Paul Laurence Dunbar* (New York: Dodd, Mead & Co., 1962), 9.

xiii   "We will not be satisfied": W. E. B. DuBois, *An ABC of Color* (New York: International Publications, 1963), 31.

xiii   "The only thing": Inaugural Address, March 4, 1933, in *The Public Papers and Addresses of Franklin D. Roosevelt,* vol. 2, *The Year of Crisis, 1933* (New York: Random House, 1938), 11.

xiv   "Southerners, by reason of seniority": Joseph P. Lash, *Eleanor and Franklin* (New York: W. W. Norton & Co., 1971), 516.

xiv   "To get publicity": Gunnar Myrdal, *An American Dilemma: The Negro Problem and Modern Democracy* (New York: Harper & Row, 1944), 48.

xiv   "If we wish to inspire": Special Message to Congress on Civil Rights, February 2, 1948, in *Public Papers of the Presidents of the United States: Harry S Truman, 1948* (Washington: U.S. Government Printing Office, 1964), 126.

xiv   "I can hear you say": Ralph Ellison, *Invisible Man* (New York: Random House, 1947), 11.

xv   "I can't understand": Sherman Adams, *Firsthand Report: The Story of the Eisenhower Administration* (New York: Harper & Brothers, 1961), 343.

xv   "No": Interview with Rosa Parks, in *Martin Luther King., Jr., A Documentary: Montgomery to Memphis,* ed. Flip Schulke (New York: W. W. Norton & Co., 1976), 25.

xvi   "Love must be": Lerone Bennett, Jr., *What Manner of Man: A Biography of Martin Luther King, Jr.* (Chicago: Johnson Publishing Co., 1976), 65.

xvi   Supreme Court ruled: Jack Bass, *Unlikely Heroes* (New York: Simon & Schuster, 1981), 57-76.

xvi   "He must exert": *The New York Times,* ed., *The Kennedy Years* (New York: Viking Press, 1964), 260.

xvi   a mere 118,500 votes: Governmental Affairs Institute, *America at the Polls,* ed. Richard M. Scammon (Pittsburgh: University of Pittsburgh Press, 1965), 937.

xvii   "Let the word go forth": *Public Papers of the Presidents, John F. Kennedy, 1961* (Washington: U.S. Government Printing Office, 1962), 1.

xvii   "Americans might well wonder": Arthur M. Schlesinger, Jr., *A Thousand Days: John F. Kennedy in the White House* (Boston: Houghton Mifflin Co., 1965), 937.

xviii   "For years now": Schulke, *King,* 214-217.

xix   "Don't worry": Stephen B. Oates, *Let the Trumpet Sound: The Life of Martin Luther King, Jr.* (New York: Harper & Row, 1982), 235.

xix   "Until we run out of children": *Congressional Quarterly Weekly Report,* no. 19, week ending May 10, 1963, 18.

244

xix   "We're through with tokenism": *Time*, June 7, 1963, 18.

xix   "others sailed with the wind": John F. Kennedy, *Profiles in Courage* (New York: Harper & Brothers, 1955), 21.

xx   "We are confronted primarily": *Public Papers of the Presidents, John F. Kennedy, 1963* (Washington: U.S. Government Printing Office, 1964), 469.

1. The Congressional Journey Begins

1   "The legal remedies": Kennedy, *Papers 1963*, 493.

5   correct basic injustices: Robert F. Kennedy oral history, vol. 6, interview by Anthony Lewis, December 4, 1964, John F. Kennedy Library Oral History Program, JFKC.

5   On May 17: Robert F. Kennedy appointment calendar, RFKC; Burke Marshall oral history, interview by Anthony Lewis, June 20, 1964, John F. Kennedy Library Oral History Program, JFKC.

5   Harold Greene was given: Interview with Judge Harold Greene, November 24, 1981; Marshall oral history, JFKC.

5   Kennedy urged his brother: Robert F. Kennedy and Burke Marshall joint oral history, vol. 6, interview by Anthony Lewis, December 6, 1964, John F. Kennedy Library Oral History Program, JFKC.

5-7   Robert F. Kennedy testimony before Subcommittee No. 5: House Judiciary Subcommittee No. 5 open hearings; House Committee on the Judiciary, *Civil Rights: Hearings before Subcommittee No. 5*, vol. 1, pt. 1, serials 1-4, 88th Cong., 1st sess., June 26, 1963.

6   When angered: Interview with Robert Kimball, December 11, 1981.

7   "Do you think": Ibid.

7   "since most Republicans": Joseph W. Sullivan, *Wall Street Journal*, November 7, 1963, 16.

8   (only 45 percent): *Congressional Quarterly Almanac*, 88th Cong., 1st sess., 1963, 83.

9   "Yesterday," Wirtz said: Subcommittee No. 5, *Hearings*, June 27, 1963.

9   "I think the statement": Ibid.

9-10   Fourth Congressional District: Governmental Affairs Institute, *America Votes 5, 1962*, ed. Richard M. Scamman (Pittsburgh: University of Pittsburgh Press, 1964), 311, 322, 324; 1960 county, city, and village information extracted from *The World Book Encyclopedia* (1967), s.v. "Ohio."

11   a secret poll: Memo from Robert G. Baker to Senator Michael Mansfield, June 27, 1963, Presidential Papers, JFKC.

11   "be sounded out": Memo from Nicholas Katzenbach to the attorney general, June 29, 1963, RFKC.

11   Marshall's Birmingham strategy: Burke Marshall oral history, JFKC.

11-13   Marshall's trip to Piqua: Interview with David Carver, November 4, 1981; interviews with Judge Carl Felger, Robert Fite, and Elwood Penrod, October 30, 1981; interview with Burke Marshall, November 10, 1981; for an account of McCulloch's Rotary speech, see *Piqua Daily Call*, July 3, 1963, 1, 17.

13   "a comprehensive bill": *Congressional Record,* 88th Cong., 1st sess., January 31, 1963, vol. 109, pt. 2:1538.

13-14   a chastened Robert Kennedy: U.S. Senate, *Hearings before the Committee on Commerce,* 88th Cong., 1st sess., July 1, 1963, S.1732, 72–73; July 2, 1963.

14-15   July 2, 1963, New York civil rights meeting: Meeting memo, NAACPC; Joseph L. Rauh, unpublished manuscript, 6–8.

15   five minor bills: *Congressional Quarterly Almanac,* 1963, 84–93.

16   "real liberals": Theodore Sorensen, *Kennedy* (New York: Harper & Row, 1965), 17.

16   not a burning issue: Harris Wofford oral history, interview by Berl Bernhard, November 29, 1965, RFKC.

16   531 blacks were jailed: *Washington Post,* June 1, 1963, A6.

16   "political swan song": Robert F. Kennedy oral history, vol. 6, JFKC.

16   "If we're going down": Edwin Guthman, *We Band of Brothers: A Memoir of Robert F. Kennedy* (New York: Harper & Row, 1971), 223.

16-17   At noon the next day: Audiotape log 90.3, June 1, 1963, JFKC; Sorensen memo of May 31, 1963, "Agenda for Civil Rights Meeting" and proposed "Supplemental Message on Civil Rights," Presidential Appointments log, JFKC; RFK-Marshall oral history, vol. 6, JFKC; interviews with meeting participants: Lawrence O'Brien, December 11, 1981; Theodore Sorensen, May 12, 1982; James Quigley, March 28, 1983; Francis Keppel, May 9, 1983; Wilbur Cohen, May 10, 1983; Louis Martin, December 12, 1983; Lee C. White, January 16, 1984.

17   "a straightout brawl": Audiotape log 88.4, May 20, 1963, JFKC.

17   "to stand in the schoolhouse door": Guthman, *We Band of Brothers,* 207.

17   This time the president: RFK-Marshall oral history, vol. 6, JFKC.

17   Buoyed by this success: Robert F. Kennedy oral history, vol. 3, interview by John B. Martin, March 1, 1964, and vol. 6 (Lewis), JFKC; Sorensen, *Kennedy,* 495; Sorensen interview.

18   "Sometimes you look": Theodore H. White, *The Making of the President 1964* (New York: Atheneum Publishers, 1965), 26.

18   The president immediately took over: File of Lee C. White containing summary of groups addressed by JFK, Presidential Papers, JFKC; RFK-Marshall oral history, vol. 6, JFKC.

18   "recognize the conflict": Sorensen, *Kennedy,* 26.

18   "What about racial intermarriage?": Ibid.

18   Polls showed: Poll taken between June 21-26, 1963, showed 49 percent "yes," 42 percent "no," 9 percent "no opinion"; 41 percent "too fast" (including 77 percent of Southerners interviewed), 14 percent "not fast enough," 32 percent "about right," and 14 percent "no opinion." See George Gallup, *The Gallup Poll: Public Opinion 1935-1971,* vol. 3, *1959-1971* (New York: Random House, 1972).

18   "The issue could cost me": Sorensen, *Kennedy,* 502.

18   "You've got to get it done": Senator Michael Mansfield oral history, interview by Seth P. Tillman, June 23, 1964, John F. Kennedy Library Oral History Program, JFKC.

19   "Do you think": RFK-Marshall oral history, vol. 6, JFKC.

19   In the ten weeks following Birmingham: White, *The Making of the President 1964,* 170.

19   A July *Newsweek* poll: *Newsweek,* July 29, 1963, 26.

19   "You can't count on a Congress": Ibid., 27.

19   "Our backs are to the wall": *Newsweek,* July 1, 1963, 18.

19   "We are assigning": *Newsweek,* August 5, 1963, 20.

19   "This summer we will have": *Newsweek,* June 3, 1963, 20.

20   "This," admonished Celler: Subcommittee No. 5, *Hearings,* June 13, 1963.

20–21   JFK meeting with civil rights leaders, June 22, 1963: RFK oral history, vol. 5 (Lewis, December 4, 1964), JFKC; Rauh manuscript, 5–6; Schlesinger, *A Thousand Days,* 968-971; interviews with Arnold Aronson, July 2, 1981; Marvin Caplan, July 2, 1981; Walter Fauntroy, January 9, 1982.

21   Kennedy finally endorsed: RFK-Marshall oral history, vol. 7, JFKC.

22   Subcommittee No. 5 hearings: Subcommittee No. 5, *Hearings,* July 10, 1963 (Celler); July 19, 1963 (Reuther); July 25, 1963 (Wilkins); July 26, 1963 (Tyler); July 31, 1963 (Roosevelt).

22   By August 2: figures extracted from Subcommittee No. 5, *Hearings,* August 2, 1963.

23   "If we are not careful": Audiotape log 101.4, July 29, 1963 (transcript, p. 8), JFKC.

23   from August 14 to 27: Subcommittee No. 5 closed sessions, *Minutes,* on file with the National Archives, Washington, D.C.; minutes of executive sessions, August 14, 15, 20, 21, 22, and 27, 1963.

24   To maintain order: *Time,* September 6, 1963, 14.

24   A Gallup poll: Gallup, *The Gallup Poll,* 1963.

24   "not going to bluff me": *Lima News,* August 25, 1963, 1–2.

24–26   March on Washington, August 28, 1963: *Organizing Manual No. 2: Final Plans For the March on Washington For Jobs and Freedom* (New York: March on Washington for Jobs and Freedom Committee), ECC; RFK-Marshall oral history, vol. 7, JFKC; Rauh manuscript, 10–11; Schlesinger, *A Thousand Days,* 972-973; Schulke, *King,* 89–99, 218.

26   "That guy is really good": Lee White interview.

26–27   JFK meeting with civil rights leaders, August 28, 1963: Audiotape log 108.2, August 28, 1963, JFKC; Sorensen, *Kennedy,* 505.

27–28   "There would be no FEPC": *Time,* September 6, 1963, 13.

2. Republicans to the Rescue

30   jotted down quotations: Quotations filed with Celler's papers, ECC.

30   "He never said": Interview with Don Edwards, January 29, 1982.

30–31   He simply ignored: Letter from Nicholas Katzenbach to Emanuel Celler, August 13, 1963, ECC.

31–32   Subcommittee No. 5 proceedings, September 10, 1963: Subcommittee No. 5, *Minutes,* September 10, 1963.

31   "You always have to give a member": Interview with Bess Dick, June 23, 1981.

32   should attend the markup sessions: O'Brien memo to President Kennedy, August 12, 1963, Presidential Papers, JFKC.

32   Republicans on the committee: Interviews with Benjamin Zelenko, March 9, 1982, and Nicholas Katzenbach, May 16, 1983.

32   Celler's seating arrangements: Interviews with former Congressman William Hungate (D.-Mo.), February 24, 1984, and James Cline, staff director (1984), House Judiciary Committee, March 9, 1984.

32   had no rules: Hungate interview.

32–33   Subcommittee No. 5 proceedings, September 11–12, 1963: Subcommittee No. 5, *Minutes,* September 11–12, 1963.

33   "segregation today": Guthman, *We Band of Brothers,* 207.

34   "The latest Birmingham outrage": Memo no. 7, September 20, 1963, quoting Wilkins's September 18, 1963 press conference, LCCRC.

34   Celler announced: Meeting no. 6 of full judiciary Committee, May 7, 1963.

34   "We must no longer palliate": Subcommittee No. 5, *Hearings,* June 13, 1963.

34–35   Subcommittee No. 5, proceedings, September 17–18, 1963: Subcommittee No. 5, *Minutes,* September 17–18, 1963.

35   Subcommittee No. 5 proceedings, September 25, 1963: Subcommittee No. 5, *Minutes,* September 25, 1963.

35   At Celler's request: Interview with Byron Rogers, October 14, 1981.

35   "so severe": *Dayton Daily News,* September 26, 1963, 46, WRC.

36   Subcommittee No. 5 proceedings, July 26, 1963: Subcommittee No. 5, *Hearings,* July 26, 1963.

36   Celler-civil rights leaders meeting, July 30, 1963: Memo no. 2, August 5, 1963, LCCRC; clipping from Rowland Evans and Robert Novak, *New York Herald Tribune* (no date or page number), ECC.

36–37   he promised to add: File copy of Celler's address to NAACP convention, 8:00 P.M., August 7, 1963, ECC.

37   a curious change: Kimball interview; George Meader, "Additional Views," in House Committee on the Judiciary, *Report No. 914, Civil Rights Act of 1963,* vol. 1, 88th Cong., 1st sess., November 20, 1963, 45.

37–38   Subcommittee No. 5 proceedings, October 2, 1963: Subcommittee No. 5, *Minutes,* October 2, 1963.

38   "write now": Memo no. 9, October 3, 1963, LCCRC.

38   "It's a pail of garbage": Sullivan, *Wall Street Journal,* November 7, 1963.

38   "everything under control": Katzenbach interview.

38   "Nicholas Katzenbach didn't know": Dick interview.

38   "the stronger the subcommittee bill": Zelenko interview.

39   O'Brien's September 23 memo: O'Brien memo for the president, September 23, 1963, Presidential Papers, JFKC.

39　Kennedy-Blake meeting: Audiotape log 113.2, September 30, 1963, JFKC.

39　"gut fighter": Neil MacNeil, *Dirksen: Portrait of a Public Man* (Cleveland: World Publishing Co., 1970), 188.

40　"Why," he demanded later: Minutes of leadership meeting, June 12, 1963, Republican Congressional Leadership file, EMDC.

40　Halleck meeting with Republican Judiciary Committee members, October 2, 1963: Interviews with Charles Halleck, October 27, 1981; Garner Shriver, June 23, 1981; Clark MacGregor, June 26, 1981; James Bromwell, February 12, 1982; Charles Mathias, March 22, 1982.

40　"You're not in favor": Shriver interview.

40　"Are you sure you really want": MacGregor interview.

41　Judiciary Committee proceedings, October 8, 1963: House Judiciary Committee closed sessions, *Minutes* of executive sessions on file with the National Archives, Washington, D.C.; minutes of October 8, 1963.

42　Meeting in Speaker McCormack's office, October 8, 1963: Halleck appointment book on file with University of Indiana Library, Bloomington, Ind.; Halleck and Katzenbach interviews.

42　Either they patched up: RFK-Marshall oral history, vol. 7, JFKC.

42　An angry Bobby Kennedy: Ibid.

42–43　"It wasn't a gratuitous lecture": Ibid.

43　unfairly on the defensive: *Dayton Daily News,* October 18, 1963, WRC.

43　So Kennedy told Celler: RFK-Marshall oral history, vol. 7, JFKC.

43　"Have I ever run from a cause?": Robert J. Havel, *Cleveland Plain Dealer* (no date or page number), WMFP.

43　an ironclad guarantee: RFK-Marshall oral history, vol. 7, JFKC.

43　"It won't work": Nicholas Katzenbach oral history, interview by Paige Mulhollan, November 12, 1968, LBJC.

43　"Congressman McCulloch has done it": RFK-Marshall oral history, vol. 7, JFKC.

44　attorney general be invited: Minutes of leadership meeting, October 10, 1963, Republican Congressional Leadership file, EMDC.

44–45　Judiciary Committee proceedings, October 15, 1963: Judiciary Committee, *Minutes,* October 15, 1963.

45　"What I want is a bill": *Washington Post,* October 16, 1963, A1.

45　Judiciary Committee proceedings, October 16, 1963: Judiciary Committee, *Minutes,* October 16, 1963.

45–46　two day appearance brilliant: Bromwell interview.

46　"There is no reason": *Time,* October 25, 1963, 29.

46　"thinks he has the Negro vote": *Newsweek,* October 28, 1963, 21.

46　"To weaken the bill": Copy of Aronson telegram, October 17, 1963, LCCRC.

46　"send messages": Memo no. 11, October 18, 1963, LCCRC.

46　JFK meeting with journalists: Extracted from Presidential Appointments—1963 file, JFKC.

47　worked to moderate: Copies of three proposed amendments on file with Celler's papers, ECC.

47   Judiciary Committee proceedings, October 10, 1963: Judiciary Committee, *Minutes,* October 10, 1963.

47–48 Kastenmeier-Dawson meeting, October 10, 1963: Interview with Robert Kastenmeier, June 22, 1981.

48   An appearance by Emanuel Celler: *Time,* November 1, 1963, 23.

48   "Old Libby knows": MacGregor interview.

48–49 Judiciary Committee proceedings, October 22, 1963: Judiciary Committee, *Minutes,* October 22, 1963.

49   reflected no grand design: Interview with Arch Moore, Jr., February 10, 1982.

49   "The shame of our times": Arch Moore, Jr., "Additional Views," in House Judiciary Committee, *Report No. 914,* November 20, 1963.

50–52 JFK meeting with House leaders, October 23, 1963: Audiotape log 116.7, October 23, 1963, JFKC.

52   his discussion with Halleck: Benjamin C. Bradlee, *Conversations With Kennedy* (New York: Pocket Books, 1976), 219.

52   despite warnings by Larry O'Brien: RFK-Marshall oral history, vol. 7 (Lewis, December 22, 1964), JFKC.

52–53 JFK meeting with Judiciary Committee liberal Democrats, October 24, 1963: Edwards and Kastenmeier interviews; *Newsweek,* November 4, 1963, 27–28.

53   "no immediate results": *New York Times,* October 24, 1963, 1.

53   a bitter Bobby Kennedy: RFK-Marshall oral history, vol. 7, JFKC.

53   An overloaded calendar: Halleck appointment book.

53   "a lot of heat from the president": Bromwell interview.

53   "one iota of compassion": David Hess, *Akron Beacon Journal* (no date or page number), WMFP.

53   "restless agreement": Bromwell interview; interviews with William Copenhaver, October 11, 1981, and Leslie Arends, October 8, 1982.

54   JFK-Halleck telephone conversation, October 24, 1963: Halleck and O'Brien interviews; Lawrence O'Brien, *No Final Victories* (New York: Doubleday & Co., 1974), 27–28.

54   "They couldn't understand": Halleck interview.

54–57 account of conversations and events of October 25, 26, 27, and 28, 1963: Kimball, Copenhaver, and Katzenbach interviews; interview with John Lindsay, December 11, 1981; *Newsweek,* November 11, 1963, 34–35; testimony of William McCulloch before the House Rules Committee, January 15, 1964.

56   "vital civil rights bill": Joseph Alsop, *Washington Post,* October 28, 1963, A17.

56–57 "The key figure": Anthony Lewis, *New York Times,* October 28, 1963, 1, 4.

57   McCulloch-Katzenbach telephone conversation, October 28, 1963: Katzenbach oral history, LBJC.

58   bank of Justice Department stenographers: Kimball and Edwards interviews.

59–61 JFK meeting with Judiciary Committee liberal Democrats, October 28, 1963: O'Brien, Kastenmeier, and Edwards interviews; interviews

250

with James Corman, November 6, 1981; Peter Rodino, February 1, 1982; Charles Daly, February 3, 1982; RFK-Marshall oral history, vol. 7, JFKC.

59   "create the greatest pressure": Robert W. Kastenmeier oral history, interviewed on October 25, 1965, John F. Kennedy Library Oral History Program, JFKC.

59   "conservative coalition" chart: *Congressional Quarterly Almanac*, 1963, 749.

60   JFK-Daley telephone conversation: Dictabelt transcript 28A.2, October 28, 1963, JFKC.

60   "had a right to be heard": *Congressional Record*, 88th Cong., 2d sess., February 1, 1964, vol. 110, pt. 2:1607 (Chelf repeated his October 28, 1963, remarks to Kennedy in a speech on the House floor).

61   president threatened Green: Kastenmeier interview.

62   Kimball received several telephone calls: Kimball interview.

62   Bromwell-Shriver breakfast, October 29, 1963: Bromwell and Shriver interviews.

62   Halleck meeting with Judiciary Committee Republicans, October 29, 1963: Kimball interview; *Newsweek,* November 11, 1963, 37.

62–63   JFK meeting with House leaders, October 29, 1963: Audiotape log 118.2, October 29, 1963, JFKC.

64–66   Judiciary Committee proceedings, October 29, 1963: Judiciary Committee, *Minutes,* October 29, 1963; Justice Department instructions on file with Celler papers, ECC; *Time,* November 8, 1963, 22–23; Cline and Katzenbach interviews.

66   "How did Libonati vote?" Zelenko interview.

66   41st in the Mafia's hierarchy: Ed Reid, *Mafia* (New York: Random House, 1952), 56–58.

66   "I have been told": Shriver interview.

66   "a comprehensive and fair bill": Kennedy, *Papers 1963,* 820.

66   "the possibility of civil rights legislation": *New York Times,* October 30, 1963, 22.

66   "inadequate to meet the needs": Press release of November 1, 1963, quoting Wilkins's statement of October 29, 1963, NAACPC.

66   "the mysterious origins": Arch Moore, Jr., "Additional Views," in House Judiciary Committee, *Report No. 914,* November 20, 1963, 62.

66   "greatest grasp for executive power": "Minority Report," in House Judiciary Committee, *Report No. 914,* November 20, 1963, 62.

66–67   JFK-Halleck telephone conversation: Dictabelt transcript 28A.3, October 29, 1963, JFKC.

67   placed an umbrella: Halleck interview; Murray Kempton, "Heroes on the Right," *New Republic,* November 9, 1963, 4.

67   70 disgruntled GOP congressmen: Kimball interview; Frank van der Linden, *Dayton Journal Herald,* November 8, 1963, and February 12, 1964 (no page numbers), WMMC.

67   JFK's Philadelphia trip: *Time,* November 8, 1963, 22; *Newsweek,* November 11, 1963, 37.

68   JFK press conference, November 14, 1963: Kennedy, *Papers 1963,* 846.

68–69   JFK Tampa speech, November 18, 1963: Ibid., 868.

69   "very, very difficult process": Edwards interview.

69–70   Bolling agreed: Interview with Richard Bolling, February 8, 1982.

70   Halleck press conference, November 21, 1963: Leadership press conference, November 21, 1963, Republican Congressional Leadership file, EMDC.

3. Johnson Takes Charge

71   "I will do my best": *Public Papers of the Presidents, Lyndon B. Johnson, 1963–64,* vol. 1 (Washington: U.S. Government Printing Office, 1965), 1.

72   "landslide Lyndon": *Newsweek,* December 2, 1963, 30.

72   "nostril inspections": Frank Lausche's description, related by Frank Moss in May 20, 1982, interview.

73   was merely amused: Rowland Evans and Robert Novak, *Lyndon B. Johnson: The Exercise of Power* (New York: The New American Library, 1966), 309.

74   "I don't have any budget": Hobart Taylor, Jr., interview by Stephen Goodell, January 6, 1969, Oral Histories, LBJC.

74   "I really don't have anything": O'Brien interview.

74   busily outlining the agenda: Interview with Jack Valenti, May 28, 1982.

75   inviting civil rights leaders: Extracted from President's Appointment file (Diary Backup), Box 1, November 22–29, 1963, LBJC.

75   "I was astounded": James Farmer, interview by Harri Baker, October 1969, Oral Histories, LBJC.

75   "Johnson was our enemy": Aronson interview.

75   "very rarely helped": RFK oral history, vol. 6, JFKC.

76   "is blind to color": Evans and Novak, *The Exercise of Power,* 376.

76   "No," Johnson muttered: Audiotape log 90.3, June 1, 1963, JFKC.

76   "wouldn't get passed": RFK oral history, vol. 6, JFKC.

76   asked Kenny O'Donnell: Norbert A. Schlei, memo for the attorney general, June 4, 1963, RFKC.

76   Johnson wondered to himself: LBJ's reflections related to Norbert A. Schlei as reported by Schlei in his June 4, 1963, memo to RFK, RFKC.

76   "I pass": Ibid.

76–77   LBJ's conversation with Schlei: Ibid.

77   LBJ's conversation with Sorensen: Transcript of Edison Dictaphone recording of conversation between Lyndon Johnson and Ted Sorensen, office files of George Reedy, Box 1, June 3, 1963, LBJC.

77   "very wise": RFK oral history, vol. 6, JFKC.

77   "The first priority": Valenti interview.

77–78   Busby memo: Horace Busby memo to the president, November 25, 1963, President's Appointment file (Diary Backup), Box 1, November 25, 1963, LBJC; interview with Horace Busby, May 12, 1982.

78   put together a final version: Interview with Lynda Johnson Robb, November 22, 1983; Busby interview; *Newsweek,* April 13, 1964, 27; Evans and Novak, *The Exercise of Power,* 348; John Kenneth Galbraith, *Ambassador's Journal* (Boston: Houghton Mifflin Co., 1969), 592-599.

78-79   Joint session of Congress: *Congressional Record,* November 27, 1963, pt. 17:22838-22839.

80   LBJ's television address: Johnson, *Papers 1963-64,* 1:12.

80-81   LBJ's meeting with Wilkins: President's Appointment file (Diary Backup), Box 1, November 29, 1963, with attached memos from Lee White and George Reedy, LBJC; O'Brien memo to LBJ, November 29, 1963, Confidential file, LBJC; Roy Wilkins oral history, interview by Thomas H. Baker, April 1, 1969, LBJC; press release, December 2, 1963, NAACPC; Roy Wilkins with Tom Mathews, *Standing Fast: The Autobiography of Roy Wilkins* (New York: Viking Press, 1982), 295-296.

81   "work actively for the defeat": Press release of September 13, 1963, referring to September 9, 1963, board decision, NAACPC.

81   "get them on record": Memo from Wilkins to all NAACP branches, November 20, 1963, NAACPC.

81   LBJ meeting with Young: President's Appointment file (Diary Backup), Box 2, December 2, 1963, with attached memo from Lee White, LBJC.

81   "A magnolia accent": *Newsweek,* December 9, 1963, 25.

81   first weekly Tuesday breakfast: Minutes of meeting, President's Appointment file (Diary Backup), Box 2, December 3, 1963, LBJC.

81-82   LBJ meeting with King: President's Appointment file (Diary Backup), Box 2, December 3, 1963, LBJC; Lee White memo to LBJ, December 3, 1963, Confidential file, LBJC; *New York Times,* December 4, 1963, 1.

82   LBJ's meeting with Meany: President's Appointment file (Diary Backup), Box 2, December 4, 1963, LBJC.

82   "certainly would act on the bill": *New York Times,* December 5, 1963, 26.

82   LBJ's meeting with Farmer: President's Appointment file (Diary Backup), Box 2, December 4, 1963, LBJC; Farmer oral history, LBJC.

82-83   LBJ's labor address: Johnson, *Papers 1963-64,* 1:22.

83   labor leaders told reporters: *New York Times,* December 5, 1963, 1.

83   LBJ's businessmen's address: Johnson, *Papers 1963-64,* 1:24.

83   LBJ's meeting with Halleck: President's Appointment file (Diary Backup), Box 2, December 5, 1963, LBJC; *New York Times,* December 6, 1963, 1.

83-84   LBJ's meeting with Randolph: President's Appointment file (Diary Backup), Box 2, 1963, with attached memos from Willard Wirtz and Lee White, LBJC.

84   "very damaging": *Newsweek,* December 16, 1963, 23.

84-85   Halleck made it clear: Minutes of House Republican Conference, December 4, 1963.

85   House proceedings, December 11, 1963: *Congressional Record,* December 11, 1963, pt. 18:24217-24218.

85   "I just don't think": *New York Times,* December 3, 1963, 28.

86   "I don't want to run over you": Bolling interview; *New York Times,* December 6, 1963, 1.

86   "I know something": Memo no. 19, December 23, 1963, LCCRC.

87   "press palms": *Newseek,* December 2, 1963, 28.

87   "laying on of hands": *Newsweek,* December 9, 1963, 20.

87   "This is Lyndon": *Newsweek,* December 16, 1963, 22.

87   LBJ luncheon with Texas Democratic congressmen: Ibid.

88   White House source accused Halleck: *Newsweek,* January 6, 1964, 14.

88   House minority leader reminded reporters: Ibid.

88   spent the entire Saturday afternoon: President's Appointment file (Diary Backup), Box 2, December 21, 1963, LBJC.

88   "We lost the two-thirds vote": President's Appointment file, (Diary Backup), Box 2, December 23, 1963, LBJC.

88   "Well, I'll be damned": Ibid.

88   "Bird,": authors' conversation with Lady Bird Johnson, February 21, 1967.

88–89 White House reception, December 23, 1963: *Newsweek,* January 6, 1964, 14; Evans and Novak, *The Exercise of Power,* 367.

89   bleary-eyed lawmakers: *Newsweek,* January 6, 1964, 14.

89–90 *Newsweek* poll: *Newsweek,* January 13, 1964, 23.

90   "Every parliamentary ruse": *Newsweek,* January 20, 1964, 20.

90   "I knew Howard Smith": Alfred Steinberg, *Sam Rayburn, A Biography* (New York: Hawthorn Books, 1975), 313.

91   Smith meeting with Kimball: Kimball interview.

91–92 Rules Committee proceedings, January 9, 1964: U.S. House of Representatives, *Civil Rights: Hearings before the Committee on Rules on H.R. 7152,* 88th Cong., 2d sess., January 9, 1964.

92   Rules Committee proceedings, January 14, 1964: Ibid., January 14, 1964.

93–94 Rules Committee proceedings, January 15, 1964: Ibid., January 15, 1964.

94   through all nine days: Kimball interview.

94   Rules Committee proceedings, January 16, 1964: *Hearings on H.R. 7152,* January 16, 1964.

94   LBJ's calls to civil rights leaders, January 17, 1964: *New York Times,* January 19, 1964, 1.

94   LBJ's meeting with civil rights leaders, January 18, 1964: Ibid.

95   "Poverty is a problem": Ibid.

95   LBJ breakfast with Democratic congressional leaders, January 21, 1964: Head Count, January 20, 1964, Legislation, Box 65, LBJC.

95   O'Brien "counted" Democrats: Clarence Mitchell, interview by Thomas H. Baker, April 30, 1969, Oral Histories, LBJC.

95   Mitchell considered as "unrealistic": Burke Marshall oral history, interview by Larry J. Hackman, January 19, 1970, John F. Kennedy Library Oral History Program, JFKC.

95   "walk down a corridor": Mathias interview.

95 "But this would only work": Joseph Rauh, interview by Paige Mulhollan, August 8, 1969, Oral Histories, LBJC.

96 "doesn't give an inch": Off-the-record interview with a former ADA official, November 21, 1982.

96 Johnson apologized: Interview with Joseph Rauh, August 13, 1984 (Johnson's remarks occurred during his meeting with Rauh on December 19, 1963).

96–97 LBJ meeting with Mitchell and Rauh: Valenti memo to the president, January 21, 1964, Legislative Background, Civil Rights Act 1964, Box 1, LBJC; Rauh oral history, LBJC; Rauh manuscript, 16, 21.

97 Rules Committee open hearings, January 21, 22, and 23, 1964: Rules Committee, *Hearings on H.R. 7152,* January 21–23, 1964.

97 "I thought they'd get one of us": Harris Wofford, *Of Kennedys & Kings: Making Sense of the Sixties* (New York: Farrar, Straus, Giroux, 1980), 412.

98 did not lobby the House: Marshall oral history (Hackman), JFKC.

98 Rules Committee open hearings, January 28–29, 1964: Rules Committee, *Hearings on H.R. 7152,* January 28–29, 1964.

99 Rules Committee closed session, January 30, 1964: *Transcript* of January 30, 1964, executive session on file with the National Archives, Washington, D.C.

4. Bipartisan House Victory

100–107 House proceedings, January 31 and February 1, 1964: *Congressional Record,* January 31, 1964, pt. 2:1511–1552; February 1, 1964, pt. 2:1582–1647.

103 armed with a manual: Manual on file with Celler papers, ECC.

103 assigned members of the Judiciary Committee: Title I, McCulloch, Shriver, Celler, Rogers, Libonati: Title II, Lindsay, MacGregor, Mathias, Celler, Kastenmeier, Corman, Senner; Title III, McCulloch, Lindsay, Rogers, Gilbert, Edwards; Title IV, MacGregor, Bromwell, Rogers, Libonati, Gilbert, Edwards; Title V, McCulloch, Cahill, Shriver, Corman, St. Onge; Title VI, Lindsay, Mathias, Celler, Rodino, Libonati, Corman; Title VII, Lindsay, MacGregor, Celler, Rodino, Roosevelt (Education and Labor); Title VIII, Lindsay, Mathias, St. Onge, Senner; Title IX, Kastenmeier, Gilbert, Edwards.

103 eight Justice Department attorneys: Burke Marshall, Harold Greene, Sol Lindenbaum, Norbert Schlei, Harold Reis, Richard Berg, Alan Marer, and David Filvaroff, DSGC.

105 "One of the examples": David Hess, *Akron Beacon Journal* (no date or page number), WMFP.

105 "The Constitution doesn't say": Ibid.

106 "the Brooklyn street urchin": Ibid.

107 sixth press conference: Johnson, *Papers 1963–64,* 1:259.

107 when told Saturday evening: *Washington Post,* February 2, 1964, A2.

107 The following afternoon: Halleck-Dirksen on "Meet the Press," February 2, 1964, Remarks and Releases, 1941–1969, EMDC.

107   "all we would do": Arends interview.

107–108   "Bill McCulloch and I": Lindsay interview.

108–109   Description of whip system: Rauh manuscript, 17–18; Kimball interview; memo no. 24, February 11, 1964, LCCRC; interviews with William Phillips (DSG staff director), January 18, 1982, and Jane O'Grady, November 22, 1982.

109   House proceedings, February 3, 1964: *Congressional Record*. February 3, 1964, pt. 2:1677–1709.

109   "as good as possible": Interview with William Cramer, June 24, 1981.

109   "that every member is notified": Urgent Memo to all Regional and Sub-Regional Whip Offices, from Frank Thompson, Jr., February 4, 1964, DSGC.

109–110   House proceedings, February 4, 1964: *Congressional Record,* February 4, 1964, pt. 2:1899–1933.

110   "If I were cutting corns": Rauh manuscript, 18.

110–111   House proceedings, February 5, 1964: *Congressional Record,* February 5, 1964, pt. 2:1961–2001.

111   "biggest test": *Dayton Daily News,* February 5, 1964, WRC.

111–113   House proceedings, February 6, 1964: *Congressional Record,* February 6, 1964, pt. 2:2250–2301.

112   "I almost quit": Zelenko interview.

113   "All I could see": Off-the-record interview with former House member, May 23, 1983.

113   a "nagging presence": O'Grady interview.

114   "still had to be sure": Interview with Arnold Mayer, May 25, 1982.

114   as far away as Europe: Rauh manuscript, 18.

114–115   House proceedings, February 7, 1964: *Congressional Record,* February 78, 1964, pt. 2:2462–2513.

114   "Look": Interview with Mabel McCulloch, July 1, 1981.

114   Not one Republican: *Washington Post,* February 8, 1964, Al.

115–118   House proceedings, February 8, 1964: *Congressional Record,* February 8, 1964, pt. 2:2548–2616.

117   "We've won": Caplan, Corman, and Greene interviews.

117   "But," declared George Meader: Interview with George Meader, July 16, 1981.

118–121   House proceedings, February 10, 1964: *Congressional Record,* February 10, 1964, pt. 2:2705–2805.

119   the president had called: Call to Rauh at 4:00 P.M. and to Wilkins at 4:15 P.M., President's Appointment file (Diary Backup), Box 4, February 10, 1964, LBJC; Rauh oral history, LBJC.

119   "What are you fellows doing?": Rauh manuscript, 19.

121   "triumph in itself": Kenneth Crawford, *Newsweek,* February 24, 1964, 32.

122   "I want to state": *Congressional Record,* February 10, 1964, pt. 2:2805.

122   his greatest accomplishment: Ted Knapp, *New York World Telegram,* February 12, 1964, 31.

122   "the most comprehensive": *Washington Post,* February 11, 1964, A1.

122s   LBJ telephone calls: Extracted from President's Appointment file (Diary Backup), Box 4, February 10, 1964, LBJC.

122   Rodino said: Rodino interview.

122   "we could not have done anything": *New York World Telegram,* February 12, 1964.

122   Johnson tried to rectify: Call to McCulloch at 6:55 P.M., receiving no answer, President's Appointment file (Diary Backup), Box 4, February 11, 1964, LBJC.

123   "We had imposed": O'Grady interview.

5. Senate Filibuster

125   imperiously informed: 4:45–5:10 P.M., President's Appointment file (Diary Backup), Box 4, February 11, 1964, LBJC.

125   "McCulloch insisted that": Nicholas Katzenbach, interview by Paige Mulhollan, November 12, 1968, Oral Histories, LBJC.

126   "don't have the stamina": Interview with Stewart Udall, August 9, 1982.

126   "I don't care": Rauh manuscript, 21.

127   LBJ-Katzenbach cloture discussion in White House entrance hall: Katzenbach interview; Katzenbach oral history, LBJC.

128   "Being a senator": *Time,* March 20, 1964, 23.

128   "if they're not from Montana": Interview with Frank Valeo, May 20, 1982.

128   "Mike was the most popular": Interview with Frank Moss, May 20, 1982.

128   "Mike didn't like": Interview with Gale McGee, April 28, 1982.

129   "The two-speech rule": Stephen Horn, *Periodic Log Maintained During the Discussions Covering the Passage of the Civil Rights Act of 1964* (199 pages), February 14, 1964, 6.

129   "When Johnson was majority leader": Report from Rabbi Richard Hirsch, February 5, 1964, LCCRC.

130   "You'll never get": Marshall oral history (Lewis), JFKC.

130   Robert Kennedy confided: RFK-Marshall oral history, vol. 7, JFKC.

130   "that didn't have Bob's approval": Ibid.

130   Johnson "didn't think": Ibid.

130   "If I worked out the strategy": Ibid.

131–133   Senate proceedings, February 17, 1964: *Congressional Record,* February 17, 1964, pt. 3:2882–2886.

132   had alerted James Eastland: Valeo interview.

133   Clarence Mitchell called: Memo by M. Jackson Smith, February 17, 1964, NAACPC.

134   votes for cloture were available: Horn, *Log,* February 14, 1964, 4–5.

134–135   Senate proceedings, February 26, 1964: *Congressional Record,* February 26, 1964, pt. 3:3689, 3692–3720.

135   Mitchell, who earlier that day: Horn, *Log,* February 26, 1964, 23.

135   "Javits," observed his GOP colleague: Interview with James B. Pearson, June 7, 1982.

136   "that's what Mike wanted": Manatos memo to O'Brien, February 27, 1964, files of Mike Manatos, LBJC.

136   had originally opposed: Humphrey memorandum summarizing activities on H.R. 7152 (memorandum undated, 21 pages), Legislative files, 1961–1964, Senatorial files, 1949–1964, HHHC.

136   some advance concessions: Ibid.

136   "The time has come": Henry M. Jackson tribute, *Congressional Record,* 95th Cong., 2d sess., January 24, 1978, vol. 124, pt. 1:576.

136   literally talked to himself: Humphrey memorandum, HHHC.

137   "before this is over": *Newsweek,* March 16, 1964, 38.

137   Stories of his boundless energy: George McGovern tribute in *Congressional Record,* January 24, 1978, vol. 124, pt. 1:608.

137   "had more answers": Ibid., Edward Muskie tribute, 585.

137   ill with the flu: Ibid., McGovern tribute, 608.

137   "something in the water": Tribute by Representative J. J. Pickle (D.-Tex.), who inserted column by George Christian, former press secretary to Lyndon Johnson, in *Congressional Record,* January 25, 1978, 880.

137   letter to Muriel: quoted in eulogy given by Vice President Walter Mondale at memorial services for Hubert Humphrey in Capitol Rotunda, January 15, 1978; program transcript inserted by Robert C. Byrd in *Congressional Record,* January 19, 1978, pt. 1:6.

137   a bipartisan team: Title I, Hart, Keating; Title II, Magnuson, Hruska (later resigned); Title III, Morse, Javits; Title IV, Douglas, Cooper; Title V, Long (Mo.), Scott; Title VI, Pastore, Cotton (resigned); Title VII, Clark, Case; Titles VIII-XI, Dodd.

138   fond of quoting: Interview with Stephen Horn, July 19, 1982.

138   reading to his blind father: Ibid.

138   almost as a son: Ibid.

138–139   February 28, 1964, strategy meeting: Horn, *Log,* February 28, 1964, 24–26.

139   "Not a scintilla": *Newsweek,* March 2, 1964, 20.

139   "Not a shred of truth": Ibid.

139   "I am in favor of passing": Johnson, *Papers 1963-64,* 1:328.

139   Russell on "Face the Nation," March 1, 1964: Transcript inserted by Herman Talmadge in *Congressional Record,* March 2, 1964, pt. 3:4069.

140   Humphrey on "Meet the Press," March 8, 1964: Text of "Meet the Press" interview, March 8, 1964, newspaper clipping file, September 19, 1963–July 31, 1964, HHHC.

140   Johnson's call to Humphrey: 1:00 P.M., President's Appointment file (Diary Backup), Box 4, March 8, 1964, LBJC; Hubert Humphrey interview III by Michael Gillette, June 21, 1977, Oral Histories, LBJC.

140–141   final strategy session, March 9, 1964: Horn, *Log,* March 9, 1964, 29–31.

141 Southerners held their own last caucus: *New York Times* clipping, March 10, 1964, RBRC.

141-143 Senate proceedings, March 9, 1964: *Congressional Record,* March 9, 1964, pt. 4:4741, 4742-4768.

142 Sparkman dozed...Dirksen skipped up to: *Time,* March 20, 1964, 25.

142 "no room for compromise": *New York Times,* March 10, 1964, 1.

142 suck on two lozenges: *Washington Post,* March 10, 1964, newspaper clipping file, HHHC.

143 all-time Senate wind record: *The World Book Encyclopedia* (1967), s.v. "filibustering."

143-144 new system was devised: *Congressional Record,* March 10, 1964, pt. 4:4816; Horn, *Log,* March 9, 1964, 31b-c; Mary McGrory, *Washington Star,* March 29, 1964, newspaper clipping file, HHHC; Humphrey memorandum, HHHC; Valeo interview.

144-145 Senate proceedings, March 12, 1964: *Congressional Record,* March 12, 1964, pt. 4:5042-5047, 5058-5075, 5078, 5079-5095.

144 small confederate flag: *Washington Post,* March 13, 1964, newspaper clipping file, HHHC.

145 Richard Russell revived: *Congressional Record,* March 16, 1964, pt. 4:5338-5352.

145 on St. Patrick's Day: *Congressional Record,* March 17, 1964, pt. 4:5431-5451.

145 "I am worried": Interview with John Sherman Cooper, June 2, 1982.

145 Coordinating Committee for Fundamental American Freedoms: *Newsweek,* March 30, 1964; Eugene McCarthy Collection, Minnesota Historical Society, Public Affairs Center, St. Paul, Minnesota.

145 BILLION DOLLAR BLACKJACK: Copy of advertisement in McCarthy collection.

145 Letters received by Senators Keating and Hart: Senate letter no. 2 from Mitchell to Wilkins, March 24, 1964, NAACPC.

145 Roman Hruska reported: *Newsweek,* March 30, 1964, 17.

145 Frank Church said: Ibid.

145 in a chat with Jack Steele: Horn, *Log,* March 17, 1964, 48.

145-146 Bill McCulloch, too: Ibid.

146 On March 18 Senator Humphrey: *Congressional Record,* March 18, 1964, pt. 4:5582.

146 "Hubert's speech": Horn, *Log,* March 19, 1964, 59.

146 Humphrey and Russell on "Today Show": Film of "Today Show" program, March 19, 1964, RBRC.

146 "would never understand": Horn, *Log,* March 19, 1964, 61a.

147 "I do not believe": *Congressional Record,* March 24, 1964, pt. 5:6027.

147 summarized the day's events: Mitchell summaries, NAACPC.

147 "Senate Letter Number Two": Letter from Mitchell to Wilkins, March 24, 1964, NAACPC.

147 Holding a caucus: Horn, *Log,* March 24, 1964, 65 (vote outcome related to Horn by Jerry Grinstein, chief counsel of Senator Magnuson's Commerce Committee).

147–148   Senate proceedings, March 26, 1964: *Congressional Record,* March 26, 1964, pt. 5:6415–6427, 6428–6438, 6441–6456.

147   "A battle has been lost": Ibid., 6455.

148   "The bill can't pass": Humphrey memorandum, HHHC.

6. Dirksen's Conversion

149   decided to provide frequent television: Interview with Roger Mudd, August 6, 1982.

149   Friendly noted: William Small, *To Kill A Messenger: Television News and the Real World* (New York: Hastings House, 1970), 256–257.

149–150   "gimmicky flag-pole sitting stunt": Mudd interview.

150   "I'll have to get my coat": Small, *To Kill A Messenger,* 257.

150   "It was several sizes": Ibid., 257.

150–151   Senate proceedings, March 30, 1964: *Congressional Record,* March 30, 1964, pt. 5:6527–6570, 6573–6574.

150   "a peerless order-keeper": Mary McGrory, *Washington Star,* March 29, 1964, newspaper clipping file, HHHC.

150   huge briefing books: Box 718, Senatorial files, 1949–1964, HHHC.

150   on the margins: Legislative files: Civil Rights—1964 (23.k.10.7b), HHHC.

151   "keeps my pipes lubricated": Louella Dirksen with Norma Lee Browning, *The Honorable Mr. Marigold: My Life with Everett Dirksen* (Garden City, N.Y.: Doubleday & Co., 1972), 259–260.

151   Old Doctor Snake Oil: Roger Mudd, interview by Hugh Cates, March 4, 1971, Oral Histories, LBJC.

151   "the high flyer": Interview with Andrew Glass, August 4, 1982.

151   "a legislator's legislator": Horn interview.

152   "was a superb leader": Interview with Carl Curtis, May 14, 1982.

152   "One hundred diverse personalities": *Time,* March 20, 1964, 22.

152   Dirksen told reporters: Unmarked clipping, newspaper clipping file, HHHC.

152   morning of June 11, 1963: Minutes of June 12, 1963, leadership meeting, Republican Congressional Leadership file, EMDC; Hugh Sidey, *John F. Kennedy, President* (New York: Atheneum, 1964), 401.

152   continued to call him Jack: MacNeil, *Dirksen,* 189.

152   "a fantastic help": Ibid., 205.

153   appointed a federal judge: RFK-Marshall oral history, vol. 7, JFKC.

153   neither Dirksen nor Halleck committed: Minutes of June 12, 1963, leadership meeting, Republican Congressional Leadership file, EMDC.

153   only 20.1 percent: Governmental Affairs Institute, *America Votes 5, 1962,* 114 (Wards 1–5).

153   "Senator Dirksen, nobody else": RFK-Marshall oral history, vol. 7, JFKC.

153   "How great a price": Memo by Ted Sorensen on "Tactics," "Substance," and "Drafting" of civil rights bill for meeting later that day with JFK, Presidential Papers, June 14, 1963, JFKC.

153   given a copy: Dates on Civil Rights History, entry for June 14, 1963, Notebooks, 1932–1969, EMDC.

153   Dirksen told Kennedy: Ibid., entry for June 17, 1963.

153–154   When he met the next morning: Memo from Mansfield to the president, June 14, 1963, Presidential Papers, JFKC.

154   "gauges the velocity": MacNeil, *Dirksen,* 220.

154   "I have an objection": Transcript of Halleck-Dirksen press conference, February 20, 1964, Republican Congressional Leadership file, EMDC.

154   "sort of let the thing": *Time,* June 19, 1964, 17.

154   commandeered three lawyers: MacNeil, *Dirksen,* 226.

154–155   he penned his thoughts: Entry for February 26, 1964, Working Papers, 1951–1969, EMDC.

155   "Senator Dirksen," Humphrey wrote: Humphrey memo to LBJ, March 18, 1964, Legislative files, 1961–1964, Senatorial files, 1949–1964, HHHC.

155   "Ev Dirksen didn't have": O'Brien interview.

155   February Harris poll: Memo no. 36, May 4, 1964, LCCRC.

155   Gallup survey: Gallup, *The Gallup Poll,* February 2, 1964, 1863.

157   "whole thing is timing": *Newsweek,* April 13, 1964, 31.

157   The 80 civil rights leaders: Memo no. 32, April 6, 1964, LCCRC.

157   "Let's face it": Horn, *Log,* April 2, 1964, 76.

157   "I am so conditioned": Memo no. 32, April 6, 1964, LCCRC.

157–158   Only 39 members: *Congressional Record,* April 4, 1964, pt. 5:6862–6863.

158   A quick check: *Time,* April 17, 1964, 35.

158   Humphrey fired off: *Minneapolis Star,* April 7, 1964, newspaper clipping file, HHHC.

158   "The only way we can lose": Rauh manuscript, 24.

158   "I do not want": Johnson, *Papers 1963–64,* 1:440.

158   Phil Hart's office: Murray Kempton, *New Republic,* April 4, 1964, newspaper clipping file, HHHC.

158   "We've shot our wad": Ibid.

159   factors favoring cloture: Entry for April 6, 1964, Notebooks, 1932–1969, folder 207, EMDC.

159–160   Dirksen placed on the table: *Washington Post,* April 8, 1964, A3.

160   "This is a vulnerable section": *Time,* April 24, 1964, 18.

160   Thursday morning Republican caucus: Minutes, Senate Republican Conference, April 9, 1964; *Washington Post,* April 10, 1964, A2; *New York Herald Tribune,* April 10, 1964, Legislative files: Civil Rights—1964, HHHC.

160   Of the 33 Republicans: Authors' philosophical rating has been arbitrarily determined, based on the *Congressional Quarterly Almanac's* "conservative coalition" opposition scores in 1963: "liberal," 44–86 percent; "moderate," 21–39 percent; "conservative," 0–20 percent (*CQA,* 747).

160 "palatable as possible": *New York Herald Tribune,* April 10, 1964, HHHC.

160–161 bipartisan team meeting, April 9, 1964: Horn, *Log,* April 9, 1964, 84.

161 Edward Kennedy was delivering: *Congressional Record,* April 9, 1964, pt. 6:7375–7380; *New York Herald Tribune,* April 10, 1964, HHHC.

161–162 discuss the Cherry Blossom Festival: *Congressional Record,* April 10, 1964, pt. 6:7589.

162 bipartisan team meeting, April 13, 1964: Horn, *Log,* April 13, 1964, 86–89.

162 baseball season opened: *Time,* April 24, 1964, 18; *Washington Post,* April 14, 1964, A1, A9.

162 Gone Fishing sign: Mudd interview.

162–163 The next day John McClellan: *Congressional Record,* April 14, 1964, pt. 6:7875–7876.

163 "let's try cloture": Rauh manuscript, 25.

163 bipartisan team meeting, April 16, 1964: Horn, *Log,* April 16, 1964, 92–95.

163 That afternoon Everett Dirksen: *Congressional Record,* April 16, 1964, pt. 6:8192–8196.

163 "These 10 amendments": Interview with Cornelius (Neil) Kennedy, April 26, 1982.

164 Two days earlier Bill McCulloch: Horn, *Log,* April 16, 1964, 95.

164 24-hour-a-day vigil: Memo no. 32, April 6, 1964, LCCRC; Legislative files: Civil Rights—1964 (23.k.10.7b), HHHC.

164 "The secret of passing": Horn, *Log,* March 9, 1964, 31a.

165 "This was the first time": Interview with James Hamilton, June 1, 1982.

165 decided on several strategies: Ibid.; Memo no. 32, April 6, 1964, LCCRC.

165 "There never has been": "Face the Nation" transcript inserted by Herman Talmadge in *Congressional Record,* March 2, 1964, pt. 3:4070.

165–166 met with Hubert Humphrey on March 17: Hamilton interview.

166 "get my accustomed cup of tea": Transcript of Halleck-Dirksen press conference, April 21, 1964, Republican Congressional Leadership file, EMDC.

166–167 Senate proceedings, April 21, 1964: *Congressional Record,* April 21, 1964, pt. 7:8613–8624, 8626–8643, 8649–8666.

167 regularly came over: Interview with John Stewart, May 17, 1984.

167–168 Humphrey-Dirksen conversation, April 21, 1964: Unsigned diary of John Stewart, entry for April 21, 1964 (entries begin on April 21, 1964, and run intermittently through "Final" entry of June 19, 1964), Legislative files, 1961–1964, Senatorial files, 1949–1964, HHHC.

168 "the jig was up": Stewart diary, entry for April 21, 1964, HHHC.

168 Dirksen broached the subject: President's Appointment file (Diary Backup), Box 5, April 21, 1964, LBJC; *New York Herald Tribune,* April 29, 1964, Legislative files: Civil Rights—1964, HHHC.

168 coming to Mansfield's defense: MacNeil, *Dirksen,* 230.

168–169 meeting in Mansfield's office, April 23, 1964: Manatos memo to O'Brien, April 27, 1964, files of Mike Manatos, Box 12, LBJC; O'Brien memo to the president, April 27, 1964, Reports on Legislation, Box 1, LBJC.

169 a beaming Bobby Kennedy: *Washington Post,* April 24, 1964, A8.

169 "Splendid," exclaimed Hubert Humphrey: Ibid.

169 "a most productive meeting": Manatos memo to O'Brien, April 27, 1964, files of Mike Manatos, Box 12, LBJC.

169 "now engaged": Interview with Charles Ferris, May 4, 1982.

169 The next day Dirksen submitted: *Congressional Record,* April 24, 1964, pt. 7:8991.

169 "just a mustard plaster": *Washington Post,* April 26, 1964, A13.

169 "is a matter for the senators": Johnson, *Papers 1963–64,* 1:522.

169–170 "get it done...How are you doing?" *Newsweek,* April 13, 1964, 31.

170 70 percent support: Memo no. 36, May 4, 1964, LCCRC.

170 four or five votes short: *New York Times,* April 27, 1964, 1.

170 "senators have the right": *Congressional Record,* April 27, 1964, pt. 7:9122.

170 "one week's notice": *Washington Post,* April 29, 1964, A8.

170–171 That evening at Georgetown University: *New York Times,* April 29, 1964, 1; *Washington Post,* April 29, 1964, A1.

171 convert the "unconverted": *Washington Post,* April 29, 1964, A1, A9.

171 "an emotional high": Hamilton interview.

171 bipartisan team meeting, April 29, 1964: Horn, *Log,* April 29, 1964, 128–130.

171 "You say you want": Andrew Glass, *New York Herald Tribune,* April 29, 1964, Legislative files: Civil Rights—1964, HHHC.

171–172 Johnson-Dirksen meeting, April 29, 1964: 12:18–1:00 P.M., President's Appointment file (Diary Backup), April 29, 1964, LBJC; Glass article, *New York Herald Tribune,* April 29, 1964, HHHC; Stewart diary, entry for April 29, 1964, HHHC; Dirksen appointment book, April 29, 1964, EMDC; *Washington Post,* April 30, 1964, A6.

172 Johnson-Humphrey meeting, April 28, 1964: Horn, *Log,* April 29, 1964, 130; Stewart diary, entry for April 29, 1964, HHHC.

172 The Southerners caucused: Date Book, entry for April 29, 1964, RBRC; *New York Times,* April 30, 1964, 20.

172 Russell-Dirksen-Mansfield discussion, April 29, 1964: *Washington Post,* April 30, 1964, A6; *New York Times,* April 30, 1964, 1.

172 kept in the dark: Stewart diary, entry for April 25, 1964, HHHC.

172–173 bipartisan team meeting, April 30, 1964: Horn, *Log,* April 30, 1964, 139–144.

173 got Dick Russell to agree: Humphrey memorandum, HHHC; *Washington Post,* May 2, 1964, A1, A7.

173 a "perfecting" amendment: *Congressional Record,* May 1, 1964, pt. 7:9816.

173 Humphrey-Dirksen conversation, May 1, 1964: Humphrey memorandum, HHHC; *Washington Post,* May 5, 1964, A1, A10.

173–174   "How can you say": *Washington Post,* May 5, 1964, A10; *Time,* May 15, 1694, 32.

174   Johnson-Hayden conversation, May 5, 1964: Memo for the president from Stewart Udall, May 7, 1964, Legislative Background, Civil Rights Act 1964, LBJC.

174   "never would have been here": Carl Hayden, interview by Joe B. Frantz, October 28, 1968, Oral Histories, LBJC.

174–175   meeting in Dirksen's office, May 5, 1964: Stewart diary, entry for May 6, 1964, HHHC; Horn, *Log,* May 5, 1964, 159; *New York Times,* May 6, 1964, 27.

174   "Dirksen's bombers": Mudd interview; MacNeil, *Dirksen,* 226.

175   Tommy Kuchel was as astounded: Horn, *Log,* May 5, 1964, 159.

175   "then we can go on": Johnson, *Papers 1963–64,* 1:618.

175   Mike Mansfield reported: Memo for Senator Mansfield from Jack Valenti, May 6, 1964, Confidential file, Box 56, LBJC.

175   "as per your memorandum": Ibid.

175–176   meeting in Dirksen's office, May 6, 1964: *New York Times,* May 7, 1964, 16.

176   a softie: Stewart diary, entry for May 6, 1964, HHHC.

176   "Katzenbach tells me": Memo to O'Brien from Manatos, May 6, 1964, Ex Hu2, November 22, 1963–July 16, 1964, LBJC.

176   Senate proceedings, May 6, 1964: *Congressional Record,* May 6, 1964, pt. 8:10157–10174, 10186–10209.

176   Moss became angry: Stewart diary, entry for May 6, 1964, HHHC.

177   frittering...mismanaging: Ibid.

177   bipartisan team meeting, May 7, 1964: Horn, *Log,* May 7, 1964, 160–162.

177   meeting in Dirksen's office, May 7, 1964: Ferris and Cornelius Kennedy interviews; *Milwaukee Journal,* June 19, 1964, Senatorial files, HHHC; *New York Times,* May 8, 1964, 1, 37.

177   "Dirksen," said his legal assistant: Cornelius Kennedy interview.

177   Clyde Flynn suggested: Ferris interview.

177   Ferris called Burke Marshall: Ibid.

177   "Jump at it, Charlie": Ibid.

177   "was the key": Cornelius Kennedy interview.

177   "Tommy,": Horn, *Log,* May 8, 1964, 168.

177–178   "The reports I get": Memo for the president from Stewart Udall, May 7, 1964, Legislative Background, Civil Rights Act 1964, Box 1, LBJC.

178   "couldn't argue with them": Udall interview.

178   meeting in Dirksen's office, May 8, 1964: *New York Times,* May 9, 1964, 1, 14.

178   "In our search": Johnson, *Papers 1963–64,* 1:649.

178   "because of my beloved friend": *Washington Post,* May 9, 1964, C6.

178   "I must, in candor": *New York Times,* May 10, 1964, E1.

179   "Since I left the Senate": Johnson, *Papers 1963–64,* 1:665–666.

179   memo from Mike Manatos: Memo to O'Brien from Manatos, May 11, 1964, Ex Hu2, November 22, 1963–July 16, 1964, LBJC.

179   "The whole procedure": *New York Times,* May 12, 1964, 1.

179–180   Johnson breakfast with Democratic congressional leaders, May 12, 1964: *Austin* (Tex.) *Daily Herald,* May 12, 1964, 1, newspaper clipping file, HHHC; *New York Times,* May 13, 1964, 1.

180   bipartisan team meeting, May 12, 1964: Horn, *Log,* May 12, 1964, 177–178.

180   "There is a feeling": *New York Times,* May 13, 1964, 1.

180–181   Senate proceedings, May 12, 1964: *Congressional Record,* May 12, 1964, pt. 8:10626, 10628–10646, 10667–10692.

181   "doesn't scare us": *Time,* May 22, 1964, 23.

181   "Perhaps never before": Evans and Novak, *Washington Post,* April 21, 1964.

181   czar of the Senate: Mary McGrory, *Dayton Journal Herald,* May 12, 1964 (no page number), McCulloch file, Cox Newspapers library, Dayton, Ohio.

181   "on bended knee": *Dayton Daily News,* April 26, 1964 (no page number), McCulloch file, Cox Newspapers library, Dayton, Ohio.

181   Kenneth Keating voiced: Ibid.

181   "if the Senate can't make any changes": Ibid.

181   "one note of consistency": Speech material, copy of manuscript, "Upon What Meat Doth This Our Ceasar [*sic*] Feed That He Has Grown So Great," RBRC.

181–182   meeting in Mansfield's office, May 13, 1964: Stewart diary, entry for May 13, 1964, HHHC.

182   "stayed in": RFK-Marshall oral history, vol. 7, JFKC; Stewart diary, entry for May 13, 1964, HHHC.

182   "Kennedy was the lawyer": RFK-Marshall oral history, vol. 7, JFKC.

182–183   meeting in Dirksen's office, May 13, 1964: Stewart diary, entry for May 13, 1964, HHHC; Horn, *Log,* May 14, 1964, 179–181; *New York Herald Tribune,* May 14, 1964, newspaper clipping file, HHHC; *New York Times,* May 14, 1964, 1.

182–183   "a goddamn sellout": Winthrop Griffith, *Humphrey: A Candid Biography* (New York: William Morrow & Co., 1965), 282.

183   "We have a good agreement": *Newsweek,* May 25, 1964, 33; *New York Times,* May 14, 1964, 1.

183   "bill is perfectly satisfactory": *Time,* May 22, 1964, 23; *New York Times,* May 14, 1964, 1; *New York Herald Tribune,* May 14, 1964, newspaper clipping file, HHHC.

183   "And to me, too": Ibid.

183   would reserve judgment: Stewart diary, entry for May 13, 1964, HHHC.

183   "are OK": Stewart diary, entry for May 19, 1964, HHHC.

183   McCulloch again came over: Horn, *Log,* May 14, 1964, 182.

183   "thought it would be a lot worse": Rauh interview.

183   "great victory for civil rights": Stewart diary, entry for May 19, 1964, HHHC.

183   "a much stronger bill": Aronson interview.

183 "no title": Jacob K. Javits, *Javits: The Autobiography of a Public Man* (Boston: Houghton Mifflin Co., 1981), 346.

183 "What happens if Dirksen": Horn, *Log,* May 15, 1964, 197.

183 "cut our throats": Ibid.

184 Democratic caucus proceedings, May 19, 1964: Stewart diary, entry for May 19, 1964, HHHC; *New York Times,* May 20, 1964, 34; *New York Herald Tribune,* May 20, 1964, 11.

184–185 Republican caucus proceedings, May 19, 1964: Minutes, Senate Republican Conference, May 19, 1964; *New York Times,* May 20, 1964, 34; Stewart diary, entry for May 19, 1964, HHHC; MacNeil, *Dirksen,* 235; Neil Kennedy interview.

185 "It's a gargantuan thing": *New York Times,* May 20, 1964, 34; *Worthington* (Minn.) *Daily Globe,* May 21, 1964, newspaper clipping file, HHHC.

185 "No army is stronger": *New York Times,* May 20, 1964, 34; MacNeil, *Dirksen,* 235; interview with Hugh D. Scott, Jr., May 11, 1982.

185 Roger Mudd noted: Mudd interview.

185 "carrying out on the surface": Moss interview.

186 a "dramatic development": Mitchell Senate letter no. 11, May 22, 1964, NAACPC.

186 "when Dirksen turned around": Scott interview.

186 Republican caucus proceedings, May 20, 1964: Minutes, Senate Republican Conference, May 20, 1964; *New York Times,* May 21, 1964, 26.

186 "serious reservations": *Worthington* (Minn.) *Daily Globe,* May 21, 1964, newspaper clipping file, HHHC.

186 Republican caucus proceedings, May 22, 1964: Minutes, Senate Republican Conference, May 22, 1964; *Washington Star,* May 22, 1964, A6; *New York Times,* May 23, 1964, 1, 10.

187 "Right now": *New York Herald Tribune,* May 25, 1964, 1, 4.

187 two Republican caucus proceedings, May 25, 1964: Minutes of morning and afternoon conferences, Senate Republican Conference, May 25, 1964; *New York Times,* May 26, 1964, 27.

187 "we have consensus": *Washington Post,* May 26, 1964, A2.

187 "I believe that consensus": Ibid.

187–188 Johnson-Cannon meeting, May 26, 1964: 11:45 A.M., President's Appointment file (Diary Backup), Box 5, May 26, 1964, LBJC; Howard Cannon's response to authors' question transmitted through his press aide, Michael Vermatti, August 19, 1982.

188 "did not mention this": Interviews with former Edmondson staff members John Criswell, September 29, 1982, and Michael Reed, September 30, 1982.

188–189 Senate proceedings, May 26, 1964: *Congressional Record,* May 26, 1964, pt. 9:11917–11943.

189 "many changes have been made": Memo (unsigned) from Justice Department, May 26, 1964, Legislative Background, Civil Rights Act 1964, Box 1, LBJC.

189 "Coverage in all the titles": Memo no. 40, June 1, 1964, LCCRC.

189 "basically agreed with us": MacGregor interview.

190   Mike Mansfield announced: *Congressional Record,* June 1, 1964, pt. 9:12274.

190   until after the June 2 primaries: *Newsweek,* June 1, 1964, 19.

190   time had come to vote: Stewart diary, "final dictated thoughts," entry for June 19, 1964 (covering June 1–19, 1964), HHHC.

190   "bull through this week": Stewart diary, entry for June 19, 1964, HHHC.

190   Dirksen took ill: Ibid.

190   Russell continued to press: *Congressional Record,* June 2, 1964, pt. 9:12436.

190   "impossible to get any votes": *Congressional Record,* June 3, 1964, pt. 9:12535.

190   "Why does he wish to go over": *Congressional Record,* June 4, 1964, pt. 10:12643.

190   "we need more time": Humphrey memorandum, HHHC.

190   "largest church in Iowa": Interview with Jack Miller, May 27, 1982.

190–191   Archbishop of Dubuque: Glass interview; interview with David Brody, director, Washington Office, Anti-Defamation League, B'nai B'rith, August 2, 1982.

191   "we ought to bend": Miller interview.

191   rump meeting of Republican conservatives, June 5, 1964: Stewart diary, entry for June 11, 1964, HHHC; *Washington Post,* June 6, 1964, A2.

191   "tended to be a choleric": Scott interview.

191   "seniority-is-everything school": Pearson interview.

191   "Bourke had the feeling": Miller interview.

191–192   Senate proceedings, June 5, 1964: *Congressional Record,* June 5, 1964, pt. 10:12807–12820, 12822–12828, 12831–12854.

192   "Our latest count": Mitchell telegram to Wilkins, June 5, 1964, NAACPC.

192   Senate proceedings, June 6, 1964: *Congressional Record,* June 6, 1964, pt. 10:12859–12862, 12873–12874, 12877–12878.

192   "I knew if Hruska": Humphrey memorandum, HHHC.

192   convivial drink: Brody interview.

192   "was to Everett Dirksen": Ferris interview.

192–193   "would get Everett Dirksen's agreement": Katzenbach interview.

193   "Well, Dick,": Humphrey memorandum, HHHC.

7. Triumph in the Senate

194   the jobless rate: *Washington Post,* June 6, 1964, A1, A2.

194   two U.S. aircraft, *Washington Post,* June 8, 1964, A1.

194–195   Senate proceedings, June 8, 1964: *Congressional Record,* June 8, 1964, pt. 10:12933–12934, 12943–12968.

195   a memo to Larry O'Brien: Memo from Katzenbach to O'Brien, June 8, 1964, Reports on Legislation, LBJC.

195   "22 years ago today": Memo from Juanita Roberts, June 9, 1964, President's Appointment file (Diary Backup), Box 6, LBJC.

195   Manatos's cloture "head count": Head count on cloture, files of Mike Manatos, Box 6, June 8, 1964, LBJC.

195   Senate proceedings, June 9, 1964: *Congressional Record,* June 9, 1964, pt. 10:13050–13099, 13118–13119, 13125–13219 (Byrd speech).

196   "I stood with you": Letter from Robert C. Byrd to the president, December 7, 1963, Legislation: LE/HU, Box 65, LBJC.

196   a relaxed dinner: Glass interview.

196   Johnson-Humphrey 7:30 P.M. telephone conversation, June 9, 1964: Humphrey memorandum, HHHC.

196   Johnson-Humphrey second telephone conversation, June 9, 1964: Press Releases, June 9, 1964, Press files, HHHC.

196   "exuberant, optimistic, bouncy self": Cecil E. Newman, "Editor Watches From Gallery as Senate Passes Cloture Motion," *St. Paul Recorder,* June 16, 1964, newspaper clipping file, HHHC.

196   three last-minute calls: Newman article, HHHC.

196   "didn't need to be told": Interview with Ralph Yarborough, August 26, 1982.

197   handed Phil Hart a note: Humphrey memorandum, HHHC.

197   "Although there often was rivalry": Curtis interview.

197   Dirksen's activities, evening of June 9 and morning of June 10: *Time,* June 19, 1964, 18.

197   only six blacks: Newman article, HHHC.

197–199   Senate cloture proceedings, June 10, 1964: *Congressional Record,* June 10, 1964, pt. 10:13307–13337; *Time,* June 19, 1964, 15–18.

198   "lacked the fire": Newman article, HHHC.

198   no attempt: Ibid.

198   Twice he gulped pills: Ibid.

199   Humphrey crossed the aisle: unidentified clipping, newspaper clipping file, HHHC.

199   kept his own tally sheet: Newman article, HHHC.

199   announced on the air: Mudd interview.

199   tears stood in other eyes: Aronson interview; interview with Dr. Steven Ebbin, member of Mansfield's staff, March 15, 1984.

199   Raising his arms: Hubert H. Humphrey, *The Education of a Public Man: My Life and Politics* (Garden City, N.Y.: Doubleday & Co., 1976), 283.

199   prepared to support cloture: Mitchell oral history, LBJC.

199   "It's all right": *Newsweek,* June 22, 1964, 26.

200   Lyndon Johnson's response: Letters on April 23 and May 27, 1964, from Johnson to the President of the Senate and the Speaker of the House of Representatives requesting additional aid for Alaska, Johnson, *Papers 1963–64,* 1:526–527, 719–720.

200   made Air Force Two available: Interview with Milton Fairfax, Gruening staff member, December 13, 1982.

200   "I am prepared": Gruening statement to Humphrey on Senate floor, *Congressional Record,* May 13, 1964, pt. 8:10765–10766.

200   Monroney had concluded: Interviews with Mary Ellen Miller, January 23, 1983, and with John Burzio, staff member on Commerce Committee for Senator Monroney, February 23, 1983.

201   ADA Liberal Quotient Rating: Americans for Democratic Action "Liberal Quotient—1963," Wisconsin State Historical Society, Madison, Wisconsin, as reported in an interview with Lloyd Velicer, March 7, 1983.

201   "made a 'thing' ": McGee interview.

201   "favored full debate": Moss interview.

201   "I courted Dirksen": Edgar Berman, M.D., *Hubert: The Triumph and Tragedy of the Humphrey I Knew* (New York: G. P. Putnam's Sons, 1979), 51.

202   Twenty states: U.S. Senate, *Hearings before the Committee on Commerce on S.1732,* 88th Cong., 1st sess., pt. 2:1316–1380.

202   another dozen: Ibid.

202   "I supported civil rights legislation": Interview with J. Caleb Boggs, May 18, 1982.

202   "the living faith": *Congressional Record,* June 10, 1964, pt. 10:13320.

202   "That's wrong": Curtis interview.

202–203   A Gallup poll: Gallup, *The Gallup Poll,* June 10, 1964, 1884.

203   Keating received: *Congressional Record,* June 4, 1964, pt. 10:12650.

203   Milton Young: Curtis interview.

203   Church lobbyists prevailed upon: Hamilton interview.

203   "Inasmuch as the pastor": Ibid.

203   "The last thing a senator wants": Valeo interview.

203   "at the heart of free government": Norris Cotton, *Norris Cotton Reports To You From the United States Senate,* newsletter no. 7, June 25, 1964.

203   "no appetite to explain": *New York Times,* May 26, 1964, 27.

203   "more to do": *Chicago Daily News,* June 11, 1964, 16, newspaper clipping file, HHHC.

204   Senate proceedings immediately after cloture vote, June 10, 1964: *Congressional Record,* June 10, 1964, pt. 10:13327–13330.

204   suddenly realized: Hubert H. Humphrey, *Beyond Civil Rights: A New Day of Equality* (New York: Random House, 1968), 96.

204   "Adoption of this amendment": Stewart diary, entry for June 19, 1964, HHHC.

204–205   a disheartened Russell: Russell's conversation with Mitchell, reported in Humphrey's *The Education of a Public Man,* 284.

205   "It is the law of the Senate": Letter from Russell to Frank H. Williams, June 17, 1964, Civil Rights box, RBRC.

205   "to refrain from violence": Letter from Russell to Guy Hornsby, July 25, 1964, Civil Rights box, RBRC.

205   "Dick Russell had ability": Harry S Truman, *Memoirs,* vol. 2, *The Years of Trial and Hope* (Garden City, N.Y.: Doubleday & Co., 1956), 494.

205   first person Lyndon Johnson contacted: Evans and Novak, *The Exercise of Power,* 51.

205   rarely made a move: Ibid.

206   "was not a man": Lady Bird Johnson, interview by Hugh Cates, June 28, 1977, Oral Histories, RBRC.

206   affectionately called "Uncle Dick": Ibid.

206   remarkable knowledge of Civil War history: Herman Talmadge, interview by Hugh Cates, April 21, 1971, Oral Histories, RBRC.

206   new president called: unidentified clipping, newspaper clipping file, RBRC.

206   dates of Johnson-Russell meetings: Date Book, entries of January 12, 16, 18, 27, 28, and 29, 1964, RBRC.

206   amazing them: Lady Bird Johnson oral history, RBRC.

206   Humphrey wearily returned: Stewart diary, entry for June 11, 1964, HHHC.

206   "Since I am sure that cloture": Personal and Family papers, 1919–1978, A-E (tally sheet filed with papers), HHHC.

206–207   Humphrey's meeting with floor captains, June 10, 1964: Stewart diary, entry for June 11, 1964, HHHC.

207   Senate proceedings, afternoon of June 10, 1964: *Congressional Record,* June 10, 1964, pt. 10:13330–13419.

207   "let us go home": Ibid., 13420.

207   meeting in Mansfield's office, June 11, 1964: Stewart diary, entries for June 11 and June 19, 1964, HHHC.

207   Senate proceedings, June 11, 1964: *Congressional Record,* June 11, 1964, pt. 10:13434–13438, 13442–13445, 13447–13471, 13473–13507.

207   "picked up speed": Stewart diary, entry for June 11, 1964, HHHC.

207   "I wanted to perfect": Miller interview.

207   "to look for accommodation": Stewart interview.

207   "Oh, Hubert": Ibid.

208   "Let me be the first": Wilkins's letter to Dirksen, June 12, 1964, NAACPC.

208   Senate proceedings, June 12 and 13, 1964: *Congressional Record,* June 12, 1964, pt. 10:13641–13670; June 13, 1964, pt. 10:13694–13703, 13708–13726.

208   fulfilled a presidential commitment: 11:30 A.M., President's Appointment file (Diary Backup), Box 6, June 15, 1964, LBJC; Rodino interview.

209   "To expedite": Bipartisan Civil Rights Captains News Release, June 15, 1964, Press Releases, Box 5, Press Files, HHHC.

209   Senate proceedings, June 15, 1964: *Congressional Record,* June 15, 1964, pt. 10:13799–13822, 13825–13827, 13830–13832, 13834–13840.

209   "Once cloture was invoked": Pearson interview.

209   "This is extremely embarrassing": Stewart interview.

209–210   Senate proceedings, June 16, 1964: *Congressional Record,* June 16, 1964, pt. 10:13871–13902, 13904–13906, 13909–13910, 13913–13947.

209   "senators began to get": Stewart diary, entry for June 19, 1964, HHHC.

210   Dirksen exchanges with Long, Dominick, and Mechem, June 16, 1964: Ibid.

270

210   Strom Thurmond and Sam Ervin both promised: Ibid.'

210   a message Humphrey received: Humphrey, *Beyond Civil Rights,* 96; Humphrey, *The Education of a Public Man,* 285.

210   An operation: Operation successfully performed by Dr. Stuart Arhelger, newspaper clipping file, HHHC.

210–211   Senate proceedings, June 17, 1964: *Congressional Record,* June 17, 1964, pt. 11:14179–14197, 14200–14216, 14219–14240.

211–213   Senate proceedings, June 18, 1964: *Congressional Record,* June 18, 1964, pt. 11:14275–14281, 14283–14287, 14294–14319, 14326–14336.

212   tears welling in his eyes: *Time,* June 26, 1964, 17.

212   "sounded like the death scene": Memo no. 42, June 19, 1964, LCCRC.

213   "this is a dreadful mistake": *Newsweek,* June 29, 1964, 17.

213   declined to suggest: Curtis interview.

213   "did not twist my arm": Goldwater's response to authors' question, transmitted through Ellen Thrasher, appointments secretary, February 8, 1983.

213–215   Senate proceedings, June 19, 1964: *Congressional Record,* June 19, 1964, pt. 11:14432–14504, 14506–14511.

214   "We had to get Mike angry": Humphrey memorandum, HHHC.

216   a "major step": Johnson, *Papers 1936–64,* 1:787.

216   "landmarks of my life": Ralph G. Martin, *A Man For All People: Hubert H. Humphrey* (New York: Grosset & Dunlap, 1968), unnumbered page 113.

216   "I marveled at the way": Moss interview.

216   had lost 20 pounds: Richard McGowan, *New York Daily News,* June 20, 1964, newspaper clipping file, HHHC.

216   walked out on the east front steps: *Minneapolis Morning Tribune,* June 20, 1964, newspaper clipping file, HHHC.

216   An hour later: Humphrey, *Beyond Civil Rights,* 97.

216   "Never in my 15 years": Ibid.

216   a late evening dinner: Stewart diary, entry for June 19, 1964, HHHC.

216–217   "His role was absolutely critical": Humphrey, *The Education of a Public Man,* 277.

217   "torn between the pride of victory": Martin, *A Man For All People,* unnumbered page 113.

217   Tragedy also struck: *New York Times,* June 20, 1964, 1, 54; article by Paul Hoffman inserted by Michael Mansfield in *Congressional Record,* July 2, 1964, pt. 12:15793.

217   "Joining the legions": "Bipartisan Civil Rights Newsletter," no. 76, June 19, 1964.

8. The Bill Becomes Law

218   "A message from the Senate": *Congressional Record,* June 22, 1964, pt. 11:14630–14631.

218   a joint press release: *New York Times,* June 20, 1964, 1.

219   a June 18 memo: Memo from O'Brien to the president, June 18, 1964, Confidential file, LBJC.

219   McCulloch originally leaned: Memo from O'Brien to the president, June 15, 1964, Reports on Legislation, Box 1, LBJC.

219   Charlie Halleck, meanwhile: Memo from O'Brien to the president, June 18, 1964, Confidential file, LBJC; *Washington Post,* June 19, 1964, A8.

220   objections to Celler's request: *Congressional Record,* June 22, 1964, pt. 11:14631.

220   dropped in the hopper: Ibid., 14672.

220–222   House Rules Committee open hearings, June 30, 1964: U.S. House of Representatives, *Civil Rights: Hearings before the Committee on Rules on H.Res. 789,* 88th Cong., 2d sess., June 30, 1964.

222   Behind closed doors: House Rules Committee closed session, *Transcript* of June 30, 1964, executive session on file with the National Archives, Washington, D.C.

222   Reopening the doors: House Rules Committee open hearings, *Hearings on H.Res. 789,* June 30, 1964.

222–223   Bolling moved: House Rules Committee closed session, *Transcript,* June 30, 1964.

223   a strident speech: *Congressional Record,* July 1, 1964, pt. 12:15597.

224–226   House proceedings, July 2, 1964: *Congressional Record,* July 2, 1964, pt. 12:15869–15897.

225   As Smith yielded the floor: *Dayton Daily News,* July 3, 1964, WRC.

225   rare standing ovation: Ibid.

226   The first man on his feet: Ibid.

226   who announced the word: *Congressional Record,* July 2, 1964, pt. 12:15831.

226   cried the elated New Yorker: Ibid., 15832.

226   "The act which has just been passed": Ibid.

226–228   Bill signing ceremony, July 2, 1964: *Dayton Daily News,* July 3, 1964, WRC; *Newsweek,* July 13, 1964, 17.

227   "I am about to sign": *Public Papers of the Presidents, Lyndon B. Johnson 1963–64,* vol. 2 (Washington: U.S. Government Printing Office, 1965), 842–844.

228   had mysteriously disappeared: Lady Bird Johnson, *White House Diary* (New York: Holt, Rinehart & Winston, 1970), 174–175.

228   "turmoil is a sign of birth": Subcommittee No. 5, *Hearings,* May 8, 1963.

228   His house was picketed: David Hess in *Akron Beacon Journal* (no date or page number), WMFP; photographs of pickets in front of McCulloch's Piqua home carrying signs, "Is Bill McCulloch anti-white? He voted for the Civil Rights Act," WMFP.

228   "How do you tear hatred": Robert J. Havel, *Cleveland Plain Dealer* (no date or page number), WMFP.

228   "No statutory law": Ibid.

229   "To create hope": *Congressional Record,* July 2, 1964, pt. 12:15894.

229 "All this": Kennedy, *Papers 1961*, 2.

Conclusion

231 52.4 percent of black Americans: John P. Davis, ed., *The American Negro Reference Book* (Englewood Cliffs, N.J.: Prentice-Hall, Inc., 1966), 106–107.

231 ("the best vote"): Interview with Representative James L. Oberstar (D.-Minn.), June 20, 1980.

232 the time for effective: Martin Luther King, Jr., *Why We Can't Wait* (New York: New American Library, 1964), 15–26.

232 "all due deliberate delay": Ibid., 18.

232 "risen from colonial bondage": Ibid., 22.

232 spread to 800 cities: *Congressional Quarterly Almanac*, 1963, 334.

233 "We saw this": Interview with Andrew Young, October 28, 1982.

234 had Richard Russell been willing: *Milwaukee Journal*, June 19, 1964, Senatorial files, Box 718, HHHC.

235 "if I didn't get out in front": Doris Kearns, *Lyndon Johnson and the American Dream* (New York: Harper & Row, 1976), 191.

235 "private dickering": *Newsweek*, June 22, 1964, 25.

235 "such high visibility": Ferris interview.

235 "a tacit understanding": Valeo interview.

236 had Senator Russell allowed more voting: *Milwaukee Journal*, June 19, 1964, HHHC.

236 "It seemed to me": Humphrey memorandum, HHHC.

237 "in the hope that some development": Letter to Thurman T. Scott, April 30, 1964, Civil Rights box, RBRC.

237 "We have no intention": Telegram to W. H. McKenzie, Jr., May 1, 1964, Civil Rights box, RBRC.

237 a backlash vote: Ibid.

237 ("I voted for"): Transcript of Halleck-Dirksen press conference, May 7, 1964, Republican Congressional Leadership file, EMDC.

237 "Wallace won't affect": Andrew Glass, *New York Herald Tribune*, May 13, 1964, 17, newspaper clipping file, RBRC.

237 "Last MEMO": Memo no. 44, July 6, 1964, LCCRC.

238 "the value above all others": Wilkins speech inserted by Representative Robert Nix (D.-Pa.) in *Congressional Record*, June 24, 1964, pt. 11:14948–14949.

Appendix

239–242 Major provisions: *U.S. Code Congressional and Administration News*, 88th Cong., 2d sess., 1964, vol. 1, 287–319.

Index

Index

277

Kastenmeier, Robert W., 4, 45, 46, 52, 62; Dawson, meets with, 47-48; and public accommodations amendment, 34; subcommittee bill, support of, 59; and voting rights amendment, 32

Katzenbach, Nicholas deB., 56, 100, 122, 141, 227; and bipartisan Senate leaders, 168-169, 171; Celler, strategy letter to, 30, 42; compromise bill (House), negotiates, 57; Dirksen, cocktail hour with, 192-193; and Halleck, 42; House leaders, meetings with, 50-52, 62; Johnson cloture advice to, 125, 127, 130; Kennedy, Robert F., accompanies to House Judiciary Committee hearing, 44, 46; and markup sessions, Subcommittee No. 5, 32; and McCulloch, 11, 43, 54; Senate negotiations, H.R. 7152, 174, 176, 177; subcommittee bill (House), 38-39; substitute bill (Senate), explains to Celler and McCulloch, 183; vote prediction, Norton, Cotton, Hickenlooper amendments, 195; Wallace, confrontation with, 17

Keating, Kenneth B., 156, 167; attends interdenominational religious convocation, 170; Katzenbach, conversation with, 183; mail received by, 145, 203; McCulloch, complaint about, 181

Kelly, Edna F., 117

Kennedy, Cornelius, 163, 174, 177, 184

Kennedy, Edward M., 144, 161, 211, 217

Kennedy, Ethel (Mrs. Robert), 161

Kennedy, Jacqueline B. (Mrs. John), 53, 70, 71, 79, 97

Kennedy, Joan (Mrs. Edward), 161

Kennedy, John F., xix, 44, 96, 151, 155, 227, 234; Alabama National Guard, federalizes, 17, 33; Blake, Eugene Carson, meeting with, 39; characteristics of, 15, 18, 68; civil rights, commitment to, 16, 18, 161; and civil rights leaders, meeting with, 20-21; civil rights legislation, submits to Congress, 1-2; and civil rights message to Congress, 1; Daley, call to, 60; death of, 70, 97-98, 196, 206; Democratic congressional leaders, meetings with, 69, 81; Democratic platform, disavows civil rights plank in, 4, 232; Dirksen, dealings with, 152-153; and doubts about introduction of civil rights legislation, 5, 19, 22; and Eisenhower civil rights bill, 134; Florida Chamber of Commerce, addresses, 68-69; funeral ceremonies of, 74, 75, 226; Halleck, calls, 54, 66-67; House congressional leaders, meetings with, 49-52, 62-63; House

Judiciary Committee liberal Democrats, meets with, 52-53, 59-61; Inaugural Address, xvii, 229; Johnson, dealings with, 73, 76-77; Kennedy memorial, civil rights bill as a, 78-79, 90; legislative strategy for H.R. 7152, 4, 67, 124, 153; legislative success, 8, 15, 89; literacy bill, submits to Congress (1962), 130, 236; Mansfield, tribute from, 215; and March on Washington, 25, 26; and McCulloch, 13; members of Congress, dealings with, 87; Philadelphia, travels to, 68; and presidential civil rights responsibilities, xvi; press conference of, 68; press support for H.R. 7152, campaigns for, 46, 56; and Smith, Howard, 84; tax reduction bill, gives priority to, 23; and television address about civil rights, xx, 17, 34; unfinished agenda, 126, 133, 216

Kennedy, John F., Jr., 46

Kennedy, Robert F., 57, 122, 161, 227, 235; and Alabama University enrollment of Hood and Malone, 17; Celler, critical of, 42-43; characteristics of, 3, 18, 97-98; civil rights legislation, encourages brother to send to Congress, xix, 16, 19; commitment to preserve House bill in Senate, 125, 130, 156, 182, 234; House Judiciary Committee, testifies before, 44-46; House leaders, meetings with, 50; Johnson, dealings with, 73, 75, 77; jury trial amendment, negotiations with Mansfield and Dirksen, 168-169; Katzenbach, memo from, 11; legislative strategy for H.R. 7152, 42, 43, 153, 156, 201; liberals, critical of, 53; and Libonati, 66; Senate Judiciary Committee, testifies before, 135; and Senate negotiations for H.R. 7152, 174, 181-183; Subcommittee No. 5 of the House Judiciary Committee, testifies before, 4, 5-8; vice presidential nomination, grass roots backing for, 151

Keogh, Eugene J., 104, 120, 122

Kimball, Robert, 94, 103, 146; compromise bill, assists in negotiating, 54-57; Higgs, call from, 62; Smith, conversation with, 90

King, Martin Luther, Jr., 19, 185, 222, 226; Birmingham protests, participation in, xviii, 11; civil rights legislation, calls for, xix, 232; Detroit march, participates in, 24; Johnson, dealings with, 77, 81-82, 94-95; Kennedy, John F., meetings with, 220; letter from Birmingham jail, xviii; Montgomery bus boycott, participation in, xvi; and speech delivered at

283

194; House, passed by, 37; Johnson,
support of, 81, 83; retaliation
against, Kennedy's fear of, 22-23,
32; Senate, consideration of, 133,
134; Ways and Means Committee,
approved by, 29
Taylor, Hobart, Jr., 74
Teasdale, Kenneth, 129, 174
Thompson, Frank, Jr., 108-109, 122
Thurmond, James Strom, 19, 143, 145,
209, 210, 212
Time, 27-28
Tisci, Anthony, 66
Tobey, Charles W., 211
"Today Show" (television program):
Humphrey-Russell appearance on,
146
Toll, Herman, 4, 61, 65
Tower, John G., 208
Trade Expansion Act, 15
Truman, Harry S, xiv, 72, 76, 200, 205
Tuck, William M., 48, 61, 106
Turkey, aid to, 232
Tyler, Gus, 22

Udall, Stewart L., 126, 177-178
unemployment, 194
United Auto Workers (UAW), 14, 22,
96
United Nations Charter, Senate passage
of, 232
Urban League. *See* National Urban
League

Valenti, Jack, 77
Valeo, Francis, 135, 168, 203, 235
Victoria, Queen, 79
Vietnam, 168; Buddhist protests in, 15
Volstead Act, 184
voting rights (Title I), 32-33, 47-48, 109,
195

Waggonner, Joseph D., Jr., 220, 223
Wall Street Journal, 7
Wallace, George C., 17, 33, 152, 237
Walters, Herbert S., 180, 192, 195
Warren, Earl, xv, 138
Washington Cathedral, 184
Washington, D.C., climate of, 21-22
Washington, George, 21
Washington, Kenneth, 173-174
Washington Post, 56, 96, 122

Washington Star, viii
Waters, Bernard J., 174
Ways and Means Committee, House of
Representatives, 23, 29
Webster, Daniel, 132, 184
Welsh, William B., 134, 201
Weltner, Charles L., 225
White, Lee C., 80, 82, 175
Whitten, Jamie L., 115
Wilberforce University, 86
Wilk, Joseph, 166
Wilkins, Roy, 114, 119, 206; at bill
signing for H.R. 7152, 226-227; Bir-
mingham bombing, holds press con-
ference about, 34; Dirksen, letter to,
207-208; Johnson, meets with, 80-81,
94; Kennedy, John F., meets with,
26; Mitchell, communications from,
147, 185, 192; NAACP annual con-
vention, addresses, 238; Subcommit-
tee No. 5, testifies before, 22
Williams, Camilla, 25
Williams, Frank H., 205
Williams, John Bell, 120, 220
Williams, John J., 192, 195, 196, 199,
202
Willis, Edwin E., 64-65, 94, 106, 112,
222
Wilson, T. Woodrow, 126, 184
Wirtz, W. Willard, 8-9
World Bank. *See* International Bank for
Reconstruction and Development
World War II, xiv, 22, 96, 226, 232;
and Cannon, Howard, 187;
Johnson, mission during, 195;
McCulloch, enlists in Army during,
10
Wright, Zephyr, 82

Xenia, Ohio, 86

Yarborough, Ralph W., 70, 192, 195,
196
Yates, Sidney B., 153
Young, Andrew, 233
Young, John A., 222
Young, Milton R., 192, 195, 203, 215
Young, Whitney M., Jr., 26, 75, 81, 94,
227

Zelenko, Benjamin, 30, 66, 112

About the Authors

CHARLES WHALEN served in the U.S. Congress, representing Ohio's third district, from 1967 until 1979. His career there was marked by special distrinction in foreign policy. He was a member of both the Armed Services Committee and the Foreign Affairs Committee. He was U.S. delegate to the 32nd United National General Assembly in 1977, and U.S. delegate to Special General Assembly Session on Disarmament in 1978. In 1976 columnist Jack Anderson named him one of the "Top Ten" House members.

Mr. Whalen's involvement in civil rights dates from an earlier period when, as a member of the Ohio General Assembly, he was a sponsor of the 1963 Public Accommodations Law and author of the 1965 Fair Housing Act. A native of Dayton, Ohio, he earned a B.S. from the University of Dayton in 1942. He spent World War II as an army lieutenant, mostly in the India-Burma Theater. Returning in 1946, he won a masters degree in business administration that same year from Harvard University. After six years as a vice president in his family-owned Dayton Dress Company, he joined the department of economics at the University of Dayton and continued to teach there throughout his twelve years in the Ohio state legislature. Since retiring from Congress he has been president of New Directions, a citizen-interest foreign policy organization; a fellow at the Woodrow Wilson International School, and an adjunct professor in the School of International Service at American University. He is the author of *The House and Foreign Policy: the Irony of Congressional Reform; Your Right to Know*; and (with four House colleagues) *How To End the Draft: the Case for an All-Volunteer Army*.

BARBARA GLEASON WHALEN has been a columnist for the Dayton (Ohio) Journal-Herald, an account executive for Dayton's Yeck and Yeck Advertising Agency, and continuity director for Station WHIO-TV in Dayton. She was born in Detroit, Michigan, and raised in Sidney, Ohio. She holds a B.A. degree from Marymount College in Tarrytown, N.Y. She and Charles Whalen were married in 1958 and are the parents of four sons and two daughters. The Whalens now live in Bethesda, Maryland.

Picture Credits

The signing, July 2, 1964. 1. Charles Halleck (R.-Ind.); **2.** William McCulloch (R.-Ohio); **3.** Walter Fauntroy, Washington representative, Southern Christian Leadership Conference; **4.** Peter W. Rodino (D.-N.J.); **5.** George Meany, president, AFL-CIO; **6.** President Lyndon B. Johnson; **7.** Martin Luther King, Jr., SCLC; **8.** Whitney Young, National Urban League; **9.** Richard Bolling (D.-Mo.); **10.** Emanuel Celler (D.-N.Y.); **11.** John V. Lindsay (R.-N.Y.); **12.** John D. Dingell (D.-Mich.); **13.** John W. McCormack (D.-Mass.); **14.** James Roosevelt (D.-Calif.); **15.** Warren G. Magnuson (D.-Wash.).